American Politics and Public Policy

MIT Studies in American Politics and Public Policy
Martha Weinberg, general editor

1. *The Implementation Game: What Happens After a Bill Becomes a Law,* Eugene Bardach, 1977.

2. *Decision to Prosecute: Organization and Public Policy in the Antitrust Division,* Suzanne Weaver, 1977.

3. *The Ungovernable City: The Politics of Urban Problems and Policy Making,* Douglas Yates, 1977.

4. *American Politics and Public Policy,* edited by Walter Dean Burnham and Martha Wagner Weinberg, 1978.

American Politics and Public Policy

Edited by
Walter Dean Burnham and
Martha Wagner Weinberg

The MIT Press
Cambridge, Massachusetts, and London, England

This book was set in Baskerville by A & B Typesetters, Inc., Concord, N.H., printed on R & E Book and bound in Holliston Roxite cloth by Halliday Lithograph Corporation in the United States of America.

Library of Congress Cataloging in Publication Data

Main entry under title:
American politics and public policy.

(MIT studies in American politics and public policy; 4)
Includes bibliographical references and index.
1. United States–Politics and government–1945-
–Addresses, essays, lectures. I. Burnham, Walter Dean. II. Weinberg, Martha Wagner. III. Series.
JK21.A463 320.9′73′092 78-17304
ISBN 0-262-02132-3

Contents

Jeffrey L. Pressman (1943–1977). Photo by Richard Reihl. MIT Historical Collections.

Preface

Jeffrey L. Pressman died unexpectedly in March 1977, at the age of 33. Jeff was our cherished colleague, esteemed for his intelligence and professional acumen, for his warmth, compassion, and integrity. He had a singular ability to listen to and understand others. He conveyed a sense of such good humor and concern that those with whom he dealt—his teachers, colleagues, and students—all came to regard him as a friend.

At the time of his death, Jeff was considered to be one of the outstanding young scholars of American politics in the country. He had published a study of conference committees in Congress, a seminal article on mayoral leadership, a widely influential book on implementation of federal policy, a detailed case study of federal programs and city politics, and two collaborative studies of representation and legitimation in the Democratic party. In addition, he had established a reputation for being one of the finest teachers of both graduate students and undergraduates at MIT and at Dartmouth.

Jeff Pressman loved politics—studying politics, teaching politics, discussing politics, and participating in politics—and his enthusiasm was contagious. His interest in government was not only academic. He cared deeply about public affairs and immersed himself in them because he genuinely felt that government at its best could improve people's lives.

Jeff was above all a person who thought of politics not only as the object of scholarly study but also as a subject in which everyone could share his interest. One of Jeff's most conspicuous talents was his ability to analyze research and to extract from very specific data the most useful kinds of general conclusions about American politics. Remarkably, he made everyone think well about politics, not always an easy task to accomplish.

After Jeff's death we asked ourselves what suitable memorial we could fashion. Our thoughts quite naturally turned to a book of essays by some of his many friends on contemporary issues of politics and public policy in the United States. In keeping with Jeff's approach to studying politics, we decided to ask contributors to the volume to focus on an issue that interested them and to discuss it as they might have discussed it with Jeff.

We knew that he would have wanted anything done in his name to be actively useful to others in the ongoing task of understanding political affairs. For this reason we also asked that contributors to this volume deal with subjects that help explain the points of intersection of American politics and public policy—the complicated linkages among government institutions, public officials, and substantive policy which Jeff analyzed so penetratingly in his own work. (We also knew that he would have wanted us to get quickly to the point, to indicate clearly the significance of our subject, to write with organization, clarity, and, if possible, wit. But these are canons of presentation to which we can only aspire.)

The categories in which we have chosen to group the essays—electoral politics, presidential leadership, the legislative process, urban politics and public policy, and implementation—may appear to be loosely defined, since each of the essays addresses not only its particular subject but also the behavior of the institutions of American government and the policies they make. However, the significance of the categories for us is that each is one in which Jeff was acknowledged to be expert. In this sense his own work served to structure the book. The fact that many of the essays take the form of case studies is also reflective of Jeff, for another of his talents was his ability to describe cases and to draw general theory from them.

The enthusiasm with which our proposal for this book was received reflects more truly than our words can the esteem in which Jeff was held by his professional colleagues. The spirit which the contributors to this volume have shown reflects Jeff Pressman's influence on others, for he made it his task to foster a harmonious and collegial professional environment. His colleagues became his friends and his friends became friends of each other. We are extremely grateful to the contributors and to the editorial advisory board of the American Politics and Public Policy series for their devotion to this project.

These essays are written by outstanding scholars. We think they will be of interest to students, scholars, and others who are vitally interested in the problems of American politics and public policy in the 1970s. Jeffrey Pressman did far more than many twice his age to shape the study of these problems. We hope and believe that he would have enjoyed reading this collaborative tribute to his memory, just as we are confident he treasured the company of those whose writings are represented here.

Walter Dean Burnham
Martha Wagner Weinberg

Contributors

Eugene Bardach, The Graduate School of Public Policy, The University of California, Berkeley

Lawrence D. Brown, The Brookings Institution

Walter Dean Burnham, Massachusetts Institute of Technology

Demetrios Caraley, Columbia University

Thomas Cronin, The University of Delaware

Philip B. Heymann, Harvard University Law School

Jack Knott, The Graduate School of Public Policy, The University of California, Berkeley

Martin Levin, Brandeis University

Frank Levy, The Urban Institute

Michael Lipsky, Massachusetts Institute of Technology

William Ker Muir, Jr., The University of California, Berkeley

Robert T. Nakamura, Dartmouth College

Benjamin I. Page, The University of Wisconsin

Nelson W. Polsby, The University of California, Berkeley

Francine Rabinovitz, The University of Southern California

Martin Rein, Massachusetts Institute of Technology

Denis G. Sullivan, Dartmouth College

Martha Wagner Weinberg, Massachusetts Institute of Technology

Aaron Wildavsky, The Russell Sage Foundation

Douglas Yates, The School of Organization and Management, Yale University

Part I

Electoral Politics

Chapter 1

The 1976 Election: Has the Crisis Been Adjourned?

Walter Dean Burnham

Every American election is a discrete event. In due course, this event is joyfully and exhaustively chronicled by journalists and political scientists. The 1976 election is no exception. Think of the personal dramas of this election: the meteoric rise of Jimmy Carter from obscurity to the presidency, the cliff-hanging battle between Gerald Ford and Ronald Reagan for the Republican nomination, the closeness of the contest between Ford and Carter. These dramas have evoked an outpouring of books and analyses of remarkable volume in the short time since the election was decided.

But if 1976 is a discrete event, like all other elections it is also part of a flow, a moment in our political evolution. Analysis of an election as a moment in historic time, linked indissolubly with other moments in past and future, must differ from event analysis. Above all, the election must be fitted into the context of social and economic change if it is to be properly understood. The need for this is particularly compelling at the present, when many of the traditional, implicitly accepted orderings of electoral politics have disintegrated. When the contextual landscape is murky—and it has never been murkier than it is today—the digging must go even deeper than usual. That is the object of this essay. It is an exercise in studying the "deep background" of the 1976 election.

Since the early 1960s the United States has passed through major crises of an intensity and variety unknown in recent times. Their names form a familiar litany: the Kennedy assassination, the escalation of the Vietnam War and its eventual—and highly predictable—loss, the domestic upheavals of 1967-68, the Nixon presidency and its abrupt, tragicomic end, the oil crisis, and the worst economic slump capitalism has known since before World War II. Quite a large number of things in American life, things in which government is directly involved, have gone very wrong in a very short period of time. It is natural, therefore, for the observer to suspect that the crisis as a whole is greater than the sum of these parts—that more than bad luck or the characterological deficiencies of individual leaders must be blamed for this disarray.

A conjunctural crisis of politics occurs when political settlements, and the operational ideologies that justify and sustain them, collapse. This collapse, in turn, occurs when conditions in the society and the economy have made the political settlement irrelevant to the point where large parts of the population come to regard it as oppressive. With desperate brevity one might summarize this deep-background context of the 1976 election as follows. The political settlement which grew out of the New Deal and World War II had two essential elements. Domestically, politics came to be articulated as "interest-group liberalism," as an activity involving the interactions of the acknowledged and legitimate leaders of major peak groups with each other, and with government. Party leaders played a pragmatic, "brokerage" role. Enduring differences on economic-allocation issues divided most Democrats from most Republicans, but these differences were narrow and grew narrower over time. At the same time, the interventionist role of the federal government was—and until the early 1960s remained—very limited. It was limited most of all in those domains of potential public policy where "social" rather than economic regulation or intervention was involved. In a very real sense, the Lockean individual who stood at the base of the country's hegemonic political ideology was "saved" from the implications of depression, war, and empire by being transformed into the Lockean group.[1]

In the international arena, the political settlement that unfolded after 1945 was imperial or "globalist," and militantly anti-Communist. The United States, confronted with an international challenge to its well-being, saw the new needs of the existing order of things interact with the liberal activism of our leaders to produce, eventually, its nemesis: the Vietnam War. On the way, it necessarily created new structures of power in the "military-industrial complex" and—among many other things—linked the peak trade-union leadership to the Warfare State not only on grounds of ideology but, increasingly, on grounds of direct economic interest as well.

The electoral history of the past dozen years and more has been in large part the chronicle of this political settlement's disintegration. The old rules by which politicians and political scientists tend to live break down in such circumstances, and all sorts of peculiar things happen. For underneath the collapse of any political settlement is a refusal of assent to the "old politics," the accepted ways of doing things, a refusal that spreads, like a contagion, from one group of citizens to another. Moreover, the refusal of one group to perform the role stereotypically assigned to it in society will, rapidly enough, engender bitter opposition from members of other groups who find their values threatened.

The big accelerator of this process in the 1960s was, of course, the war. But the Wallace voters of 1968 were not in the main motivated by opposition to the fighting in Vietnam, but by opposition to the tremendous increase of federal intervention into social domains formerly the preserve of local governments or private arrangements. In short, for many who left the old Democratic party coalition by that door—and for others who were tempted to do so but until 1972 did not—the problem was that blacks were not "keeping their place," and, what was worse, they were being supported by northern middle-class liberals and by the federal government itself.

The wavelike escalation of ghetto riots and student demonstrations moved a very large part of interest articulation altogether outside the well-known (and well-blocked) institutional channels. The very legitimacy of these channels was challenged, with the crescendo of protest centered on the 1968 Democratic convention. The pressure to restabilize that party by making it more representative was overwhelming. Out of the 1968 fiasco came the network of changes in Democratic convention rules that shifted the focus of selection away from the back rooms and toward the primaries and that—very significantly—relied upon quasi-proportional representation formulas for ingesting the proper number of scheduled minorities into the delegations.[2]

In retrospect, it appears to have been inevitable that one of the chief institutional victims of the collapse of the postwar political settlement was the party system. The Goldwater triumph in the 1964 Republican convention had demonstrated how very tenuous the welfarist consensus at the top had been in the United States, and how very powerful the appeals of laissez-faire ideology continued to be. But it also led to a party debacle in the short term, and it appears to have been the starting point in the process of erosion of GOP strength among voter groups, including affluent students, which had hitherto supported the party. Was the GOP a "usable" opposition any longer? Despite Nixon's victories of 1968 and 1972, this question has recurred, formulated in various ways, ever since. It remains unresolved to the present day. What is not in dispute is that there is now an extreme imbalance in size between the two major components of the party system, whether measured in terms of individual party identification or in terms of such "grass-roots" support measures as the percentage of state legislature seats won by each party.

Quite naturally, then, much recent analysis of the problem of party disintegration has focused on the internal dynamics of the majority party. It is clear that the war and social-issue cleavages ruptured this party in 1968 and 1972. The so-called pragmatists of the party's prowar wing had as their chief opponents not the Republican opposition but the newer middle-class liberal Democrats for whom the cold-war formulas of the old political settlement were not merely irrelevant but positively abhorrent in the context of the Vietnam conflict as they understood it. The candidate of the "pragmatists" won the 1968 nomination, but four years later the continuing pressure of war and social-issue cleavages, coupled with revised party rules which more accurately represented the current balance of forces within the party, led to the victory of their opponents. The upshot, among other things, was the demonstration of a political truth often buried in myth. "Pragmatists" and broker politicians act as they do under normal circumstances because the interests they defend are best protected by this style of behavior. When circumstances change and these interests are threatened, they can and do become as ideologically rigid, as polarized, as the veriest purist conducting a political jihad.[3]

But these internecine convulsions exposed even deeper issues. No two-party system can credibly exist for very long if politics becomes acutely polarized along more than a single dimension. As a result of the 1964, 1968, and 1972 elections, large but constantly shifting minorities of voters (and sectoral interests) found themselves losers in elections of unusual general-issue importance.[4] If the Republican party had become unprecedentedly shrunken and unattractive to the electorate as a whole, the Democratic party—by the very fact that it was in executive power from 1961 to 1969 and by virtue of its "incompatible" nominations of 1968 and 1972—had become identified as a central part of the problem. When to all of this was added the disastrous Nixon presidency, hard on the heels of an almost equally disastrous Johnson presidency, it was scarcely surprising that by the mid-1970s the strength of partisan identification had plummeted; that surveys repeatedly demonstrated a massive public loss of confidence in the working of our political institutions, especially the parties; and that writers like me were talking of "American Politics in the 1970s: Beyond Party?" or asserting flatly that *The Party's Over.*[5]

With this sort of crisis-ridden background, the 1976 election was early the focus of anxious attention by pundits and politicians. On the right loomed the specter of Ronald Reagan, a leader of some charisma who was exceptionally well suited to the image requirements of the electronic media. As for the Democrats, it was very hard to see how the party's antagonistic fragments could ever be welded together behind a nominee who could create enough intraparty consensus to win. At the very least, this fragmentation, coupled with the rules, appeared virtually to ensure a multiballot convention for the first time since the rise of television in 1952, and thus, paradoxically, to give unanticipated scope to power brokers at the convention.

As is usual in disordered and unstructured conditions, the expectations of politicians and pundits were confounded by the event. This was less noticeable on the Republican side. Had Ronald Reagan and his supporters conceded less to President Ford and worked harder, they might have ousted him. As it was, Ford's incumbency and the influence of the more cosmopolitan business interests within the party were just enough to secure his nomination. Even this, however, could not hide the continuing rightward shift of the GOP. The choice at Kansas City was between conservative and far right: the once-prominent liberal wing of the party, though still showing its prowess by winning senatorial elections in industrial states, is now virtually powerless in the councils of the party as a whole.

The real surprise was the remarkable return to consensus in the Democratic nomination process. Jimmy Carter, a former one-term governor of Georgia, and a man almost wholly unknown as late as early 1975 to political elites, much less to voters, won a first-ballot nomination. This was such a break with long-term traditions and shorter-term expectations that an adequate explanation of it is essential to understanding what is happening to American electoral politics. The Carter campaign tactics were brilliantly designed to fit the disordered conditions I have discussed. From a strategic point of view it resembled nothing quite so much as a "revitalization movement" aimed at reintegrating the disintegrated, with a minimum of disturbance to the cultural or material values of hegemonic interests. As a Southerner, Carter first had to purchase credibility by demonstrating that he could defeat George Wallace in his home region. Carter did so, but the leverage he won thereby went far beyond this. Because of George Wallace's very existence—and the ruinous popular reaction against Democratic presidential nominees in the South and elsewhere which was linked to him—any successful non-Wallace Southern Democrat would appeal broadly to other Democrats looking for a national winner.

Additionally, Jimmy Carter campaigned as an "outsider," as one not in any way part of the Washington "establishment," and hence as one who could in no way be considered (like all his rivals but Wallace) as part of the problem. His was a campaign fought on personalist grounds, stressing his religious beliefs, the purity of his moral commitment, and the need for comprehensive but nonpartisan reform in the way government did its business. From very early on, it was clear to liberals and conservatives that the former had not much to hope from, and the latter rather little to fear from, a Carter administration. All of this, it should be stressed, fitted very well the pervasively disgusted mood of the electorate in 1976. It was an electorate heavily populated with voters who were alienated but who at the same time sought credible reassurance that their continuing belief in the old-time symbols of the American political religion was not vain.[6]

Of course, success is often its own justification in politics. But it is hard to escape the judgment, in retrospect, that this centrist, vaguely revitalizationist campaign succeeded within the Democratic party as well as it did because the older structures of opposition were already crumbling away. This crumbling was reflected in the weakness of all of Carter's major initial opponents. In fact, the only men who were to give Carter much trouble after the Massachusetts primary in March were Senator Church of Idaho and, especially, Governor Brown of California. Brown, after all, was a still newer face—but one preaching the same gospel of a new, retrenched, and self-denying liberalism whose popularity fitted the exhausted and bewildered mood of the country at large. He remains Carter's most formidable opponent within the Democratic party. His 1976 career, like Carter's, epitomizes the new politics of the 1970s: change the faces with ever-increasing speed, but keep the dream and the system that spawns the dream.

The chief significance of the 1976 Democratic convention was that it was captured by a campaign identical in many of its essentials to campaigning in a Southern Democratic gubernatorial primary. There was irony in all this, the latest of countless ironies in the twentieth-century history of our electoral politics. The reformers of 1972 were defeated by changing circumstances and by superior technique in utilizing the reforms which they themselves had created. Carter's success in gaining the nomination meant the sudden adjournment of the politics of confrontation within the Democratic party. Both parties to that confrontation had exhausted and to a considerable degree discredited themselves. Carter's surge represented what E. E. Schattschneider long ago called the most devastating of all political strategies: the ability, when the time is ripe, to change the subject.

With the Vietnam War long over, and in the wake of the worst economic slump since before World War II, it could be expected that the setting of the 1976 election would be utterly different from that of any previous election of recent years. Even the most cursory review of the survey data reveals the attitudinal effects of this. Among the respondents in the postelection voting study at the Michigan Center for Political Studies, the preoccupation with economic malfunction was enormous. Among those who identified a "single most important problem" facing the country, 31 percent selected unemployment, 26 percent chose inflation, and another 13 percent gave a variety of economics-related replies—in all, a total of 70 percent. By contrast, public-order problems were selected as the "single most important" by 8 percent (5 percent choosing crime/violence specifically); the energy crisis by 4 percent; social-welfare issues by 4 percent; all foreign-affairs items by 3 percent; all defense-related items by 2 percent; and race-relations problems by 1 percent.[7] Foreign-policy and defense issues were probably less salient in 1976 than at any time since 1948 or earlier. The salience of "social-issue" problems had largely evaporated. The salience of economic problems was much higher in 1976 than it had been at any point in the preceding quarter-century.

One would expect that these stimuli would work to restore the New Deal coalition, including the South—largely because of Carter's regional identification. To a limited extent this coalition materialized, especially by contrast with the losing McGovern coalition of 1972. Thus, the Gallup surveys reveal that the heaviest pro-Democratic swings between 1972 and 1976 were, in order: Southerners (+26); self-identified Democrats (+22); people who describe themselves as moderates in ideology (+22); people in blue-collar occupations (+20); and males (+20). Conversely, the voters among whom Carter's appeal was weakest relative to McGovern's were: people aged 18 to 21 (a swing of −5); blacks (−4); people living in cities of 500,000 or over (+2); Republicans (+5); people describing themselves as liberals in ideology (+5); people making $20,000 a year or more (+7); and Westerners (+8). Similarly, a review of the internal polarizations in voting-group categories shows a maximum *decline* from 1972 to 1976 among age, community size, region, and ideology, and a very sharp *increase* of polarization in the category of party identification and, especially, income and occupation.[8]

All of this sounds at first blush as though "happy days were here again" in 1976. But the striking feature of this election, as of its immediate predecessors, was its pied results at different levels of the election. At the grass roots—state legislative outcomes, or the elections for the House of Representatives—the Democrats secured more than two-thirds of the seats. The Republicans were reduced to depths plumbed before only in the 1932-36 period and in the special case of 1964. They quite failed to bounce back from the Watergate-induced rout of 1974. But the presidential election was extremely close. Carter won only 51.1 percent of the two-party vote. By one criterion of closeness (the minimum number of votes theoretically needed to change the result in the electoral college), 1976 turns out to be the third-closest presidential contest in the last century and a half, exceeded in that regard only by the elections of 1876 and 1884. Nor was there any doubt that Ford was an economic conservative, and that the Republican party was significantly more disliked by the electorate than the Democratic party, largely because the GOP in the minds of many voters was associated with big business.[9] Instead of a relatively comfortable victory—let alone a victory by the landslide projected by the polls of midsummer—Carter barely squeaked through, gathering just enough fragments of the New Deal coalition to edge past the incumbent. Why was this so?

First of all, Gerald Ford was the incumbent. In this century only three sitting presidents have been defeated for election (in 1912, when the majority party was split in two, in 1932 in the face of economic disaster, and in 1976). But Ford's pardon of Nixon clearly rankled among many voters in 1976, and it is quite possible that this act in the end cost him the election.[10] Moreover, Ford was a nonelected incumbent who had never, even as vice-presidential candidate, faced the voters in a national election. Yet when the Michigan interviewers asked voters what they liked about the candidates, Ford's two chief assets loomed very large in the responses: his personal qualities (as a "nice guy," trustworthy) and, especially, his experience. These two categories together constituted 69 percent of all favorable references to Ford, compared with 34 percent for Carter. Carter's positive rating on personal characteristics was slightly higher than Ford's overall (with heavy emphasis on sincerity and morality), but a much higher proportion of respondents than in Ford's case were favorable to him because they perceived him as friendly to the little man and as the candidate of his party. But in any case an incumbent's stock in trade is his experience, and incumbents are accordingly hard to defeat as a rule.

Second, both candidates were widely perceived as less than satisfactory: 80 percent of all references to Carter's leadership qualities were negative, as were 76 percent of similar references to Ford's leadership qualities. While Carter appears to have "won" the debates overall, his lead was neither large nor "deep."

Third, it is worth stressing again that presidential elections in our time are overwhelmingly plebiscitary events in which voters have been induced over the years to choose on increasingly personalistic grounds. The whole of Carter's campaign was heavily oriented—as in any Southern Democratic primary—toward stressing this personalistic side of campaigning until about five weeks before election day. But "pure" personalism is not yet completely dominant in voter choice. As the summer went on, Carter's overwhelming lead in the polls shrank to the vanishing point; as the campaign went on, Carter's strategy shifted toward group-oriented policy appeals to the bedrock constituencies of the national Democratic coalition. It was at that point, and not before, that his slide stopped—for personalism is a two-edged sword. Ford as a person was at least as attractive overall as Carter was, to judge from the evidence; and being an incumbent of stable and well-known views, he profited from the ambiguity that surrounded Carter's campaign.

Fourth, while the election turned on economic issues, they appear to have cut in different ways than they once did. There is good reason to suppose that the evolution of the American political economy over the past generation has produced a kind of "two-nations" phenomenon. It has been true for a long time that the relative concern over inflation and unemployment varies significantly by social class. People in the lower half of the income-occupation structure tend to be preoccupied with unemployment problems, while concern with inflation issues becomes relatively greater the higher the respondent's position is in the class structure.[11] But this propensity was probably heavily reinforced by the extreme unevenness of the impact of the 1974–75 slump, both geographically and occupationally. Recovery from the slump's effects also appears to be moving at very different rates of speed within the occupational structure. Moreover, while factory workers have seen little or no rise in real income after taxes for the past decade, businessmen, professionals, and people in the higher reaches of the federal service have clearly done much better than this. One survey from the NBC poll of voters on election day makes this point quite graphically. Respondents were asked whether their family's finances were generally in better, the same, or worse shape than they were a year earlier. The results, stratified by income, are reported in table 1.[12]

Differentiation of voting in terms of these responses appears to have been quite sharp. Of those respondents reporting improvement (22 percent of the total), 30 percent voted for Carter. This compares with a Carter percentage of 51 among those reporting no change (48 percent of the total), and 77 among those who feel worse off (28 percent of the total). Similarly, only 36 percent of those in this survey who believed that inflation was the most important economic problem voted for Carter, while fully 75 percent of those whose primary economic concern was over jobs and unemployment voted for the Georgian. It is also worth noting that 38 percent of the Democratic identifiers in this survey thought themselves worse off, while only 15 percent considered themselves better off than a year earlier. Among Republican identifiers, the proportions reversed: 13 percent thought themselves worse off and 35 percent thought themselves better off in 1976 than in 1975.

Given these divisions, the mystery would seem to deepen except for one basic fact of the 1970s: the heavy and growing class skew in electoral participation. Evidence is overwhelming that non-

Table 1. "Two Nations?" Responses to NBC Poll Question about Family Finances by Income Level, 1976

Perceived Change in Family Finances since 1975	Family Income				
	Less than $5,000	$5,000-9,999	$10,000-14,999	$15,000-24,999	$25,000 and over
Better	9%	13%	26%	27%	14%
Same	56	50	51	50	46
Worse	35	37	30	27	17
Percentage of Respondents	9	20	26	27	14

Table 2. The Case of the Disappearing Voters: Turnout and Partisanship in Two New York Metropolitan Counties, 1940-1976 (Percentage of potential electorate)

	1940	1952	1960	1972	1976
Bronx					
Voting	75.6	68.8	63.6	47.0	36.4
Nonvoting	24.4	31.2	36.4	53.0	63.6
Democratic	51.0	41.6	43.2	25.9	25.8
Republican	24.2	25.7	20.2	21.0	10.4
Other	0.4	1.5	0.2	0.1	0.2
Westchester					
Voting	81.8	81.6	78.6	69.1	61.0
Nonvoting	18.2	18.4	21.4	30.9	39.0
Democratic	30.7	26.3	34.0	25.5	27.5
Republican	51.0	54.9	44.5	43.4	33.1
Other	0.2	0.4	0.1	0.2	0.4

voting is concentrated in the lower half of the American socioeconomic structure. The evidence is equally strong that, as turnout has decayed in both presidential and off-year elections from 1964 on, it has fallen more rapidly—both absolutely and relatively—among low-participation social groups than among those whose members participate most.[13]

Viewed at the aggregate level, the national presidential turnout of 54.6 percent in 1976 is mediocre enough, with lower rates of participation found in our past only in 1920, 1924, and 1948. But even this low turnout is masked, to a considerable extent, by the remobilization of the Southern electorate since 1948. If we exclude the Southern states from analysis, the 1976 participation rate of 56.8 percent is the lowest of all time, marginally lower even than 1920 and 1924. It stands 14.3 percent below the 1960 level, and 16.1 percent below the turnout rate achieved in the 1940 election. The detailed census survey of voting and nonvoting for 1976 is not yet available, but it is possible to obtain a sense of the magnitude of this problem by looking at the presidential turnout in selected New York metropolitan-area counties. One, the Bronx, has become nationally infamous for the concentration of urban social problems within its borders. The other, Westchester County, is not wholly free of these problems nowadays but remains an older and generally prosperous suburban bedroom for

New York City. Table 2 graphically reveals what has happened to turnout in both counties since 1940.

The decay in participation even since 1972—hence, with the 18-to-20-year-old vote held constant—is considerable in both counties, but especially in the Bronx; where it was 22.6 percent of the 1972 base, compared with 11.4 percent of the 1972 base in Westchester. Had the 1940 turnout levels been reached in 1976, at least 350,000 more people would have come to the polls in the Bronx than actually did so, compared with an additional 131,000 in Westchester. The picture is similar in California: predominantly Chicano and black-slum congressional districts in Los Angeles, the 25th and 29th respectively, were carried overwhelmingly by Carter with turnout rates of 28.1 percent and 36.2 percent respectively. The suburban 20th and 27th, however, had participation rates of 59.9 percent. Both were carried by Ford; it was the raw-vote pluralities he received in affluent, high-participation districts like this that helped him win a statewide plurality of 139,960.[14]

In the concrete situation of 1976, excessive emphasis ought not, perhaps, to be placed on this massive decline in voting participation in attempting to account for the election's partisan outcome. For example, Everett Ladd insists that an "inversion" has occurred in the demographic structure of liberalism and conservatism since the New Deal era.[15] Even if something of a shift back again is discernible in 1976, it would be very misleading to assume that the old class-ethnic polarities had been restored to anything like their pristine state. The data in table 2, limited as they are, hint as much. The outcomes of 1940 and 1976 in New York State were similar in the aggregate, with narrow Democratic victories in both elections. Very broadly, the decline in the Democratic share of the potential electorate in places like the Bronx has been matched by a decay in the Republican share of the electorate, both in the party's traditional upstate bastions and in the rapidly growing suburbs.

Thus, in New York at least, the interaction of these two processes produced a narrow Carter victory, but one grounded quite differently from FDR's 1940 victory in that state. The general argument still stands, especially if states like Illinois or California are taken into account: had lower-status voters participated even at the rates of 1960 or 1964, the presidential election of 1976 would not have been very closely decided. But perhaps one reason why they didn't participate at those levels is the growing extent to which the Democratic party has come to appeal to some sectors of the better-off electorate, as Ladd indicates. It is the "majority party" of a declining fraction of the adult population. It is important to note in this respect that turnout for Congress was still lower (51.0 percent nationally). Yet Democrats won handily with 57.6 percent of the two-party vote, compared with Carter's 51.1 percent. Put another way, Carter won with the support of 27 percent of the adult population, congressional Democrats with the support of 29 percent.

It is, in fact, this divergence between outcomes at different election levels which is of central importance in analyzing the meaning of the 1976 election. Taken together, the evidence presented by Ladd and others, the narrow balance between likes and dislikes for each candidate in the 1976 CPS study, the high levels of suspicion and distrust of leadership and political parties found in all recent surveys, and the turnout pattern all suggest a profound blurring of political images in the public mind. The dissolution of the partisan link between electors and elected continues its course. One chief symptom of this has been the now abundantly documented divergence of presidential and congressional voting coalitions. The election of 1976 extended and perhaps reinforced this recent pattern. The historic decline of the Republican party at the grass roots continued. In the northern and western states, for example, the party's state-legislature representation hit lows not even reached in 1936 or 1964.

The evolution toward distinct voting coalitions at different election levels has given incumbents of both parties an increasing, personalized protection. The election for the House of Representatives showed almost exactly the pattern described by a number of recent writers.[16] That is, the partisan distribution of outcomes in seats without incumbents tended to have a single mode close to the 50 percent mark, while incumbents tended to score lopsided victories over their opponents. Of the 74 supposedly vulnerable Democratic freshmen elected in the Watergate landslide of 1974, only three lost their seats.[17] Indeed, of all 267 incumbents in the non-Southern states, only 11 (4.1%) lost their seats.

Table 3. Anticipated Consequences of Two Models for Congressional Outcomes

Category	Incumbent-Insulation Model	Party-Salience Model
Vote in CDs with incumbents, 2 terms or more	Swings paralleling national, little effect on outcomes because of bimodality (already existing landslide margins for incumbents of both parties)	Swings paralleling national; significant effect on outcomes because of relative closeness
Voting swing in CDs with incumbents, 1 term (freshmen up for reelection)	Strong countercyclic swing favoring freshmen of both parties	Swing paralleling national, large-scale loss for freshmen of party with adverse nationwide swing
Vote swing, open seats (no incumbents)	Strong convergent swing toward 50% (greater than national swing for losing party, countercyclical swing against gaining party)	Swing paralleling national in *both* categories (D and R at last election) of open seats
Heterogeneity of vote swing across all CDs	Tends toward maximum	Tends toward minimum
Amplitude of seat swing (losses or gains for a given party in HR representation)*	Tends toward minimum	Tends toward maximum

*Another, somewhat more technical, way of putting this is to say the swing ratio ("predicted" by the cube law to be 2.80 to 1 in the long run) approximates a minimum under the incumbent-insulation model and a maximum under the party-salience model. Empirical verification of this expectation is clear-cut. Thus, in the five-election sequence 1884-92, the swing ratio reached an all-time high of 8.62. In the five-election sequence 1968-76, it reached an all-time low over the past century of 0.97.

This literature on the increasing insulation of incumbents in congressional elections implicitly presupposes its opposite: a more or less tight partisan linkage in the electoral process. From such a linkage comes a constraint on the divergence of electoral coalitions along office-specific lines—what might be called, in short, the electoral foundation of party government. Table 3 presents schematically what each of these models implies for leading categories of aggregate electoral performance in congressional elections.

Considerations of space preclude as detailed an analysis as one might wish, but let us briefly compare the elections of 1874-76 and 1974-76 with these models in mind. (For obvious reasons, these comparisons incorporate all congressional districts except those in the eleven ex-Confederate states of the South.) An attractive feature of this comparison is the existence of certain rough comparabilities in the two sets: a modest Republican electoral upsurge after a preceding rout for the party (a Democratic swing in the two-party vote of −1.8 percent in 1874-76, and of −2.1 percent in 1974-76); an incumbent Republican administration with scandals in the immediate political background; and economic hard times. If we look first at the pattern of partisan outcomes by incumbency status in the elections of 1876 and 1976, we note immediately a startling difference in the two configurations (charts 1 and 2). The move toward much greater heterogeneity of outcomes for incumbents is clear-cut. It should also be noted that the proportion of seats with incumbents is, of course, much larger in 1976 than in 1876 (60.6 percent in 1876, 86.7 percent in 1976).

Similarly, the swings reported in table 4 reveal a strong conformity with the patterns to be anticipated as we move from a party-salience situation (1876) to a more personalized incumbent-insulation situation (1976). In 1876, the nationwide swing entailed the loss of their seats by 32 Democratic incumbents, 30 of whom were freshmen (24.4 percent of Democratic incumbents), as well as 7 Republican incumbents (12.5 percent). But in 1976, a slightly larger swing was associated with the loss of only 7 Democratic incumbents out of 241 running (2.9 percent), and 4 Republicans out of 122 running (3.3 percent). As is obvious from table 4, movements among these categories of districts have a personalized heterogeneity which did not exist a century earlier.[18] A

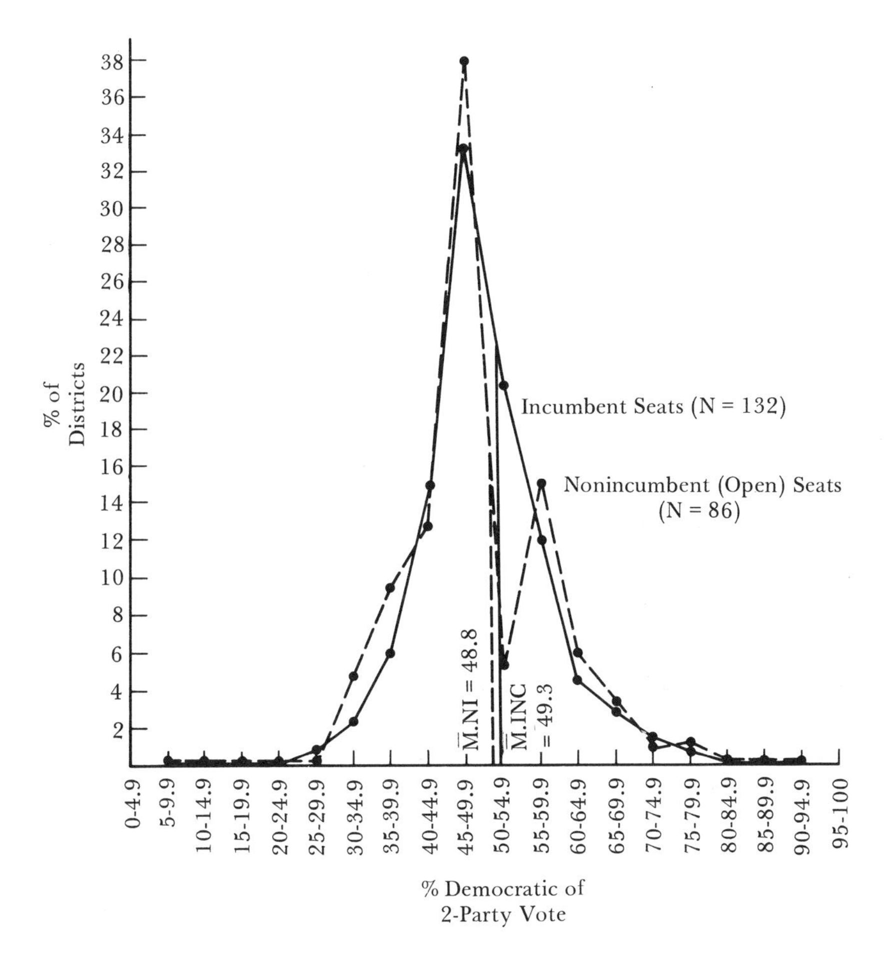

Chart 1. 1876: Distribution of Contested Seats, Non-South, by Incumbency Status

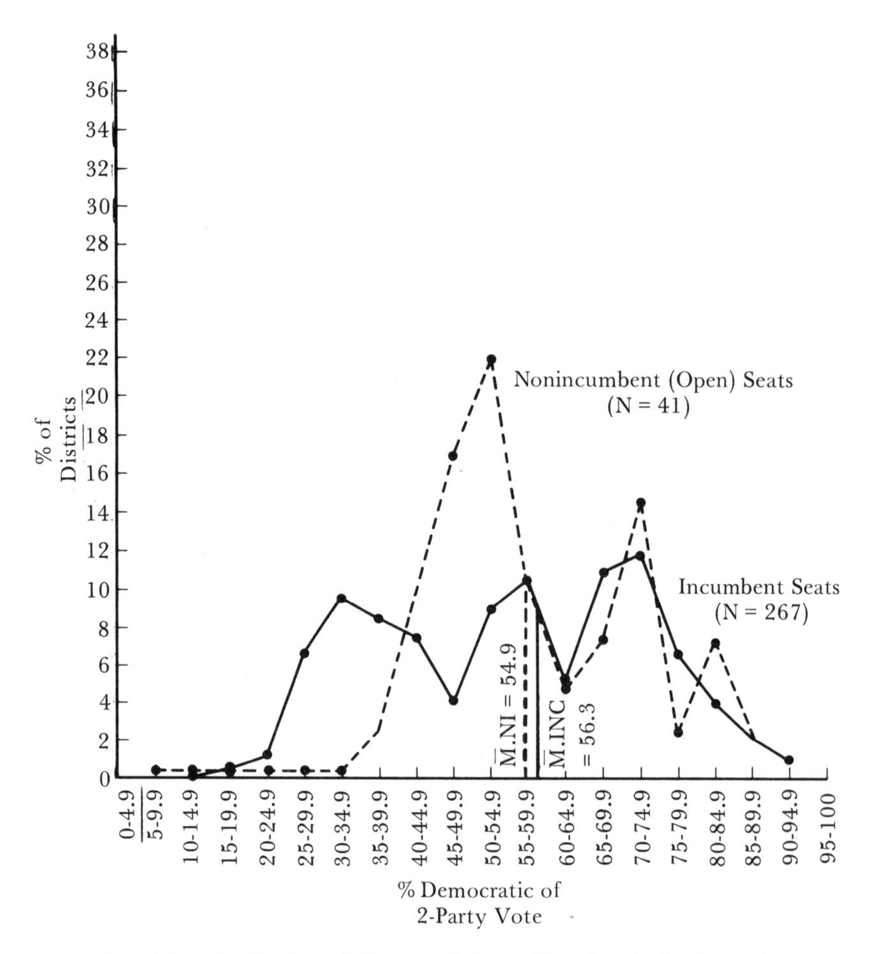

Chart 2. 1976: Distribution of Contested Seats, Non-South, by Incumbency Status

study of the heterogeneity of swing across all non-Southern districts likewise produces results in conformity with the two models. Thus, in the tightly partisan-constrained British electoral universe, a 4.7 percent Conservative swing between 1966 and 1970 was associated with a variance of 6.8; the 1874–76 Republican swing of 1.8 percent with a variance of 24.8; and the 1974–76 Republican swing with a variance of 76.7, a threefold increase over the past century.

There is no question that the changing technology of political campaigning—the growth of congressional staffs, the increasing capacity and interest of incumbents in concentrating on constituency service, and the steeply rising use of the congressional frank—has contributed heavily to this denationalization of electoral forces in the United States.[19] But the rapid and quite massive recent shifts in this direction are also part of a general crisis of politics in which political parties have lost their salience as cue givers for voting among decisively large minorities of voters. This increasing personalization of electoral politics critically affects not only electoral outcomes but the power relations among elective institutions at the national level. As electoral coalitions diverge and become more office-specific (actually, candidate-specific), the result is a profound behavioral reinforcement of the constraints which the separation of powers imposes on coherent policymaking and coordination. Put more bluntly, the emergence of these patterns implies a massive and, so far as we can tell, permanent reinforcement of institutional deadlock and the hamstringing of the presidency as an institution of national leadership.

To this we may add two other considerations. In the first place, we have Jimmy Carter himself: a man who owed little in his rise to the major interests surrounding the Democratic party, or to major leadership circles within the party itself. His style is technocratic and "above party." As he owed little to congressional Democrats in his rise to the presidency, so they owe little to him now. Second, there are abundant reasons to believe that the general crisis of capitalism into which we are now entering requires the formulation of the kinds of programs a Carter would tend to prefer: rational, comprehensive, highly complex, and with each major part crucially depending for its success on securing enactment of every other major part. Such is obviously the rationale

Table 4. Two Models: The Cases of the 1874-76 and 1974-76 Congressional Elections*

	1874-76				1974-76			
Category of District	N 1876	Mean % D, 1874	Mean % D, 1876	Swing to D, 2-party	N 1976	Mean % D, 1974	Mean % D, 1976	Swing to D, 2-party
D incumbents, 2 terms or more, 76	18	58.9	56.5	−2.4	95	71.8	68.6	−3.2
D incumbents, 1 term (elected 74)	62	55.3	52.2	−3.1	60	58.2	62.7	+4.5
Open seats 76 won by D 74	38	58.1	54.7	−3.4	25	70.4	62.3	−8.1
Open seats 76, won by R 74	46	44.9	44.4	−0.5	17	40.1	48.9	+8.8
R incumbents, 1 term (elected 74)	17	44.9	44.7	−0.2	17	46.4	35.0	−11.4
R incumbents, 2 terms or more	28	42.2	42.4	+0.2	79	40.6	36.5	−4.1
Total H.R., non-South	209	51.2	49.4	−1.8	293	57.1	55.0	−2.1

*Non-Southern districts only. Based on percentage Democratic of two-party vote, in all districts where major-party opposition existed in both years of each pair.

behind the energy program. Other areas, notably taxation, will appear to require similar treatment. Yet, if the history of our dispersed, nonsovereign political system teaches us anything, it is that Congress is unlikely to approve any such sweeping policy packages in any conditions other than those of overwhelming, immediate crisis. The syndrome of drift and mastery about which Walter Lippmann wrote more than a half-century ago was a crucial part of American experience, even when partisan links across separated branches of government were much more powerful than they are now.[20] A fortiori, the structural conditions favoring drift have become more deeply entrenched than ever.

Some years ago the historian Eric McKitrick wrote a seminal article which compared the effectiveness of Union and Confederate war efforts during the Civil War.[21] His analysis centered on a crucial comparative fact: the Union had powerful political parties, the Confederacy had no parties at all. The existence of these parties in the North meant two things for Lincoln's leadership. First, his own Republican/Union party gave him invaluable and predictable support at crucial times and created an essential institutional bond between him and Congress on the one hand, and between him and the war governors of the states on the other. Second, the existence of a powerful and structured Democratic opposition gave Lincoln essential information on the nature, scope, and effectiveness of the opposition to the war effort. In the Confederacy, on the other hand, the war effort was vitiated at every stage. The president and vice-president, coming from very different political traditions, were constantly at loggerheads; so were Jefferson Davis and the Confederate Congress. State-governor opposition to the centralizing thrust of war was also endemic. The Confederacy was a political system in which opposition, unchanneled by party, seeped in here, there, and everywhere, to the detriment of its capacity to achieve the most elemental collective purposes.

The truth of the matter is that in a modern state political parties are required not only to give some substance to nominal democracy, but to act as channels of information and power through which political leadership can penetrate the society.[22] If the short-term interests of concentrated economic power and campaigning politicians are promoted by a disintegration of party linkages between rulers and ruled, their broader interests—both as individuals and as members of the hegemonic class—may be very seriously compromised in the not-so-long run. In the American system, above all, the price for creating the support of mass electorates and cadres of activists—a support essential to the accumulation of power resources by executives—is the existence of some organized force able to overcome the fragmenting which the institutional structure mandates. Moreover, it may well be said that the essential job of the chief executive is to manage the capitalist political economy as a whole, both domestically and in its relationships with other political economies and states. It seems probable that today this management requires not only the existence of working instrumentalities for executive power accumulation, but the use of the power accumulated to secure assent to policies that will seriously affect both the position of organized interests and the daily habits of most Americans. If so, the progressive disappearance of party—a disappearance that successful candidates for office these days are capitalizing upon—would appear to favor political instability and ineffective performance on a scale without recent precedent.

Of course, one cannot have a resurgence of political parties (or a creation of new and more relevant ones) just by wishing for it. A price has to be paid by our various power elites to realize their purposes within the existing order. The shape of the 1976 election gives scant evidence that they are either willing to pay it or even able to perceive that it must be paid if political stability and effectiveness are to be minimally realized. My own judgment, then, is that the outward symptoms of crisis have recently been transformed, but the crisis itself endures. How will the contradictions that feed it be resolved within the existing structure of our political system? Will they be resolved at all without a breakdown of the system at some point? These remain the unanswered riddles of the 1976 election.

Notes

1. Probably the best single discussion of the tensions involved is Theodore Lowi, *The End of Liberalism* (New York: Norton, 1969), Chapters 2-4. See also the discussion in Grant McConnell, *Private Power and American Democracy* (New York: Knopf, 1966).

2. For a useful discussion of these changes and their relationship to the nomination process, see Denis G. Sullivan, Jeffrey L. Pressman, Benjamin I. Page, and John J. Lyons, *The Politics of Representation: The Democratic Convention 1972* (New York: St. Martin's Press, 1974). See also Denis G. Sullivan, Jeffrey L. Pressman, and F. Christopher Arterton, *Explorations in Convention Decision Making: The Democratic Party in the 1970s* (San Francisco: W. H. Freeman, 1976).

3. Sullivan, Pressman, Page, and Lyons, *Politics of Representation*, pp. 116-134.

4. See, for example, Norman H. Nie, Sidney Verba, and John R. Petrocik, *The Changing American Voter* (Cambridge, Mass.: Harvard University Press, 1976), Chapters 12-15; and Arthur H. Miller, Warren E. Miller, Alden S. Raine, and Thad A. Brown, "A Majority Party in Disarray: Policy Polarization in the 1972 Election," *American Political Science Review* 70 (1976): 753-778.

5. Walter Dean Burnham, "American Politics in the 1970s: Beyond Party?" in William N. Chambers and Walter Dean Burnham, eds., *The American Party System*, 2nd ed. (New York: Oxford University Press, 1975), pp. 308-357, and David Broder, *The Party's Over* (New York: Harper & Row, 1972). For a somewhat more optimistic view, see John G. Stewart, *One Last Chance: The Democratic Party 1974-76* (New York: Praeger, 1974).

6. See particularly the sobering data and report by Louis Harris Associates in a survey commissioned by the U.S. Senate, *Confidence and Concern: Citizens View American Government*, U.S. Senate, Committee on Government operations, 93rd Cong., 1st sess. (Washington, D.C.: Government Printing Office, 1973). The Michigan CPS 1976 study shows comparable findings.

7. Michigan CPS 1976 election study, frequency counts, Variable 3689.

8. The standard deviations of the presidential vote among the usual broad groups of Gallup's surveys increased for Party from 21.3 to 28.2; for Income from 4.7 to 9.0; and for Occupation from 2.9 to 6.5. For Ideology, on the other hand, the standard deviation declined from 23.3 to 18.0; for Region from 5.1 to 2.7; and for Age from 5.1 to 2.7.

9. For example, in the postelection survey the question was asked as to whether given groups had too much, enough, or too little influence. Big business led among 24 groups (77 percent said too much, 14 percent about right, 3 percent too little) in responses in the "too much" column. Next came labor unions (64 percent too much) and black militants (49 percent too much).

10. In fact, this is quite the largest single negative-mention item concerning Ford in this study.

11. See the evidence reported by Douglas A. Hibbs, Jr., "Economic Interest and the Politics of Macroeconomic Policy" (Cambridge, Mass.: Center for International Studies, M.I.T., paper C/75-14, 1976), esp. pp. 24-40. This article was published in abridged form in the *American Political Science Review*, December 1977.

12. Typescript, "NBC Election-Day Poll, 1976."

13. Since 1964, the U.S. Bureau of the Census has been asking questions as part of its extensive Current Population Reports, Series P-20, about voting participation in presidential and off-year congressional elections. These reports have grown more detailed over the years. While the detailed reports for 1976 are not available at the time of writing, the longitudinal patterns for 1966-74 are clear-cut.

Category	Turn-out, 1968	Turn-out, 1972	Shift 1968-72	Normal-ized Shift, 1968-72	Shift 1966-74	Normal-ized Shift, 1966-74
Propertied middle-class (professional, managerial farm owners)	81.7	79.7	−2.0	−2.4	−10.0	−14.3
Nonpropertied middle class (clerical sales)	77.4	72.8	−4.6	−5.9	−14.6	−22.5
Upper blue collar (craftsmen, service)	66.9	60.4	−6.5	−9.7	−14.7	−26.3
Lower blue collar (operatives, laborers)	57.5	49.5	−7.0	−11.3	−12.5	−27.1

14. Data from California *Statement of Vote,* relevant years; population base for 1976 districts, *Federal Register* 42, no. 79 (April 25, 1977): 21129; and *Congressional District Data Book,* 1974 California supplement. It is entirely characteristic that the absolute level of turnout declined from 1968 through 1976 by 9.3 percent and 17.4 percent in the poor/minority districts—CDs 25 and 29, respectively—but only 4.8 percent and 3.0 percent in the affluent suburban CDs 20 and 27, respectively.

15. Everett C. Ladd, "Liberalism Upside Down," *Political Science Quarterly* 91 (Fall-Winter 1977): 577-600.

16. For example, Burnham, "American Politics in the 1970s," pp. 322-333; Edward R. Tufte, "The Relationship between Seats and Votes in Two-Party Systems," *American Political Science Review* 67 (1973): 540-554; and Tufte, *Data Analysis for Politics and Policy* (Englewood Cliffs, N. J.: Prentice-Hall, 1974), pp. 96-101.

17. Allan Howe (Utah 1); Tim L. Hall (Illinois 15); Richard VanderVeen (Michigan 5). Howe was involved in a local personal scandal; VanderVeen ran in the solidly Republican district from which Gerald Ford came, at a time when Ford was at the top of the Republican ticket; and Hall represented an also normally Republican district in an exceptional year for the GOP in Illinois.

18. More formally, the variance across these categories of seats increased from 1.96 in 1876 to 49.0 in 1976, or by 25 times.

19. The best single discussion of this so far is Morris Fiorina, *Congress: Keystone of the Washington Establishment* (New Haven: Yale Fastback, 1976). The mechanisms which incumbents use to entrench themselves are spelled out thoroughly. See also David R. Mayhew, *Congress: The Electoral Connection* (New Haven: Yale University Press, 1974).

20. Walter Lippman, *Drift and Mastery* (New York: 1914).

21. Eric McKitrick, "Party Politics and the Union and Confederate War Efforts," in Chambers and Burnham, *American Party System*, pp. 117-151.

22. Note the discussion of this in Giovanni Sartori, *Parties and Party Systems: A Framework for Analysis* (Cambridge: Cambridge University Press, 1976), 1:41-42. Sartori is much more preoccupied with the evils of hegemonic claims on the society by "monopolistic" parties (such as the Communists), and with problems of political order, than with the possible uses of parties as collective vehicles of democratization; but the point he makes is in any case important.

Chapter 2

Party Democracy and Democratic Control

Robert T. Nakamura and Denis G. Sullivan

The presidential selection reforms of the 1960s and 1970s raise profound questions about the relationship between parties and democracy. This paper examines these questions in the light of recent convention research.[1] Specifically, we shall place nomination process changes—principally those in the Democratic party—in the context of four basic models of party democracy. Since each model makes different assumptions about the rationality of voters and motivations of elites, each one makes different predictions as to the consequences of reform.

Our analysis is in three parts. First we shall describe four basic models of party democracy and identify the characteristics of the two most critical to the current debate. Second, we shall examine criticisms that recent presidential nominations changes have produced a new and unrepresentative party system, thereby diminishing the quality of citizen choice. Third, we shall analyze these criticisms using our recent research on presidential nominations.

Each model of party democracy describes a different kind of party organization to maximize voter satisfaction. Two basic dimensions seem to underlie the differences, one motivational and the other organizational. The motivational dimension involves either the primacy of issues or the primacy of winning (see chart 1). The organizational dimension involves the preference for a

Chart 1. Party Models of Democratic Control

		Organizational Dimension	
		Centralized, Hierarchical Party Organization	Decentralized, Nonhierarchical Party Organization
Motivational Dimension	Issues as Primary	Responsible party model	Participatory model
	Winning as Primary	Party as firm	Pluralist-organizational model

centralized-hierarchical organization or a decentralized nonhierarchical organization. We shall briefly describe each model, its prescribed reforms, and then examine in some detail the characteristics of the two models most critical to the current debate.

The Responsible Party Model The party is a centralized, disciplined, hierarchical organization primarily motivated by the desire to advance agreed-upon issue positions.[2] This position is found in *Toward a More Responsible Two-Party System* and more recently in James McGregor Burns's proposals to the 1974 midterm Democratic party conference. Elections in this model are educational and designed to show voters their true latent interests. Disciplined and clear-speaking parties are necessary to simplify real choices for relatively uninformed voters. Specific reforms favored by the advocates of this model are clear party membership requirements to provide the party with the means to discipline elected officials who do not live up to the party's issue commitments, and regular party conferences to establish the party's line.

The Party as Firm In this model parties are vote-maximizing, disciplined organizations whose only motivation is the winning of office. Policies are products presented to voters to maximize vote yields. The analogy is to a business firm and has been developed by academics such as Anthony Downs and others.[3] Such parties are said to discover and provide what voters want. Voters are assumed to be relatively fixed in their issue preferences. While this model is actively discussed within political science, there is no movement in America holding that a more perfect democracy would be achieved by its adoption.

The Participatory Model In this model issues are primary and the party is decentralized.[4] The individual participant is the fundamental unit, and so the model prescribes maximizing participation opportunities for individuals. Party activities are intended to help individuals discover and clarify choices. The structural reforms favored by advocates of this model include affirmative action, proportional representation, primaries, openness, and due process requirements for delegate selection meetings. While the participatory premise of this model is not often fully articulated, the prescriptions that follow from these premises were actively advanced within the Democratic party during the 1960s and 1970s.

The Pluralist-Organizational Model This model—considered most descriptively accurate by party theorists and professional politicians—prescribes the modern nominations system prior to the Democratic party's reforms of the 1960s and 1970s.[5] Parties are said to consist of reasonably stable coalitions; the electoral task of each party is to mobilize its coalition's members. Issue positions are evaluated in terms of their capacity to mobilize existing supporters, rather than of their correctness. Each party's coalition consists of groups who tolerate each other in less than perfect harmony. The ever-present possibility of internal conflict encourages the use of decentralized decision making as a device for holding the party together. Specific reforms under this model tend to increase the influence of party regulars, who value unity and winning, and to reduce the influence of issue activists who would split the party.

The recent dispute over changes in presidential selection procedures has occurred principally between the holders of the participatory and pluralist-organizational models of democracy. This is so because insurgents in the Democratic party have centered their demands on increased participation opportunities and justified them by the participatory tradition in democratic thought. Their opponents, the party regulars, have responded to these attacks using as their arguments the pluralist-organizational model. Since these two models were—and still are—central to the dispute over the Democratic party's reform rules, as well as other changes, we will examine these positions in greater detail.

The dispute over the proper role of party in presidential

selection centers on the role of elections in democracy and the appropriate patterns of voter consultation and consent. The pluralist-organizational model assumes the quality of democracy to be a function of interparty competition. The organizational health of each party—freedom from internal division—determines the quality of democratic choice presented to voters. The participatory model assumes, on the other hand, the quality of democracy to be a function of popular participation in internal party affairs. As parties, through extensive internal conflict, learn what voters want and clarify their own offerings, the quality of voter choices in the general election will improve. A listing of the essential characteristics of these two models is contained in chart 2.

Chart 2. Two Alternative Views of Party Democracy

The Organizational Model	The Participatory Model
Voters lack the incentives, information, and interest to formulate consistent or realistic opinions about how they should be governed.	**Voters** have specific and detailed opinions about how they want to be governed. They want and will use the opportunity to make their positions clear to leaders.
Parties should be run exclusively by professional politicians who 1. are motivated by the desire to win elections; 2. value party as their means of winning elections; 3. use as their standard for judging issues and nominees the usefulness of each for winning the election and unifying the party.	**Parties** should be open to issue-oriented activists who 1. are motivated by the desire to improve public policy by advancing specific issue positions; 2. place a high priority on advancing principled issue positions and a correspondingly low priority on considerations (such as party unity) that would compromise or distort those principles; 3. use as their standard for judging issues and nominees their "correctness" according to the activists' personal standards.
Participation in party nominations should be limited to insure the maximum room for maneuver on the part of professional politicians. Great care should be taken to preserve resources for the coming campaign, including unstated or vague issue positions.	**Participation in party nominations** should be open to insure the widest airing for issue positions and to guarantee the selection of a nominee whose positions have been clarified by an open process.

Chart 2. Two Alternative Views of Party Democracy (continued)

The Organizational Model	The Participatory Model
Campaigns should be waged in terms voters will find meaningful. Nondivisive appeals are best: symbols of party identification, ethnic or interest-group loyalties, issues on which a consensus exists. Elections are a test of candidate and party competence rather than a contest of principle. Parties tend to vary their appeals only incrementally from previous years, a tactic related to party or organizational survival.	**Campaigns** are primarily educational events. Candidates have the obligation to clarify their issue positions and the differences between themselves and the opposition. Voters are to be educated about the advantages and disadvantages of each party's offerings. Parties may vary their electoral appeals significantly from past years because they are responding to current concerns.
Democratic choice consists of the voter's picking the party whose current appeal or past performance has most satisfied him. Choice is made easier by the simplification of party appeals and each party's criticism of the other.	**Democratic choice** consists of picking the candidate whose detailed issue positions are most in agreement with the voter's.
Election outcomes decide who gets to exercise governmental power. The party in power has an incentive to act responsibly because it wants to win the next election, and the out-party points out deficiencies for the same reason.	**Election outcomes** are binding contracts between the public and officials. Officeholders are expected to behave according to the issue positions of the campaign.
Conclusion The quality of democracy is dependent on the organizational strength of political parties.	**Conclusion** The quality of democracy is dependent on the degree of participation exercised by voters within parties and in the electorate.

Each model serves as an ideological justification for advancing the power position of the disputants. By adopting the participatory model, insurgents justified demands for openness in the name of democracy, and rules that opened up the party reduced the power positions of those controlling party offices. Party regulars, on the other hand, cited the pluralist-organizational model to justify their dominant position, again in the name of democracy, and the inadvisability of sharing it with the insurgents. But the dispute is not entirely one of power; both models are rooted in important philosophical traditions, each with a particular conception of democracy.

The Democratic party's rules changes reflected a movement away from the pluralist-organizational model toward the participatory model. Specifically, the opportunities for participation were increased and the role of party leaders as professional intermediaries was reduced.

A New Class of Presidential Elite?

The Democratic party's rules changes favoring greater participation by voters and activists in internal party affairs—principally in determining the presidential nominee—have produced a strong reaction from the supporters of the pluralist-organizational model. They argue that the rules changes have reduced the capacity of the party to carry out its democratic function of choosing nominees popular with the voters and effectively presenting them in the general election. The weakening of party organization, then, reduces the competitiveness of the parties in the general election. This, in turn, lessens the effective level of citizen choice.

The crux of the criticism of the new nomination system is that the newly empowered participants are *not* representative of the party's rank and file or of the party's electoral coalition. Furthermore, it is said that this new group of participants indulges its own policy preferences instead of anticipating electoral preferences. Thus greater participation, according to this position, reduces the ability of the Democrats to present candidates attractive to voters, and the unilateral weakening of one party diminishes the effectiveness of two-party competition.

Perhaps the most sustained and complete critique of participation in the new system is that advanced by Jeanne Kirkpatrick and her colleagues in their interpretation of recent presidential nominating conventions (see *The New Presidential Elite*).[6] Using as her principal evidence interview and questionnaire data from Republican and Democratic delegates to their respective 1972 presidential conventions, Kirkpatrick argues that 1972 marked the entrance of a "new breed" into the presidential elite. The imputed characteristics of this new presidential elite—membership in the middle class, skill in the use of media, commitment to ideological remedies for governmental problems, unrepresentativeness of the general population, and indifference to the true distribution of preferences—are a litany of the pluralist-organizational model's advocates' objections to the participatory model. The basic criticism is that the participants favored by the new system of presidential selection make the party system less able to perform its democratic function. In the name of participatory democracy, the real prospects for pluralist-organizational democracy have been lessened, and an unrepresentative and insensitive system has been put in its place.

Because of her research, Kirkpatrick's description of the characteristics of the new class is much more precise than the impressionistic evidence provided by previous commentators. She has identified the source of the "new breed" with changes in society. Our society has larger numbers of "symbol specialists"—owing to more elaborate systems of education and communication—than has ever been the case before. Examples of convention delegates who are "symbol specialists" are college-educated professionals, such as teachers, professors, authors, publishers, clergymen, social scientists, and social workers, as well as their spouses. The significance of the new breed lies in their role as shapers of new moral codes and new political priorities. Their political beliefs tend to be weakly supportive of parties, ideologically holistic, and are held with an intense moralism that precludes compromise.

The new elite, according to Kirkpatrick, is important because the triumph of the participatory model has created a permeable Democratic party organization. Primaries, open state conventions, proportional representation, affirmative action, and generally complex procedures have advanced the new elite at the expense of organizational loyalists. Finally, and most importantly, the consequence of their participation has been the growing inability of the parties to represent the majority of the people. The new breed, in short, are unlikely to submerge their own beliefs long enough to learn what the electorate wants and consequently are poor judges of what is popular. The final result is, in the author's view, the decline of parties as organizations and the alienation of voters from the party system.

Kirkpatrick's work raises many specific methodological and substantive questions. Here we will deal primarily with the validity of the argument as it relates to the proper role of party in democratic control.[7] Kirkpatrick's charges can be divided into two main categories: the biases of the party's new participatory system and the shortcomings of the new breed as the agent of party democracy.

The New System and the New Class

The charge that the Democratic party's participatory process gives some people advantages over others is neither new nor in itself a cause for concern. Rules always affect the distribution of power by raising or lowering the costs of participation. What is significant is the specific formulation, made by Kirkpatrick and others, that the organizational loyalists (who in their model are the agents of party democracy) have been unfairly disadvantaged by the new rules, while the new class has unduly benefited.

The general thrust of the new rules has been toward greater participation. Rules governing state and local delegate selection conventions, for example, have opened the process through a variety of devices: the requirement that such meetings be publicized in advance, the writing and enforcement of rules for determining who will be permitted to participate, holding such meetings during an election year when citizen interest is likely to be higher than in an off year, and so forth. In a general sense, one could argue that such rules disadvantage party leaders who could have held such meetings early and in secret and restricted participation to their own circle. Greater participation, however, does not mean that party leaders must automatically lose. All it means is that party leaders must compete with nonleaders for influence. If party leaders are able to mobilize sufficient numbers of followers, then they can prevail. The appearance of bias stems from recent convention outcomes in which party leaders have been out-organized by insurgents.

Democratic party rules governing the running of primaries also are said to have an effect. In part, some of this effect is unintended. Lengle and Shafer argue, for example, that the complexity of rules governing state conventions and caucuses led many states to adopt the primary route.[8] This means that voters have a greater say in the selection of delegates, while the groups that mobilize voters—primarily candidate organizations—have the greatest say. Professional politicians and organizational loyalists—distrustful of internal party divisions, and concerned with winning—commit themselves later than issue activists, who merely search for a candidate with whom they agree. Thus the candidate organization—with its need for manpower to move into many primaries and its few material rewards—becomes inordinately dependent on issue activists.

The rules governing primaries do not in themselves preclude the involvement and influence of party professionals and organizational loyalists. The lengthy primary and convention process provides many opportunities to make judgments on professional criteria (information becomes more readily available about who is popular and which issues are useful), and it is apparent that picking a failing candidate does not preclude joining a winner at a later point. This process—with its increasingly rapid pace of primaries toward the time of the nominating convention—may even enhance the influence of party organizations where they exist. Candidate organizations apparently organize thoroughly for the early primaries but find themselves spread thinner and thinner as time progresses. The candidate who can make an effective alliance with a functioning party organization in the later primary states has an advantage over his rivals. Thus the value of party organization—when it is capable of delivering primary votes—is probably great under any system that includes primaries.

Probably the clearest effect of the new rules is that they benefit people who participate and those who can organize participants effectively. The bias is said to come from the emphasis on participation. One stereotype of the party loyalist is the machine politician who has an essentially working-class following. While he may be able to mobilize these people for a general election—where the symbol of party and the promise of patronage are salient—they are not likely to take advantage of subtler participation opportunities, like candidate caucuses and issues discussions. The stereotype of the issue activist is that of an energetic middle-class person (often female) with an equally middle-class and active following. Such people are not only likely to participate but to actively create opportunities for participation.

Whatever the element of truth in these stereotypes, opportunities to participate are much more likely to be used by the middle class than the working class. This does not mean, however, that middle-class participants are homogeneous, that they are all or even principally issue activists, or that their participation is entirely at the expense of organizational concerns.

Varieties of Middle-Class Ideologies

The literature on citizen participation in party politics assumes that there are only two types of participants: purists and professionals. Issue purism is indeed a documented middle-class political style. Study after study has found it in presidential nominating conventions. But it must also be clear that issue purism is not the only middle-class political style, merely the most widely documented one. If there are many middle-class political styles (or more elaborately, middle-class ideologies), then the advantage gained by the middle class through opportunities for political participation need not lead to the dominance of issue activists.

We will merely sketch out some other middle-class styles we have encountered in our convention research, in order to indicate that the range is much greater than assumed at present. First, many Republican delegates and some Democrats could be classed as managerial technocrats. The prototype is a businessman who works in a large organization and emphasizes the "competence" of his preferred candidate, distrusts elaborate left-right ideologies, prefers "problem-solving" approaches, and often does not express any particular loyalty to the party as an organization (but may do so to a candidate's organization). Second, there are the organizational purists whom we encountered in the 1972 convention supporting the centrist candidates. Usually these people are taken for professionals—they may be party politicians, minor officeholders, loyal workers—because they tend to participate through party organizations. But they have deep-seated issue commitments, often centrist, which are hidden by their nonissue language. When the nominee is someone who does not share their centrist positions, the criticism of the organizational purist becomes an issue-oriented one. McGovern, they argued, should not be the nominee because his issue positions were wrong.

A third plausible configuration for middle-class participants is that of the candidate loyalist. These are people who, for example, committed themselves to Jimmy Carter on largely personal and non-ideological grounds, such as religious affinity or regional pride. Their commitment was hardened and reinforced during the lengthy primary process, and their judgment reaffirmed by the developing backing of voters. It might be that the protracted process of presidential nominations will increase the numbers and importance of this group.

It is possible to generate other types of middle-class styles, but the important point is that increasing middle-class participation opportunities do not necessarily mean that issue purism will predominate.

Are Issue Activists Party Wreckers?

A second criticism of issue activists is that they reduce the capacity of the Democratic party to unite behind the nominee and to wage an effective campaign against the Republicans. Here the relevant event seems to have been the badly divided 1968 convention and Hubert Humphrey's loss in a close election to Richard Nixon. The criticism of issue activists as rigid ideologues, willing to substitute their personal judgments for the collective wisdom of party leaders, has often been made. It extrapolates from their known characteristics (a deeply felt concern for issues) to their likely behavior.

The role of conventions in legitimating the nominee and symbolically uniting the party for the coming campaign, we have argued elsewhere, is becoming its real function.[9] As the nomination is increasingly decided in advance through primaries and mutual adjustment among candidates, the convention ceases to have a candidate selection purpose beyond acting as an Electoral College. This leaves as a central item the legitimation function.[10] So the argument that issue activists, advantaged by the new system, are less likely to unify than are professionals has serious implications.

This charge against issue activists is peculiar in light of recent experiences. It was the so-called Eastern Republican Establishment, led by Governor Nelson Rockefeller, who failed to unite behind the nomination of Barry Goldwater in 1964. It was from the ranks of the regular Democrats, followers of Hubert Humphrey, Edmund Muskie, and Scoop Jackson, that the bitterest criticisms of George McGovern's 1972 nomination came.[11] The single recent exception, that of the 1968 Democratic convention, is instructive. "Party wreckers," in two of the three most recent divided conventions, have been the followers of regular candidates and not the issue activists usually pictured as playing this role.

Among our findings from the 1976 Democratic and Republican conventions is that nominees have more resources to placate issue activists than they do to placate professionals who have lost. Issue activists, we have shown, will tend to unify behind the nominee when that person demonstrates movement toward their favored positions. Carter did this through concessions on rules (involving women and blacks), specific platform planks, and most importantly in the selection of a liberal vice-presidential candidate. Ford also was able to get the backing of conservative issue activists supporting Ronald Reagan through concessions on the platform and vice-presidency. In both these cases, issue activists, precisely because they place a value on issues, could be moved to legitimate by the nominee's issue appeals. Rather than a reason for dividing the party, concern over issues—at least in these two recent cases—has been the basis for unifying behind the nominee. The case of the Democrats in 1968 can be interpreted in this light. The Humphrey forces refused to concede on the compromise wording of the Vietnam platform plank, and by winning this test of strength the Humphreyites deprived their opponents of an excuse for backing the nominee.

Professional politicians, on the other hand, are less likely to legitimate on the basis of issue concessions. They value, by definition, winning power, and think of issues as means rather than ends. Thus they are not likely to respond to what they interpret to be issue shifts by the nominee. When a candidate lacks the prospect of electoral victory, as McGovern seemed to in 1972, there is little that he can do to placate many professionals who do not support him.[12] Commitment to organization apparently does not extend to supporting the party's nominee whoever he may be.

Conclusion

The triumph of the participatory model of party democracy over the organizational model has fundamentally altered the Democratic party's presidential nominating system. It has opened up that process to greater participation, and the principal beneficiaries of those participation opportunities seem to have been middle-class activists. The charges made against this new system by proponents of the organizational model, however, do not stand up to critical analysis. The groups advantaged by the process are not homogeneous, they are not necessarily more or less representative than the party organization people they have replaced (using as a test of representativeness the capacity to mobilize supporters), and their participation does not necessarily guarantee continued internal divisions in the Democratic party.

Notes

The authors wish to acknowledge the helpful comments on our manuscript made by W. D. Burnham and Laurence I. Radway.

1. See Denis G. Sullivan, Jeffrey L. Pressman, Benjamin I. Page, and John J. Lyons, *The Politics of Representation: The Democratic Convention of 1972* (New York: St. Martins, 1974); Denis G. Sullivan, Jeffrey L. Pressman, and F. Christopher Arterton, *Explorations in Convention Decision Making* (San Francisco: Freeman, 1976); Denis G. Sullivan, Jeffrey L. Pressman, F. Christopher Arterton, Robert T. Nakamura, and Martha W. Weinberg, "Candidates, Issues, Caucuses: The Democratic Convention, 1976," in S. Maisel and J. Cooper, eds., *The Impact of the Electoral Process* (Beverly Hills: Sage, 1977); and the same authors' series of articles on the Republican convention of 1976 in *Political Science Quarterly* 92 (Winter 1977-78).

2. E. E. Schattschneider, *Party Government* (New York: Rinehart, 1942), and *Semi-Sovereign People* (New York: Holt, Rinehart and Winston, 1960); Committee on Political Parties of the *American Political Science Review* (chaired by Schattschneider), *Toward a More Responsible Two-Party System* (New York: Rinehart, 1950); James McGregor Burns, *The Deadlock of Democracy* (Englewood Cliffs, N.J.: Prentice Hall, 1963). For a review of the dispute over this model, see Evron Kirkpatrick, "Toward a More Responsible Two-

Party System: Political Science, Policy Science, or Pseudo-Science?" *American Political Science Review*, LXV (December 1971): 965-990.

3. Anthony Downs, *An Economic Theory of Democracy* (Boston: Little, Brown, 1957); Otto A. Davis, Melvin J. Hinich, and Peter Ordeshook, "An Expository Development of a Mathematical Model of the Electoral Process," *American Political Science Review* 64 (June 1970): 426-448.

4. While this model has not been fully articulated in any single place, its features can be found in the internal Democratic party debate over convention rules. Some of them are described in Austin Ranney's analysis of those proceedings, "The Democratic Party's Delegate Selection Reforms, 1968-76," p. 204, in Allan Sindler, ed., *America in the Seventies: Problems, Policies and Politics* (Boston: Little, Brown, 1977). James W. Ceaser, in *The Theory and Development of Presidential Selection* (Princeton: Princeton University Press, forthcoming), Chapter 7, develops portions of this model in his discussion of the Progressives' views on presidential selection. See also Denis Sullivan et al., *How America is Ruled* (New York: John Wiley & Son, forthcoming). Despite the frequent use of Woodrow Wilson's arguments by adherents of the responsible party model, Ceaser persuasively argues that Wilson's conception emphasized leadership rather than party as the mechanism for empowering leaders through a process of direct popular participation (internal party democracy, issues and elections).

5. For a discussion of this model applied to conventions, see Nelson W. Polsby, "Decision Making at the National Conventions," *Western Political Quarterly* 13, no. 3 (September, 1960): 609-617. Robert A Dahl, *A Preface to Democratic Theory* (Chicago: University of Chicago Press, 1960) presents the theoretical context; for the political culture of the model, see the discussion of the professional political style in James Q. Wilson, *The Amateur Democrat* (Chicago: University of Chicago Press, 1966).

6. Jeanne Kirkpatrick, *The New Presidential Elite* (New York: Twentieth Century Fund-Russell Sage, 1976). Her critique that activists produced an unrepresentative convention is cited by Nelson W. Polsby and Aaron Wildavsky, *Presidential Elections*, 4th ed. (New York: Scribners, 1976), and Ranney, "Delegate Selection Reforms." For a discussion of issue activism, see Wilson, *Amateur Democrat*, Chapter 12, "The New Party Politics: An Appraisal." Political style in the Democratic conventions of 1960 and 1968 and the Republican convention of 1964 is described with insight by Aaron Wildavsky in *The Revolt Against the Masses* (New York: Free Press, 1971), Chapters 12-14. John Soule and James Clarke, "Amateurs and Professionals: A Study of Delegates to the 1968 Democratic Convention," appears in the *American Political Science Review* 64 (September 1970): 888-899.

7. For a more thorough discussion of methodological and other theoretical points, see Denis G. Sullivan, "A Review of Jeanne Kirkpatrick, *The New Presidential Elite*," *American Political Science Review*, in press.

8. James Lengle and Byron Shafer, "Primary Rules, Political Power, and Social Change," *American Political Science Review*, LXX (March 1976).

9. See Sullivan et al., *Explorations in Convention Decisionmaking*; Sullivan et al., "Candidates, Caucuses and Issues."

10. Sullivan et al., *Politics of Representation.*

11. Ibid.

12. Denis G. Sullivan, "Exploring the 1976 Republican Convention's Party Unity: Appearance and Reality," *Political Science Quarterly*, 92 (Winter 1977-78).

Chapter 3

Interest Groups and the Presidency: Trends in Political Intermediation in America

Nelson W. Polsby

Jimmy Carter is the latest in a lengthening line of American politicians to claim a direct and unmediated relationship with the American people. Like Richard Nixon, George McGovern, Eugene McCarthy, Robert Kennedy, and other recent candidates for high public office, President Carter has taken the view that interest groups and state and local party organizations as they are traditionally constituted in the American political system have become largely irrelevant for electoral success, and likewise in the subsequent processes of governing. It is my intention in this essay to explore the meaning and the merits of this view because, if it is correct, it signals a distinctive shift in the character of the American political system from a "pluralist" or "polyarchal" democracy to something nearer a "direct" or "plebiscitary" or "mass" democracy. And even if it is not wholly correct, by considering how closely it approaches the truth, we may be able to catch a glimpse at some aspects of the future of American politics.

The first thing that should be said is that it is largely true that presidential nomination processes have passed out of the hands of interest group and party leaders and into the hands of state primary electorates, various sorts of professional technicians, and the mass media. Because this revolution in the party system has taken place only in the last dozen years, the litany of meaningful changes cannot be recounted too often.

Rather than seeking alliances with and commitments from state party organizations or interest groups allied to factions within state party organizations, candidates for the presidency are increasingly obliged to mount their search for delegates by building their own personal organizations, state by state. This is necessary because in general state party organizations cannot deliver the vote for the candidates of their choice in primary elections in which opposing candidates are effectively advertised or for other reasons enjoy high name recognition. Consequently, candidates must themselves advertise and promote high name recognition.

The mounting of a presidential campaign has come more and more to resemble the production of a Broadway show. A company is created that sells tickets, books theaters, writes a script (frequently known as "the speech"), and advertises the star. Individual contributions are solicited through the mail. As these build up, candidates become eligible for federal matching funds, provided by law to assist candidates successful in their initial fundraising efforts. With these funds, they can advertise themselves further and campaign in additional state primaries.

In general, it was party elites or party staff people acting with their tacit consent who created this situation by rewriting the rules of national conventions. Beginning with the Democrats in 1968, rules were written requiring delegates to future conventions to meet such a variety of stringent criteria that recourse to primary elections seemed to many state parties the only sensible method of assuring compliance and preventing successful challenges to their right to seat delegates at all. Primary-selected delegates grew from around one-third of the total to around three-quarters. The composition of primary electorates and the special characteristics of elections as mechanisms of deliberative choice of course came under scrutiny. It was observed that while primary electorates were invariably far more numerous than the party bosses who in the past had so often picked delegates to the national conventions, party bosses were frequently more sensitive than primary electorates in anticipating the composition of the electorate in the general election. Smaller minorities—especially those not designated as especially deserving by party rules—became harder to include in overall coalitions. Occasionally critics could point to horrible examples in which small percentages of the total eligible electorate turned out in sufficient numbers to elect as delegates people whose views on public policy varied drastically from those of party leaders, the rank and file, or the great bulk of the general electorate. Of such stuff, it was said, the McGovern debacle of 1972 was made.

National party conventions are no longer deliberative in any meaningful sense, since delegates come not to trade and bargain but to register the results, as they are more and more often legally required to do, of the primary elections in their respective states. Thus it is now far more desirable for a candidate to be the first choice of some substantial number of delegates—and in this context it now appears that 30 percent, Jimmy Carter's "magic number" in 1976, is very substantial indeed—than to be the second choice of 90 percent of all delegates. In such a strategic situation, coalition building between party factions, in which second choices are sometimes settled on as commanding a wider consensus, is a waste of time. Deliberation, mutual accommodation, give-and-take, all have become obsolete in the affairs of the national parties as the presidential nominating process has come to be dominated by the rivalry of theatrical companies, the star system, and the straightforward registration of first choices only at primary elections—which are proclaimed as "wins" by the national television networks no matter how close the margin between winners and losers.

Successful participants in this new system seem to be drawing two lessons from the experience. First, they evidently have come to believe that this system is genuinely one that is free of mediation processes. And second, at least in the cases of both President Nixon and President Carter, they seem to believe that contemporary circumstances have sharply reduced the need to exhibit traditional presidential concerns with coalition building in order to govern. The argument I would be inclined to make is that while both these conclusions are far from foolish deductions from the facts of genuine change in the presidential nomination process, they are nevertheless off the mark. The relations between president and people are still powerfully mediated, although by somewhat different processes and agencies than before. And presidents still need interest groups and must build coalitions of the older kind to govern successfully.

The main vehicle by which presidents bypass interest groups and reach the people "directly" is the medium of television, supplemented by the major wire services, news magazines, and other national news publications. Ample experience, however, as well as the formal findings of research, has shown that these news media are anything but neutral transmission belts. Rather, obeying their own organizational imperatives, craft norms, fashions, and accepted practices, the news media select and transform events. Politicians gain and lose from these processes of selection and transformation. Jimmy Carter, to take a famous example, was a substantial gainer in the early skirmishing leading up to the 1976 election because the networks took the view that in Iowa, the first state to select delegates, the strength of the uncommitted position (which actually attracted the most delegates) was not reportable news, while Carter's achievement of second place (first among those candidates present in the state) was. Similarly, the winner of the relatively small and insignificant—but early—New Hampshire primary attracts enormous amounts of national publicity as compared, let us say, with the winner of the much more consequential (in terms of delegates) Massachusetts primary a couple of weeks later. This illustrates how national publicity becomes a currency that can be cashed in in future state primaries: New Hampshire, because it is a very early primary, far outweighs Massachusetts, although in terms of delegates, the currency that candidates are ostensibly competing for, the reverse holds true.

To argue that the choices the media make in treating the news exercise a significant influence over what millions of Americans perceive as reality is not to imply that these choices are typically made in a spirit of partisanship or irresponsibility. It merely implies that a systematic understanding of the criteria that underpin these decisions is fundamental to an understanding of how communication between citizens and leaders is mediated in contemporary America. Communications specialists who have independent access to neutral organs of news transmission—Washington reporters, columnists, television news producers, and so forth—increasingly set the agenda for politicians. They raise the questions to which politicans must give their attention, they define what is important and what is trivial, what is acceptable in terms of answers and other behavior, and what is unacceptable.

In part, it is the conscientiousness of these specialists in seeking out and giving sympathetic treatment to novel and previously neglected voices in society that has sparked the rise to political influence of new sorts of interest groups. These groups, frequently—and for the most part erroneously—billed as grass-roots organizations, have taken on a new weight in American politics, in some cases achieving special recognition for their clientele in party rules and in law. Such groups include militant advocates speaking for the women's "movement" and "youth," black groups and certain other previously disadvantaged ethnic minorities (some of whose leaders have also exercised significant influence in situations favoring traditional interest groups), and groups specializing in the mobilization of rectitude such as Common Cause and various organizational offshoots of Ralph Nader.

I do not wish to argue that groups of this sort are especially worthy or especially unworthy as compared with state party organizations, labor unions, farmers' groups, associations of businessmen, or other interest groups organized on traditional lines around the economic or status needs of their clientele. Rather, what I am suggesting is that many of these newer sorts of groups—the ethnically based groups are the main exceptions—arise and are sustained by different means than traditionally organized intermediate groups. These new groups are to an unprecedented degree the creatures of the mass media, in that it is their power to command news coverage and to be taken seriously by the news media that in some cases brought them into being and in all cases sustains their political influence.

For good or ill, a political system having intermediation processes such as these is the sort of political system that is emerging in the United States. But instead of reaching directly into the homes of individual and atomized voters, political leaders broadcast to publics mobilized and organized around certain principles of attentiveness and inattention. Leaders must be seen to be doing certain things and avoiding certain other things.

Three recent events in which modern mediation processes played a part may suggest a little of how they work. One is the dismissal of Senator Thomas Eagleton as vice-presidential candidate on the Democratic ticket in 1972. Another is the resignation of Bert Lance as director of the Office of Management and Budget in late 1977. The third is the nonselection of John Dunlop as secretary of labor by President-elect Carter in 1976. It was widely assumed that Dunlop had a good chance to be Jimmy Carter's secretary of labor since, like another Carter adviser, James Schlesinger, his prior association with the Ford administration had ended in an honorable departure in which his personal integrity and political astuteness had to some degree been vindicated. Moreover Dunlop was known to be the first, second, and third choices of George Meany and the dominant faction of organized labor for the job as "their" ambassador to the new administration. In indicating this preference, Meany had given due regard to a norm that prescribes a measure of independence from the labor movement for the secretary. Dunlop was not himself a labor leader but a college professor and dean, an academic specialist on labor relations with a long record of practical experience as an impartial arbitrator of labor disputes.

It may well be that President Carter never intended Dunlop to have the job, but it is at least intriguing to note that the appointment was strenuously opposed by leaders of black and militant women's groups, who believed that in his prior government service and as dean at Harvard Dunlop had been unsympathetic to their aspirations. One interpretation of the course of events is that in a straight fight between one set of interest groups—labor—and another—black groups and the women's movement—over who was to be secretary of labor, it was not the traditionally organized group that won, even though the fight was held in their own bailiwick. It is not recorded that labor exercised a comparable veto over the appointments of black citizens and women in the Carter administration. The appointment of black and female Americans to administration positions was extensively monitored in the press, however, which in due course came to refer to these two groups, with the addition of Spanish-Americans and native Americans, as virtually the only "interest groups" whose progress was worth tracking. This, once again, was a news decision made by independent news specialists, but it was not a decision empty of political consequences, since such decisions serve to confer legitimacy on groups and their political claims—and to withdraw it as has been happening, for example, in the case of American Jews.

Another facet of contemporary political intermediation is revealed by the Eagleton case. Once it was discovered by the mass media that Senator Eagleton had not disclosed episodes of hospitalization for severe depression, it was only a matter of time before his colleague Senator McGovern had to remove him from the Democratic ticket. Why was this a foregone conclusion? Interested readers can search in vain through "responsible" journals of news and opinion for a serious discussion of hospitalization and recovery from mental illness as a disqualification for public office, not to mention a comparison of Eagleton's life history with that of the Republican vice-presidential nominee, Spiro T. Agnew, who had never been institutionalized or diagnosed as mentally distressed. In fact the news media rapidly reached a consensus that Eagleton had to go, but so far as an outsider could tell, it was not based on a discussion of the merits of the case so much as on the chagrin of media people at Eagleton's lack of candor with them. George McGovern, a nominee whose success depended not on the building blocks of interest-group alliances within the Democratic party but on these very same news media, had no real choice but to dismiss Eagleton forthwith.

Here we can note that one characteristic of the newer style of political intermediation is that it is done in the sunshine. It is easy enough for anyone who has the price of a newspaper, or access to the televised evening news, to see what advice a political leader is getting from the news media. One difficulty with such arrangements is that when politicians must announce themselves and their preferences on national television, they tend to get locked into positions before they come to understand one another's point of view. Deliberation and negotiation, in which mutual accommodation and mutual learning are encouraged, are hard to arrange without causing one or more public figures embarrassment. Participants are tempted into confrontation politics and moralism in order to look good. And of course in looking good they may to an unaccustomed degree actually be good. But there are dangers here as well as opportunities.

The unfortunate affair of Bert Lance illustrates several of these themes. The news media uncovered enough of the story of Lance's financial difficulties to embarrass a Senate committee into withholding what would probably have been a routine extension of a deadline to sell his interest in a Georgia bank. Many charges and countercharges were exchanged in the newspapers and on nationwide television. No improprieties of any sort were alleged about Mr. Lance's conduct of official business, but many irregularities in his prior financial activities were uncovered and publicized.

The question is this: To whom does a president turn when a trusted associate becomes a political liability? By what means are political liabilities balanced off against political assets so that a given administration can carry net assets on its political books without unduly constraining the president from counseling with associates of his own choosing? A president who relies upon traditional forms of intermediation has actual flesh and blood political associates and allies all over the nation to whom he can turn. He can ask their indulgence, consult and confer with them. All this is on the whole unavailable to a mass-media-oriented president, or to a president whose direct links to the people are in fact dependent upon access to the mass media, which he shares with reporters and editors who may or may not agree with him but in any case cannot bargain or consult with him.

So far my argument is simply that while there has been a shift in intermediation processes, it is not the case that modern forms of political intermediation free political leaders from important constraints. By trading George Meany for Walter Cronkite, presidents and presidential candidates may have achieved a kind of freedom, but only at a price. The Dunlop, Eagleton, and Lance cases suggest what sort of price is involved. In a large-scale society based upon appeals from leaders to followers for their votes, it is evidently impossible to escape the effects of political intermediation as a set of institutions and processes in some sense separate from leaders and followers, even as they link them.

A sizable number of conventional notions exist about the behavior of political intermediaries in large-scale political systems. Intermediary groups are supposed to interpret the desires of ordinary people to leaders, and to inform publics as well as tutor their expectations about the activities of government. They recruit and train leaders for politics, identify social problems, and suggest solutions. And they conduct long-range political education, helping to form the loyalties of citizens toward the state and providing legitimacy, a provisional sort of acquiescence to the underlying political order upon which the state can rely. Intermediary organizations teach political obligations to citizens and inform citizens of their political rights.

Traditional agents of intermediation thus include the nuclear family and the extended family, the school, the primary or communal groups such as exist in a workplace or church or neighborhood, or a voluntary association organized for the purpose of promoting some shared interest. It has been apparent for some time that various trends in modern society have eroded the monopoly that these institutions once held over the time and the loyalty of Americans, and so it is no surprise to learn of their decline as monopolists of political intermediation. The private automobile, a comprehensive network of roads, and the telephone have expanded the potential for individual communication enormously and have consequently attenuated the tyranny of geographical propinquity in determining the options that people have in adopting one or more organizations as their political intermediaries of choice. Television has had somewhat different effects. Since it is not an interactive medium, it has increased the power of a few who are at the focus of its attention and assured that certain sorts of standardized information are readily available, on a virtually universal basis. Political representation has more and more become a specialized, even a professionalized, activity. Finally, the rules of politics are being rewritten to reflect all these trends and in some sense to facilitate them. National party conventions, for example, once were conducted primarily for the purpose of discovering what the delegates wanted to do. Today they are even more frequently run according to scripts worked out by television consultants so as to maximize their advertising value to the viewing public.

If there is a political aristocracy today in national politics, it consists of people who are well known. If the hand that rocked the cradle once ruled the world, today the fingers that mash buttons in television control rooms have unexpected powers. Intermediaries now put a premium on the varied crafts of persuasion by means of mass media. In this situation, direct and material interests are bound to become relatively less important as compared with symbolic interests. Thus we can observe the rebirth of ideology. One doubts that a decade ago unsatisfactory unemployment statistics for black Americans could have been traded off against the control of foreign policy toward the continent of Africa. Today, as the educational level of black Americans rises and they, like all Americans, are hooked into a national communications network, they become reachable by symbols, and such trade-offs become thinkable.

To what extent do newer methods of intermediation perform the social functions that earlier fell to the old? It is undoubtedly too early to say in a definitive way. Clearly political education continues apace. Demands are made upon the political system in the name of citizens and blocs of citizens. The government seems to enjoy more than enough legitimacy to get its routine work accomplished without difficulty. If there are any nagging doubts about the newer forms of political intermediation, they surround the issue of accountability. On this issue, many traditionally organized political intermediaries are also vulnerable. To what extent does George Meany represent his rank and file? And how does he know? We can be fairly confident that on one great set of issues, civil rights, labor union leadership was far in advance of the attitudes of their rank and file, and in part because of the rather sluggish methods of accountability that prevail in the labor movement, they were able to get away with it more or less with impunity.

The accountability of the leaders of the newer interest groups, such as Common Cause or the Ralph Nader organizations, to the people in whose behalf they ostensibly speak is equally tenuous. Their capacity to deliver the votes of the people they organize directly is at the least highly questionable. Their real clients are news media managers. So long as news and television people believe in the rectitude of Ralph Nader and defer to him and his judgments, politicians will feel obliged to do so as well, and Nader can continue to claim to be an authoritative interpreter of the desires of people at the grass roots.

It will no doubt come as a disappointment to some observers that current trends in political intermediation do not include greater accountability and hence greater openness and democracy in some larger sense. In fact it can be argued—indeed, it frequently is argued—that groups equally deserving as the ones that have gained ground have lost ground because of their propensity to organize along traditional lines. In particular, the groups traditionally served by city machines—geographically compact, ethnically homogeneous neighborhood groups, for example—may well be suffering greatly. Women with a history of activism in political parties may be at a disadvantage compared to women with a history of activism in the women's movement. Life, as presidents increasingly have occasion to remind us, is unfair, and illustrations of that uncomfortable maxim can be found in the field of political intermediation as readily as in any other.

The newer methods of intermediation operate unevenly in the political system. They have far more to do with the election of presidents or governors of large states than with nominations and elections to Congress. They involve the manipulation of relatively ephemeral attitudes and nontransferable loyalties. For these reasons one must sharply question whether it makes sense for any president to believe that the type of intermediation that got him nominated and elected is adequate to the formation of a governing coalition.

For the purpose of governing, alliances with relevant factions and blocs in Congress and with national interest groups not necessarily organized on the new principles are highly desirable. Efforts to ignore, bypass, or run roughshod over such groups by appealing over their heads to the people are doomed on at least two counts. First, the appeal to public opinion itself is likely to fail because of the ephemerality of mass public attitudes on most issues and because of the nontransferability of a president's popularity (when the president is popular) to the objects of a president's desires. Second, even if by some unusual combination of circumstances public opinion does for once yield to a president's entreaties, the effects may or may not reach Congress or influence congressional disposition of an issue. Congressmen after all have their own constituencies and their own means of reaching them, and they may find themselves ill disposed toward a president who prefers to deal indirectly with them through what they may interpret as coercion rather than face to face and in a spirit of mutual accommodation.

For a president who wants nothing of Congress, and likewise nothing from traditional interest groups, it may be entirely feasible to live according to the dictates of a strategy that is concerned exclusively with renomination and reelection. But if a president means to do more than hold onto office, he will have to face the pockets of pluralism that remain in the political system and somehow deal with them. If Common Cause and other reformers succeed in their efforts to reduce the capacity of congressmen to facilitate their own reelections, it may well be true in some future time that presidents will be able to get their way on matters of public policy by direct appeals to public opinion. At the moment, however, checks and balances preclude this under ordinary circumstances.

No resounding peroration is possible. Traditional interest groups, based upon geography and economic self-interest, still exercise meaningful influence in Congress. So (with a few exceptions) do state and local party organizations, where these have traditionally been strong. In the presidential nomination process, however, these groups have lost ground to groups more approved of by the mass media and organized on different principles. The enormous growth in the influence of the media over the presidential nomination process has led presidents to believe that a high level of public approval for themselves is the central resource needed to govern, and that the attainment and maintenance of high popularity is relatively unconstraining as compared with the constraints of bargaining with interest groups. I have tried to suggest why I believe both these notions are debatable if not false.

Part II

Presidential Leadership in American Politics

Chapter 4

Jimmy Carter's Theory of Governing

Aaron Wildavsky and Jack Knott

Seek simplicity and distrust it.
Alfred North Whitehead

Why has it been so difficult for observers to determine what President Carter believes or will try to do in office? The reason is that we have all been concentrating on the wrong aspect of his words as predictors of his deeds. President Carter is not an ideologue of policy; he has flexible views on substantive policies, such as tax reform, medical care, and busing. Like most of us, as the times and conditions change, he can and does change his mind.

Our hypothesis is that Carter's basic beliefs are about procedures for making policy, procedures about which he speaks with passion, determination, and consistency. He is concerned less with particular goals than with the need for goals, less with the content of policies than with their ideal form—simplicity, uniformity, predictability, hierarchy, and comprehensiveness. Therefore, if there is a danger for President Carter, it is not that he will support unpopular policies, but that he will persevere with inappropriate procedures. The question is whether he views his procedural criteria merely as rough guidelines for formulating public policy or as immutable principles of good government. If they are hypotheses about governing, subject to refinement or abandonment in the face of contrary evidence, there is no reason for alarm, but if he does not allow his theories of governing to be refuted by experience, we all are in for hard times.

Of all the Democratic presidential candidates in the primaries, Jimmy Carter was criticized most for his alleged vagueness on policy. Some people saw him as a fiscal conservative who would cut government spending; others wondered about possible plans for costly social programs. Actually, his campaign staff put out numerous papers outlining his proposals on issues ranging from abortion to busing to welfare.[1] The problem was not so much that he did not say specific things about issues as that he placed greater emphasis on methods, procedures, and instruments for making policy than on the content of policy itself.

The response of Stuart Eizenstat, Carter's chief "issues" adviser, to a question about what issues would dominate the campaign, will serve as an illustration. Eizenstat grouped the issues into three types: one concerned the absence of long-range federal planning, a second concerned openness; and a third dealt with government reorganization.[2] The emphasis of all three was on administrative instruments, not on policy outcomes. (Long-range planning, like openness and reorganization, is not a policy but an instrument used to produce policies.) If faith in intellectual ability to put it all together is any sign, Carter on public policy is more of a planner than a politician.

Carter on Procedures

In contrast to the other candidates, Jimmy Carter made numerous statements during the campaign and during his term as governor of Georgia (1971–75) in which he explicitly emphasized principles of procedure for making public policy. Although we are aware of the possibility that these statements are in part rhetoric, his ideas do comprise a coherent philosophy, with recurrent and identifiable themes about how government ought to work, and we shall show that as governor of Georgia he put them into practice.

In his own words, a major purpose of reorganizing the federal government is to "make it simple." He favors "drastic simplification of the tax structure,"[3] "simple, workable, housing policies,"[4] "simplification of the laws and regulations to substitute education for paper shuffling grantsmanship,"[5] "simplification of the purposes of the military," and a "fighting force that is simply organized."[6] Rather than the "bewildering complexity" we now have, he wants to create a "simplified system of welfare."[7] His praise goes out to the state and local governments that have devised "simple organizational structures."[8]

How does he intend to simplify? When Carter became governor of Georgia he reduced the number of agencies from 300 to 22. He has proposed a similar nine-tenths reduction in the number of units at the federal level, from the present 1,900 down to around 200.[9] His general rationale seems to be the fewer agencies the better. Carter, it is fair to say, does not manifest a federal bias.

According to Eizenstat, another way Carter will simplify administrative structure is "to make sure that duplicating functions are not performed by one agency and that, in fact, we don't have a situation whereby duplicating programs are being administered by more than one agency."[10] Carter has stated repeatedly that one of the purposes of his proposal to introduce "zero-base budgeting" (as he did in Georgia) is "eliminating duplication and overlapping of functions."[11] In restructuring the defense establishment, he would like to "remove the overlapping functions and singly address the Defense Department toward the capability to fight."[12] In our terms, Carter favors intellectual cogitation over social interaction.

The Uniform Approach to Policy

A third way President Carter intends to simplify policy is through uniformity. He plans to reform the welfare system by providing a uniform national cash payment varying only according to cost of living.[13] He intends to standardize the tax structure by eliminating loopholes, thus treating all income the same.[14] To create uniformity, Carter would grant a direct subsidy for new housing.[15] Also he would standardize medical treatment—"We now have a wide disparity of length of stay in hospitals, a wide disparity of charges for the same services, a wide difference in the chances of one undergoing an operation"—and make criminal justice uniform by "eliminat[ing] much of the discretion that is now exercised by judges and probation officers in determining the length of sentences."[16]

"There's just no predictability now about government policy," Carter has complained, "no way to tell what we're going to do next in the area of housing, transportation, environmental quality, or energy."[17] He believes in "long-range planning so that government, business, labor, and other entities in our society can work together if they agree with the goals established. But at least it would be predictable."[18] And, "The major hamstring of housing development is the unpredictability of the Federal policies. . . ."[19] In agriculture, the greatest need is a "coherent, predictable, and stable government policy relating to farming and the production of food and fiber."[20] In foreign affairs, other nations are "hungry for a more predictable and mutually advantageous relationship with our country."[21] Unpredictability led Carter to condemn Henry Kissinger's policy of no permanent friends and no permanent enemies with these words: "I would . . . let our own positions be predictable."[22]

Shared Goals Make Predictable Policies

If only we agreed on long-range goals, according to Carter, we could work together to make our policies predictable. The format of his thinking follows: long-range planning entails explicit delineation of goals; once goals are known (and agreed upon), policies become predictable. This predictability reduces conflict and increases cooperation. Note that predictability does not come from intensive interaction about continuous adjustment of policies but by intellectual agreement on original goals.

Carter's theory of conflict shows how he would expect to deal with a recalcitrant cabinet: "The best mechanism to minimize this problem is the establishment of long-range goals or purposes of the government and a mutual commitment to these goals by different Cabinet members. . . ." By getting early agreement, "I can't imagine a basic strategic difference developing between myself and one of my Cabinet members if the understanding were that we worked toward the long-range goals."[23] When asked how he would resolve differences with Congress on foreign policy, Carter answered, "I hope that my normal, careful, methodical, scientific or planning approach to long-range policies . . . would serve to remove those disharmonies long before they reach the stage of actual implementation."[24]

A major Carter campaign criticism of President Ford was that Ford "allowed the nation to drift without a goal or purpose."[25] By contrast, as governor of Georgia, Carter's administration had tried to identify long-range goals: " . . . during the first months of my term, we had 51 public meetings around the state, attended by thousands of Georgians, to formulate specific long-range goals in every realm of public life. We spelled out in writing what we hoped to accomplish at the end of two, five, or even 20 years. . . ."[26] Only if government has clearly defined goals, Carter believes, will people be prepared to "make personal sacrifices." One of his favorite quotes from the New Testament is, "If the trumpet give an uncertain sound, who shall prepare himself for the battle?"[27] But suppose others prefer to march to different music? How would Carter contend with conflict?

Openness may not be a form of godliness for President Carter, but it must come close. He has proposed an "all-inclusive 'sunshine law' . . . [whereby] meetings of federal boards, commissions, and regulatory agencies must be opened to the public, along with those of congressional committees."[28] In his own mind Carter connects openness with direct access to people. He favors giving the people access to governmental decision making, and as president, to speak directly to them. He values openness "to let the public know what we are doing and to restore the concept in the Congress that their constituents are also my constituents. I have just as much right and responsibility to reach the people for support as a member of Congress does." Carter planned (and we have already experienced) a revival of Franklin D. Roosevelt's fireside chats;[29] he also intends to accept "special responsibility to by-pass the big shots," to act, as it were, as the people's lobbyist.[30] Should his policies be thwarted by special interests, Carter says he will go to the people—at times identifying himself *as* the people. In reviewing experience with consumer legislation in Georgia, Carter said, "The special interest groups prevailed on about half of it. I prevailed—rather the Georgia people prevailed—on the other half."[31] What is consistent in these proposals is Carter's opposition to the intermediate groups—the lobbyists who stand between government and citizens or the palace guard that stands between a president and his cabinet—that obstruct his concept of comprehensive policymaking.

President Carter prefers to make changes comprehensively rather than "timidly or incrementally." As he has put it,

> Most of the controversial issues that are not routinely well-addressed can only respond to a comprehensive approach. Incremental efforts to make basic changes are often foredoomed to failure because the special interest groups can benefit from the status quo, can focus their attention on the increments that most affect themselves, and the general public can't be made either interested or aware.[32]

The same theory stands behind efforts at government reorganization:

> The most difficult thing is to reorganize incrementally. If you do it one tiny little phase at a time, then all those who see their influence threatened will combine their efforts in a sort of secretive way. They come out of the rat holes and they'll concentrate on undoing what you're trying to do. But if you can have a bold enough, comprehensive enough proposal to rally the interest and support of the general electorate, then you can overcome that special interest type lobbying pressure.[33]

In a word, "The comprehensive approach is inherently necessary to make controversial decisions."[34]

Part of Carter's political theory, then, is to change everything at once. Comprehensive change enables one both to identify the public interest by considering the merits of opposing claims and to serve that interest by making opponents fight on all fronts simultaneously, thus diluting their forces while concentrating one's own. The bigger the change, the greater the public attention—and the more likely it becomes that the public interest will prevail over private interests.

Inclusiveness is central to Carter's idea of comprehensive reform. "A complete assessment of tax reform in a comprehensive way" is a characteristic Carter phrase. He wants to "establish comprehensive proposals on transportation and energy and agriculture";[35] he favors a "comprehensive nation-wide mandatory health-insurance program" and a "drastic reorganization of the health care services in the U.S."[36] Although we could go on, one more foreign affairs example must serve: since "the old international institutions no longer suffice," Carter feels, "the time has come for a new architectural effort."[37] Because "those who prefer to work in the dark, or those whose private fiefdoms are threatened" care only about themselves, such special interests will prevent inclusive decision making.[38] To avoid this pitfall, Carter wants to restructure the federal bureaucracy, the health system, the welfare system, the tax system, the criminal-justice system, and international institutions.

According to Carter, the comprehensive approach offers a final, decisive solution to problems. On the basis of experience with government reorganization in Georgia, he has become a leading advocate of what is called the one-step process.[39] Carter aims at achieving an "ultimate and final and complete resolution of New York City's problems, fiscally."[40] In the Middle East, he wants to devise an "overall settlement rather than resuming Mr. Kissinger's step-by-step approach"[41] President Carter contends that with Soviet cooperation we can achieve "the ultimate solution" there.[42]

Predictable, Uniform, Simple

No one could object to making governmental policy predictable so that people know what to expect. But is predictability consistent with uniformity—another managerial quality that President Carter seeks? To be more precise, is predictability for one agency (and its clients) compatible with predictability for others? One could get broad agreement, for instance, on smoothing out the economic cycle by maintaining a steady low level of unemployment. A major instrument used to accomplish this objective is to vary the level of government spending, but it becomes evident immediately that predictability in employment (assuming that it could be achieved) and predictability in expenditure policy are mutually exclusive. Similarly, predictability for recipients of governmental subsidies means that all who meet the qualifying conditions would receive the guaranteed sum. Predictability for governmental expenditures (and, quite possibly, for taxpayers), however, requires fixed dollar limits, not open-ended entitlements. Yet if there are limits, potential beneficiaries cannot know in advance how much they will get. Since all policy results cannot be predictable, decisions about whose life will be predictable and whose won't are political as well as administrative.

The same holds true for uniformity and simplicity. Uniformity based on one criterion—say, population—means diversity on others, such as wealth or race or geography. Imagine that President Carter wishes to make good a promise to subsidize the arts, an intention we would like to see realized. Will money be allocated by population (which favors urban density), by region (which favors rural areas), by need (which favors those who do the least), or by past performance (which means that those who have will get more)? With a uniform policy, all these differences cannot be taken into account simultaneously.

Comprehensiveness, in the sense of fundamental and inclusive change, often contradicts predictability and simplicity. Fundamental changes, precisely because they are far-reaching, are unlikely to be predictable. The cost of the food-stamp program grew from an expected few hundred million dollars to more than $8 billion, and one of the unanticipated consequences of indexing Social Security against inflation was that it threatened to bankrupt the system. Thus, acting inclusively so as to consider all (or almost all) factors impinging on a particular problem at a specific time is by its very nature opposed to predictability, which requires that programs established in the past not be undone in the near future. Zero-base budgeting, the epitome of comprehensiveness, requires reexamination of all major programs every year; this is the very opposite of predictability.

With Slices for All, How Large a Pie?

Uniformity also lives uneasily with comprehensiveness. Programs that are both uniform and comprehensive may be too expensive. For example, if public housing must be provided everywhere on the same basis or not at all, there may be no public housing. Similarly, a desire to establish a uniform level of benefits across all welfare programs for all eligible citizens might force a choice between much higher taxes or much lower benefits. "Cashing out" all benefits from food stamps to Medicaid and Medicare might add up to so large a sum that it would be voted down by Congress. Hence, the choice might be between a variety of disparate programs or much lower levels of benefits. Upgrading all eligibles to the highest level of benefits will increase costs, and downgrading all to the lowest level will increase need. Thus uniformity may come at too high a price in suffering or in opposition.

A word should be said about the relation between uniformity and individuality. We do not always equate fairness with being treated like everybody else; on occasion, we would like to be treated as individuals. To be uniform, regulations must place people into large and homogeneous categories. Every effort to take account of special characteristics in the population leads to further subdivision of categories and to additional provisions in the regulations. This effort to treat people in terms of their individual characteristics is what makes for proliferation of rules and regulations.

President Carter's desire for uniformity has led him to advocate a single principle of organization whereby administrative agencies are formed on the basis of function or purpose.[43] Carter would have all activities involving education or health or welfare or crime, to mention but a few, in the same large organization. As a general rule, one can say confidently that no single principle or criterion is good for every purpose. Suppose that reducing dependency on welfare is a major purpose of the Carter administration. Would this mean that education for employment, rehabilitation in prisons, improvement of health, mitigation of alcoholism, and Lord knows what else should be administered under welfare?

The New Look: Top-Light and Bottom-Heavy

Carter's urge toward simplicity has led him to advocate reorganization of the federal government. Leaving aside campaign rhetoric about 1,900 federal agencies (a sum that equates the tiny and trivial with the huge and important), to reduce the number of agencies at the top of the hierarchy necessarily would increase the number at the bottom. If there were only ten big departments, each could have 190 subunits; if there were ten subunits at each level, an issue would have to go through nineteen bureaus before it was decided. The president might find this simpler because fewer people would be reporting directly to him. But Carter might also discover that finding out what is going on is more difficult. The existence of gigantic departments makes it hard for anyone—Congress, secretaries, interest groups, citizens—to see inside. Conflicts between different departments about overlapping responsibilities and conflicts that reveal important differences are submerged under a single departmental view.

One of the few things that can be said about organization in general is the very thing President Carter denies—namely, that a considerable quantity of redundancy (yes, overlap and duplication) must be built into any enterprise.[44] When we want to make sure an activity is accomplished, as in our lunar missions, we build in alternative mechanisms for doing the same thing so that one can take over when other mechanisms fail. Efficiency, the principle of least effort, must be coupled with reliability, the probability that a given act will be performed. A naive notion of efficiency, for example, would suggest that elderly and infirm persons be provided with either a visiting service or an office which they can come to or call. The more we wish to assure actual delivery of services to the elderly, however, the more we must invest in multiple methods. Of course, there must be a limit to redundancy, but if we ever succeeded totally in eliminating all overlap and duplication, most things would work only once, and some things not at all. It is ironic that administrative reforms in the public sector often aim at monopoly or concentration of power, while reforms in the private sector often aim at competition or dispersion of power.[45] Our constitutional mechanisms for dealing with abuse of power, the separation of powers, and checks and balances are after all forms of redundancy. The House and Senate and presidency overlap in jurisdiction and duplicate functions. That is why they quarrel, and why we have been safe.

Carter's criteria cannot guide choice. The proverbial character of the criteria—look before you leap, but he who hesitates is lost—becomes apparent when they are paired with other equally desirable criteria: the elimination of overlap and duplication detracts from reliability; predictability must go with adaptability; uniformity is worthy, but so is recognition of individual differences.

President Carter's criteria for decision making are individually contradictory and mutually incompatible.

Zero-Base Budgeting: How Well Did It Work in Georgia?

The practical embodiment of Jimmy Carter's administrative theory is zero-base budgeting. Here, if anywhere, we can learn what it would mean for Carter to practice what he preaches. Being caught between revolution (change in everything) and resignation (change in nothing) has little to recommend it. Yet this is what a zero-base, start-from-scratch, comprehensive approach requires. If one could actually start from scratch each year, the only zero part of the budget would be its predictability, for zero-base budgeting is ahistorical. The past, as reflected in the budgetary base (common expectations as to amounts and types of funding), is explicitly rejected. Everything at every period is subject to scrutiny. As a result, calculations become unmanageable. Figuring out how other things would look if most things were changed defeats the best efforts. Consequently, attempts to apply intelligence to programs about which something can and needs to be done are buried under mounds of paper. The trivial swamps the important, because if everything must be examined, nothing can receive special attention.

According to the originator of zero-base budgeting, Carter as governor concentrated his time on "reviewing policy questions, major increases and decreases in existing programs, new programs and existing capital expenditure, and a few specific packages and rankings where there appeared to be problems." In other words, he devoted time and energy to increases and decreases from the previous year and to a few problem areas, just as his predecessors had done.[46]

Interviews with participants in zero-base budgeting in Georgia (85 percent of whom thought no shifts in spending had been made, while the other 15 percent thought shifts had occurred but were unable to specify any) show that when fiscal conditions changed in 1974 and 1975, Carter asked for entirely new budget submissions.[47] Why? Departmental budget analysts in Georgia explained that priority rankings changed under different funding levels. But the point is that a budgetary process must be able to accommodate change; if a budget has to be altered every time funding levels change, then zero-base budgeting really is a label for unknown and unspecified future procedures.

The main product of zero-base budgeting is literally a list of objectives. Rarely are there resources for more than the first few. The experience of federal commissions on national priorities, for instance, is that there is no point in listing 846 or even 79 national objectives because almost all the money would be gone after the first one or two. Carter knows this. But he would argue that zero-base budgeting makes agencies supply alternatives. Unless they are assured of being rewarded for reducing the size of programs, however, agencies will manipulate the priorities, placing politically sensitive and otherwise essential items at the bottom, so as to force superiors to increase agency income. This might explain why Carter did not lower the zero-base cutoff point to include lower-priority items when there was an increase in funds or raise the cutoff point when there was a decrease in funds.[48]

On balance, the people who conducted the interviews feel that the zero-base system has benefited Georgia's administration because it has increased information about, and participation in, the budgetary process. However, these increases might just as well have resulted from introducing *any* novel procedure that centered attention on the budget. The investigators also believe that as participants gain more experience, shortcomings will be overcome. Perhaps; it is always possible to believe that more of the same will lead to improvement.

Measuring "Success" in the Carter Era

The overwhelming emphasis that President Carter puts on procedural instruments could leave his administration vulnerable to massive displacement of goals by having success defined, at least within the administration, by the degree of governmental effort rather than by the degree of social accomplishment. To use prisons as an example, the amount agencies spend, the number of new programs initiated, and the uniformity of procedures could replace increase in rehabilitation or reduction in crime as measures of success.

By emphasizing agreement about objectives, as Carter does, such critical problems as how to relate people and activities so that citizens get good results tend to be subsumed under generalities about the desirability of having objectives. If public agencies must have objectives, they prefer a greater rather than a lesser number, so that the consequences of agency activities are likely to fit under at least one. Moreover, public agencies tend to have multiple and conflicting objectives because different people want different things. The objective of limiting the costs of medical care can (and does) coexist, for instance, with the opposing objective of increasing the quantity and quality of such care. Reconciling the differences is made no easier by telling bureaucrats that this strategic behavior—staking out multiple objectives so they can always claim they have achieved something—has become sanctified as a virtue.

If our views have any credence, why, then, has Carter come to hold untenable beliefs about procedures for making policy? Perhaps they were inculcated at Annapolis, but one could just as well argue that Carter chose to go there because he wanted an instrumental approach to decision making.[49] No doubt his father's influence was important ("My daddy . . . was a meticulous planner like me"),[50] but this could have become mere compulsiveness instead of a well-developed pattern of work and thought. No candidate since Herbert Hoover, the Great Engineer,[51] would have thought it important to talk to the public about so arcane a subject as zero-base budgeting, going so far as to include it in five-minute television spots, as Carter did last year. But let us remove the burden from Carter and place it where it belongs, on ourselves, by asking why a highly intelligent political executive might interpret his experiences so as to reinforce his personal belief in an instrumental-cum-technological view of public policy making.

At the outset we can dispose of the cynical view that Carter's ideas on procedures are purely political—that favoring efficiency, opposing the "bureaucratic mess" in Washington, promising more service at less cost are simply noncontroversial positions that project a useful image of the candidate as an effective manager.[52] Reorganization not only suggests rationality but is also a useful cover for gaining control over positions and agencies (see Carter's proposal that the president appoint the chairman of the Federal

Reserve Board).[53] Coordination often is a synonym for coercion. To all this we reply, "Yes, but." Yes, politicians are (and ought to be) political, but Carter pursues his procedural proposals above and beyond the call of duty or interest—and acts on them. No one who has read Carter's gubernatorial messages or observed the consistency and tenacity with which he personally pursued zero-base budgeting, reorganization, and all the rest can doubt his commitment.[54] Carter cares, and Carter acts. Why, then, does he persevere with unsuitable procedures for public policymaking?

Will Carter Be a Good Executive?

Scientists may love surprises, but men of affairs do not. For a scientist, the less predictable the consequences of a theory, that is, the more surprising the conclusions, the better the theory. The further the theory leads us from what we know, the more important and promising it is considered. Businessmen and politicians prefer predictability; things should be as they seem, and surprises are nice if they happen to the competition. The attraction of planning (private and public) is that this element of the unexpected has been domesticated, its will subject to our own, at least on paper.

Carter believes he can avoid many of the pitfalls of planning by applying himself to Washington's problems with energy, intelligence, and a demand for excellence.[55] We agree—in fact, we think it is these attributes, and not his procedural principles, that have brought Carter whatever success he has enjoyed as an executive. (Other life forms experience a phenomenon called "adverse selection," in which general success is mistakenly attributed to specific attributes that are then wrongly selected as worthy of propagation.)

Yet as mistaken in his procedural approach as we think he is, Carter may be on solid ground in an area that we have not covered—the area of public confidence. Our president recognizes (and has emphasized) that citizens have a right to understand their government if they are being asked to support it, which might motivate him to prefer procedures that enhance the appearance of simplicity and predictability in governmental activity, in order to achieve that support.

A concern for appearances as a prerequisite for obtaining support to undertake action apparently animates Carter's behavior in other areas as well. His three election campaigns (for state legislature, for governor, and for president) may be fairly characterized as socially conservative, whereas Carter's presidential actions thus far have been politically progressive. He takes care to make citizens feel he is one of them, even if the whole electorate will not be able to agree with his proposed programs. As governor of Georgia, Carter's need to keep close to the electorate limited his financial aspirations for state spending, but he did spend new monies for the rural poor, for the mentally handicapped, for prisoners, for those who had the least. (And after Watergate, no one should look down upon efforts to improve the appearance as well as the performance of government.)

We are concerned that President Carter will pursue procedures regardless of their efficacy and will regard opposition to his procedural prescriptions as, if not exactly the work of the devil, at least irrational, a product of ignorance and special interests not subject to the usual rules of evidence. The comprehensive, scientific approach, which is supposed to work to promote harmony, has the absence of conflict as a basic assumption. If agreement does not result from openness, if seeming support for long-range goals breaks down under short-range pressures, will the president be able to tolerate the frustration?

The Carter recipe for controlling conflict is to make it boil over; comprehensive change will force opposing interests into public arenas where a president can confront and overcome battling parties. But how often can this be done? Agitating some interests some of the time is not the same as upsetting most interests most of the time. Interests are lots of people who depend on government, the very same people to whom Carter must appeal for support. If Carter can space his appeals out so as not to be fighting on every front at once, there may be a chance for success; otherwise, he (and the nation) may be in for a difficult time.

"He-the-People"

President Carter has promised to go directly to the people, both to incorporate and transcend group interests. Incorporation works by including virtually all groups in the initial stages of policy formation. Through co-optation, Carter hopes to commit most groups to support his programs (or at least not to oppose them vigorously). Transcendence works by investing hierarchy with morality. In order to reflect the people's will, the best way to organize government is to make it democratic at the bottom and centralized at the top.[56] President Carter, then, as chief hierarch and ultimate definer of the public interest, leaps over group interests through direct contact with the populace. "He-the-people" Carter would rather interpret the inchoate desires of the mass of people than bargain over who gets what the government offers.

Carter's theory of governing suggests opportunities for leadership but also obstacles to success. To reorganize the executive branch, the president will have to overcome both its clienteles and their elected representatives. To put through major reforms, Carter will need financial support from a Congress accustomed to making its own budget. Should presidential initiatives falter, private interests may appear to have triumphed over the public's interest. According to his own philosophy, Carter will be compelled to appeal to the people to protect his programs. But in the end, even the people may prove ungrateful; for if citizens fail the president, it will appear that they have given in to private interests instead of standing up for public duties.

The most worrisome aspect of Jimmy Carter's theory of public policymaking is his assumption that discussion will lead to agreement on long-term objectives, and that agreement will assure support for present programs. Carter's views on conflict could survive only if past objectives were to determine future administration. This view of policy politics is untenable because the price of agreement is likely to be vagueness and because administration involves altering ends by changing means. When specific acts call for choice between how much inflation versus how much employment, or how much preservation of natural resources versus how much consumption, it becomes evident that agreement in general need not mean (and often has not meant) agreement in particular. Since conditions change, the agreements that Carter negotiates in time of plenty may have to be renegotiated in periods of austerity.

Jimmy Carter as President

What, then, is Jimmy Carter likely to do as president? Contingency may overwhelm concern. Another huge oil price increase, a resurgence of inflation, or a military involvement may do more to shape what a president does than his own initial ideas worked out under much different circumstances. Personality may prevail over policy. From listening to FDR's policy pronouncements, who would have predicted his eagerness to abandon the deflationary, low-spending policies advocated during his first presidential campaign? Confronted with crises, many policies pass away, but often long-learned modes of problem solving remain. FDR's administration was characterized by eclecticism. There was a willingness to try and a readiness to abandon programs—an incorrigible optimism as well as a love of conflict—even when it led to contradictions, perhaps precisely because they gave Roosevelt room to maneuver. These operative administrative theories proved more permanent indicators of FDR's behavior than did his past policies. So too, we think, Jimmy Carter's theory of governing will better indicate behavior in office than what Carter says about substantive issues.

Like most Americans, we voted for Carter and worried about him at the same time. Contrary to our fears, there is evidence that Carter can (and does) learn from experience. On busing, for example (we are not passing judgment on the correctness of the position but rather on Carter's approach to the problem), Carter realized that wealthy parents often avoid it by sending children to private schools or by moving out of the area. Despite good intentions, it is mostly black children who get bused and pay the price. The policy achieved neither the immediate objective of school integration nor the more distant objective of better school performance. The president's proposal has been to substitute a voluntary program for the mandatory one. Carter's emphasis is on changing the school system from within by putting blacks in administrative and teaching jobs.[57]

Another area in which Carter's policy indicates a positive response to past unsuccessful attempts is in handling racial and civil disturbances. As governor of Georgia, Carter learned that the normal, massive presence of state troopers during civil disorders not only served to aggravate the situation but used up enormous police resources. So Carter set up biracial community civil-disorder units composed of three persons dressed in civilian clothes. After the disorder, the units were replaced by permanent local committees.[58] When Carter tried to influence the choice of legislative leaders in Georgia, however, he learned this caused more trouble than it was worth, and he vowed not to do it with Congress. Many more examples exist, but the question is, Will Carter apply the same standards to procedures, including procedures for handling conflict, as he does to policies?

Since taking office, it would be fair to say that none of Carter's policy proposals, however desirable, has met his own criteria. Reform of welfare on a comprehensive basis, for example, has proved incompatible with fiscal restraint and with the demands of states and cities for financial relief. Perhaps the most interesting situation exists in Congress. Carter's earlier difficulties may be ascribed to inexperience and to the fact that he was used to dealing with a legislature that stayed in session only a few weeks. Even after the White House started to pay more attention to Congress, the difficulty persisted, largely, it appears, because of a lack of interest in congressional preferences. It is one thing to try to convince legislators to adopt the White House position and another to act as if their preferences were not worth considering. If one behaves as if policy were already set after initial discussion, all that remains is implementation.

Read this as a cautionary tale for President Carter and his supporters. There is after all no reason to believe that former President Ford followed better procedures or even that Ford paid much attention to procedures. Because Carter is explicit about his own philosophy and cares about procedures, we have been able to be critical. But people who care are also likely to perform. If too concerned, however, such people might substitute rigidity for right action. Having been forewarned, perhaps Carter will be forearmed to search for weaknesses in his strengths.

Notes

1. "Jimmy Carter Presidential Campaign Issues Reference Book," July 24, 1976. Cited hereafter as "Issues Reference Book."

2. "Issues: Clearer and More Detailed," *National Journal Reports,* July 24, 1976, p. 1028.

3. "Head-to-Head on the Issues," *U.S. News and World Report,* September 13, 1976, p. 21.

4. "Issues Reference Book," p. 20.

5. Ibid., p. 13.

6. "Interview on the Issues—What Carter Believes," *U.S. News and World Report,* May 24, 1976, p. 19; "Issues Reference Book," p. 30.

7. "Issues Reference Book," p. 13.

8. Jimmy Carter, *Why Not the Best?* (Broadman Press, 1975), p. 147

9. "Jimmy Carter: Not Just Peanuts," *Time,* March 8, 1976, p. 19.

10. Stated by Stuart Eizenstat, Carter's policy adviser, in *National Journal Reports,* July 24, 1976, p. 1029.

11. *New York Times,* April 2, 1976, p. 2; *U.S. News and World Report,* May 24, 1976, p. 19.

12. "The View from the Top of the Carter Campaign," *National Journal Reports,* July 17, 1976, p. 1002.

13. *U.S. News and World Report,* May 24, 1976, p. 23; James P. Gannon, "The Activist: Carter, Despite Image of Outsider Favors Do-More Government," *Wall Street Journal,* April 2, 1976, p. 23.

14. "What Carter Would Do As President," *U.S. News and World Report,* July 26, 1976, p. 18.

15. "Issues Reference Book," p. 20.

16. *U.S. News and World Report,* May 24, 1976, p. 23, and July 26, 1976, p. 18.

17. Ibid., May 24, 1976, p. 18.

18. "Jimmy Carter on Economics: Populist Georgia Style," *Business Week,* May 3, 1976, p. 66.

19. "Excerpts from an Interview with Jimmy Carter," *New York Times,* March 31, 1976, p. 20.

20. "Issues Reference Book," p. 15.

21. "Carter: Seeking Clearer Goals," *Time,* May 10, 1976, p. 24.

22. *U.S. News and World Report,* May 24, 1976, p. 19.

23. *National Journal Reports,* July 17, 1976, p. 997.

24. "Excerpts from the Interview with Carter on his Concepts in Foreign Policy," *New York Times,* July 7, 1976, p. 12.

25. "Carter Says Ford Fails to Check Nation's 'Drift,' " *New York Times,* August 18, 1976, p. 1.

26. Carter, *Why Not the Best?*, p. 114.

27. Jimmy Carter, National Press Club. Announcement Speech for Democratic Presidential Nomination, December 12, 1974.

28. "Issues Reference Book," p. 14; Albert R. Hunt, "Carter and Business," *Wall Street Journal,* August 12, 1976, p. 15.

29. *U.S. News and World Report,* September 13, 1976, p. 20.

30. "Carter Tells Film Stars about Poverty in the South," *New York Times,* August 24, 1976, p. 17.

31. *National Journal Reports,* July 17, 1976, p. 998.

32. Ibid., p. 999.

33. "State Structural Reforms," ibid., April 5, 1975, p. 506.

34. Ibid., July 17, 1976, p. 999.

35. *U.S. News and World Report,* September 13, 1976, p. 21.

36. *Wall Street Journal,* April 2, 1976, p. 23.

37. Eleanor Randolf, "Carter Hits 'Lone Ranger' Foreign Policy of Kissenger," *Chicago Tribune,* June 24, 1976, p. 5.

38. Carter, Announcement Speech, December 12, 1974.

39. *National Journal Reports,* April 5, 1975, p. 506.

40. "Excerpts from an Interview with Jimmy Carter," *New York Times,* March 31, 1976, p. 20.

41. *U.S. News and World Report,* July 26, 1976, p. 18.

42. "Where Jimmy Carter Stands on Foreign Policy," *Chicago Tribune,* May 8, 1976, p. 10.

43. This principle has had a long history, having been proposed in 1911 by the President's Commission on Economy and Efficiency: "Only by grouping services according to their character can substantial progress be made in eliminating duplication." Quoted in Peri E. Arnold, "Executive Reorganization and Administrative Theory: The Origin of the Managerial Presidency," a paper presented at the 1976 Annual Meeting of the American Political Science Association, Chicago, Illinois, September 1976, p. 6.

44. Martin Landau, "Redundancy, Rationality, and the Problem of Duplication and Overlap," *Public Administration Review* 29, no. 4 (July/August 1969): 346-358.

45. Lewis Dexter has emphasized that modern Western society has followed the route of competition, not monopoly, as a means to clarify issues and procedures. He cites the example that U.S. antitrust laws are "deliberately designed to impose redundancy and duplication on industry." See Lewis Anthony Dexter, "The Advantages of Some Duplication and Ambiguity in Senate Committee Jurisdictions," p. 174, Temporary Select Committee of the United States Senate on Committee Jurisdiction (chairman Adlai Stevenson) first staff report, September 1976.

46. Peter Phyrr, *Zero-Base Budgeting: A Practical Management Tool for*

Evaluating Expenses (New York, John Wiley and Sons, 1973), p. 97, quoted in Aaron Wildavsky, *Budgeting: A Comparative Theory of Budgetary Processes* (Little, Brown, 1975), p. 295.

47. George S. Nimier and Roger H. Hermanson, "A Look at Zero-Base Budgeting—The Georgia Experience," *Atlanta Economic Review*, July-August, 1976, pp. 5-12. In 1974 there was an increase in available funds, and in 1975 a decrease.

48. Ibid.

49. See, for example, Vice Admiral Hyman G. Rickover's speech delivered in Brooklyn on April 9, 1958, p. 5, in which he complains about inefficiency in bureaucracy: "If over-organization lengthens our lead time we must heed Thoreau's cry of 'simplify, simplify.' "

50. Quoted in Bruce Mazlish and Edwin Diamond, "Thrice Born: A Psychohistory of Jimmy Carter's Rebirth," *New York*, August 30, 1976, p. 32.

51. Hoover was an unrelenting champion of organization by "major purpose under single-headed responsibility" as a means for making agencies easier to manage and more efficient. See Arnold, "Executive Reorganization," pp. 13-14, 20. Securing broad reorganization authority subject to congressional veto is also the approach Carter took in Georgia and hopes to repeat in Washington. See *U.S. News and World Report*, July 26, 1976, p. 17.

52. Although Carter, like any good engineer, knows it is not possible to maximize simultaneously in more than one dimension, his language sometimes suggests the opposite: " . . . I assure you that my primary concern will be providing the maximum amount of services for the least cost." State of Georgia, *Governor's Reorganization Message*, March 1, 1971, p. 18.

53. The Reorganization Act in Georgia, for instance, removed an entire administrative level, leaving those positions open to appointment by the governor. See T. McN. Simpson III, "Georgia State Administration: Jimmy Carter's Contribution," a paper delivered at the 1973 Annual Meeting of the Southern Political Science Association, Atlanta, Georgia, November 1-3, p. 10.

54. For a discussion of Carter's contribution to Georgia administration, see ibid.

55. Carter's qualities as an executive are evoked in the instructions he gave to members of the study group involved in making recommendations for reorganization in Georgia: "Studies of this nature are a full-time job. You cannot drop by to chat with a department head for a few minutes and then go back and write a report. If that were all that is required, I would do the study myself during the next two months. Somebody has to get out in the field and find out what is really happening and why. That is not a part-time job; it means spending eight hours a day working with the state employees and another four or five hours that night analyzing what was learned. It means writing and rewriting the report so that each point is clearly and concisely stated, backed by adequate detail, able to stand up to any question and practical for implementation." State of Georgia, *Governor's Reorganization Message*, p. 18.

56. In New York City, John Lindsay "rationalized" the city administration by consolidating and eliminating all intermediate structures, thus forming the "Office of Collective Bargaining." It soon became the sole target of public-employee union demands, thereby greatly strengthening the union's position. In Jack Douglas's apt description, the rationalization "swept away all the hedgerows behind which he [Lindsay] could have hidden." See Jack D. Douglas, "Urban Politics and Public Employee Unions," in *Public Employee Unions: A Study of the Crisis in Public Sector Labor Relations* (San Francisco: Institute for Contemporary Studies, 1976), p. 103.

57. "Issues Reference Book," p. 21.

58. Ibid.

Chapter 5

Small Program, Big Troubles: Policy Making for a Small Great Society Program

Thomas E. Cronin

This is the story of a small, well-meant, presidentially endorsed program that failed to do much of what it was supposed to, but somehow survived anyway. It is also the story of an embattled program that demonstrated bureaucratic tenacity and resilience in the face of the political forces and political institutions that controlled its fate. It is of particular interest because its small size allows a close examination of what went awry, and the strength and determination of the groups antagonistic to it are representative of those that thwart high hopes in a variety of domestic policy ventures.

The National Teacher Corps was set up to bring a new breed of teachers to schools in poverty areas. Passed as a section of the Higher Education Act of 1965 (P.L. 89-320, Title V, Part B), the enacting legislation was meant to help lay a part of the foundation of Lyndon Johnson's Great Society. It established a small program to send teams of talented college graduates to study education and to teach under the supervision of specially recruited experienced teachers. The program retained a special place in Johnson's heart, and he retired to Texas in 1969 considering it one of the successes of his administration.

In fact, however, the Teacher Corps never accomplished many of its objectives. Its history is virtually an application of Murphy's

Law to politics: almost everything that could go wrong did go wrong. The program was poorly planned, hastily enacted, badly implemented, and inadequately evaluated. Debilitating local resistance, changes in mood, faulty analogies, and unexpected outcomes only dimly foreseen are all part of the story.

The Genesis of the Teacher Corps

Policy proposals come to the White House in dozens of ways, but presidential commitment to policy "reform" is likely to develop (1) once a problem is widely recognized, (2) when a suggested remedy appears to be a logical extension of previous efforts, (3) when it has incubated for a time among congressional and professional constituencies, and (4) when it can earn political credit for a president.

Each of these elements was present at the time President Johnson embraced the Teacher Corps idea. Johnson and his staff had become aware that each year nearly a million children dropped out of school and that the children of as many as five million families in low-income areas were denied high-quality education. According to Johnson, the danger existed that a whole generation of poor children would become unskilled dropouts, unemployed or delinquent. Everyone was aware, too, that the best teachers generally migrated to wealthy or middle-class communities. A national teacher shortage existed, and this shortage was especially pronounced in poverty-area schools.

Programs to encourage volunteers to serve in poverty areas were certainly not novel. For years, community-conscious university students had maintained small organizations that sent volunteers to settlement houses, centers for the mentally retarded, and Indian reservations. Also, the concept of a federal service corps, in the guise of the Civilian Conservation Corps of the 1930s, had been one of the most popular aspects of the New Deal.

In the early 1960s, in the light of increased attention to domestic poverty, many people suggested that if the nation sent idealistic young people to help the poor abroad, perhaps it should offer the same opportunities for service among poor people at home. President Kennedy proposed a "domestic Peace Corps" in his January 1963 State of the Union address.[1] After Kennedy's death, antipoverty legislation was passed, creating a program (VISTA) that encouraged volunteers to serve one year, working directly with social workers and local community councils. The Teacher Corps was visualized as a channel for similar commitments to educational institutions.

The notion of recruiting experienced teachers to work in hardship posts had been tried in a few places and found to be "successful," notably in Prince Edward County, Virginia, which had experienced a long and bitter struggle over public school desegregation. There, after the county board of supervisors had closed the schools for four years to avoid integrating them, the Kennedy Administration took upon itself the task of securing money from foundations, corporations, and others to subsidize Prince Edward County "Free Schools" for the county's blacks (and a handful of whites who elected to come). About a hundred teachers were recruited; they set up ungraded schools where novel teaching techniques were encouraged. The experiment was judged successful, winning favorable attention in the press and among liberal members of Congress.[2]

A year or so later a noteworthy experiment in recruiting and training Peace Corps returnees for urban teaching assignments had begun at Cardozo High School in Washington, D.C. Though small, this program was distinctive: it stressed a need to have young teachers experiment with and develop curriculum materials that would be meaningful to urban youngsters, and it placed teacher training in the local public school rather than at the university school of education. It caught the attention of several members of Congress, one of whom, Senator Gaylord Nelson, was sufficiently impressed that he proposed an amendment to the Elementary and Secondary Education bill of 1965 modeled almost entirely on the Cardozo project.

Intellectual support also had been building for something like the Teacher Corps as several individuals tried their hand at prescribing remedies for the ills of the newly rediscovered "other America." An important contribution to this discussion was an article by John Kenneth Galbraith which appeared in *Harper's* in March 1964. Galbraith urged President Johnson to designate one hundred of the poorest urban and rural poverty areas as eligible for special federal funds to upgrade educational, recreational, and transportation facilities. One key to his detailed plan was the creation of an elite body of teachers "ready to serve in the most remote areas, tough enough and well-trained enough to take on the worst slums, proud to go to Harlan County or to Harlem"—a Green Beret Teacher Corps.[3]

The idea of a Teacher Corps was also politically attractive. Johnson had seen at firsthand the popularity of Roosevelt's Civilian Conservation Corps and National Youth Administration, and he was aware of the substantial political credit gained by President Kennedy for establishing the Peace Corps. He knew too that a National Teacher Corps was another way to show that he cared deeply about poor people. He liked the image of himself as a supporter of the underdog. As a former teacher and principal, the most illustrious graduate of San Marcos State Teachers College found the notion of a Teacher Corps especially appealing. Finally, political competitiveness may have encouraged him to embrace the proposal, since otherwise credit for the Teacher Corps idea would largely have accrued to a Kennedy brother.

The precise motives of Johnson were always hard to pinpoint, for as the late White House wire service reporter Merriman Smith pointed out, in Johnson's case "hypnosis, mind reading and truth serum probably could not have separated political motive from deep concern."[4] But all the elements necessary for presidential commitment to a new policy were present when Johnson decided to champion the Teacher Corps, even if in themselves they do not account for his decision: a problem existed; the federal government was already involved in similar activity; members of Congress, intellectuals, and interest groups had brought the idea to the attention of the White House; it was a variation of the already popular Peace Corps; it was politically feasible; and, finally, it would promote the president's proclaimed mission of ending poverty.

The Congressional and Presidential Initiatives

When political scientists call the president America's "chief legislator," they imply that he can virtually write, shape, and obtain passage for legislation in which he is especially interested. But even when, as with the Teacher Corps, the president is generally successful in "putting a law on the books," members of Congress and various lobbies often exert considerable influence in shaping and altering the character of a federal program, though the program continues to be labeled "the president's."

Moreover, the president himself seldom has time for detailed involvement in the formulation of domestic policy plans, and usually less time for monitoring subsequent implementation and evaluation. This circumstance is seldom the presidential preference. Rather, it is in large part due to a necessary presidential preoccupation with national security and economic policy. Concern about the crises of the moment constantly distracts the White House from critical stages of program drafting and administration. The amount of presidential-level attention that policies receive in the drafting stage plays an important role in determining their success, but presidents and their White House aides are often unaware or unappreciative of significant choices made at this level.

In the case of the Teacher Corps, the program idea was originally the brainchild of several senators, notably Edward Kennedy and Gaylord Nelson. William Spring, an aide to Senator Nelson, was impressed with the Galbraith article of 1964 and moved by what he observed at the Cardozo urban teacher training project. He was also on the lookout for meritorious legislation which his senator could sponsor. He would later recall in an interview, "Another thing that got us interested in this program was that Senator Nelson had just transferred from another Senate committee and was joining the Senate Labor and Public Welfare Committee. We, his staff aides, felt that he needed an issue to get his feet wet, an issue that would let him get deeply involved in his committee and show his interest in the committee's sphere of interest."* Spring took it upon himself to "touch base" with the US Office of Education in HEW, with the major educational lobbies, with the people who ran Cardozo-style experiments around the country, and with a variety of education deans and school officials. With Office of Education (USOE) assistance, Spring drafted a bill for Senator Nelson.

Educational lobbies and USOE were unenthusiastic. They

*Interview quotes without footnotes come from a series of interviews conducted by the author.

worried about federal control of local educational efforts and expressed concern about duplication of efforts.

At the White House, President Johnson, having completed much of the unfinished legislative agenda he had inherited from his predecessor, was impatiently setting out an even more ambitious agenda of his own. He was hungry for new ideas. As one of his aides put it, "Johnson was like a bottomless barrel, it seemed to me that we had to keep pouring ideas and proposals onto him." The Great Society messages of 1965 illustrated the president's mood. Johnson had pledged to assemble the best thought and the broadest knowledge "from all over the world" to find the answers to the problems of urban decay, poverty, and inadequate housing. He had specifically singled out the classrooms of America as one of the chief sites on which the Great Society must be built.[5]

By 1965 Johnson had presided over passage of both the Economic Opportunity Act (1964) and the landmark Elementary and Secondary Education Act (1965). He was understandably delighted at his growing reputation as "the education president" but wanted further recognition that he was doing more for education and more for poor people than any other president. So Johnson now decided to follow up his earlier achievements by making sure that good teachers would be available to use these new monies. The assumption was that effective teachers were a critical part of education; hence the need for a program that would get especially able teachers to move into hardship posts.

The president's point man for education legislation was Douglass Cater, a veteran Washington reporter whom he had recruited from a research center at Wesleyan University. It became Cater's responsibility to work on educational policy matters with the major lobbies, appropriate members of Congress, and department officials. His job was to piece together ideas and proposals that came to his office, assess their merit, and bring the best to the president's attention.

Cater read Galbraith's article. Soon thereafter he was visited by staff aides to Senators Wayne Morse, Kennedy, and Nelson, all of whom were enthusiastically supporting Teacher Corps bills of one kind or another. Cater was also aware of hearings then taking place in the Senate that focused on these various ideas. About this time he was asked to draft the president's forthcoming address to the National Education Association, and Cater recalls that he decided to insert the call for a National Teacher Corps in an early version. This was one way of bringing it to the president's attention and, if approved by him, of generating public support. Johnson readily approved.

Thus, on July 2, 1965, Johnson surprised an audience of 7,000 educators with this announcement:

In the next few days I will propose a National Teacher Corps to enlist thousands of dedicated teachers to work alongside local teachers in city slums and in areas of rural poverty where they can really serve their Nation. They will be young people, preparing for teaching careers. They will be experienced teachers willing to give a year to the places in their country that need them most. They can bring the best in our Nation to the help of the poorest of our children.[6]

Nothing that could legitimately be called "research" had been done on the idea—at least not at the White House. Nor had the idea been subject to systematic evaluation at the staff level or in the Bureau of the Budget. The process was far more casual. It was assumed that the Teacher Corps would be a relatively modest undertaking. No new organization or new federal agency was envisaged. Indeed, it was assumed that it was no more than a variation on existing teacher fellowship programs, based on the Peace Corps model and with the purpose of injecting a sense of mission and idealism into teaching. Questions such as who would pay for it, how much might it cost during the next few years, and what would be its criteria of success or failure were given little consideration.

It may surprise some readers to discover that a president will announce new programs or that staff assistants to a president will even suggest them to him without careful scrutiny. But in politics to be deliberate is often to be indecisive. Reaching out for "new ideas" and adopting "innovations" is common practice for politicians, especially Democrats, who are constantly being asked, How are you going to solve this problem? What have you done for us lately? Why aren't you trying harder to improve things? At the time, Johnson enjoyed a working majority in Congress, and he wanted to make use of this luxury while it lasted. And Johnson personally had a voracious appetite for new legislative proposals. As one Johnson aide said, "Basically, our philosophy was to get things started. The philosophy that Lyndon Johnson had was to keep a full legislative plate before the Congress."

The Absence of Clear Goals

From the beginning the Teacher Corps program was a hybrid. Its sponsors in Congress had diverse models in mind. Little thought was given to precise objectives by the president or his staff. This was left to the subgovernment of Senate aides, USOE staff, and educational organization representatives. The Office of Education had not advocated the new program and had in fact initially questioned its merit. The resulting legislation was a compromise, a quick response to an impatient White House request for a program. The charter was drafted, modified, and eventually enacted, but Congress left the details of implementation and evaluation exceedingly vague.

The fundamental dilemma as to whether the Teacher Corps was professional or voluntary seems never to have been resolved by the White House or Congress. In the Galbraith-Edward Kennedy view the need was for experienced and highly qualified teachers who would be sent to poverty-area schools and be given higher pay, some variation of "combat pay," for going to these hardship posts. But Senator Gaylord Nelson, employing the Peace Corps analogy, adopted the philosophy that Teacher Corps personnel were really engaged in volunteer service, motivated by idealism and altruism, dedicated to learning how to teach and to "reforming" education at the same time.

Part of the reason that things were left so vague was an overeagerness to justify the program's existence before the jury of suspicious congressional committees and to capture support from added constituencies. As one politically attentive aide at the Teacher Corps recalled, "We used every argument we could when we were selling the Teacher Corps idea because we had to in order to win support. There was no other way you could do it. You had to use every bit of evidence you could however valid or invalid, so we sold it as a manpower program to some people, and just about everything else that was related, and along the way we certainly were guilty of overpromising."

Later, as criticism mounted from Congress, educational lobbies, and local school officials, the Teacher Corps searched for additional tasks, symbols, and selling points. With the program under growing pressure to justify itself in the absence of a clear legislative intent, the corps' charter continuously expanded. A bright idea would be brought to the director's attention, would gain almost immediate acceptance, and would be hastily incorporated into the guidelines. A communication overload developed between the Washington "front office" and the local programs across the country. Here is a short list of some of the targets specified at one time or another:

to attract highly motivated people to the teaching profession;

to improve the quality of education for poor children;

to improve the quality of teacher training models;

to help remedy the nation's teacher shortage;

to reform local schools by introducing community service activities;

to reform the curriculum in schools that teach poor children;

to provide an opportunity for altruistic service;

to encourage coordinated efforts among school, community, and university;

to provide jobs for returning veterans;

to improve the quality of education on Indian reservations, behind the walls of juvenile correction institutions, and in state prison systems;

to retrain experienced educational personnel serving in local educational agencies.

By 1970, an outside management consulting firm discovered seven broad Teacher Corps objectives embodied in the enabling legislation and some 45 explicit goals embraced by the Washington office. Most of these were worthy goals, but a national program can plainly become so preoccupied with public relations efforts to enhance its prestige that it neglects the less glamorous work that makes up its true purpose.

Conceptual Inadequacies of the Program

A lack of precise objectives was not the only problem resulting from the hasty drafting of the Teacher Corps proposal. The lack of forethought behind the plan was also reflected in some serious conceptual weaknesses. The analogy to the Peace Corps upon which the plan was based was faulty, some of the program's purposes were questionable, and its multiple goals were in partial conflict with one another.

Because the pressure for immediate action and a show of results in political areas is intense, it is often tempting to build programs by analogy, to use what appears to work in one area to generate offspring in another. As its name suggests, the immediate parent of the Teacher Corps was the Peace Corps, which had its beginning about four years earlier. The Peace Corps analogy transferred to the Teacher Corps a burden of exaggerated hope, which subsequent events were to modify for both programs, and it applied the Peace Corps model of short-haul voluntarism to a teacher-training program that hoped in contrast to produce dedicated professionals with a long-haul commitment to education of the disadvantaged. Role ambiguity often resulted: was the Teacher Corpsman a volunteer in training or a teacher in service? But in another way, the analogy was unhappily quite appropriate: the disenchantment of host countries with Peace Corps volunteers had a close analogue in the struggle the Teacher Corps had to confront over the local autonomy of host schools and schools of education.

It would be unfair to criticize too harshly the planners who adapted the Peace Corps model for wholesale application to the quite different area of education. To do so is to forget the whole spirit of soaring enthusiasm which surrounded the beginnings of the Peace Corps, and some of the baneful results of that program could not have been foreseen. In any case, the purpose here is not so much to criticize as it is to outline the limitations that seem to be inherent in the exercise of presidential initiative.

Forecasts of a national teacher shortage also figured importantly in the case for a Teacher Corps, which was seen as one answer to the shortage. It was emphasized by the bill's sponsors that in 1965 there was an annual shortage of 118,000 teachers. In recommending to President Johnson that the Teacher Corps be tripled in size,

HEW Secretary John W. Gardner in late 1966 argued that the Teacher Corps was an "ideal device" to help remedy the shortage of qualified teachers. However, two years later, that shortage had become a decided surplus. Warnings that this would occur had been sounded earlier, but few officials had listened. The initial tactic of the directors of the Teacher Corps was to respond that there was no surplus of qualified teachers who knew how to work with children who have special needs in poverty areas. However, by 1973 the Teacher Corps did begin adapting to the reality of a teacher surplus by stressing that the corps would become a teacher retraining rather than teacher recruitment program. (See table 1.)

Another assumption that influenced the Teacher Corps held that it was important to cut the high school dropout rate, which averaged about 900,000 students yearly in the 1960s. Both the Kennedy and Johnson administrations strongly endorsed "stay in school" campaigns, and the Teacher Corps was viewed as another effort in this direction. Yet some studies show little evidence that dropouts suffer financially, emotionally, or intellectually by quitting school before graduation. Usually, their problems were as great *before* dropping out of school. Thus, it is open to question whether merely preventing students from dropping out was a valid goal.[7]

Table 1. Corps Member Data

Cycle	Year	No. of Interns Started	Teachers in Retraining	Ratio Interns: Teachers
1	1966	1,279	213	6:1
2	1967	930	155	6:1
3	1968	1,029	171	6:1
4	1969	1,330	222	6:1
5	1970	1,223	204	6:1
6	1971	1,385	231	6:1
7	1972	1,534	272	5.6:1
8	1973	1,358	951	1.4:1
9	1974	735	1,873	1:25
10*	1975	220	3,770	1:17

Source: Teacher Corps
*Estimate

The Program's Location and Its Consequences

On occasion, a major presidential priority is given over to a new agency designed specifically to bypass existing bureaucracies. The space program was located in NASA rather than in the Air Force because it was feared that the Air Force might view the space race and the goal of getting a man on the moon as secondary to its major raison d'être. No such decision was even considered with the Teacher Corps, partly no doubt because the president had already set up several new agencies (HUD, OEO, and DOT, which he was then pressing for), and partly because the Teacher Corps was viewed at the White House as complementary rather than competitive with other US Office of Education responsibilities.

As noted, certain USOE veterans were skeptical about the idea of a Teacher Corps. Some believed that existing grant programs already permitted and encouraged local authorities to develop improved teacher training programs. It was feared that a Teacher Corps might be viewed as an indictment of existing practices; many within USOE had come from institutions in the field and had helped organize and run those "existing practices." Others were wary of the political consequences of sending reform-minded young people to conventional school systems in areas represented in Washington by ever-attentive members of Congress. But even though many in the USOE opposed the Teacher Corps proposal, the office backed the president. It was hardly about to resist a president who was then dominating the national legislative process.

Educational and teacher college lobbies urged that the corps be an Office of Education program, because they wanted to make sure they would have some control over the new venture. Once the program was lodged in the office, business-as-usual naturally prevailed, and the educational interest groups were dutifully consulted and "taken into account." The US commissioner of education delegated Teacher Corps staff work to career bureaucrats in the USOE, who not surprisingly enjoyed especially close ties with the nation's schools of education. These career staff viewed themselves as educational professionals and came to this new task with previous experience running and staffing NDEA (National Defense Education Act) teacher fellowship and teacher training institute programs, always, of course, in close collaboration with the schools of education.

Supporters of the Teacher Corps based many of their hopes on the belief that what was wrong with education and schools of education could be overcome by an infusion of talented liberal arts graduates with a minimum of traditional teacher training. The emphasis would be on learning and experimentation on location in poverty-area schools. However, any hope that the Teacher Corps could bypass or otherwise jolt the established schools of education was thwarted by the final legislation and by these early planning or consultation strategies. The whole approach amounted to a vote of confidence in schools of education. The legislation was patterned after existing programs and stated that "the Commissioner is authorized to . . . enter into arrangements with local educational agencies, after consultation in appropriate cases with State educational agencies and institutions of higher education. . . ." The teaching teams would be afforded time by the local educational agency "for a teacher-intern training program" to be carried out in cooperation "with an institution of higher education." USOE officials, with a business-as-usual approach, encouraged the schools of education to make out applications and to organize local Teacher Corps programs much as they were accustomed to doing with other programs.

Most schools of education have long been in the business of preparing teachers and, to put it mildly, view themselves as the experts in the business. To them, the Teacher Corps was just a new program promising extra federal money and a chance to try "innovations" which often meant a slight shift of emphasis toward black history or urban sociology. As one observer of this early stage of implementation described it, "Office of Education officials wanted to work only with schools of education and they were very conscious of not wanting to hurt any of their friends in the education groups. The flaw was their reliance and hope that schools of education would use this money differently than they were using other funds coming from the same source. It was just another case of good money following bad money." A few years later, even the director of the Teacher Corps would conclude that he had not realized how resistant to change the schools of education would be: "Schools of education were of necessity the main people we dealt with, our contracts and contacts were with them and this turned out to be a bad decision. I didn't realize until after a couple of years how difficult they are to work with . . . unless you know that the whole school of education is going to support the program and is supportive of change and innovation, it probably is best to stay out and save the federal money."

Enactment

The Teacher Corps legislation moved briskly through Congress. It was enacted a mere eighteen weeks after President Johnson called for its passage. Johnson succeeded in winning quick passage for the Teacher Corps because he was enjoying an unusually friendly Congress, owing in large measure to the landslide of 1964 that brought dozens of new liberals to the House. Most of the educational lobbies felt obliged to go along with the president because he had so recently done so much for education. In addition, the Teacher Corps amendment was tagged onto the Higher Education legislation, soon to pass. The Teacher Corps itself was not subject to much discussion, legislative debate, or hearings. Indeed, several members of the House felt the bill was being brought up so quickly that they did not have a chance to deliberate, and that it was just another example of President Johnson's bulldozing legislative tactics.

As enacted, the purpose of the Teacher Corps was to strengthen the educational opportunities available to children in areas having concentrations of low-income families and to encourage colleges and universities to broaden their programs of teacher preparation. To do this, the Teacher Corps was mandated to attract and train inexperienced teacher-interns who were available for teaching and in-service training in teams led by an experienced teacher. School systems and universities were asked first to decide on their training plans in this area and then how the Teacher Corps could help them get from where they were to where they wanted to go. In common with countless other federal programs, they had to develop a program proposal with their plans, needs, and budgets. Ideally, members of the community, students, and diverse educators in the community would participate in the drawing up of the plans. In practice, most plans were devised by a few faculty members at schools of education in cooperation with some local school principals or a nearby school superintendent.

The plans had to be approved by the appropriate state educational agency (a perfunctory obstacle) and then submitted to the Teacher Corps, where a panel of educational consultants evaluated the proposals and made recommendations for funding of those proposals that showed the greatest promise. Most proposals were for at least a two-year period. A major objective emphasized at all stages of the program was the goal of attracting persons who would be superb in working with disadvantaged young students but who had not previously considered teaching as a career.

Initial Implementation and the Office of Education

The location of the Teacher Corps in USOE and the selection of its leaders explain part of the problems it was to experience in its implementation. The White House and Congress virtually forced the program on USOE. Yet it was left to the office to breathe life into the general intentions outlined by the political authorities. As it turned out, however, the office was not well endowed with special knowledge about teaching low-income students. USOE was accustomed to administering federal grant-in-aid or loan programs; few if any of these had explicit objectives that might alter the way local authorities operated. To date, the major function of the Office of Education had been to enlarge the size of the educational economic pie rather than to impose "change" programs on localities. But the Teacher Corps was different; it was intended to prod and stimulate, to create a new model. During the initial planning for the program, Office of Education officials sought counsel from outside professionals, calling several conferences with specialists from schools of education and from a few state and local systems that had shown special interest in the preparation of teachers for low-income students. These advisers opposed the idea contained in the initiating legislation of recruiting well-trained, experienced public school teachers from one part of the country and sending them to poor school districts elsewhere. The idea of "combat pay," proposed by Galbraith and others, was rejected because teacher unions would be opposed to income disparities. The general concept of recruiting an elite corps of experienced teachers was considered problematic. How would a school system protect itself from troublemakers? Would Teacher Corps units be used to integrate southern school faculties? What about seniority? What about local control over schools? The concept of bringing in outsiders was seen as radical, upsetting, and politically unacceptable. In this way, the problems of professionalism and localism became issues even before the Teacher Corps came off the drafting boards.

Funding also proved to be an important problem. Money was appropriated only a few weeks before the program's field operations began with training of Teacher Corps interns. Because of late and uncertain funding, the Teacher Corps had to be organized in less than two months. In this time it solicited, reviewed, and approved over forty contracts with universities and somehow selected and recruited over 1,200 college graduates. The administrative imperative was to get the program running, get the money to the field, and worry later about spelling out clear objectives or providing for evaluation procedures. It was perhaps an act of faith that highly motivated new people and new federal money properly mixed would somehow liberate teacher training from traditional practices.

Attracting leadership also proved difficult. The Teacher Corps went without a director for nearly a year after the legislation was passed. Then its first director, Richard A. Graham, came to the Teacher Corps as an outsider to the field. Trained as an engineer, he had previously been a public relations specialist and an overseas country director for the Peace Corps. He had not been a teacher, held no degrees in education, and had not worked within a university. But he did have commitment and energy. Modeling himself after the Peace Corps' Sargent Shriver, he waged a tireless campaign to sell the Teacher Corps to Congress and to the public. He was to find, however, that the most difficult selling job was convincing his own associates and superiors within the USOE.

Much as Shriver had sought to differentiate Peace Corps from State Department and overseas AID personnel, so the Teacher Corps now tried to differentiate itself from the traditional USOE. Several "noneducators" were recruited to staff the Washington office. Some had been active in the Peace Corps, others enjoyed political ties to the Congress. Administrative headaches plagued them from the start. Because initial funding was late, the Washington office was not able to participate systematically in candidate selection, and many mistakes were made. Then, too, in that first year an old-boy network was at work in which seasoned USOE veterans, temporarily assigned to the Teacher Corps, alerted their friends at the schools of education that here was another federal contract they could get in line for. Late congressional funding also made it impossible for the Washington office to pay the recently recruited Teacher Corpsmen during the first several weeks of the 1966 school year, prompting an unusually high dropout rate in the first months of the program. Some 51 percent of entering Teacher Corps interns and 50 percent of the experienced teachers, or Teacher Corps team leaders, quit.

The director of the Teacher Corps resented being submerged within a bureau within an agency within a department. The program was losing its identity and, in the minds of its loyal cadre of leaders, its integrity. Major skirmishes were waged over stationery and secretarial allotments. Teacher Corps director Graham persisted in seeking expanded legislative and executive branch commitments. He spent countless days on Capitol Hill in pursuit of votes. At the same time Graham sought out every chance to convince his own commissioner of the merits of expanding and granting greater independence to the Teacher Corps. He campaigned publicly for more status for the Teacher Corps, eventually openly supporting efforts to secede it from the USOE.

Thus in the early years the Teacher Corps staff consisted largely of two groups: the USOE old guard, moderately resistant to innovation, adept at foot-dragging, attentive to the wishes of the educational lobbies, and the young, enthusiastic, and conspicuously inexperienced new people trying to replicate the Peace Corps. The sometimes unseemly struggle between old and new people, often between those with and without education school doctorates, created image problems and made staff recruitment more difficult.

Meanwhile, what was the White House doing while one of the president's pet programs hit these snags? It did very little, if it was aware of them at all. Although the president is nominally chief administrator of the government, it is extremely difficult for an activist president to follow the operations of individual programs, as the case of the Teacher Corps illustrates. One of Johnson's aides says, "We just didn't monitor much. The White House staff can't really go out and look at programs, and even when we do we probably don't get accurate evidence. You really have to go out with a team of specialists and stay for awhile, look over the books, and get involved. And that was impossible. It might be possible to have some spot checks into trouble situations with trouble shooters but we just didn't have very much time for that either."

Conflict with Local Educators

The Johnson White House assumed too readily that the Teacher Corps would be welcomed by local communities, schools of education, and local schoolmen, as other nations had welcomed the Peace Corps. But from the beginning there were critics. The name "National Teacher Corps" was changed after a year or so to "Teacher Corps," to minimize or at least try to mute the role of Washington. Several prestigious schools of education said they would work with the Teacher Corps only if they could design and run their own programs. Others were miffed if not explicitly insulted by the premise that existing programs were not accomplishing what was needed.

Perhaps the greatest shock for the Teacher Corps was its confrontation with the personnel of participating schools. Teacher Corpsmen were young, and they were mainly from liberal arts schools. They believed schools of education and most teachers had failed students in low-income areas and that "it was time for a change." Teachers and principals in most of the public schools where they served had graduated from local teachers colleges, majoring in education rather than in liberal arts. They were generally more cautious, more satisfied with the way their schools served the community. More important, they controlled the schools, so conflict was almost inevitable.

Local school systems generally favored the Teacher Corps notion in the abstract, but they often discovered that having outsiders in their midst, with different values and a decidedly youthful impulse to change the existing order (or at least complain about it) was considerably more than they had bargained for.

Invariably, the Teacher Corps members worked with each other and became separated from regular teachers. Many interns, contrary to "professional" norms, identified with and befriended their students. More often than not, the Teacher Corpsmen were frustrated by the lack of support from regular teachers and blamed them for the problems of the disadvantaged. It became a vicious cycle: interns implying that the older teachers were to blame and urging sweeping reforms; older teachers saying the Teacher Corps people were troublemakers and naive about education.

A few years after the program had been in operation a visitor to Teacher Corps schools was as likely to hear deep-seated resentment as well-deserved praise. As a superintendent in southern Illinois who had worked with at least a score of Teacher Corps interns put it, "They were sloppy and offensive. There were several draft dodgers in the group. I don't think they were really interested in teaching, and they certainly were not disciplined. You see, they were too different, they really weren't our kind of people. I'd have to say, honestly, that they were really, when it comes right down to it, a bunch of *heathens.*" No one in the planning stages of the Teacher Corps had anticipated this clash in values and life-styles, though some of them might have been headed off by better program design or pilot-project testing. Incentives might have been developed to make older teachers less resentful and jealous, and to make Teacher Corpsmen more understanding of their beliefs and ways of doing things. Little or nothing of this sort was devised ahead of time, and neglect of such details came back to haunt the Teacher Corps. Local principals complained to Washington, to the participating school of education, and sometimes to their congressman that they wanted more control over selection and appointment of Teacher Corps personnel. Schools of education complained of too much red tape in the application process and of too many delays in funding or guidance from Washington.

But the real taming of the Teacher Corps reform derived from the way in which local schoolmen used the federal program funds to further their own interests. There was nothing exactly devious about this practice. In the first place, the guidelines of the program called for local control. Local schools of education, the very institutions that were to be the object of Teacher Corps reforms, were given substantial discretion for recruiting Teacher Corps members, designing curriculum, and organizing highly decentralized operations. Despite the burst of presidential level publicity about reform and innovation that preceded the implementation of the Teacher Corps, local school principals and local schools of education believed that the funds were available in order for them to do better at the job they were already doing.

The Washington Battles over Control and Funding

At the same time that the Corps was sinking into the quagmire of ill-defined objectives and implementation difficulties, with next to no White House attention, presidential involvement with the program continued—confined, however, to publicity and legislative persuasion. Johnson often spontaneously praised the Teacher Corps as a "symbol of new hope for America's poor children."[8] He also made personal appeals to Congress for money to assure that the Teacher Corps got off the drawing boards and into the classrooms. In 1967 the White House obtained barely enough funding to keep the Teacher Corps alive.

At about the same time, local school superintendents demanded the right to select local team leaders and have more of a say in screening prospective team members for their system. This was an obvious attempt to gain control over the program and to insure that the "new people" were compatible with the existing order. Washington officials balked at first but then consented, as the educational lobbies and conservative members of Congress argued the merits of more local control. Eventually USOE aides reasoned that this concession was necessary for program survival and even rationalized that if the local system felt too threatened and lacked "change-oriented people" to start with, it was highly unlikely that the Teacher Corps could take root anyway.

The Teacher Corps experienced its greatest congressional difficulties in 1967. Easy and quick passage of the 1965 bill did not imply easy appropriations. On the contrary, precisely because many in Congress resented the manner in which it had been rushed by them initially, they were ready to exact retribution. Rep. Edith

Green (D-Ore.), together with several House Republicans, offered various amendments designed to increase local control. One journalist summed up the Teacher Corps' growing congressional problems this way: "The Teacher Corps has few jobs and little money for congressmen to disperse. It questions the value and relevancy of current practices in teacher training. It illuminates the failure of public schools to reach and elevate large numbers of disadvantaged children. No wonder it's under attack."[9]

The most influential critic of the Teacher Corps was Congresswoman Green, a former public school teacher and staff member for the Oregon Education Association. She was known as persistent, stubborn, knowledgeable, and decidedly partial to local and state school officials. She felt that the regular students at teachers colleges who were earning their own way or perhaps borrowing under NDEA might be just as dedicated to teaching as Teacher Corpsmen. She insisted that the special attention and subsidies to Teacher Corps members would encourage a form of elitism and divide the teaching ranks.[10]

> I am suggesting that I don't think this [the Teacher Corps] necessarily goes to the heart of the problem. I don't think we have made enough of a study of the slum school to know how we can attract and retain teachers there. Maybe it is going to be by a big salary increment. Maybe it is going to be through means of compensatory education . . . , with very small classes. There are a lot of alternatives that should be explored. I think to say that the Teacher Corps is the answer is perhaps a superficial answer.[11]

The White House cautioned that Green should not be allowed to get too upset, that compromise over jurisdictional (local versus federal control) matters could be lived with, although USOE officials should not have to accept substantive compromises that would materially damage the program. But jurisdictional compromises turned out to involve substance.

Teacher Corps officials took a conciliatory approach to nearly any member of the Congress who had complaints. Organizational survival depended on it, or so it seemed to them. Consequently, one former Teacher Corps aide reports, "Our first priority was to put programs in our Senate and House Appropriations Committee members' districts. Second, we tried to put programs in the districts of members of Congress serving on our authorization committees, and last, we tried to have the programs spread around the fifty states." In this way, "we hoped the program would become a salesman for itself and thereby win congressmen [in whose districts programs were operating] over to our side."

Though the Washington office was successful in locating programs in appropriate congressional districts, this priority had the effect of inhibiting a concentration of funds in any one locality or in a limited number of universities. This is a common problem for new federal programs. But a program that has its funds thinly scattered around thirty states when its initial funding is less than $20 million often has difficulty attracting talented local leadership or the commitment of local political elites. The question that arises is how can the federal government initiate pilot projects in order to test new types of programs without being obliged to conduct them simultaneously in every state and community?

Despite the careful selling of Teacher Corps programs and intensive lobbying on their behalf, by late 1967 Edith Green and her allies in Congress had been successful in changing the character of the National Teacher Corps. Some of these changes were manifest in amendments to the Teacher Corps legislation in 1967. Others were brought about by private consultations with HEW officials, committee reports, or merely the volume of congressional attention and criticism aimed at the program. The net effect was that the Teacher Corps was no longer a national program; it became a series of local programs, locally controlled. Local schools and local Teacher Corps teams chose teaching approaches and curriculum emphases pretty much at their own discretion. This satisfied most educational lobbies and school people and made it more likely that local principals would select trusted friends within their own school to serve as Teacher Corps team leaders, insuring that however idealistic or even radical the Teacher Corps interns might be, the program would be closely monitored and controlled by local hierarchies.

By 1968 most HEW officials were frustrated at the amount of time required to defend the Teacher Corps. Said one, "I have worked with at least one hundred pieces of legislation that have been made into law. The most difficult of those hundred has been the Teacher Corps—absolutely without question. . . ."

Table 2. Teacher Corps: Authorizations and Appropriations FY 1966 – FY 1976 (in millions)

Fiscal Year	Authorized	Appropriated
1966	$ 36.1	$ 9.5
1967	64.7	11.3
1968	33.0	13.5
1969	36.1	20.9
1970	80.0	21.7
1971	100.0	30.8
1972	100.0	37.4
1973	37.5	37.5
1974	37.5	37.5
1975	37.5	37.5
1976	37.5	37.5

Source: "Teacher Corps Past or Prologue?" *Report by the National Advisory Committee on Education Professions Development* (Washington, D.C., July 1975); US Budget, Fiscal Year 1977.

The Executive and Congress Lose Interest

As the Johnson Administration moved into its lame-duck phase and as the Nixon presidency took hold, the life of the Teacher Corps became very much a congressional matter. Congressional "angels" of the Teacher Corps, like Senators Nelson and Edward Kennedy, and House members like Rep. John Brademas (D-Ind.), were sought out continuously by Teacher Corps officials trying to extend the life of the program, enlarge its funding, and liberate it from the interior of the USOE labyrinth.

Until fiscal 1972 the program's funding gradually increased, rising from $11.3 million in fiscal 1967 to $37.4 million, although it remained well below authorized levels. After 1972, its appropriation was fixed at $37.5 million annually. (See table 2.)

By 1971, when the 1972 budget was drawn up, the Nixon administration had indicated little interest in this Democratic program. Teacher Corps officials had attempted to gain endorsement of the program from the Nixon White House but gained neither access nor attention. Said a former Teacher Corps senior aide, "Not only don't they know about the Teacher Corps, they don't care about us." The director was reassigned in early 1971, and for over a year the Teacher Corps was again allowed to drift.

Yet the program continued. Late in the first Nixon administration, it won a measure of bureaucratic independence and was transferred from its home bureau to the office of the commissioner of education. In 1973–74, it ran 94 projects in 158 school districts and 93 institutions of higher education. And later in the 1970s it became primarily a means to support demonstration projects for retraining educational personnel in poverty-area schools. The Teacher Corps became locked in limbo: its supporters couldn't make it grow, its detractors couldn't kill it.

Resistance to Evaluation

During its lengthy fight for survival, the Teacher Corps tried to minimize evaluations of its operations. Aides acknowledge that during its early years the program hierarchy was defensive toward researchers and evaluations. "The director would always dispute their findings and say that on the contrary the program results were really great. He was an optimist and disregarded the critical evaluations of any type." Since the program was doing rather poorly by many objective yardsticks, the corps' reluctance to undergo vigorous examination was understandable.

The only sort of evaluation that the program's directors would accept was a rose-tinted one. One such evaluation attempt came in the form of a "Special Report on the Teacher Corps" issued in 1967 from the presidentially appointed National Advisory Council on the Education of Disadvantaged Children. As is frequently the practice of such councils, this analysis was exclusively the work of a few staff in collaboration with a few hired consultants. The report was superficial. Prepared for White House transmission to Congress during debate over future funding for the Teacher Corps, the report glossed over the problems facing the agency and emphasized only the enthusiastic support enjoyed by some local programs. It contained no data, many half-truths, and a few completely inaccurate statements.

In-house capabilities for research and evaluation at the Teacher Corps were always puny. The Teacher Corps was defensive about this but claimed that inadequacy of funds, time pressure, and the practical necessity of generating publicity and accentuating "successes" made it impossible to undertake evaluation. However, evaluation aides in Teacher Corps staff positions were underused, bypassed, and soon disillusioned. Moreover, a presidentially appointed advisory council on the Teacher Corps was similarly disregarded, save as a potential lobbying ally. A prominent state school official who served on this council in the late 1960s summed up its role in this way: "[This] advisory council I serve on is more window dressing than actual service—[it is] used to get higher federal appropriations. Staff does as it pleases after the meetings." In lieu of systematic evaluation, the staff settled for letters from mayors and school superintendents who praised the existing program and called on Congress to expand it. The staff accentuated solicited "success stories" whenever possible and diverted problems as much as it could from attention by White House and Congress.

The corps' reluctance to submit to real evaluation was an understandable strategy, but it had serious consequences. The substitution of puffery for study doubtless misled some members of Congress and the media, by portraying a program in a growing administrative morass as an outstanding success. Rep. John Brademas, for instance, proudly referred to the Teacher Corps as "one of the most innovative and successful education programs which Congress has initiated" and claimed that it had been "remarkably successful in meeting the purposes that Congress has assigned it."[12] Even worse, the refusal to do serious in-house research left the corps blind to problems in its objectives and operations, unable to justify itself before congressional skeptics, without an understanding of the import of proposals to alter it, incapable of recasting itself.

The Results of the Teacher Corps

Despite the Teacher Corps' early reluctance to submit to evaluations, enough evidence exists to render some sort of judgment on its effectiveness. On the whole, the record of the Teacher Corps must be judged unfavorably. The Teacher Corps has done little to promote its declared objectives and has proved far costlier than anticipated. Thus, according to figures provided by the USOE, in the early 1970s it cost well over $20,000 to train a single Teacher Corps intern over a twenty-month program.

The high cost of educating a Teacher Corpsman might, of course, be worth the investment if most of the recruits stayed in teaching, continued to work in areas with large concentrations of low-income students, and brought to their jobs special abilities and commitment, as the program originally promised that they would. This has not been the case. Attrition has been high. Fifty-one percent dropped out of the first cycle and 27 percent from the second. About 10 percent of the interns have dropped out in more recent cycles. Additional surveys suggest that close to 30 percent more did not plan to stay in teaching even though they completed the program. Thus only about half of them would have entered teaching even without the program. Moreover, of the corps alumni who plan to teach, a third or more do not plan to work in "disadvantaged" schools. Consequently, of the individuals who begin Teacher Corps training, perhaps a mere third or so actually become teachers in poverty areas.

How cost-effective, then, is the Teacher Corps? Ten years after its beginning, government officials are unable to answer this question. In a report to the president and the Congress in July of 1975, the National Advisory Council on Education Professions Development could only rather weakly observe:

It would be helpful in assessing the Teacher Corps to know how it compares in terms of cost effectiveness with other teacher education programs. We would like to be able to offer some evidence, but we lack satisfactory data.

There are only crude, incomparable data available on the costs of educating teachers. Nor have we been able to calculate a true cost of educating teachers in the Teacher Corps, either pre-service or in-service. Until better data are available, comparisons are not possible.[13]

Of course there are those who ask whether the $37.5 million now going annually to the Teacher Corps might not be more effectively invested elsewhere, but the Teacher Corps and HEW officials are apparently not about to provide the information and evaluations needed to make such rational calculations. And so it goes.

Another major goal of the Teacher Corps was to bring fresh new talent into the schools, but studies for the Ford Foundation completed in the early 1970s found little evidence that Teacher Corpsmen were statistically different from teachers ordinarily attracted to the education profession. It is clear that in the beginning the Teacher Corps attracted a good many people who would not have otherwise joined the ranks of the teaching profession, but significantly it was these corpsmen who tended to have one of the highest dropout rates from the program. Moreover, according to one estimate, the brightest of America's young adults were not being attracted to the program in its first years: "most interns scored in the lowest quartile of the Graduate Record Examination."

Another objective of the program was to spur reform in teacher training and make schools of education more sensitive to the needs of disadvantaged pupils. Social psychologist Ronald Corwin offers evidence that though new courses were introduced under the sponsorship of the Teacher Corps at numerous schools of education, there was little evidence that either these new courses or the presence of the Teacher Corps on campus had any real impact on improvements within the participating education schools.[14] Frequently, it turns out, the Teacher Corps was viewed as a short-term undertaking, staffed by temporary or junior faculty. When Teacher Corps grants or the university's good will toward the Teacher Corps ran out, the program and its temporary faculty were expendable. This problem was of course exacerbated by the national Teacher Corps' own policy of trying to spread the funds to all the states, with emphasis on politically significant districts.

Conclusion

By Washington standards, the Teacher Corps was a modest undertaking. But in spite of its modest size, its variety of good intentions, and its earnest objectives, it failed to do much of what was expected of it. Eventually it would become merely one more teacher-training grant program for schools of education and local school systems, a program comfortably controlled by its clientele.

In fairness to the officials who administered the Teacher Corps, it must be pointed out that they worked under difficult conditions. Presidential interest was substantial, but it was evidenced almost entirely in symbolic and public relations efforts. Congressional support waxed and waned. Educational associations, which never wanted a centralized program that would threaten existing schools of education, worked to minimize the role of the Washington office. The war in Vietnam and escalation in defense budgets came at precisely the same time that Teacher Corps expansions might have taken place. Once a program that seemed likely to grow with national revenues, it became a program that had to compete with less threatening and more cherished subsidy programs. Small and unsure of itself from its creation, the Teacher Corps quickly got pushed to a back burner.

What lessons can we draw from the fate of the Teacher Corps?

1. *The need for prompt action conflicts with the need for thorough analysis and scrutiny of proposals.* When the Teacher Corps was established, conventional wisdom held that the answer to poor education in poor schools was to recruit and train better teachers for these schools. It seemed like common sense to senators, to presidential assistants, and, in this case, to President Lyndon Johnson. Much of what the federal government attempts to do is based upon such common-sense assumptions; some programs grow, some fade away. The Teacher Corps offers a good example of how common-sense solutions can go awry.

The assumption that small bands of Teacher Corps interns could change the system was in retrospect an assumption egregiously oversold. To have expected these recent college graduates, new to teaching and new to the community, viewed with suspicion by the long-term teachers, without clearly defined responsibilities and with academic course loads at nearby universities consuming much of their time, to change the quality of education in the nation's toughest schools was as unrealistic as it was altruistic. That hopes were inflated became clear as several school systems from Boston to Cairo, Illinois, threw the Teacher Corps out. Not only did the intern-participant dropout rate average nearly 30 percent in the first three or four years in each two-year training cycle but an equally high percentage left the teaching of low-income students a year or two later.

At least some of the problems that the corps was to encounter could have been anticipated. However, the political pressures of the moment meant that the Teacher Corps legislation was enacted with little forethought or planning. The dilemma facing politicians is clear: rush reform and risk failure or study reform and endanger passage.

2. *The need for clear objectives conflicts with the need to build political support.* In the case of the Teacher Corps, the drive for passage and funding meant that program officials promised to attain an ever-expanding roster of goals. Paralyzing conflicts among goals became endemic; some were due to the program's poor initial planning, but others arose because the administrators promised too much. In any event, the corps committed itself to so much that it was able to do very little.

3. *Federal reform often will arouse local resistance; local control often will impede federal reform.* The establishment of a federal reform program means that local authorities, for some reason or other, have failed—or revenue in sufficient quantity is not available. In general, however, the same interests that led to error or inaction at the local level are likely to oppose and try to co-opt federal action. The Teacher Corps, for instance, foundered because it was first resisted and then ultimately controlled by the very local teachers colleges and school systems it had been designed to change. Established interest groups are usually more concerned with what they might lose than with what they might gain. As this example shows, in the case of reform programs jurisdictional compromise is fraught with substantive significance. Efforts to bring reform programs under local control are often disguised efforts to gut them.

4. *Congress and the president are often unable (or unwilling) to monitor the implementation of newly enacted programs effectively.* Neither the president nor his senior domestic policy advisers were aware of the major difficulties besetting the implementation of the Teacher Corps. Top HEW officials were aware of many of them but did not pass the word to a White House increasingly consumed with the war in Vietnam. Congressmen who were advocates of the Teacher Corps in its early days often became emotional in their defense of it. Just as they had been overly optimistic in their early claims for what it might accomplish, so now they became overly charitable in their claims for what it had achieved. Teacher Corps officials controlled most of the information flow to the Congress (and to the White House). And "evaluations," if they can be called that, were made by those who were implementing the program.

5. *Co-opted reforms can become self-perpetuating.* The very interests that struggle to thwart a program may ensure its continuance once they have seized control of it, even though, like the Teacher Corps, the program never fulfills its promise. Ironically, support for the program grows as sponsors, participants, and beneficiaries acknowledge their self-interest. To paraphrase Daniel Webster, the Teacher Corps is a small federal effort, but there are those who love it.

More generally, it is plain that the implementation strategies of the Teacher Corps were not directly related to goal achievement. Improvement of education in poverty areas was approached indirectly through teacher-training programs in which trainees were under no contract to work in depressed-area schools. Providing assistance to school superintendents and principals with few use restrictions for money received parallels the Economic Development Administration's arrangements with World Airways in Oakland, California described by Pressman and Wildavsky.[15] Similarly, the strategy of rushing a reform through Congress and risking failure of the program, as opposed to studying it in advance and endangering passage, directly parallels Daniel P. Moynihan's general finding in *Maximum Feasible Misunderstanding*, a study of community action in the war on poverty.[16] The findings in this case study also illustrate many of the factors that Bardach points to as complicating the implementation process.[17] Specifically, these factors in the Teacher Corps case include ambiguous executive decisions; major policy changes that violate standard operating procedures of agencies; a large number of officials who act independently on an issue; and too much leeway given to the organization implementing policy.

Finally, we see in the Teacher Corps another phenomenon that several analysts have found in other policy areas, in which grant recipients focus on *program outputs* rather than *policy outcomes.* In this case, what counted was the training of the Teacher Corps interns rather than an assessment of how the education of children in poverty areas was improved.

Making governmental programs work effectively and efficiently is plainly an exacting task. Public officials need encouragement and help in these functions, and they deserve to be praised when they are successful. We need case analyses and comparative studies of both successful and unsuccessful governmental operations to learn how programs can be shaped and guided to achieve intended objectives.

Notes

1. John F. Kennedy, "State of the Union Address, 1963," *Public Papers of the Presidents of the United States* (Washington, D.C.: Government Printing Office, 1964), p. 13.

2. US Senate statements and testimony of Senator Edward M. Kennedy, William Vanden Heuvel, and Dr. Neil Sullivan, *Hearings on S. 600,* Part III, Subcommittee on Education of the Committee on Labor and Public Welfare, 89th Cong., 1st sess., June 11, 1965, pp. 1346-1351, 1362-1368, 1428-1437.

3. John Kenneth Galbraith, "Let Us Begin: An Invitation to Action on Poverty," *Harper's Magazine,* March 1964, p. 26.

4. Merriman Smith, *A White House Memoir* (New York: Norton, 1972), p. 36.

5. Lyndon B. Johnson, speech at University of Michigan, May 22, 1964, *Presidential Papers* (Washington, D.C.: Government Printing Office, 1965), pp. 705-706. See also Doris Kearns, *Lyndon Johnson and the American Dream* (New York: Harper and Row, 1976).

6. Address to the annual convention of the National Education Association, July 2, 1965, *Public Papers of the Presidents of the United States* (Washington, D.C.: Government Printing Office, 1966), p. 718.

7. See Jerald G. Bachman, Swazzer Green, and Ilona Wirtanen, *Dropping Out—Problem or Symptom*? (Ann Arbor: University of Michigan Institute for Social Research, 1971).

8. Lyndon B. Johnson, statements, April 20, 1967, February 28, 1967, and June 29, 1967, *Public Papers of the Presidents of the United States* (Washington, D.C.: Government Printing Office, 1968), pp. 248, 455, 667-668.

9. John Egerton, "Odds Against the Teacher Corps," *Saturday Review,* Dec. 17, 1966, p. 71.

10. Rep. Edith Green, *Hearings on H.R. 6230,* Elementary and Secondary Education Amendments of 1967, Committee on Education and Labor, US House of Representatives, 90th Cong., pp. 215-216.

11. Rep. Edith Green, "A Congresswoman Discusses the Politics of Education," *Phi Delta Kappan,* February 1966, p. 232.

12. Rep. John Brademas, *Congressional Record* 116, no. 96 (June 11, 1970), H. 5477.

13. *Teacher Corps: Past or Prologue*?, a report by the National Advisory Council on Education Professions Development, July 1975, p. 19.

14. These generalizations derive from a study of the Teacher Corps funded by the Ford Foundation and directed by Professor Ronald G. Corwin of Ohio

State University. Findings cited here are from Corwin's report to Ford, entitled "The Fate of a National Program for Educational Reform" (mimeo, 1971). See also Corwin's book, *Reform and Organizational Survival: The Teacher Corps as an Instrument of Educational Change* (New York: Wiley, 1974).

15. See Jeffrey L. Pressman and Aaron Wildavsky, *Implementation* (Berkeley: University of California Press, 1973).

16. Daniel P. Moynihan, *Maximum Feasible Misunderstanding* (New York: Free Press, 1969).

17. Eugene Bardach, *The Implementation Game* (Cambridge, Mass.: The MIT Press, 1977).

Chapter 6

Ask Not What Our Presidents Are "Really Like"; Ask What We and Our Political Institutions Are Like: A Call for a Politics of Institutions, Not Men

Martin Levin

In the past few decades Americans have developed an inordinate interest in learning what our presidents are "really like." Barbara Walters merely gave voice to this national obsession when she earnestly asked Gerald and Betty Ford whether they slept in twin beds. Journalists have always focused on personalities and explanations emphasizing the importance of individual actors and their character traits, but the publication of James David Barber's *Presidential Character* has given this popular interest a scholarly legitimation. The editor of a leading national newspaper told me that both journalists and political scientists have been greatly influenced by Barber's analysis and by Richard Nixon who seemed to prove Barber's point. I agree with his assessment. For instance, in *Marathon: The Pursuit of the Presidency,* Jules Witcover of the *Washington Post* defends media focus on the 1976 candidates' personality and character on the grounds that the Johnson and Nixon experiences taught them how important these factors were.

In the spring of 1976, journalists, many political scientists, and most of Washington started asking, "What is Jimmy Carter like?", and "What is he likely to do in office?" But to answer the question of what any president is likely to do in office by analyzing what he is like misdirects our understanding of policy making. In this essay I want to make two broad points. First, a descriptive one: presidential policymaking is primarily a function of the interaction between the president and the elements and institutions of our political system. Presidential personality, background, and attitudes on particular issues are less influential; moreover, their impact on presidential behavior is mediated through their interaction with institutional and situational factors. In the language of political strategy, what a president will do in office is less a function of what he is like than of what we do to him: the kind of demands we make of him and how we make them. By "we" I mean the rest of the political system; not so much "the people" as political organizations–labor organizations, state and local party organizations, religious, ethnic, business, professional, and "public interest" organizations, the bureaucracy, Congress, and state legislatures. In politics, knowledge may not be power, but organization surely is the key to power. Mass participation in politics, even in elections, is not as significant as the participation of organizations. And within organizations, it is the actions of their executives and permanent staffs that are most significant.

My second point is prescriptive: we need a politics of institutions, not men; a presidency that is shaped and influenced by the rest of the political system; a Madisonian conception of the presidency, especially among those writing about it, which sees it as part of the web of government. This is opposed to the dominant postwar view of those in and out of politics that the presidency is the government. We also need a different conception of the role of other political institutions, particularly Congress, which emphasizes their ability to contribute to policy making and to speak for the national interest. We should focus on increasing the power and stature of these other institutions rather than diminishing that of the presidency. In this way, policy making would reflect more of a Madisonian balance among competing institutions, interests, and organizations, a sharing of power. Such an arrangement, especially with a Presidency more open to these influences, seems likely to produce better policies because they would be more responsive and subject to more error detection and correction.

I am not, of course, proposing a narrow and naive view of our political system in which the president is merely a political cash register upon which groups bang out their demands. On the contrary, in a mass democracy like ours there has to be more reliance on leaders than on the led, even when the latter are organizations. Indeed, the attitudes and behavior of the led are to a considerable degree shaped by their leaders' cues. Thus a democracy increases rather than diminishes the need for outstanding leaders. What I am proposing, however, is that we should rely on the institutions and organizations these persons lead, and that policy should be the product of the interaction between a competitive plurality of these institutions and organizations. In the following pages I will sketch the view opposing my two points. Then I will provide some historical and contemporary material from six presidencies which I think supports these points. Finally, I will suggest a critical look at this "politics of institutions."

The Presidency Is the Government

Among both practitioners and academics the dominant postwar view of the presidency and of national policy making in general has been that the presidency is the government. William Andrews summarized this view as it was expressed in the early 1960s: "[They] allowed for no other national political or governmental leadership than the President's. He was called upon to be absolute Number 1 in each area of activity of the national government. . . . So far as Congress entered the picture at all, it followed the President. The President was alone in the driver's seat. At best, Congress was a loyal helpmate . . . at worst, it was an aggressive backseat driver, grabbing at the steering wheel, fighting to put on the brakes, threatening to overturn and destroy the whole vehicle. 'One of the few political truths about the American system of government,' wrote Walter Johnson, 'Is that the President alone can give the nation an effective lead.' "[1] In this view, for the presidency, checks and balances, the separation of powers, are either an anachronism or a Republican "cover" (or a Democratic one, when there is a Republican White House) designed to oppose the president's policies. (I do not refer to this view by its usual label of the "strong" or "activist" presidency. The essence of this view is not activism or strength but the almost complete predominance of the presidency over other institutions and interests in national policy making. Furthermore, a strong and activist presidency is not excluded from the model of policy making by competing institutions and organizations which I am advocating.)

After Vietnam and Watergate, for the first time in the postwar era there was significant dissent from the presidency-is-the-government view, even among some of its leading advocates, such as Arthur Schlesinger, Jr., and James MacGregor Burns. However, this switch in institutional preference seemed to be due to their reaction against these and other specific policies. Thus, if and when the "good guys" got back in the White House, it seemed likely that these writers would switch back again, and indeed, as soon as Carter entered the White House that began to happen.

A major reason for the widespread and long-lasting acceptance of this view of the presidency seems to be the popularity of one of its major corollaries, that the presidency is best able to stand for the public or national interest. Accordingly, a president ought to represent something more than the sum and resolution of interest-group conflicts. He ought to be something different than a broker of interests. If there can be such a thing as a public interest on a given issue, according to this view, there is not likely to be a voice for it from any institution other than the presidency.

Later I will discuss the merits of this traditional view of the public interest and the presidency. My point here is to analyze why it is so widely held. One important element seems to be that, as Louis Hartz argued persuasively, America has always had a liberal tradition, and the strong, activist Presidency has always been advocated as the single voice that could achieve what have come to be thought of as liberal goals. Thus, even erstwhile opponents of an "imperial presidency" and associated policies such as the Vietnam War keep gravitating back to the presidency-is-the-government view. For instance, in 1977 the Senate moved toward deregulating the price of natural gas, with liberal opponents of regulation of a wide variety of areas such as airline fares and broadcasting joining for the first time with conservatives and oil-state senators. President Carter opposed deregulation and criticized the Senate for yielding to "special interests." He was joined by recent critics of the presidency such as the old socialist and Vietnam dove Murray Kempton, who said that Congress was showing itself to be responsive only to narrow and parochial interests and thus had forfeited all right and ability to speak for the nation as a whole. On the other hand, Kempton went on, Carter's opposition to deregulation shows us once more that only the president can speak for and serve the single national interest against these narrower interests.[2]

Support for this view is even more strongly held at the White House, as Thomas Cronin's interviews of the presidential staffs of Kennedy, Johnson, and Nixon indicate. The first two consisted of liberal activists, the third of conservative activists. But all voiced impatience and frustration with all other elements of the government, especially with the Cabinet departments and the bureaucracy. These feelings were best summarized by one White House aide who said, "Everybody believes in democracy until he gets to the White House and then you begin to believe in dictatorship, because it's so hard to get things done. Every time you turn around, people just resist you, and even resist their own job."[3]

There is another view of the presidency that tends to run counter to my prescriptive argument, as well as reinforcing the presidency-is-the-government view: interpreting presidential behavior on the basis of character and personality. These two views are not usually thought of as being closely associated, but I will suggest some of their common assumptions and values. The character and personality view is most elegantly voiced by James David Barber, who focuses on presidential personality—personal style and political world view, as well as the climate of expectations and the power situation with which the president's personality interacts. For Barber, the core of personality is character: "The way the President orients himself toward life—not for the moment, but enduringly. . . . [It] grows out of the child's experiments in relating to parents, brothers and sisters, and peers at play and in school, as well as to his own body and the objects around it."[4] In character he focuses on two dimensions—"activity-passivity" and "positive-negative affect toward one's activity," which refer to how much energy an individual invests in his activity and how he feels about what he does.[5] From this Barber has derived four character types for analysis: "active-positive," "active-negative," "passive-positive," and "passive-negative."

This is not the place to deal with the significant problems in Barber's methodology and his theory constructions and testing. (See Alexander George's perceptive and balanced effort.)[6] Instead, I wish to discuss the potential political and policy effects of this interpretation of presidential behavior and the values underlying it. Barber's scholarly and provocative analysis and other excellent examples of psychobiography, such as Alexander and Juliette George's *Woodrow Wilson and Colonel House: A Personality Study,* seem to me to have reinforced and legitimized the predilection in both journalism and the popular mind to explain policy making in terms of personalities and individual character traits. This interest in what our presidents are really like leads to a political fatalism which seems to assume that once we elect someone president, he is beyond our control.[7] In this view, to understand and anticipate a president's behavior we ought to know his character traits. This contributes to a false ideology of personalism that in turn tends to legitimize quiescence and political passivity on the part of citizens, organizations, and institutions in the face of presidential power. It tends to develop a political voyeurism which seeks to identify and personalize the traits and tastes of public leaders so as to have a personal figure with whom to identify. It reflects and reinforces our tendency to look for a father figure in the presidency. (It does, however, help the media because it is easier to talk about personality than about structures, institutions, and complex issues; it is also easier to convey personality to an audience.) Thus, this view does not contribute to a politics of institutions rather than of men. Most importantly, it is refuted by recent history, which indicates that we can influence a President's policies, which satisfies democratic values and often improves the policies themselves through error detection and correction.

The character and personality view of presidential behavior tends to flow from the same activist values and assumptions that underlie the presidency-is-the-government view. Barber, for example, emphasizes the virtues of the active-positive type of president. Active-positives (FDR, Truman, Kennedy) "display personal strengths which enable them to make of that office an *engine of progress*."[8] As Alexander George has argued, Barber does not give sufficient consideration to the risks associated with active-positive presidents: "The historical example [of these risks, which Barber] cites [is] FDR's effort to pack the Supreme Court [and it] is hardly reassuring in this respect."[9] By contrast, Barber is critical of passive-negatives (Coolidge, Eisenhower) because they leave "vacant the *energizing,* initiating, stimulating possibilities of the role."[10] He notes, but does not elaborate on it, that in certain historical circumstances passive-negatives can provide a "breathing spell" for recovery after a frantic period in politics.[11]

From a policy perspective the most serious flaw in Barber's analysis is his failure to make qualitative distinctions among actual levels of activity and positivity.[12] The presidency-is-the-government writers, such as Neustadt, also fail to do this with regard to activism. Perhaps the most important of these distinctions is the question of the values that an active and positive president will pursue. Like Neustadt, Barber tends to be more concerned with creating an efficient machine—one that moves briskly and feels positive about itself, so it won't be self-destructive. Indeed, he wants the office to be an "engine of progress." But neither he nor Neustadt is very explicit about where they think this engine should be going, toward what goals and the achievement of what values. Neustadt's *Presidential Power* is about how a president should obtain and keep power. There is almost no discussion of ends: Neustadt tends to treat power as if it were an end in itself and as if it could be exercised in a neutral fashion; Barber treats activism and positive affect in a similar manner. Of course, their New Dealish, liberal Democratic sympathies do show through. But they tend to avoid explicit discussions of values, as if there were societal consensus on where we want the presidency to take us and on how to get there; as if the goal of "more progress" meant the same thing to everyone. This is part of the corollary noted earlier—the presidency is best able to stand for the public or national interest. The dubious assumption behind it, which these writers reflect, is that if the president wants it, it must be good; after all, he is elected by all the people. So he must be more representative of the national interest than others, elected to represent parochial interests.

A Politics of Institutions, Not Men

A presidency open to both a variety of interests and views and to the task of brokering among them results in a policy-making process that is bumpy, indirect, unsightly, wearing on the president, and sometimes even inefficient. But tidiness has never been the source of our political system's virtues, nor is efficiency our highest political goal. Indeed, by the mid-twentieth century, politics seems to have replaced economics as the "dismal science" in most democracies trying to deal with social problems through policy intervention. They have found it difficult to move men and organizations to obtain agreements and social action. The more political institutions are open to a variety of interests and pressures, and the more leaders see their role as brokering among them, the harder will it be to move people and organizations and secure agreements. However, as I have argued elsewhere at length, for a democracy such difficulties are probably appropriate and have positive value.[13] In this age of omnipresent government, everyone ought to have a chance to slow government down before it acts in order to search for alternatives, including no government action at all. This may cause some inefficiencies, but it maintains democratic values through a more representative politics and policymaking. The compromises inherent to an open politics with dispersed power may alter a policy's objectives and reduce its effectiveness, but they seem to be the essence of representative policy making in a large, heterogeneous society.

However, the most significant point here is that policymaking characterized by competing institutions, each of which–including the presidency–is open to a variety of interests and pressures, is more efficient and wiser in the long run. We cannot expect the president or any policymaker to be completely free of error or even to come close. Thus these competing institutions and interests can make a major contribution as sources of error detection and correction. The failures of Vietnam and Watergate, for instance, can be read as instances in which the presidency was resistant to error correction. By contrast, Eisenhower was able to avoid an inappropriate and untimely US intervention in Indochina because of his openness to error detection and the vigorous efforts of competing institutions. The ultimate success in the Watergate case was the work of competing institutions–the courts and the Congress, operating independently of each other, with no central guidance.[14]

Nevertheless, I do not think that presidents will voluntarily open themselves to this type of policy making. First, the view that the presidency is best able to stand for the national interest is accepted at the White House and reinforced by popular support. Second, as George Reedy has persuasively argued, structural characteristics of the office run in the opposite direction. "The environment of deference [in which the President operates], approach[es] sycophancy. . . . [It] helps to foster another insidious factor . . . a belief that the President and a few of his most trusted advisers are possessed of a special knowledge which must be closely held within a small group lest the plans and the designs of the United States be anticipated and frustrated by enemies."[15] Third, and related to all this, presidents seem to have adopted the view that since they ultimately must take the responsibility for most national policy making, they should not have to share the decision making with others who do not share that responsibility and its risks.

These factors are manifested in a plebiscitary conception of the presidency held by others besides Richard Nixon. Using the rhetoric fasionable today, President Carter has deplored the growth of an imperial presidency. Yet his emphasis on direct access to the people, without any intermediate bodies, is central to a plebiscitary presidency. He often talks of "special interests" as the obstacle to desired policy. If he does not get his way, Carter has promised to go directly to the people, as he did in his legislative battles in Georgia.[16] Mayor Lindsay of New York City also did not like "deals" and bargaining with special interests, power brokers, party bosses, and union bosses, which were all morally tainted. Nor did President de Gaulle, who spoke so contemptuously of political parties and had an explicitly plebiscitary presidency, with direct access to the people. Similarly, in his first administration and in the 1972 election, Nixon even set himself apart from the rest of his own executive branch. President Carter seems so different from Nixon that maybe this potential similarity tells us something about our current political system and how the institution of the presidency is evolving. Perhaps with the decline of political parties, all presidents will take this plebiscitary, no-intermediate-groups approach.

If presidents will not open themselves voluntarily to a more competitive Madisonian policy making, then to improve error detection and correction these other institutions and organizations must take the initiative and press their views on the White House. This will be difficult because of the presidency's predominance for over forty years. But a place to start is Aaron Wildavsky's suggestion that "the institutional lesson . . . is not that the Presidency should be diminished but that other institutions should grow in stature. . . . The wisdom of a democracy must be in its 'separate institutions sharing power'. . . . The first order of priority should go to rebuilding our political parties because they are most in need of help and could do most to bring Presidents in line with strong sentiments in the country. . . . [A] party provides essential connective tissue between people and government. . . . So does Congress; strengthening its appropriation process through internal reform would bring it more power than any external threat could take away. The people need the vigor of all their institutions."[17]

Of course, one person's error correction is another's obstructionism; one person's error is another's statesmanship and principled behavior. Underlying part of this analysis of alternative policy-making processes is value conflict: the simple preference for a particular policy which is associated with one institution at a given time. For instance, the presidency plays an important error-correcting role for the rest of the system. But there is much more than value conflict here. First, there is the question of balance: the presidency as an error-correcting device is widely advocated and accepted, but we seem to have lost the perspective in which the presidency also needs to be subject to some error detection and correction. Second, both the White House and these other institutions and organizations commit errors. Thus the crucial question is which one can more readily admit error and thus contribute to correction. Because of the dominance of the presidency-is-the-government view and the office's structural features discussed by Reedy, the presidency seems to be less able to admit error publicly than Congress and some interest groups. This is probably the strongest argument for more competitive, plural policymaking. Reedy in effect suggests that the nature of the modern presidency has largely vitiated its own error-detection abilities. It has thrown up around itself a fog of dissonance reduction: "If I am the President and I do this, given all that I alone know, all my unique responsibility . . . , then it *must* be right." Vietnam and Watergate are striking examples of this, but much recent presidential policy making has fit this pattern.

Pressure, Error Correction, and Responsive Policymaking

An examination of some issues in the Truman and Kennedy presidencies and brief discussions of the other postwar presidencies will illustrate the two themes of this essay. In the instances of successful error detection and correction, the president's personality and openness to different views may have been contributing factors, but the pressure on him from other institutions and organizations seems to have been at least as influential. In the cases in which presidential error correction failed to occur, it seems to have been a product of inadequate pressure from others (especially congressional abdication of responsibility) as well as of the president's personality and views on the issue.

Truman and Kennedy

The policies toward Israel and on civil rights in the Truman and Kennedy administrations are best understood by analyzing the demands made on these presidents once in office rather than by looking at their prepresidential careers, attitudes, or behavior. Most organizations and coalitions interested in these issues were and are shrewd enough to ignore the question of what a president is "really like." Instead, they concentrate on how they can pressure him and the other organizations and institutions in our political system. Jewish organizations did this with Truman and have continued to do so successfully since then.[18] Since the 1940s blacks and their allies have followed the same strategy with general success, as the Truman and Kennedy administrations indicate. In both instances blacks were faced with administrations that at the outset were at the most moderate on civil rights, but they eschewed any fatalistic acceptance of the prepresidential record and used pressure to turn both into administrations that were quite progressive on civil rights for their day. These cases will be examined in some detail because they are instances in which both presidents were at almost every step reluctant to pursue the policies pressed on them. Thus while these cases hardly constitute proof, they are suggestive of this essay's arguments, especially concerning the relative influence of personality and background compared to pressures from other institutions and organizations.

Before becoming president, Truman had no personal or policy predispositions toward Zionism. Indeed, whether it was his own personal predilection or merely political expediency in his area of Missouri, Truman's and his wife's behavior was publicly cool to Jews. Yet on balance Truman's policies as president greatly benefited Zionism. They were strikingly the product of demands made on him and on congressional and party leaders by the Jewish community, which was a significant element of his party's coalition and strategically concentrated in states with large electoral votes. This in turn produced political pressure on Truman from his own White House staff. All this occurred despite Truman's own ambivalence and despite strong counterpressures within the executive branch. As Snetsinger has shown, it is only a "popular myth" that Truman was an unswerving supporter of Israel.[19] His support was a function of political pressure and thus oscillated quite a bit.

Shortly after he assumed office, a State Department memo sternly warned Truman, as if he were still the junior senator from Missouri, that there would be Zionist pressure on him but that there were also other "interests in that area which are vital to the U.S.," and "that the whole subject is one that should be handled with the greatest care." For the next five years, State, Defense, and the military pressured Truman for policies unfavorable to the creation and support of Israel. In the face of this range of counterpressure, Truman's policies, which became more pro-Zionist over time, were always marked by ambivalence and backtracking. Truman later complained that "there'd never been anything like [the Jewish pressure] before and there wasn't after. Not even when I fired MacArthur, there wasn't."[20] Even as he acquiesced to this pressure, he wrote in his *Memoirs* that he resented the "rather quarrelsome and emotional" pressure of the Zionists. "I kept my faith in the rightness of my policy in spite of some of the Jews. When I say 'the Jews,' I mean, of course, the extreme Zionists. . . . Most Americans of the Jewish faith, while they hoped for the restoration of [the] Jewish homeland, are and always have been Americans first and foremost."[21] This corresponds with how others remember his attitudes at the time. At the White House, Eddie Jacobson, Truman's former business partner in Missouri, asked him to take the important symbolic step of receiving Chaim Weizmann, the leading international Zionist. Truman, according to Jacobson, became "abrupt in speech and very bitter. . . . In all the years of our friendship he had never talked to me in this manner. . . . [He told me] 'how disrespectful and how mean' some of the Jewish spokesmen had been. I suddenly found myself thinking that my dear friend, the President of the U.S., was at that moment as close to being an anti-Semite as a man could possibly be."[22]

These pressures were effective, however, not because of their persistence or moral superiority but because they were followed by other forms of political action and by political events that were in part orchestrated by Jewish leaders. Through 1947 and 1948, competing political pressures on the Palestine question from the left and the right continued to intensify as the political future of Truman and the Democrats continued to darken. Both Henry Wallace and Governor Dewey took positions supporting Israel. In early 1948, Truman and the Democratic party were stunned when an American Labor party candidate for Congress, Leo Isaacson, beat the Ed Flynn-backed Democrat in a normally safe Democratic district in the Bronx by an almost two-to-one margin. Wallace had campaigned for Isaacson and criticized Truman for "talk[ing] Jewish but act[ing] Arab."[23]

As early as 1947 all elements of the Democratic party in New York State (the state chairman, Ed Flynn of the Bronx, Emmanuel Celler of Brooklyn, and antiorganization liberals) warned Truman of the loss of New York both in the convention and the election unless a staunchly pro-Zionist policy were followed. In 1947 Paul Fitzpatrick, the New York Democratic state chairman, told Truman that "if the [anti-Zionist policy of the British] goes into effect it would be useless for the Democrats to nominate a State ticket for the election this fall."[24] As the 1948 convention approached, New York State delegates warned their county chairmen of rebellions in Jewish districts.[25] Truman continually reacted to this pressure and to competitive threats. Britain's Foreign Secretary Bevin complained at one of their conferences that he was handicapped because the Palestine negotiations were "made the subject of local elections."[26]

All this pressure was in effect brought to focus on Truman by the reaction of his White House staff. As early as 1946 David

Niles, his special assistant, was a major conduit to Truman for Zionist opinions and exhortations. In late 1947 and early 1948 Zionist pressure led presidential assistant Clark Clifford to advocate a pro-Zionist policy largely in terms of domestic politics and as a keystone to the 1948 election strategy. In May 1948 Truman's ambivalent policy toward Israel ended with US recognition of Israel as a state within minutes of its proclamation of independence, strong support in the ensuing war, and a continued honoring of his campaign commitments in 1949 after the war ended.

Truman's very significant pro-civil rights policies were developed through a similar pattern of political pressure. In this policy area, Truman's prepresidential views and actions were ambiguous. More importantly, they were the product of the same type of coalition expediency in Missouri that he was to face as president, rather than of his own background or personal preference. Truman's symbolic and substantive presidential civil rights policies were quite progressive for the 1940s and were important building blocks for later aspirations and more advanced policies. The relative influence of various factors is capsulated in an off-the-record comment to a young political scientist in the late 1950s, which as far as I know has never been printed before. After completing an interview with the former president on another topic, the researcher said that he wanted Truman to know that he had always admired him for his strong stands on civil rights. Truman replied matter-of-factly, "Well yes that's true. . . . But you know I never really cared much for the Negra [sic]. Most of them are lazy. . . . They aren't clean. . . . But when you are President, you have got to be for the Negra [sic]." Truman of course did not "have to be for the Negro" just as he did not have to be reelected; indeed, few thought he would be. Hoover wasn't reelected, nor was Johnson or Ford. But Negroes and their allies were strategically positioned elements of the national Democratic coalition. In the face of significant pressure, he moved for them and helped his administration survive politically, as well as producing responsive public policy.

Merle Miller states that "privately Mr. Truman always said 'nigger'; at least he always did when I talked to him [in the 1960s]. That's what people said when he was growing up [in]

Independence, a Southern town."[27] But as much as he was a product of Independence, he was also a product of Boss Tom Pendergast's statewide political machine. Its base was Kansas City, which with St. Louis had a sizable black population and a total black vote of 130,000. So whatever his personal views were, as a senator he at times spoke out for civil rights in Missouri, even in the face of opposition. In the Senate he voted for the civil rights proposals of the day, but he told a southern senator, "You know I am against this [1938 antilynching] bill, but if it comes to a vote, I'll have to vote for it. All my sympathies are with you but the Negro vote in Kansas City and St. Louis is too important."[28]

As president, Truman faced a good deal of pro-civil rights pressure from organized blacks and their allies (the NAACP and A. Philip Randolph and his union), just as FDR had. Like FDR, Truman and his advisers viewed blacks as an important element of the New Deal coalition. Influentials in the Democratic party and his administration, ranging from big-city bosses to Clark Clifford, urged Truman to court the black vote, especially as his election prospects looked dim.

The significance of this pressure—along with his bleak election prospects—in shaping Truman's actions can be seen from the existence of strong counterpressure from southern Democrats who were influential in the party and in Congress. Southern support had been crucial in getting Truman the vice-presidential nomination at the 1944 convention. Thus throughout the mid-1940s Truman's continuing movement toward support of civil rights was always ambivalent, halting, and largely symbolic. The South was still an element in the New Deal coalition, though with the significant increase in black voters in northern states, the South's relative coalition influence was declining.

Throughout 1946 racial violence and lynching increased in the South, often involving returning black veterans, especially those demanding to register to vote.[29] Truman, however, resisted pressure to create the President's Civil Rights Committee until December 1946, following the Democratic congressional election defeat.[30] In February 1948 he sent a civil rights message to Congress which precipitated a furious southern reaction. Therefore at the July 1948 convention he was still reluctant to antagonize further the southern allies of the New Deal. It was largely the big-city Democratic bosses with the support of a smaller group of liberals at the convention who gave Truman a stronger civil rights plank than he wished.[31] In June 1948 A. Philip Randolph threatened a campaign of civil disobedience and nonregistration for the draft if the new draft law went into effect without a desegregation provision. In late July 1948, after the convention, Truman issued Executive Order 9981 desegregating the army.[32]

The state of Israel and the blacks benefited from Truman's policies, but it is also significant that Truman prospered as well. His 1948 election victory was a stunning upset. Truman had many political disadvantages and made several political errors, but after the 1946 election defeat, he was able to make significant corrections. An important aid in this was his staff, which was quite responsive to intermediate groups and their pressures. It is difficult to attribute the presidential votes of even one ethnic group to particular policies, but most observers feel that the adoption of policies favored by blacks and Jews greatly helped Truman keep these groups in the New Deal coalition. Both blacks and Jews were concentrated in states that had both a large number of electoral votes and very narrow victory margins for Truman. He carried Ohio, California, and Illinois by less than 4,000, 9,000, and 17,000 votes, respectively.

The development of President Kennedy's civil rights policies indicates a similar pattern. There was little in Kennedy's prepresidential background or actions on which to predict his presidential civil rights policies, which eventually were rather progressive. Politically and personally, Kennedy probably had less exposure to the race issue than the average northern Democratic politician of his time. Arthur Krock, the *New York Times* columnist and family friend, said, "I never saw a Negro on the level of social terms with the Kennedys in all my years of acquaintance with them. And I never heard the subject [of race] mentioned."[33] Kennedy's court historian, Arthur Schlesinger, could only describe his prepresidential attitudes and behavior on civil rights as "sympathetic but detached."[34]

Pressures on Kennedy with regard to race and poverty began in his presidential campaign. He reacted with promises to combat Appalachian poverty, his "stroke of the pen" speech, and his effort to get Martin Luther King released from jail, though race was barely mentioned in the Kennedy-Nixon debates. When he became president, these pressures grew much greater. The early 1960s brought sit-ins, freedom rides, and voting rights demonstrations which by the standards of the times involved quite a bit of civil disorder. Within Kennedy's own party coalition, liberal congressmen and their allies were pressing for legislation, while in a different approach, NAACP lawyers were bringing desegregation lawsuits. Yet Kennedy clung as much as he could to a modest approach to civil rights, because he perceived the counterpressures as being even greater. Most objective observers would agree that in 1962 civil rights still lacked widespread support among whites, and southern counterpressure was especially influential in Congress. Through early 1963 Kennedy seems to have continued to think that civil rights legislation was politically unnecessary, unlikely to pass, and that efforts to pass it were likely to harm other legislative goals.

Nevertheless, by the end of 1962 Kennedy had moved a long way in the direction of greater civil rights. The Justice Department brought many southern voting suits, and in 1961 it sent 600 deputy federal marshals to protect freedom riders in Alabama. The National Guard was brought in to the University of Mississippi to protect James Meredith, and Kennedy federalized the Alabama National Guard and sent Deputy Attorney General Katzenbach to present Governor Wallace with a federal court desegregation order as he stood in the "schoolhouse door" at the University of Alabama. Kennedy followed the latter two actions with eloquent national television speeches criticizing resistance to civil rights. However, in all these cases it was a question of reacting to some specific crisis or court order; the actions were not initiated by the president, nor were they institutionalized civil rights policies. Indeed, Kennedy resisted pressure to introduce civil rights legislation until 1963. In 1961 Ted Sorensen had told the Leadership Conference on Civil Rights that Kennedy would not introduce such legislation and instead would rely on powers available to him through executive action. When congressional liberals introduced their own legislation in 1961, the White House dissociated itself from them. Moreover, in the field of executive action Kennedy moved quite slowly unless pressured. During the campaign, for instance, he had scoffed at Eisenhower for failing to desegregate federal housing programs by a mere "stroke of the pen." But that stroke took Kennedy almost two years.

Kennedy's strategy was to maintain "consensus" with both southern congressional support and black and white liberal support, but pressure from civil rights actions and anti-civil rights counterattacks finally shifted him. The confrontations between civil rights protesters and the police (and their dogs) in Birmingham in the spring of 1963 were a significant turning point, and the pressure on Kennedy to do more continued throughout 1963, reaching a high point with the huge (by pre-Vietnam standards) and peaceful civil rights march on Washington in August. Even before the march, the pressure led Kennedy to propose comprehensive civil rights legislation to Congress, and following the march, Kennedy worked hard for it in Congress and gave speeches supporting civil rights and criticizing segregationist violence. In light of the counterpressure in Congress and elsewhere, all this was quite progressive for the times, and it was almost exclusively the product of pressure from the civil rights movement and its allies in Congress and the Democratic party. As Fairlie, who otherwise is critical of Kennedy for creating excessive expectations, accurately concludes, Kennedy "waited until violence had actually erupted, or was immediately threatened, before he intervened."[35]

Kennedy did not live to face reelection, and again it is difficult to attribute votes to particular policies. A factor that must be added to the effect of the Democratic civil rights policies is that the 1964 Republican candidate was especially antithetical to blacks. Yet it is striking that Kennedy's Democratic successor, Lyndon Johnson, increased the Democratic proportion of the black vote from about 65 percent in 1960 to 95 percent in 1964.

Some Other Postwar Cases

A brief examination of some cases in the other postwar presidencies will also illustrate the themes of this essay. In several cases we find significant and successful error detection and correction of presidential policies through the interaction between the White House and other institutions, interests, and organizations. In other cases these institutions and organizations made inadequate efforts to press their views, or the president was not open to such pressures. These cases certainly do not constitute proof, but the commonality of the pattern among so many different presidencies does seem suggestive.

Perhaps the most striking and successful presidential error correction comes in a too-often forgotten but very important case: President Eisenhower and Indochina. Briefly, in 1954 as the French were being defeated in Indochina, they privately asked the US for intervention; later they specifically requested air strikes to relieve the besieged garrison of Dienbienphu. Eisenhower and his influential secretary of state, John Foster Dulles, seemed inclined to give such aid, though the former would do so only with congressional approval. (Ike spoke of a "row of dominoes" falling if Indochina were lost.) There was consultation with eight bipartisan congressional leaders, including the Senate minority leader, Lyndon Johnson. Most of the Democrats (including Johnson) opposed intervention, and all eight pressured Dulles first to seek the support of allies such as Britain. He did and failed to get any; the possibility of intervention ended. The significance and irony of this case need hardly be remarked on today.[36]

Eisenhower followed a similar pattern of interaction with Congress in two other major foreign crises. He went to Congress for resolutions authorizing American intervention in the Formosan Straits in 1955 and in the Middle East in 1957. Congress supported intervention in both. However, in a striking illustration of the presidency-is-the-government view, its proponents were critical of Eisenhower's actions. They felt it represented an abdication of presidential responsibility and authority in an area that should be dominated by the executive.[37] Rossiter, for example, said it was a "brake on his progress toward the stature of a great President."[38] Finer argued that the president's power to dispose of "the armed forces abroad is not limited to the Constitution."[39] In another delicious irony we find Koenig quoting with approval Senator Fulbright's remark that "for the existing requirements of American foreign policy we have hobbled the President by too niggardly a grant of power."[40]

By contrast, as Reedy and others indicate, while he was evolving his Vietnam policy Lyndon Johnson was not open to the variety of congressional and other pressures which might have led to error detection and correction. Vietnam was an unsuccessful policy for the nation and for Johnson, who was in effect forced to resign;

earlier the war had weakened his ability to carry out his ambitious Great Society programs.

Ironically, Johnson had been superbly successful in the Senate as an open broker of a variety of interests. Reedy thinks it was the structure and nature of the presidency that led to a different approach in Vietnam, and the Nixon White House's similar approach gave credence to his argument. However, in both cases it is hard to distinguish the effects of the office and the effects of waging an unpopular war. Gerald Ford's White House seems to have been different, but he did not have the war. Barber explains Johnson's approach to Vietnam in terms of personality. Both elements probably were influential, but I suggest that another factor may have been significant. My reading of 1965 to 1968 suggests inadequate pressure by Congress, party leaders, and other members of the Democratic coalition such as labor and civil rights leaders. They waited quite a while before they began to think independently about US policy in Vietnam, and most were not aggressive in making their doubts known to the administration until as late as 1967 or 1968. More importantly, many potential critics, such as some civil rights and congressional leaders, allowed themselves to be bought off by administration support of their goals in other areas. To be sure, the White House is powerful. But party and congressional leaders should have viewed their self-interest in a long-term perspective and understood that the White House was not only bringing itself down but also splitting the entire Democratic coalition.

The Reedy and Barber views—one emphasizing the nature of the office, the other the personality of its occupant—help explain why Nixon isolated himself so much on Watergate. But this is too simple a picture of Nixon's policymaking. In other areas, he showed himself open to a range of views in the first White House, such as sponsoring a national income-maintenance program and new policies toward China and Russia. Most of the ideas and pressures in these areas came from within the White House, but even on Vietnam (especially with regard to Cambodia in 1970) Nixon responded, though slowly, to outside pressures.[41] Thus there is some possibility that Nixon might have been open to warnings from his party and congressional leaders on the dangers of Watergate to his popular support. However, as with Johnson and Vietnam, such warnings were not forthcoming, and the near absence of national leaders in the weak Republican party contributed to this. Of course, Nixon did nothing to reverse the decay of his party.

Gerald Ford's presidency does not fit Reedy's model. It seemed open to error-correcting pressures. The most significant instance seems to have been his struggle for the nomination. From his dumping of Vice-President Rockefeller to his trimming on a whole variety of issues on which he had been criticized by the party's conservative wing, Ford was open to such error correction from his party's coalition. He and his advisers correctly read the distribution of influence within their party's coalition and acted boldly, as in the Rockefeller decision. Although he also had the powers of incumbency going for him, his responsiveness to these influences does seem to have been crucial in saving the nomination for him (and perhaps beneficial for his party, because he was probably its most effective candidate for the general election).

What about President Jimmy Carter? I have discussed his emphasis on direct access to the people, without any intermediate bodies; his attacks on "special interests"; and his representation of himself as standing above them in a direct relationship with the people. However, there is reason to believe that Jimmy Carter will make policy, at least in part, in response to pressures from leading elements of his coalition. Near the end of his presidential campaign, Carter changed his views on a number of substantive policies, such as tax reform, the Humphrey-Hawkins bill, abortion, and busing. At the time of this writing, after six months in office, his response to changing circumstances has been significant. Some would even say that after firing off strong salvos of rhetoric, he has fallen back too often and too quickly: the Sorensen CIA nomination, removing several water projects from his initial "hit list," the international human rights controversy, the $50 tax rebate, and even some elements of his "moral equivalent of war" against the energy crisis. After some aloofness, he has begun to work with some groups such as civil rights organizations, who had strongly criticized his alleged neglect of blacks, and the maritime unions on the issue of US crews.

Yet Carter also shows signs of resisting error correction with regard to the *procedures* for making policy rather than with its substance. As Knott and Wildavsky persuasively argue, "If there is a danger for President Carter, it is not that he will support unpopular policies, but that he will persevere with inappropriate procedures. . . . He is not an ideologue of policy."[42] He seems more concerned with the procedures for policymaking than with policymaking itself. He advocates, and in fact followed as governor of Georgia, the procedures of the old "scientific management" approach: simplicity, uniformity, predictability, hierarchy, and comprehensiveness. Some of his pronouncements on policy may have been campaign rhetoric or legislative bargaining chips, but his beliefs about procedures seem sincere, even passionate, and as governor he practiced what he preached.

Congress is a good source of error correction. Thus another disturbing sign has been the Carter White House's unrealistic attitude toward Congress and the distribution of power between the two. In some ways it is as if nothing had been learned from the Johnson and Nixon experiences. For instance, a Carter aide told a reporter after the congressional investigation that led to the resignation of OMB director Bert Lance that the Carter entourage's greatest surprise in Washington was the recognition of Congress's political power and the real sense of challenge and opposition to the White House that is felt there when congressional opinion runs against the president.[43] In the Lance case the White House damaged itself by acting as if it were still dealing with the Georgia legislature.

My reading of the other postwar presidencies suggests that while Carter's personality and character have been pretty completely formed now that he is fifty-three, to a great extent his presidential behavior can be shaped by how citizens, organizations, and institutions interact with him. In the face of complex policy issues, they should not shirk this task. The themes of this essay were echoed by the National Urban League's Vernon Jordan when he spoke about the Carter administration's policies toward blacks: "I do not believe Jimmy Carter is an insensitive man. He cares, and he has our interests in his heart, but it is our job to get them out of his heart and head and into public policy."[44]

A Critical Look at This "Politics of Institutions"

I have suggested that rebuilding our political parties would contribute much to creating more plural and competitive national policymaking. Nostalgia is powerful but often misleading. Strengthened parties would greatly aid our politics in many ways, in addition to improved presidential error correction. But this does not seem to be a realistic expectation. As Edmund Burke observed, "Circumstances . . . give in reality to every political principle its distinguishing colour and discriminating effect. The circumstances are what render every civil and political scheme beneficial or noxious. . . ."[45] The circumstances for American parties have not been favorable for the past thirty years, and they do not seem likely to change. The social basis for strong parties is eroding. As income and educational levels increase, the proportion of people who identify with the major parties has been declining. On a policy and ideological level, the picture is even darker. Almost all considerations of parties in the postwar period and all the "reforms" either have been explicitly directed at weakening parties or have had that effect.

The circumstances do not seem much more favorable for other organizations and institutions that might contribute to error correction for national policymaking. In the past decade Washington has seen a great proliferation in the number and activity of so-called "public interest" lobbying organizations (Common Cause, Nader affiliates, Energy Action, among others), and they seem to have given a greater balance to the inputs of national policymaking. But even without considering these organizations' policy bias, it is too early to know what their long-run significance will be. Moreover, it seems likely that they will not be an adequate substitute for either strong parties or a strong Congress.

Perhaps we can look for a bit more aid from Congress than from the parties, but the situation is still quite uncertain because as Nelson Polsby once said, "Congress has a hard time standing on its 1,070 feet." For the most part this has been more of a problem during the past decade than earlier in this century. One source of strength, direction, and focus for Congress would be strong, aggressive leadership. Today many have high expectations in this regard for Speaker O'Neill and Majority Leader Byrd. My advocacy of strengthened congressional leadership rests on mechanisms to increase institutional centralization rather than on a search for strong men. Individual congressmen should sacrifice part of their own influence to committees, party caucuses, and a leadership group of three to six persons based on the office of Speaker or majority leader. But my feeling is that the weakness of recent congressional leadership has been more a function of the members' unwillingness to have strong leaders than the weakness of the particular leaders involved. Even if O'Neill and Byrd were temporarily able to assert strong leadership, I do not think congressmen will allow it in the long run. The strength of the reform, democratic, participatory ethos that has been carrying the day in our society for the past quarter century is increasing. This ethos has come into Congress in the past decade, and it strongly militates against the centralization of power there. With a few exceptions, recent congressional "reform" has largely meant weakening the leadership and other centralizing forces in this large, structurally fragmented body. (The somewhat increased strength of party and regional caucuses probably will add some centralization and discipline to Congress, but at the same time many committee chairmen have been weakened. More importantly, these caucuses' power relies on the sufferance of their members, whose willingness to sacrifice some of their individual influence has been limited.)

Congress's tendency to abdicate policy-making responsibility and therefore power may be even a greater factor militating against a pattern of national policymaking by competitive institutions. This tendency is a major source of the growth of presidential power in the field of foreign affairs.[46] But the congressional flight from responsibility also has been occurring in the less excusable area of domestic policy.[47] The most serious instance of this has been with respect to spending. Congress could have more power here, but until very recently it seems to have been content with taking credit for individual pieces of spending and letting presidents take the heat for cutting appropriations. In part this was a major issue in the Nixon impoundment controversy, though it was hidden behind liberal and conservative labels. The first few years of the new, strengthened congressional budget process do not seem to indicate a major reversal in Congress's behavior in this area. For one thing, the congressional budget committees and the budget process itself need a central direction which has thus far been lacking. Congress's failure to make real inputs into the policy implementation process is another instance in which it has missed an opportunity to seize some responsibility. After the Great Society there was much loose talk around Washington about the need for better implementation of legislation, but as far as I can tell Congress has done almost nothing in this area. Its interest in oversight still seems to be merely seeing that the money is spent honestly.[48] This is not likely to change, because of the absence of political incentives for Congress to become genuinely interested in implementation.

The absence—in the nation and among congressmen themselves—of a conception of Congress as a competent and legitimate voice for the national interest is perhaps the most formidable obstacle to the development of national policymaking by competitive institutions. Since the presidency and Congress are both fallible, a crucial question is which one is more likely to be able to admit its errors publicly. There seems to be reason to believe that Congress and some interest groups are more able to do this than the presidency, which means that when the occasion arises congressmen must stand up and say that an error has been made (or is about to be made), that the public interest is not being served, and that they have as much ability as the president to perceive the public interest accurately. For instance, congressmen advocating the deregulation of natural gas should be willing, if they so believe (as many do), to say that this policy is in the national interest and that continued regulation, as was advocated by President Carter, is not.

Congressmen will only be willing to do this, and can only do it effectively, if both the nation and congressmen themselves view the institution as being competent and legitimate. However, it now seems that neither of them do, because since Franklin D. Roosevelt almost every president has acted in such a way as to preempt Congress's opportunities to make such statements and act in this way. At the same time, Congressmen have reinforced this preemption by their abdication of policy-making responsibility and their particular disinclination to make statements about their conception of the public interest. During the Eisenhower and Nixon-Ford administrations there were frequent exceptions to this congressional abdication, and often this resulted in significant competitive policymaking and error correction.

Nevertheless, these exceptions seem to have done little to

change anyone's conception of Congress. Perhaps this is because throughout this period the presidency-is-the government view was eloquently advocated by many academic and popular writers, with almost no writers expressing a contrary view. The high point came in the early 1960s with the wide popularity of books like Neustadt's and Rossiter's. The effect of these writings, together with its own behavior, was that Congress may have undergone a "labeling" process, in which a given trait is attributed to a person so insistently or over such a long period of time that it becomes internalized and acquires the force of a self-fulfilling prophecy. In the case of Congress, it has been described and thought of as lacking in public-interest competency so much that congressmen seem to have come to believe it and act as if they cannot fulfill this role. (Such internalization is probably even more likely among the brightest congressmen, who are more likely to be exposed to such ideas.) It has been said that early in the Carter administration Congress began to reassert some of its power as it did during Nixon's time, but even if this continues, it involves power relationships. Yet nothing seems to be happening in word or deed that would alter the conception of Congress as an inadequate spokesman for the public interest.

There is one other critical point to consider about the call for a politics of institutions. There seem to be significant limits to the possibility of its developing, but if it did develop, what would be some of its consequences? One possibility is that it would be too much of a good thing. Plural, competitive policymaking produces error correction and tends to satisfy the goal of representativeness. Yet there is a dilemma here. What in one person's view may be responsiveness and error correction in presidential policy may to the next be unprincipled opportunism. Although the evidence is indirect and sketchy, it seems that a major element determining a leader's trustworthiness and legitimacy in the eyes of the people is his consistency. Thus the trade-off here seems to be between a presidential policymaking that tends to be responsive and subject to error correction and a loss in presidential popularity. My own preference is for the former, since modern presidents seem so likely to suffer declines in popularity anyway.[49] Yet this trade-off should be kept in mind when evaluating the suggestions made here.

Some Concluding Thoughts

In the past few decades popular and academic interest in personality have deflected a proper appreciation of the importance of institutions and organizations. During the eighteenth and nineteenth centuries the persons and institutions most important in shaping national policies were often other than the president. In the twentieth century, this has changed less than we might think if we exclude periods of war and the Great Depression. For instance, ten years from now will Presidents Nixon and Ford be seen as the dominant forces behind the foreign and domestic policies of their eight years in office? Perhaps not. Was President Eisenhower or the Supreme Court or Congress more influential in shaping the domestic policies of the 1950s? Nevertheless, we will and should continue to look to the executive branch for the execution of policy, especially foreign policy. Yet much has been written on the presidency, with comparatively little attention to the thousands of other top officials in the executive branch. The initiation and development of policies—and later their day-to-day implementation—also will be done by persons *and* by institutions other than the presidency.

Of course, persons do shape institutions; analyzing the interaction between the two is essential to understanding policymaking. However, since the 1930s, first because of domestic and then because of foreign crises, we have overemphasized the importance of presidential leadership. One of the aims of this essay is to help restore the proper balance to our political perspective.

A final consideration is that process isn't everything, not even when the process is competitive and involves multiple institutions sharing power. We ought to be even more concerned with the values and ends that these institutions will pursue. As we consider what we want from our institutions, including the presidency, we must first know who *we* are and what *we* want.

Notes

My thanks to Gene Bardach and Frank Levy for their perceptive comments on an earlier draft.

1. William Andrews, "The Presidency, Congress and Constitutional Theory,"

in Aaron Wildavsky, ed., *Perspectives on the Presidency* (Boston: Little, Brown, 1975), p. 26.

2. Murray Kempton, "Spectrum" broadcast, CBS News, September 28, 1977.

3. Thomas E. Cronin, "Everybody Believes in Democracy Until He Gets to the White House: An Examination of White House-Departmental Relations," *Law and Contemporary Problems* 35 (Summer 1970).

4. James David Barber, *Presidential Character: Predicting Performance in the White House* (Englewood Cliffs, N.J.: Prentice-Hall, 1972), pp. 8, 10.

5. Ibid., p. 11.

6. Alexander George, "Assessing Presidential Character," *World Politics* 36 (January 1974).

7. Proponents of this view have suggested that its approach be used to evaluate and screen presidential candidates. But for several reasons, especially given the type of analyses necessary to do this, it does not seem to be feasible to make it a significant element in the selection process.

8. Barber, *Presidential Character*, p. 270 (emphasis added).

9. George, "Assessing Presidential Character," p. 250. Barber acknowledges that FDR's court-packing effort indicated that active-positives "in their haste to make things happen, may too quickly and easily knock down the 'formalities' that hold the democratic order in place." Barber, *Presidential Character*, p. 173.

10. Barber, *Presidential Character*, p. 246.

11. Ibid., p. 145.

12. Elsewhere I have tried to make these qualitative distinctions in an analysis of the less-than-successful policymaking by two "active-positive" political executives—John Lindsay and McGeorge Bundy. For instance, I analyzed four major cases in which Bundy made decisions: the Vietnam War, New York City school decentralization, university endowment investment policies, and congressional tax-reform policy for foundations. In each, Bundy's decision flowed from an active-positive stance, but in each the resulting policies were highly unsuccessful in terms of both society's and Bundy's self-interest. His activism was characterized by what I call an "apolitical supra-rationalism." And it took place in a nonpluralistic power setting: Bundy was not constrained by other actors or institutions, because he sat at the top of an organizational hierarchy and held a disproportionate share of resources. Martin A. Levin, "McGeorge Bundy and Four Cases of Apolitical Supra-Rationalism: Vietnam, New York City School Decentralization, Investment Policy for University Endowments, Tax Reform for Foundations" (in progress).

13. Martin A. Levin, *The Political Dilemmas of Social Policymaking*, Chapter 5 (forthcoming).

14. Indeed, Congress for the most part was reluctant to act and had to be pressured initially by a few of its members, some of its leaders, and indirectly by the courts and the press. Even the latter two acted more in response to

pressure than as bold initiators. Judge Sirica seems to have been nettled by the initially uncooperative defendants, especially McCord; the *Washington Post* yielded to its prodding reporters who in turn were stimulated by allegedly aggressive informants.

15. George Reedy, *The Twilight of the Presidency* (New York: New American Library, 1971).

16. In a perceptive analysis of his gubernatorial actions and campaign statements, Knott and Wildavsky predicted that as president, Carter would act as the "ultimate definer of the public interest, leap[ing] over group interests through direct contact with the populace. [He] would rather interpret the inchoate desires of the mass of people than bargain over who gets what the government offers. Nor will he content himself with being the mediator of contending interests, merely keeping the score and announcing the winners. Group interests breed devisiveness, while the public interest breeds unity. Instead, 'he-the-people' will interpret their victory." Jack Knott and Aaron Wildavsky, "Jimmy Carter's Theory of Governing," *The Wilson Quarterly*, Winter 1977, chap. 4, this book. When congressional leaders and committee investigators criticized OMB director Bert Lance, whom some called the "deputy president" in Carter's administration, Lance made a lengthy defense and counterattack which, he said, was directed to "the American people as the jury" in this case.

17. Aaron Wildavsky, "The Past and Future Presidency," *The Public Interest*, 41, Fall 1975.

18. For instance, instead of belaboring the question of whether in his heart Nixon was friendly to Jewish interests and Israel, these organizations pursued their interests with both carrot and stick. The complicated question of whether they were successful with Nixon before Watergate and if so, why, is beyond the scope of this essay. The point here is that they did not passively despair about the "real Nixon" but chose instead the course of action and pressure.

19. John Snetsinger, *Truman, the Jewish Vote and the Creation of Israel* (Stanford, Calif.: Hoover Institution Press, 1974).

20. Merle Miller, *Plain Speaking*, (New York: Berkeley Medallion Books, 1973) p. 234.

21. Harry S. Truman, *Memoirs* (New York: Doubleday, 1958).

22. Snetsinger, *Truman*, p. 75.

23. Ibid., p. 80.

24. Ibid., p. 30.

25. Ibid., p. 99.

26. Ibid., p. 47.

27. Miller, *Plain Speaking*, p. 195.

28. William C. Berman, *The Politics of Civil Rights in the Truman Administration* (Columbus: Ohio State University Press, 1970), p. 9.

29. Ibid., p. 44.

30. Ibid., p. 55.

31. Ibid., p. 112.

32. Ibid., p. 116.

33. Clay Blair, Jr. and Joan Blair, *In Search of Kennedy,* (New York: Berkeley Publishers, 1976) p. 515.

34. Arthur Schlesinger, Jr., *A Thousand Days,* p. 928.

35. Fairlie, *The Kennedy Promise* (Garden City, N.Y.: Doubleday, 1973), p. 244.

36. Chalmers Roberts, "The Day We Didn't Go to War," in Theodore Lowi, *Legislative Politics, U.S.A.* (Boston: Little, Brown, 1962).

37. Andrews, "The Presidency, Congress, and Constitutional Theory," p. 27.

38. Clinton Rossiter, *The American Presidency* (New York: Harcourt Brace, 1960), pp. 168-169.

39. Herman Finer, *The Presidency: Crisis and Regeneration* (Chicago: University of Chicago Press, 1960), pp. 88-89.

40. Koenig, *The Chief Executive* (New York: Harcourt Brace, 1964), p. 210.

41. Nixon the conservative was responsible for the first White House sponsoring of a form of negative income tax, his Family Assistance Plan (FAP). This grew out of an openness to pressures, all of which came from within the White House. But there was a significant range of debate, from the liberal Democrat Daniel Patrick Moynihan to the conservative Republican Arthur Burns, reflecting pressures and potential new supporters outside the White House. Similarly, Nixon the old cold warrior, in responding to staff initiatives, was responsible for creating a significant new era in our policy toward China, as well as an active détente with the Soviet Union. Even on Vietnam, Nixon was responsive, though slowly, to pressures from quite outside the White House. He did in fact slowly end the war. The pressures both from Congress and citizens following the US 1970 invasion of Cambodia were responded to rather directly. The invasion ended within the prescribed time, and the troop withdrawal began relatively soon after that.

42. See chap. 4, this book.

43. "A Politically Costly Affair for the President," *New York Times,* September 22, 1977.

44. *New York Times,* July 22, 1977. (Interview with Vernon Jordan.)

45. Quoted in Irving Kristol, "Decentralization for What?" *The Public Interest* 11, Spring 1968, p. 17.

46. Arthur Schlesinger, Jr., "Congress and the Making of American Foreign Policy," *Foreign Affairs* 51, October 1972.

47. John Johannes, "Where Does The Buck Stop?—Congress, President, and

the Responsibility for Legislative Initiation," *Western Political Quarterly* 25 (September 1972): 396-414.

48. There has been more congressional interest in the evaluation of programs, but it has been focused on the ultimate outcome of a program after it has been implemented rather than on the prior issues of whether the program is being implemented according to the legislative objective, at what cost, and with what delay. For more on this distinction, see Levin, *Political Dilemmas of Social Policymaking.*

49. John Mueller, "Presidential Popularity from Truman to Johnson," *American Political Science Review* 64 (1970): 18-34.

Chapter 7

The Roots of American Leadership: Political Style and Policy Consequences

Douglas Yates

Few subjects are more intriguing to the political scientist as citizen and scholar, and at the same time more difficult to fathom, than the character of American political leadership. This may not be the subject that most political scientists address in their research, but it is still a unifying thread in a diverse discipline. There must be few in the profession who do not feel drawn to speculate on the presidential sweepstakes or on races for the state house and city hall. After all, there can be no avoiding the obvious and enduring challenge: if you are an astute student of politics, surely you can say something useful about this or that candidate for president, governor, or mayor. And surely you can predict how a candidate will appeal to a constituency and fare against an opponent better than a journalist or the man in the street. I believe that it is precisely because the analysis and handicapping of political leaders cuts so close to the bone of professional esteem or understanding that so few scholars venture into this realm, where academic wisdom can be so easily refuted by election results and actual policy outcomes.

Having lost many bets on election results and misjudged the character of many political leaders, I do not intend in this paper to fall into a trap of my own making. Nor do I propose that political scientists invest significant scholarly effort trying to outdo journalists as inside dopesters, offering short-order glimpses of how a Jimmy Carter is running in New Hampshire or whether Bella Abzug is capable of winning in New York. What I do believe is that political scientists must spend more time analyzing and arguing about the fundamental character of political leadership, broadly understood. And as will be clear in what follows, I have a notion of character that is quite different from recent approaches to the subject. Simply put, I believe political scientists must learn a lot more about the basic roots, traits, and evolution of American political leadership before they can say much that is useful about any particular candidate.

The simplest and yet most intractable question is, What kind of people offer themselves as leaders in American politics? Where do they come from and what are their roots, economic, social, educational, geographical, political? Do these roots manifest themselves in any persistent and significant configurations? Do the roots of leadership change over time in American politics, and if so, how? Further, what political styles spring from (or correlate with) different kinds of social, economic, and geographical backgrounds? What are the main traits associated with different styles? Finally, what are the implications of different political styles for the behavior of leaders, once in executive office, as administrators and public-policy makers? These questions constitute a large map for analysis, but I suspect that unless we try to combine and relate the consideration of roots (background) and political style with executive policy-making conduct, our portrait of political leaders will inevitably be truncated. We will have described only one part of the elephant.

There are several analytical traps in the study of political leadership. First is the trap of what might be called "demographic" determinism. If we find that a large number of congressmen are lawyers or that foreign policy officials graduated from Ivy League universities, we may think we have discovered something. But unless that demographic evidence is linked to a substantive political style and an assessment of what difference that style makes for executive leadership, our "discovery" is apt to be quite empty. Consider the complaints, recently heard, that there are too many lawyers in government. What does this mean? That it is bad for the democratic spirit to study torts? That lawyers negotiate and compromise too much? That they are too client-oriented where clients are constituents or interest groups? It appears we have no theory here, only an intriguing fact. And without a theory of the meaning of roots or background for political style and executive leadership, demography will not take us far.

A second analytical trap is that of psychological determinism. In some recent studies of political leadership, the emphasis on a leader's psychological and family history is so strongly emphasized that broader political forces and policy problems are made to seem trivial by comparison.[1] Analytically, the focus is narrowed at both ends: background is reduced to psyche and family experience, and the policy-making environment is seen as a dim backdrop against which the self-destructive leader or happy warrior plays out the internal and inevitable logic of his personal style. In my view, the greatest difficulty with this approach is that since the main evidence of a leader's distinctive personal style is read into executive behavior after the fact, we have a hard time knowing what independent effect (if any) particular policy problems and events have on any leader's psyche. What would Lyndon Johnson's presidential psyche have looked like if Vietnam had been a problem that afflicted Dwight Eisenhower (and what would have happened to our beaming Ike)? How would Woodrow Wilson have reacted to World War II and Franklin Roosevelt to the aftermath of World War I? These are obviously mean questions, but the psychological view, if taken too seriously, may lead close to a political version of the pathetic fallacy, in which nature is seen to mirror and express human feelings.

A third analytical trap in the study of leadership lies at the opposite pole from psychological determinism—"institutional determinism." In some political science writings, the leader is depicted as the "ghost in the machine," the virtual prisoner of laws, bureaucratic institutions, policy processes, and public events. Indeed, political scientists have historically found so much richness in their study of institutions and policy-making processes that it is no wonder that the character and importance of individual leaders are sometimes dwarfed by the larger political environment.

I have chosen to view the three approaches sketched above as containing analytical traps. Indeed I believe they do, but one should not forget that each of them illustrates an important aspect of political leadership. My suggestion is that while by themselves they are incomplete, one can gain their analytical benefits without incurring the costs by adopting the strategy of integrating the related themes of roots, political style, and policy-making performance.

To make this argument stick, I must start at the beginning with the backgrounds of American political leaders. My argument simply is that roots (or backgrounds) are important because they have a strong influence on political style and performance in executive office. My key assumption is that the characters of political leaders have roots beyond psyche and family experience—roots that are found in neighborhood or region, social-class origins, educational background, and in one political movement or another, each of which provides particular kinds of motivations, issues, and supporters.

Considering our major political leaders and not just presidents, there is clearly an aristocratic strain in American political leadership which is found in men like Roosevelt, Kennedy, and Nelson Rockefeller. Then there are those products of modest, small-town backgrounds, usually heartland America: Hoover, Nixon, and Eisenhower. And there is the strain of relatively uneducated leaders who started out in poor communities in the South, the border states, and urban ethnic neighborhoods: Al Smith, Lyndon Johnson, Harry Truman, and George Wallace. There is, of course, no accident in the fact that these social backgrounds correspond to persisting political tendencies in our party system: the rural Democratic South, the ethnic Democratic North, the small-town Republican base of what we sometimes call Middle America. Since these distinctions do not depend simply on class, region, or ethnic group, I use the admittedly loose concept of political roots to signify different clusters of political, geographical, educational, and social traits.

To take a fourth case, a number of our recent political leaders seem to me to display a highly moralistic and crusading political style and to have distinctive political and social roots as well. This is a style that compelled attention in the election campaigns of Senators Eugene McCarthy and George McGovern. It is a style that is well known to any New York resident who was governed by the administration of John Lindsay. I think it is also a style that would have been familiar to observers of Woodrow Wilson and to admirers (and critics) of two-time presidential candidate Adlai Stevenson. It is a style characterized by idealism, strong moral purpose, and high expectations for American society. I call political leaders with this distinctive style moralists and suggest that they present another important type of American political leadership.

So far I have suggested that political leadership in America springs from clearly identifiable roots and that these roots shape political style and have important implications for executive conduct in office. To reiterate, I will attempt to identify four different leadership types. One type is the "aristocrat" (Roosevelt, Kennedy, and Rockefeller); a second is the political leader from small-town America (Hoover, Eisenhower, Nixon, Ford) whom I will term the "manager"; a third is the "populist" leader like Harry Truman, Lyndon Johnson, or George Wallace; and a fourth is the "moralist" like Woodrow Wilson, Adlai Stevenson, George McGovern, or John Lindsay.

We need now to sketch out these types in somewhat greater detail in order to show how backgrounds (roots), political style, and executive performance interact in American politics and policymaking. But I should say at the outset that my aim is not to create rigid analytical categories in which political leaders can be mechanically placed. Clearly my plan of attack requires some crude distinctions—the identification of some broad leadership types and their dominant traits—but it seems obvious to me that few actual political leaders precisely replicate the ideal type. I am particularly interested in those political leaders who seem to blend one or more of the roots and traits associated with the different ideal types of American political leadership. Having stated these caveats, I do not want to retreat too far. My argument is that there are fundamental class, geographical, and educational differences among American leaders and that these differences powerfully shape political style and policy-making performance.

The Aristocrats

Of the four leadership types introduced in this paper, the aristocrats may be the most recognizable; they are surely the most socially distinct. Nelson Rockefeller eating blintzes on the Lower East Side of New York and Franklin Roosevelt with his jaunty cigarette holder come to mind as familiar and vivid images of this leadership type. In addition to Roosevelt and Nelson Rockefeller, we can think of Averell Harriman, Herbert Lehman, and to some extent John F. Kennedy as further examples of the type. I qualify Kennedy's assignment to this category because this type is essentially rooted in the Anglo-Saxon Protestant upper class located in the cities and suburbs of the northeast, while Kennedy was at least by origin an Irish Catholic from Boston. The fact that Kennedy came to display many traits of the aristocrat in politics reflects the larger social fact that barriers to entry into the American upper class have not been entirely rigid, and the Kennedys of Choate, Harvard, Hyannis, and Palm Beach certainly resemble their Wasp rivals (at least in their social experience) far more than their ward-leader cronies from Irish neighborhoods.

The roots of the aristocrats are simply stated: wealth, social status, expensive prep schools and universities, summer estates, Groton, Harvard, Yale, Hyde Park, Pocantico Hills. The aristocrat springs from a very special social world, one that very few Americans know anything about and one that contains very few voters. The mystery of aristocratic leaders is that they have been able to reach out from their exclusive social background to appeal to a mass electorate. But there are explanations for this perhaps surprising success. Aristocrats like Roosevelt, Rockefeller, and Harriman were able to gain early political experience in high appointive governmental positions as a result of family connections. In the same vein, few Americans enjoyed the early opportunity afforded John Kennedy to learn about government in the family living room at the Court of St. James. A second and obvious explanation for the aristocrats' success is that money helps to win elections—and certainly to get started and taken seriously in political clubhouses. If John Kennedy's career does not demonstrate this point conclusively, Nelson Rockefeller's surely does.

The aristocratic strain in American leadership is particularly distinctive for the political style it generates and for the performance of America's aristocrats in higher executive office. The style of aristocrats resembles, more than anything in our national experience, Disraelian conservatism in England, or Tory democracy, in which a political leader puts himself forward (to a mass electorate) as the best man, the best able to govern, and the most worthy of support by reason of personal skill and wisdom. Notice that this is not an appeal based on ideology or party but rather on the personal characteristics of leadership. As Samuel Beer has described the main tenets of Tory democracy,

> This body of thought stresses the importance of strong government and includes a view of the nature of the governing process and of the personal qualities that governors must have if government is to be strong and effective. It does not disdain the need for foresight in those who govern or for a tradition to guide them. But it is deeply suspicious of attempts to subject the process of governing to an explicit and comprehensive social philosophy from which imperative programs are derived. It would rather trust men of the governing class to do "what is necessary" in any particular set of circumstances. As the nature of governing requires wide discretion for the governors, the capacities of the governing class justify their independent authority.[2]

It is, of course, not surprising that Tories should resort to that claim in England, where class-based political demographics go so strongly against them. What is interesting is that a version of it has worked so often in the United States. My suggestion is that with suitable local variations the American aristocratic style draws on the same political wellspring as Tory Democracy: it ultimately involves a politics of social deference and confidence in leaders of wealth and social status. Thus, as readers of the *New York Daily News* used to say in man-in-the-street interviews, you can trust a Rockefeller because you know he does not need to steal from the public till. By extension, you can place confidence in a Franklin Roosevelt because he has the background and breeding to take care of the public—almost like a latter-day Dutch patroon working on a larger stage. You can feel confident about a John Kennedy because of his wit, civility, and sense of personal self-confidence.

So far I have placed perhaps too much emphasis on the voter's imagined perceptions. What I am more interested in is the political style that our aristocratic leaders have consciously used to appeal to a broader political electorate, and there the point seems to me to become plain. Roosevelt's ideology, no less than Kennedy or Rockefeller's, was a murky thing. He certainly didn't run on it;

rather, he emphasized his personal ability to run the country on behalf of his compatriots: first Dr. New Deal, then Dr. Win-the-War. One further implication of this political style is that ideology is a very flexible thing. It is an accoutrement of leadership, not the thing itself. Thus a Roosevelt can move between many points on the compass of government intervention; a Rockefeller will shift with great speed from a liberal to a conservative incarnation, and a John Kennedy will present a vague and even bewildering stance on civil rights. What the aristocrat offers is himself, the best bred and most qualified to govern. The particulars of this style are by now quite familiar. To take Roosevelt, Rockefeller, and Kennedy again, what stands out in their style is the appearance of elegance, civility, and reassurance. If you think about it, who was Franklin Roosevelt or anyone else to say that all America had to fear was "fear itself?" One might reasonably have feared the depression and unemployment, but how reassuring a theme it was in a time of trouble. To take John Kennedy as a second example, what was the point of the "myth" of Camelot, the emphasis on high culture in the White House? It is hard not to conclude that the reaching for a style of wit, culture, and "grace under pressure" was a democratic version of an ancient political strategy: make the ruler, in his person, an object of faith, loyalty, admiration, and awe. The aristocrat, on this reading, practices a political style that is curiously distant from the ordinary political culture. Indeed this political and social distance turns out to be the aristocrat's strength, for it permits the style of elegance, reassurance, and paternalism to prosper.

What is also significant is that the aristocrat's political style fits well with the image of the presidency or governorship as it has evolved in recent decades. It seems to me that we have come to expect from our chief executives a level of ceremonial and symbolic activity that the aristocrat is well equipped to provide. That is, if to an increasing extent political leadership requires an appearance of mastery and self-confidence in meetings with foreign heads of state, legislative delegations, angry interest groups, and television press conferences, then the aristocrat's knack for appearing commanding and stylish, for appearing in charge, is particularly useful for this facet of modern executive leadership in America.

Still, I think it sells the aristocratic leaders short to say only that they perform with high style, like a Kennedy, or are masters at appearing assured and in command before the press, like a Nelson Rockefeller. What is more important is that the aristocrat's basic sense of self as the person best able to govern and solve problems appears to have persistent implications for their executive leadership. The main point is that since they do not define themselves by party, issues, or ideology, the aristocrat brings a highly flexible, adaptive attitude toward public-policymaking. Such flexibility in policy may have seemed a very desirable commodity when employed to adjust the turbulent events of the depression and World War II. But it can also lead to a suspicion that a political leader lacks any strong commitment to principle or an enduring sense of public purpose—criticisms made of Kennedy and Rockefeller and, for that matter, of Roosevelt himself.

As a final point, the aristocrats I have identified display in their executive conduct a fondness for and ease with power and politics that further reinforces the central notion of the gentleman "to the manner born." Roosevelt, Kennedy, and Rockefeller all strike one as leaders who relished the use of power and enjoyed the bargaining and horse trading of politics. My suspicion is that, given the aristocrat's style of being above the game of politics, it is that much easier to play the game without anxiety and remorse. It becomes a kind of sport that one plays hard and attentively—an exercise in the "common touch" and a price of entry to governance and "public affairs."

Some of our ablest political leaders have possessed the central elements of the aristocratic style. At their best, they have displayed the political skill, shrewdness, and flexibility that Burns attributes to Roosevelt in *The Lion and the Fox.*[3] But in other moods, the aristocrat can seem dangerously imperious and self-aggrandizing, as when Nelson Rockefeller set out to build his Athens on the Hudson in the Albany Mall government center.

The Moralists

The moralists have social and economic roots that most closely resemble the aristocrats', but their style and executive conduct are very different. Just naming the moralists establishes the obvious difference: Wilson, Stevenson, McCarthy, McGovern, John Lindsay, and Paul Douglas (in the Senate). The moralist leaders have several social roots in common, but not all have the same backgrounds—there is more than one strand. Many of the moralist leaders come from upper-middle-class families with considerable means but not the great wealth of a Rockefeller or a Kennedy. Many of the moralists share a background in the professions and have impressive educational credentials. And to a surprising extent moralists also have strong religious backgrounds. Many are the sons or grandsons of Protestant ministers.

Although there are clear differences among the moralists (Lindsay and Stevenson, for example have a more patrician background than McGovern or McCarthy), none would be easily confused with an aristocrat like Rockefeller, a middle-class, main-street American like Eisenhower, Nixon, or Ford, or a "populist" like Al Smith, Huey Long, or George Wallace. Indeed, if you ask yourself which political leaders can easily be imagined as professors or ministers and which cannot easily be imagined as businessman, socialites, labor leaders, or farmers, the answer should point (by subtraction) to candidates for the moralist style. The reason for this is clear: the moralist places primary emphasis in his world view and political style on ideas and principles and is apt to identify the central problems of American society in moral terms. This emphasis on moral issues—uplifting the spirit of America, ending racism in cities, or fighting against an evil war in Vietnam—lead the moralist leader into the role of reformer and often into a stance as crusader for some cherished cause.

In terms of political roots, the origin of the moralists in the highly educated, religious, and professional segments of American society is by now no surprise. In the late nineteenth century, good-government reformers fighting against the corruption of the urban machines frequently possessed those same social characteristics. As James Wilson has shown,[4] the latter-day reformers who joined reform democratic clubs in large cities also tended to be highly educated, upper-middle-class professionals prepared to fight for principles and substantive issues and against patronage and political accommodation.

That leaders from our professional upper-middle-class should adopt a moralistic world view and be the main champions of "ideas" in politics is also perhaps no surprise. Unlike the aristocrat who is to the manner born and defines his role in terms of personal skills and capacity to govern, the moralist has gone through an educational process, whether in his academic, professional, or religious background, that promotes a taste for abstract thinking and a concern for ideals, rules, and principles. Put simply, the moralist believes that ideas and moral convictions are or should be at the center of politics. The moralist leaders I have listed have by no means all been intellectuals–some far from it. But their political styles display in common an "uplifting," schoolmasterly, even preachy style: Wilson on the League of Nations, Stevenson on the quality of life in America, Lindsay on racism and poverty in the cities, and McGovern and McCarthy on the evil of Vietnam.

I suspect that many moralists are attracted to government because they implicitly believe in the spirit of their Puritan ancestors, in the doctrine of the "good ruler"[5] which relies on men of virtue to steer a straight and honest course in public affairs. The main problem of politics and public policy, on this reading, is to get "good" people into government and, at the same time, "to kick the bums out." Just think of the number of times a reformer has run against a big-city political boss using almost precisely this political liturgy. Or think of the number of antiwar and anti-Watergate candidates spawned in recent years who practice the same politics of purification.

If my characterization makes the moralist seem too much the boy scout, too facile in his moral convictions, this is not entirely my own fault. It is how moralists like Wilson, Stevenson, McCarthy, McGovern, and Lindsay have chosen to present themselves, and I believe that their successes and failures in executive office are closely tied to their moral definition of the proper role of American political leadership. The moralists seem to live and die by the same sword of principle. Woodrow Wilson is probably the classic case: a man whose ideal image of himself as a peacemaker made him first the "savior of Europe" and then the frustrated architect of the League of Nations. There are other cases too. McCarthy and McGovern, whose moral convictions on Vietnam brought them close to power but then left them as bitter prophets, sound increasingly like common scolds. Or John Lindsay, whose commitment to improving the lot of the urban poor led him directly into a confrontation with the home owners and policemen who determine elections and who had been cast as the bad guys in Lindsay's urban morality play.

Still one must not forget that in good times the moralist leaders have shown real strengths in both political style and executive conduct. Wilson, Stevenson, McCarthy, and Lindsay were able, as candidates, to use the bully pulpit of American politics to dramatize issues, mobilize new constituencies, and in general to present a strong and clear message of program and policy. To merely say they were issue oriented is to rob them of the vitality and urgency they brought to their issues. When in executive office, the moralists have fought hard for their policies, have often taken unpopular positions, and have won respect for their integrity and determination.

At the same time, the moralists' political style and executive performance have certain common characteristics that explain in part why they seem to encounter as much political trouble as success. The first difficulty with the politics of morality is the reverse side of its strength. That is, to the extent that a leader seriously espouses a particular issue or course, to that extent he is trapped by the issue if it fades from view; in any case, he is stuck with the issue's opponents. McGovern's commitment to the antiwar issue and Lindsay's espousal of the problems of the urban poor had these characteristics. However, the moralist's political weaknesses go well beyond this perhaps inevitable consequence of advocating strong policies and principles. In the course of fighting for their ideas and policies, the moralists have appeared cold, aloof, and remote. The stern preacher and reformer often displays a stiff, humorless quality that squares uneasily (if at all) with the backslapping, horse-trading, hail-fellow style normally associated with the American politician. As a consequence, the moralists have been criticized for being self-righteous and arrogant in their political leadership, and in some cases for talking over the heads of the American people. In public office, the moralists have drawn criticism for being difficult to deal with, stubborn, and uncompromising.

The moralists' style has two facets that tend to support these impressions. First, Wilson, Lindsay, McGovern, and McCarthy all shared a vision that divided the world into good and bad guys and infused their ordinary political dealings. Opponents of the League, white ethnics, regular "pols," and Vietnam hawks were all branded by one moralist or another as enemies of truth, justice, and the American way, and there was little political communication and accommodation across these moral chasms. Given this vision of the world, the moralists have experienced acute difficulty reconciling the demands of principle and power politics. They seem to be offended by back-room politics, patronage, and vote swapping. In the main, they repudiate this style of politics but invariably find they must use these political instruments in order to govern. Whether it is Wilson dealing with the Republicans over the peace conference, Lindsay dealing with the municipal union leaders, or the antiwar moralists dealing with the "regulars," the result is the same: a stance of being above politics and viewing politics as a dirty business that antagonizes many players who believe they too have a rightful place in the game of politics.

The Managers

A third type of American political leader comes from small-town America, particularly the Midwest, is apt to be a member of the Republican party, and displays a political and executive style characterized by pragmatism and problem solving and a desire to increase administrative efficiency (and usually decrease waste) in government. I call this type the manager and identify it with Herbert Hoover, Dwight Eisenhower, Richard Nixon, Gerald Ford, Robert McNamara, Charles Percy, and Donald Rumsfeld. As with the aristocrats, the social and geographical roots of the managers are distinctive. These are the leaders bred in the heartland, reflecting a small-town faith in individualism and private enterprise and the equally traditional fear of government intervention, bureaucrats, and ambitious social welfare programs. They were not born to families of great means. They did not typically receive their education at Harvard or Yale; they certainly do not consider themselves to be intellectuals or theorists of government; and they have usually shown a suspicion of the East Coast "establishment," whether defined in terms of Wall Street, the Council on Foreign Relations, big-city bosses, labor leaders, or Harvard professors.

One might locate their origins in the rising middle class of America, but to be more precise it must be added that the managers grew up in families who were neither especially poor nor especially privileged, and who worked hard, in the spirit of the Protestant ethic, to better themselves. Significantly, as *Fortune* magazine repeatedly reports, these social, economic, and geographical roots are shared by a very large proportion of major corporate executives. Thus, if there is a party of "business" in the United States, it would appear to be more than a convenient political alliance of particular politicians and businessmen. The roots go far deeper, into a cultural background that shapes world view, political style, and executive performance.

In calling this type managers, I clearly intend to link this leadership style with the "managerial" style of the American business executive. They share with the business manager certain basic premises about the way the world works: (1) successful policy depends on rationally structured and efficient organization; (2) government operations tend to be diffuse and sluggish, lacking the financial and psychological discipline of a clear-cut "bottom line"; (3) thus the key to better management is tightening up internal planning, budgeting, and accounting; (4) the executive lives in a fast-changing environment and must be able to respond quickly and flexibly to new problems and conditions (translated into political life, this often means that ideological stances are a hindrance to dextrous problem solving); and (5) the test of any good executive is the ability to set objectives and get things done.

Managers like Hoover, Eisenhower, Nixon, and McNamara all presented themselves as leaders who could improve the functioning of government and in so doing whip the bureaucracy into shape. In executive office, they relied heavily on strategies of administrative reorganization and on improved management techniques. Hence Hoover, the apostle of administrative management; Eisenhower, who formed formal chains of command and formal administrative machinery for decision making like the National Security Council; Nixon, the proponent of cabinet reorganization and management by objectives and the author of the New Federalism (an administrative solution to the problems of domestic policymaking); and, of course, McNamara, the champion of systems analysis and program budgeting.

The manager's political style clearly does not rely on the moralist's passion for issues and crusades, nor does it rest on the aristocrat's aura of personal authority and grace (with the special exception of Eisenhower, who as a war hero was able to translate an executive achievement in the largest military organization of modern times into a personal legend). One of the manager's most salient traits, both as politician and administrator, is his highly pragmatic and unideological attitude toward issues and problems. As political campaigners, the managers have tended to mount vague appeals that they will clean up corruption and waste in government and will get the bureaucracy and public spending under control. One of Nixon's main appeals was that he would bring calm and steady leadership after the years of war and protest and that he would clean up the mess in government caused by Lyndon Johnson's Great Society programs. Both Eisenhower and Nixon also ran on the claim that they would end the mismanagement of foreign policy manifest in Korea and Vietnam. Gerald Ford ran on the classic managerial theme that he had "managed" the economy effectively, had brought a steady hand to the tiller, and had done a "good job." There is little missionary zeal here and, in the cases of Hoover, Nixon, and Ford, little effort to run on personal glamor or that other mysterious commodity, charisma. Once in executive office, the managers have also shown a pragmatic and instrumental attitude in their handling of public issues. Eisenhower, for example, showed no consistent view of the use of American military force. He appeared to take his problems as they came, deciding them on a case-by-case basis and with a strong sense of political and military feasibility rather than relying on some broad conception of "hawkish" or "dovish" behavior. Thus Eisenhower sidestepped a land war in Indochina, begged off Suez, but then sent the marines into Lebanon.

If Eisenhower adopted the stance of selective and strategic problem solver, Richard Nixon displayed this managerial style to an even greater extent. My suggestion is that the great mistake made by many in appraising Nixon was to believe that he was a hard-line anticommunist and would be guided in office by his ideological commitments. Instead, Nixon, with the substantial reinforcement of Henry Kissinger, moved to seize his policy opportunities where he found them, in Russia, China, and the Middle East. He took deliberate advantage of his prior reputation as an anticommunist to reassure the public that his openings to that communist powers did not reflect some liberal softness. The point is that Nixon defined his policy by the problems he faced, not the reverse, and one of his real strengths as an executive was this flexible and well-timed approach to foreign policy problems that many other American policymakers had defined only in terms of holy war. Though he did not follow through on his welfare proposals, Nixon adopted a strategy of flexible and unexpected response because he believed he could clean up a policy morass and in so doing enhance his reputation as a problem solver.

Gerald Ford's accidental presidency also displayed the manager's style of pragmatic problem solving. Indeed, to the extent that Ford's overall policies seemed amorphous, it is in large part because he adapted his policies so rapidly to changing conditions: first WIN, then tougher measures; first one response to the energy problem, then another.

Administrative Solutions

The most persistent feature of the manager's style as executive lies in the search for better governmental organization and new techniques for administrative efficiency. Hence the notion of "administrative solutions" to policy problems. In this respect, it is worth noting that Eisenhower created a formal, bureaucratic structure in the White House to bring orderly decision processes to an institution that he believed had been run sloppily and inefficiently by Harry Truman and his political cronies. In precisely the same spirit, Nixon sought to centralize and rationalize the White House apparatus around his chief of staff. Ironically, a major motive for the creation of Nixon's palace guard (which was to do him so much damage) was his desire for a smooth paper flow and tightly managed staff work.

As a final point, with the exception of Ford (a long-term congressional "pro"), the managers have demonstrated little taste for and mastery of the give-and-take of politics, as if accommodation and compromise interfere with good administration, and as if the proper role of the executive is to get on with the important job of statecraft with as little interference as possible from the heavy-breathing political types in Congress, the interest groups, and the states and cities. Eisenhower stood "above politics" in this way; Nixon systematically avoided politicians in order to spend more time in private working on decisions; McNamara, to take an appointive case, was as clumsy in dealing with Congress as he was skilled in bringing rational analysis to Defense Department decisions.

In short, the managers may often govern effectively, but rarely have they triumphed as architects of new political constituencies or as the catalysts of new political issues and public moods.

The Populists

The fourth type of American leaders comes from the rural South and from urban ethnic neighborhoods. Leaders of this type tend to define themselves as outsiders fighting against Yankees (both in the South and in ethnic neighborhoods) and also against entrenched business and bureaucratic interests. They tend to be Democrats and to fight for the common man against the powerful and the privileged. They are feisty, often dramatic politicians who learn to love the rough-and-tumble of politics at the courthouse or in the city machine. Indeed, many came to be highly skillful players of the political game and eventually became powerful insiders, shrewd and durable travelers along the corridors of power in Washington and elsewhere. I call this type the populist and associate it with the leadership styles of Al Smith, Lyndon Johnson, Huey Long, George Wallace, Lester Maddox, Harry Truman (with some qualifications), James Curley of Boston, Fiorello LaGuardia, Mayor Richard Daley, and Sam Rayburn. Without the populists, American political leadership would have had less passion, less political horse trading and arm-twisting, and less color and earthiness. But it would probably also have had less belligerence, less personal idiosyncrasy, and less bearbaiting.

In terms of their social, geographical, and economic backgrounds, the populists represent a clear historical pattern. They have come from poor urban neighborhoods (South Boston and Little Italy) and small towns (Barbour County, Alabama, and Johnson City, Texas). They have as often as not had vivid and distinctive accents, whether southern drawl or Irish brogue. Their formal education was limited. If they went to college at all, it was to Southwest Texas State Teachers College or the University of Alabama, not to Harvard and Yale (like the moralists and aristocrats), or Stanford, Michigan, and West Point (as did three of the managers: Hoover, Ford, and Eisenhower). They looked to politics as a way up and out of rural and urban communities that offered ambitious young men little else in the way of opportunities for power and achievement. In making politics their career from an early age, the populists typically apprenticed themselves to the local political organization (either the courthouse or the machine) and thus learned the political trade through sustained personal involvement at the grass roots or on the sidewalks of Boston or New York. Hence, Truman and the Pendergast machine, Curley and the Irish clubhouses in Boston, Wallace and his long treks for votes across the back roads of Alabama, and Daley and the Chicago sports clubs that brought young men into politics.

More important, the populists represent a long-standing historical and ideological tradition in American politics—a tradition extending back to Tom Watson on the one hand and Tammany Hall on the other. Not quite the leaders of agrarian or immigrant revolt, the latter-day populists nevertheless speak for what they perceive to be the disenfranchised constituencies in the countryside and the melting pot. As long as the South was viewed as the stepchild of the Republic, and as long as their leaders came from relatively poor, rural backgrounds, the idea of the southern populist remained intact. His historical purpose was to improve the lot of the farmers and other country people and, in unusual cases, of blacks who shared the same economic conditions. The urban ethnic populist had a similar motivation. Whether Irish, Italian, or black, the populists have sought to fight for their group against what they perceived to be the reigning and unresponsive elites in their communities. Their point was that the urban ethnic communities had not received their fair share of services, government jobs, and political power. The depression and certainly the immigrant era in urban politics were the crucible of this leadership style, but the political legacy and memory of these "bad old days" has proved remarkably durable.

The populist leaders have also displayed many shared characteristics in their political style. Many (though not all) have been colorful, dramatizing personalities. Huey Long, the Kingfish, is an extreme example of this style of swagger and bluff. Then there is LaGuardia, who as mayor of New York rode on fire engines and read comics on the radio to the city's children. Or Lester Maddox and his bicycle. Or George Wallace and his loud, forceful talk about "pointy-headed bureaucrats" and *their* bicycles (which they allegedly couldn't park straight).

Along with this dramatizing quality, the populist leader has typically made effective use of a folksy, rhetorical style designed to emphasize his stance as a man of the people, as "plain folk," and thus to increase his appeal to the common man or, in Wallace's term, the "little people." Harry Truman, for example, was at his most forceful and persuasive as a tub-thumping political campaigner in 1948 when he adopted the stance of the little guy advocating bread and butter "lunch pail" issues and fighting against Dewey and the party of Wall Street and big business generally.

As another feature of their political style, the populists have displayed a well-developed sensitivity and skill in the use of political power. For the populists, power is not an abstract thing linked to formal authority, fine principles, or management concepts but rather a product of a rough-and-tumble, sweaty process of persuasion and bargaining. This visceral sense of power is best exemplified by Johnson and Rayburn, the masters of arm-twisting, horse trading, and various other tactics of one-on-one persuasion. It is said that few could withstand the Johnson "treatment" once they were alone in a room with him. Again, this is the close-up personal politics of the courthouse and the machine.

Once in executive office, the populists have run true to their basic political form. As presidents, governors, or mayors, they have often been described as scrappy, combative, shrewd, and stubborn. Most have retained their love for the backroom maneuver. (Remember Lyndon Johnson's attempt to create interesting political theater out of his taken-for-granted renomination in 1964 by bobbing and weaving endlessly in his selection of a vice-president.) In the main, the populist leaders have also tried to use their skills at bargaining to patch together new coalitions and compromises on policy. (That was Johnson's glory as Senate majority leader; as president he apparently hoped to bargain the entire polity into one happy American consensus.)

At the same time that they have bargained skillfully with personal acquaintances and colleagues, the populists have also often appeared belligerent and uncompromising in dealing with political enemies they did not know personally or could not bargain with on a one-to-one basis. This belligerence is apparent in Truman's and Johnson's treatment of their respective communist enemies; in Truman's dealings with his Republican enemies in Congress; and in Johnson's handling of students and other antiwar activists.

At their best, the populist leaders have been shrewd and determined executives. Truman is praised for standing the heat in his own kitchen and showing courage in difficult personal and historical circumstances. Truman, Johnson, LaGuardia, and Long have also displayed a sustained concern and compassion for the poor and those lacking in education or needing health care and other social services. At their worst, in the cases of Long, Curley, and Wallace, the populists have been demogogic, manipulative, and tainted by corruption. Johnson and Truman also were criticized for political cronyism and for tolerating corruption, and Johnson and LaGuardia, no matter how colorful they could be as showmen on a good day, were on bad days abusive, volatile, and mean-spirited.

Hybrid Styles

So far, I have argued that there are four types of American political leaders with distinctive roots, political styles, and conduct in executive office. Each of these types has a political appeal to parts of the population and a political or executive style that appeals to particular constituencies and works best on particular kinds of problems and issues. That is, the strength of any given leadership style is that it is capable of mobilizing intense support in certain quarters. But what attracts strongly also repels, and a limitation of our four leadership types is that they cannot be all things to all people. Thus, a Texas populist like Lyndon Johnson (at least before the Kennedy assassination) was always believed to face great difficulty breaking out of his southern constituency. Adlai Stevenson, George McGovern, and John Lindsay, because of their stiff-necked moralism, had consistent political difficulties with populist communities in both the North and the South. Eisenhower, Nixon, and Ford were never able to appeal strongly to the moralists' constituency, the highly educated and issue-oriented communities in the large industrial states. The aristocrats like Roosevelt and Kennedy were often viewed with suspicion, in large part because of their personal style, in the small towns of Mid-America that provide the enduring support for the managerial leaders.

It is perhaps an obvious point that distinctive political roots and style make a leader more comfortable and naturally accepted in one part of the American political culture than another. In theory, a leader without "binding" roots who could reach across the various cleavages of background and style would be a stronger political leader with a wider appeal than one tied to a narrower background. There are in fact a number of political leaders whose success in large measure has rested on their ability to transcend their roots to create hybrid styles of political leadership. This powerful synthesis of styles was apparent in Theodore Roosevelt, who combined the confidence and background of the aristocrat with the strident rhetoric and missionary zeal of the moralist. The Republican Roosevelt, as John Blum has shown,[6] was at times an enormously skillful and subtle political strategist like his cousin FDR, and at other times a bombastic and uncompromising crusader. More recently, George Romney achieved an interesting hybrid style as a manager and as a moralist emphasizing spiritual values and the politics of principle. This synthesis did not take Romney to the White House, as it turned out, but it did take him a lot further in politics than most presidents of automobile companies can expect to go. Among other recent politicians, Robert Kennedy also provides an interesting case. Robert Kennedy, far more than his older brother, offered an extraordinarily mixed style: part aristocrat (a member of the clan), part moralist (with his reputation for commitment to his principles), and part populist (with a very unusual ability to appeal to and identify with the poor and nonwhite in American society). That this collage of styles made Kennedy a particularly intriguing leader is clear. What the fluid combination of styles would have meant in executive office, we will never know.

In an older tradition of American politics, political leaders were not required to appeal to widely divergent political cultures. Nominations depended on a coalition of sectional political organizations. To a large extent, it was up to the regional and ethnic leaders to get their constituents behind the party's candidate. If Roosevelt and Kennedy did not initially inspire the South or Truman the North, it was up to party leaders to put their candidate across. With the secular decline in the strength of party organizations and with the increased fragmentation of party factions, the contemporary political leader bears far more of the burden of welding together different interests and constituencies. The growing importance of the media in political campaigns places added emphasis on the ability of a candidate to appeal to and even embody quite different political backgrounds and aspirations. The test of "Is he with us, is he one of us?" can be both a great opportunity and a great liability for the candidate who appeals directly to voters on television.

It is in this context that Jimmy Carter emerges as a quite remarkable political leader, one who has clearly been able to transcend his immediate political roots—or at least combine elements of very different political roots in his leadership style. On an early and superficial reading, Carter seemed to many observers to be just another southern populist, a Georgia governor from a small town who championed the "people" against the bureaucracy and other vested interests. However, on closer inspection, it turned out that Carter's roots and political style were far more complex and intriguing. Though a product of the rural South—and the Deep South at that—here was a leader who had broken out of this traditional background in several ways. For one thing, this was a southern boy who went to Annapolis, became a nuclear engineer, as he liked to put it, and served in Rickover's submarine corps. In addition, this was a populist who did not apprentice himself to the local political organization as a way of moving up in the world, but who returned to the South reluctantly and managed to turn his business into a successful (and much larger) enterprise. In this sense, the image of Jimmy Carter, peanut farmer, is splendidly double-edged. It evokes the South's populist roots but does double service as proof of managerial and entrepreneurial achievement (when one notices what Carter's peanut business actually amounted to).

Finally, Carter also managed to add to his persona the appearance and appeal of a stern moralist. Carter's moralism is, in fact, part Baptist fundamentalism and part post-Watergate common sense. But there is another feature too, Carter the voracious reader of books—and books on history and philosophy at that. This is the Carter of the missionary streak and the highly idealistic rhetoric calling, not unlike a Wilson or a Stevenson, for a "new spirit" and moral tone in America. In all, Jimmy Carter is a man of many parts, and most of them spring from the genuine diversity of his personal experience. That is, Carter managed to appear authentic in a wide range of roles: as farmer, engineer, as a man of the church, as a businessman, and to a lesser extent as a reflective intellectual concerned with the large issues before American society.

Carter's roots in quite different backgrounds provided the foundations for his multifaceted appeal, but there is more to it than this. In his political style, Carter made these different images and traditions work brilliantly together and reinforce one another. Thus, the populist's distrust of bureaucracy squares nicely with the manager's desire to tame bureaucracy and make government run more efficiently. And the populist southern Baptist's moralism, based on the old-time religion, combined harmoniously with the moralist's desire for a cleansed politics after Vietnam and Watergate. Of course, it may be that the synthesis of background and style that Carter was able to provide in 1976 was unique to a particular time in American political history. The joining of different traditions might prove harder in another year.

The Changing Roots of American Leadership

While the significance of Carter's achievement is still not clear, I can say with greater confidence that the roots and styles of American leadership seem to be changing in two important ways. First, I believe that the supply and political viability of my four leadership types are undergoing long-term changes. For one thing, I suspect that the aristocratic leaders will increasingly fade from view. This is in part because the great wealth of the aristocratic families has been diluted over the generations. It is also because the dominance of the northeastern industrial states has been sharply reduced in the Republican party (since Dewey) and also in the Democratic party, with the rise to power of the sunbelt (and California). Being governor of New York is no longer prima facie grounds for serious consideration at a presidential convention (as it was for both Roosevelts). To make matters worse for the aristocrat, the seeming resurgence of ethnic voting in industrial states (note well the recent New York City elections) makes the Wasp aristocrat more than ever a leader without any natural constituency. Finally, to return to my basic point about the Tory character of aristocratic leadership, I believe that there has been a persistent shift away from the politics of deference in American politics. The concept of a leader from Groton serving as the "tribune of the masses" just does not seem as plausible today.

In any case, it is hard to find many aristocratic leaders on the contemporary scene who actively pursue the tradition of the Roosevelts, Kennedy, and Rockefeller, and the leaders who have plausible roots as aristocrats are not exactly broadcasting the fact. Senator John Danforth, the scion of the Ralston Purina family, has emphasized his background as a divinity school student, lawyer, and crusading state official. There is of course still a Rockefeller in high elective office in America. But this Rockefeller came to West Virginia as a VISTA volunteer and paid his dues as the president of a small denominational college. Nevertheless, if you were looking for a state in which you could replicate Franklin Roosevelt's aristocratic appeal to depression-era voters down on their luck and money, West Virginia would be my first choice. It was also John F. Kennedy's first choice in 1960.

If the aristocratic leaders are in decline, so also may be the populist style of leadership. The legacy of the depression and Yankee-ethnic conflict in northern cities provided a durable wellspring for the populist leader's political message, but you can play on those themes for only so long, and with the rise of the New South and the movement of ethnics to middle-class neighborhoods and the suburbs, it is becoming increasingly hard to run as a "Pitchfork Ben" or as the child of Hell's Kitchen and cold-water flats. The people who once wanted to increase public services and increase benefits to the poor are now apt to be home owners and tax protestors. The populist's constituency has changed, and no one registers this shift better than George Wallace. Once a political terror, he seems more and more an antique.

If the roots of political leadership are perhaps withering at both ends of the political (social) continuum, the logical conclusion is that the number of moralists and managers must be swelling. Indeed, I believe this is the case and that recent elections suggest a continuing match-up between highly educated upper-middle-class moralists on the one hand, offering a politics of principle and a strong moral vision for America, and managers, on the other, offering an ability to solve problems, rationalize budgets, manage bureaucracies, and handle complex policy problems like energy and inflation.

The second change in the roots of American leadership is related closely to the first. Not only have the leadership types at each end of the social continuum declined, but the clear distinctions between political roots and style seem also to have diminished. No longer does a background in the South mean that you have to run in the traditional white suit, bourbon-and-branch-water tradition. Current leaders like Boren of Oklahoma, Askew of Florida, Pryor of Arkansas, and Lloyd Bentsen of Texas make that plain. In the same way, if a leader comes from an Irish, Italian, Polish, or Greek background, he no longer needs to follow in the tradition of ethnic populism—the tradition of Curley, Hague, LaGuardia, and Cermak of Chicago. New faces on the political scene make that clear: consider Jerry Brown and Hugh Carey, Ella Grasso and Mario Cuomo, Paul Sarbanes and Michael Dukakis. All of these leaders have roots in the populist tradition, but they have broken out of that narrow definition to combine their populist appeal with that of the moralist or manager. Thus Jerry Brown melds his family's Irish tradition with his well-known moralism and spartan philosophy. Dukakis is another leader with clear ethnic ties who also appears as a stern moralist. Carey and Grasso, on the other hand, seem to have combined (or sought to combine) the style of the populist and the manager.

My point is that as American society becomes more homogeneous and cosmopolitan, political leadership is apt to be less segmented, less locked into a narrow social, economic, or geographical definition. This means that leaders will increasingly combine elements of the different leadership styles and will be able to appeal across different constituencies, once separated by a more clear-cut sense of roots and style.

This increased flexibility in leadership style both strengthens and weakens political leadership. In the hands of a Jerry Brown or Hugh Carey, the synthesis of leadership styles makes for a flexible and intriguing political personality. To take a quite different case, Mayor Kenneth Gibson of Newark has combined a populist style (as a leader of the black community) with a managerial style (as an engineer and problem solver) to considerable effect.

On the other hand, the shift from a sharp definition of political roots to increasing rootlessness appears to leave some leaders caught betwixt and between. Connecticut voters had high hopes for their first woman governor, Ella Grasso, but her public political style seems tepid and shapeless. Governor Grasso seems to be caught somewhere between the ethnic/machine style of the John Bailey era and the new style of tough-minded fiscal management.

Leadership Style and the Evolution of Public Moods

As Harold Lasswell pointed out many years ago, the prominence of any given leadership style reflects the demands, moods, and political requirements of a particular era as well as the available supply of particular leadership personalities. According to this logic, there is usually a fit between a leader and his times; different times will call forth different kinds of leaders. In recent history, there appears to be an alternation between the administrative emphasis of the manager and the activist, freewheeling style of the aristocrat (or the crusading zeal of the moralist). Thus Kennedy succeeded Eisenhower with a promise of vitality and the fulfillment of "great expectations," and earlier Roosevelt succeeded Hoover with his own version of the pledge to get America moving again. At the same time, the managers came to office after long periods of expansive, highly personalized leadership. The Republican managers of the twenties came after the Wilson era, and Eisenhower after the Roosevelt era.

The notion that the demand for leadership is reactive to the deficiencies of the preceding regime is, I think, both true and a useful clue to changing styles, but it doesn't go nearly far enough.

The demands for and expectations of leadership also reflect historical events that are more specific and unpredictable than these broad cyclical fluctuations. Eisenhower was aided in his man-above-politics appeal by the inflation and reputation for corruption of the Truman years. Equally, the civil rights movement and its near relation, the urban crisis, gave added force to both moralists like John Lindsay and populists like Johnson and Wallace (populists could work either side of the civil rights issue). Vietnam was the raison d'être of the moralist leaders, McCarthy and McGovern.

The dominant events of recent history have been, in my judgment, the increased suspicion of government in the wake of costly social programs that did not seem to work and Watergate. Suspicion of government augments the appeal of managerial leaders who say they will make government work and control public spending. Watergate clearly has called forth many moralist leaders who say they will restore trust and high purpose to government. It can only be a speculation, but I suspect that the American mood in the late 1970s is divided in the first place between two different aspirations for leadership—between the desire for the moralist's sense of purpose and "spiritual uplift" and the desire for good managers who will put the house of government in order (and also avoid shrill polarizing crusades).

But there is also the appeal of the hybrid leaders, which reflects the uncertain mood of American politics. The familiar moorings of liberalism and conservatism seem to have slipped, and the traditional arguments for and against government action have become blurred in the face of issues like détente, energy, inflation, deregulation, crime, and environmental protection. The policy positions of many leaders are often, at least in terms of older verities, a strange mélange of liberalism and conservatism, as well as of moralism, populism, and managerial zeal. All of this provides an important reason why hybrid leaders who respond flexibly, using different styles and strategies to deal with different kinds of problems, have become more prominent. Thus, along with the moralists and managers, the hybrid leaders present a third political style seeking to fit itself to a dimly understood present and an emerging future in American government.

Implications for Politics and Public Policy

I have suggested that for various reasons the ranks of American political leadership will be increasingly filled with moralists, managers, and hybrid types. If this is true, what are the implications for American politics and public policy?

In the first place, it is intriguing to me that the strengths and weaknesses of the moralists and the managers are both distinct and complementary. The moralists place primary attention on defining issues and policy choices and mobilizing constituencies behind them. In a democratic system that purports to offer citizens a choice between alternative leaders and policies at least once every few years, the moralist's style aids popular choice and gives politics a sense of principle and purpose. The corollary weakness is that as executives the moralists are likely to be less adept at the craft of public management, which increasingly requires flexibility and adaptability in policymaking and problem solving.

By contrast, the managers typically do not offer strong policy positions but are often adept in steering a management course in and around the policy problems they encounter. There is a significant trade-off here. There is also a trade-off between strongly stated policies and an executive style that responds swiftly to changing problems and circumstances, between a strong philosophical advocacy of where American government ought to be going and a strong administrative emphasis on how government is going to get there—or anywhere—competently, if not efficiently.

Ideally, we would like to have leaders who combine the best traits of the moralist and the manager. And, while we are at it, it would be nice to have the strengths and skills of the aristocrat and the populist as well. For clearly the very different policy issues we now face call for the traits our leadership types offer in different measures and at different times. This, as I have said before, is the source of the hybrid leader's appeal. We would like to have it both ways (or all four ways). We would like our leaders to provide the aristocrat's authority, the moralist's commitment, the manager's desire to make the system work, plus the populist's political skill. The trouble, of course, is that if roots matter at all and if the idea of character implies some persistent definition, the emergence of a political man for all seasons should be a rare occurrence. And that leads to a final reflection on the hybrid leaders. The optimistic view is that American leaders are increasingly able to combine, through varied experiences and opportunities, elements of historically separate leadership styles. Such a leader would be protean in an authentic and useful way. The pessimistic view is that our leaders are not becoming more multifaceted and adaptive but merely more plastic. The evidence for this view is that media campaigns and government public relations can increasingly manipulate images and policies in an inauthentic way, such that a civil rights liberal can suddenly become a law-and-order sheriff without apparent challenge to any notion of integrity. Or the conservative manager can represent himself as a "man of the people." Or the crusader can decide that it is suddenly good politics to present himself as a tough manager.

This then is the central dilemma of American leadership. More than ever, we require elements of the different leadership styles, subtly and flexibly deployed. Yet we also have more reason than ever to wonder what in the world we are getting when we elect a politician to high executive office.

Notes

1. I have in mind, in particular, Doris Kearns, *Lyndon Johnson and the American Dream* (New York: Harper and Row, 1976). There is also, by now, a small shelf of recent books on the psychohistory of American leaders. By contrast, James David Barber's book, *Presidential Character* (Englewood Cliffs, N. J.: Prentice Hall, 1972), emphasizes emerging psychological traits and modes of adaptation for public life in a way that highlights the "political" dimensions of political psychology.

2. Samuel Beer, *British Politics in the Collectivist Age* (New York: Knopf, 1966), p. 247.

3. James M. Burns, *Roosevelt: The Lion and the Fox* (New York: Harcourt, Brace & World, 1956).

4. James Q. Wilson, *The Amateur Democrat* (Chicago: University of Chicago Press, 1966).

5. For a fuller discussion of this point, see Timothy Breen, *The Character of the Good Ruler* (New Haven: Yale University Press, 1970).

6. John M. Blum, *The Republican Roosevelt* (Cambridge: Harvard University Press, 1954).

Part III

Legislative Politics

Chapter 8

Cooling the Legislative Tea

Benjamin I. Page

Only occasionally do the House and Senate clash in an open and dramatic fashion. When they do, as in the appropriations dispute of 1962,[1] they draw attention to the general pattern of relations between the chambers, and to the question of what difference American bicameralism makes in the nature and quality of legislative policy.

In one sense the system of two legislative chambers is a historical accident, a result of the need to accommodate the interests of both large states and small in forming the union, with the Senate a symbol and embodiment of federalism. Yet there would seem to be more to it than that. At the time of the framing of the US Constitution there were precedents for bicameralism in Great Britain and in the American states, and as the author of *The Federalist* no. 63 (probably Madison) noted, in ancient Sparta, Rome, and Carthage, and indeed in every "long-lived republic."[2] At present, legislatures are bicameral in most of the parliamentary democracies of Western Europe and elsewhere. Unless we are to believe that constitution makers throughout the world have engaged in blind imitation, the prevalence of bicameral forms suggests that they may have substantial causes and significant effects or functions.

According to the *The Federalist,* bicameralism was designed to provide an "impediment against improper acts of legislation." In contrast to the House, which was to be the popular chamber, the Senate was to have greater expertise, in order to protect against "errors" or "blunders," and greater continuity, for stability, coherence, and responsibility in policy. Perhaps most important, the Senate was to be an "anchor against popular fluctuations," defending the people against their own "temporary errors and delusions" and ensuring that only the "cool and deliberate sense of the community" would prevail. Together, the two chambers were to protect against "schemes of usurpation or perfidy" and resist the "impulse of sudden and violent passions" or seduction into "intemperate and pernicious resolutions."[3]

The Framers, then, claimed as the main benefit of bicameralism the prevention of error through a slowing of the legislative process and provision for expertise, and in particular through resistance to temporary passions or fluctuations in public opinion. In addition they probably hoped for (but did not emphasize in the ratification campaign) some permanent resistance to majority rule and protection of such liberties or minority interests as property rights, by requiring concurrent majorities in the two bodies, one of them representing the wealthy and well-born, before legislation could be enacted. I will try to shed some light upon which, if any, of these consequences actually flow from bicameralism by examining the institutional characteristics of the House and Senate in relation to two important properties of the legislative process which vary according to contrasting theoretical views.

Some theories assert that legislative policy is determined by the preferences of equally weighted citizens. In certain economic or rational-man theories which postulate perfect information and no transaction costs, for example, each vote-seeking legislator responds precisely to the policy preferences of his constituents by supporting the most popular policies. The legislature as a whole, in turn, aggregates the preferences of equally weighted legislators. While there may be some indeterminacy in aggregating citizens' preferences (due to Arrow's paradox) or in forming legislative coalitions (owing to lack of a unique solution to this type of *N*-person game), the resulting policies embody an unbiased social choice that does not systematically count any citizen's desires unequally.[4]

Most observers of politics reject this view and maintain that for one reason or another (unequal participation, campaign money, lobbying by organized groups) citizens have unequal influence upon legislative outcomes. According to the familiar group theories of political science, for example, policy emerges from the struggle of organized interest groups. So long as it is acknowledged that not all interests are equally organized,[5] a citizen's influence varies with the money and manpower and other resources of the groups to which he happens to belong. Whether individuals or groups are taken as the primary actors, however, the chief point is that in these theories the policy-making process is one of biased competition.

The second property concerns the nature of actors' preferences. Many prevailing views of the legislative process, including theories of unbiased individualistic competition and theories of group struggle, assume that policy preferences are fixed with respect to the legislative process. In the perfect-information economic models, legislators take citizens' preferences as given and simply aggregate them. In group theories, the groups know what policies they want and fight to enact them. In both kinds of theories it is often assumed that these preferences follow automatically from self-interest.

In traditional political philosophy, however, and in the view of some participants, the legislative process itself plays a much more active part in what emerges. Citizens and groups are uncertain about which policy means would best achieve their ends. They are open to information, to new evidence, which may reveal unforeseen relationships between ends and means and may alter their policy preferences. Legislators are not just passive registers of constitutent preferences and group pressures but actively seek information and evidence. They develop expertise and gather research and testimony about the nature of problems and the appropriate means of solving them. They deliberate, individually and collectively, about what would best satisfy the needs of their constituents (or, indeed, the larger "public interest"), and they form their own judgments, subject to change when new evidence appears.

The effects we can expect from bicameralism depend heavily upon what we think about these disputed matters, the equality or inequality of citizens' influence and the nature of policy preferences. For example, neither a slowing of the legislative process nor temporary resistance to public opinion can be of much significance if the preferences of citizens and legislators are fixed: the mere passage of time will make no difference. Indeed if preferences are fully informed and reflect self-interest, the very notions of "error," "passion," and "fluctuation of opinion" among legislators or people are inconceivable. There cannot exist any need or possibility of guarding against them. By the same token, under simple social-choice or group-struggle models with fixed preferences, two identical chambers would act no differently than one. Bicameralism would have important effects only if the constituencies of the two chambers differed in some systematic fashion.

Clearly the effects of bicameralism will vary with the particular institutional features of the two chambers. Beyond a certain point it is useless to speak of bicameralism in the abstract, and one must consider how the two bodies work and what constituencies they represent. In examining some of the enduring aspects of American bicameralism, including the features that are constitutionally mandated, one must also keep in mind contrasting models of the legislative process and the theoretical views on which they are based.

Bicameralism itself, as I have noted, cannot have much effect if the possibility of deliberation is ruled out. If bicameralism takes its purest form, with the size and workings and constituencies of the two chambers identical and differing from unicameralism only by duplication, then under the assumption of fixed preferences the aggregation process in each chamber would be identical—perhaps subject only to random variations. Two such bodies would presumably act as one, with little disagreement or delay, and any delay that occurred would not alter the legislative product. Only the lower visibility and blurred accountability of a more complex legislature might reduce popular control.

If deliberation takes place in the legislative process, however, two chambers with the same initial preferences might well diverge, in the event that they unearthed differing evidence. One body might spot errors and convince the other, all the more so if they worked out a specific division of labor concerning research and testimony, or if there was a required sequence so that the second chamber would always have the results of the first chamber's investigations at hand when it began work on a piece of legislation. (To be sure, one chamber could defer to the other, so the extent of deliberation would not really be doubled.) In the United States such sequencing is constitutionally imposed for revenue bills (and is extended, by custom, to appropriations as well): the House acts before the Senate. Under these conditions, bicameralism itself may help to "cool the legislative tea"—to reduce the chance of enacting flawed legislation, that is, with provisions that would be generally acknowledged as errors or defects by those in possession of correct information.

It can be argued that the deliberative protection against error would be increased in proportion to the dissimilarity between the two bodies, since dissimilarity provides more occasions for disagreement and the seeking out and debating of conflicting evidence, on the model of an adversary system. Moreover, most of the broader effects of bicameralism (and indeed, under nondeliberative theoretical views, any effects at all) depend upon the nature and extent of the differences between the two chambers. Differences between House and Senate, then, are crucial to our exploration.

Formal qualifications of legislators The constitutional requirements concerning age and citizenship—that senators must be at least thirty years of age and nine years a citizen, compared with twenty-five and seven years respectively for the House—were once thought important for ensuring a greater maturity in the Senate and less openness to foreign influence. But now, even assuming that the original logic was correct, they are almost wholly irrelevant. Rarely are members under thirty elected to the House, and the (rather high) average age is scarcely affected by the minimum; nor do recently naturalized immigrants often attain membership in either body. Under other circumstances formal qualifications can of course be quite important, as when an upper chamber like the House of Lords is limited to a nobility largely based on inherited ownership of land. In such cases the interests represented by the two houses may be quite different, and both delay and resistance to popular will can result.

Length of term in office According to a perfect-information social-choice view, term of office should make no difference; vote-maximizing politicians would do precisely what their constituents wanted when they wanted it, regardless of whether the electoral reward was to come in two years or six. If citizens are imperfectly informed of their legislators' actions, however, term of office could be critical. Those politicians most distant from the moment of electoral truth might count on voters' faulty memories to free them from popular control,[6] which might make them even more subject to the influence of organized groups. For this reason the Senate might be somewhat more independent of popular pressure. Under the deliberation view, this increases the Senate's ability to resist the temporary passions, errors, delusions, and fluctuations of opinion that so troubled the Framers.

The arguments that senators' longer terms would result in greater stability and continuity in policy, and greater experience and knowledge of government, on the other hand, must be taken as largely illusory; the length of time between elections need not greatly affect actual tenure in office, as the current incumbency phenomenon in the House demonstrates. (Possibly the greater attractiveness of the Senate encourages more serious challenges.) It might be thought that senators' freedom from frequent reelection campaigns would allow them to devote more time to the public business, but experience offers little support for this idea. At most, the six-year term only affords a vulnerable freshman senator more time to learn his job and the art of reelection before facing the possibility of being thrown out.

Staggered terms of office, in which one third of the Senate is replaced every two years rather than the whole body every six, ensure that resistance to public opinion is counteracted by electoral sanctions gradually rather than in a surge. At any given moment some two-thirds of the senators are distant from election, so the body's accountability to the public is averaged out rather than subjected to six-year cycles. This presumably makes for more stability in the thrust of policy, although for a given length of term it should not (except through artful timing by lawmakers) affect the net extent of any antipopular bias in the legislative product. In addition it guarantees some overlap of personnel and an opportunity to pass on knowledge and expertise to new members, but the fact of length incumbency in the House has rendered this potential difference between the bodies insignificant.

The sequence of legislative action, as in the requirement that the House initiate revenue bills, can perhaps enhance the effect of bicameralism upon deliberation, by slowing the process and making sure that the second chamber waits to see the product of the first. But this effect is limited by flexibility in the concept of "beginning" work on legislation; the Senate sometimes holds hearings related to House revenue and appropriations legislation without formal introduction of Senate legislation before the House completes passage of its bill. And there is in principle nothing to prevent the second body from taking on faith the conclusions of the first (or the first from deferring to the second), thus reducing double consideration to a hollow gesture, unless their constituencies and preferences differ. Sequencing may affect which body has the greatest impact on legislation, if in fact the second body is reluctant to duplicate all the work of the first.

The powers and duties of the chambers do not appreciably differ, in the American case, except for the special role of the Senate in treaties, appointments, and impeachment. Where the powers of one body are seriously restricted, as in the extreme example of the House of Lords, the overall effects of bicameralism are more limited.

Territorial versus population representation The state basis of representation in the Senate, as opposed to the popular basis in the House, was at the heart of the original constitutional compromise of a mixed or "compound" republic. This feature of the Senate was seen as both a constitutional recognition and an instrument of protection for the sovereignty of the individual states. In practice its main effect is to give a degree of overrepresentation to the interests of those residing in certain areas, such as the Rocky Mountains and western plains, where state populations tend to be small. As Dahl has persuasively argued, this advantage can hardly be defended as helping minority interests that are especially needful of protection.[7] Like any other difference between the constituencies of House and Senate, it tends to aggravate delay and the bias toward the legislative status quo by increasing the chance of disagreement between the bodies.

The malapportionment of congressional districts, which became so acute in the first half of the twentieth century and resulted from congressional and court acquiescence in state control over districting, led to substantial overrepresentation of rural areas and small towns in the House. It thereby set up a particular kind of resistance to the popular will. It also (assuming that its effects were different in direction or greater in magnitude than those of the territorial basis of the Senate) brought about increased differences between the House and the Senate and made it harder to enact legislation. The Supreme Court's decisions on reapportionment largely removed this source of difference.

Indirect versus direct popular election In the original constitutional scheme, which endured for more than a century, senators were chosen by the state legislatures and members of the House by direct popular election. According to a perfect-information social-choice viewpoint, indirect election should make no difference: state legislators, perfectly responsive to the people, would make exactly the same choices as the people themselves. But under a view of unequal influence and attenuated popular control, a two-stage election process would further diminish citizens' hold on the Senate and thus distinguish it markedly from the House, particularly if state elections were less visible or less competitive than federal. It could permit appointment of men of wisdom and independent judgment, as the Framers hoped, or as seems to have been the case in the late nineteenth century, enhance interest-group power and outright corruption. This possible source of House-Senate differences and resistance to the public was eliminated in 1913 by the Seventeenth Amendment, which required direct popular election of senators.

Size of constituency The position of the House as the "more numerous" body, with smaller constituencies, is not actually mandated by the Constitution. That document specified two senators per state but set quotas of representatives only for the first three years and then left the matter to Congress and the census, with the provisos that each state should get at least one representative and that the number should not be more than one for every thirty thousand of population. In the initial constitutional allotment two states got only one representative each, but the average was well above two; the House was clearly intended to be the larger body and has in fact always enjoyed that status.

Again, from a social-choice perspective it is not easy to discern why citizens' preferences would be aggregated differently by a small body of representatives than by a large one; it would seem the sheerest accident if the two-part aggregation from citizens' preferences to legislators' positions to public policy did not come out the same regardless of the number of legislators and the size of the constituencies involved in the intervening step. If this is how legislatures work, we would expect constituency size to make little difference.[8]

From a group-struggle viewpoint, however, the case is quite different. Once biases in political competition are admitted, it is possible to imagine a variety of ways in which groups of different types might—because of campaign technology and resources or geographical position—have special advantages or disadvantages in influencing representatives from large as opposed to small districts. To take one example, perhaps large corporations, whose chief political resource is money, can heavily influence senatorial campaigns by paying for mass-media advertising, particularly television, but in small congressional districts, where television would wastefully scatter messages outside the target area, personal campaigning by armies of activists is more effective, and the more numerous small businessmen and professionals and others are more influential. By the same token, perhaps the influence of labor unions is heaviest in senatorial races where their money counts most, and in a limited number of House districts in which their organizational strength and manpower are concentrated. This could lead to differences between the House and the Senate in provincialism, as discussed by Huntington:[9] a Senate more responsive to modern corporate capitalism, and a House more closely tied to rural and small-town America.

A similar and especially plausible argument is that the general public has better control of senators than of congressmen, because of the greater visibility of the senatorial office. In Schattschneider's phrase, the "scope of the conflict"[10] over senatorial elections and actions may be broader, because the public has more information about its senators and is more aware of and hence better able to sanction deviations from faithful representation. If this is so, it works against other factors like the length of term in office, and it is exactly contrary to the intention of the Framers, who planned that the House would be the more popular branch and the Senate more representative of the propertied. But it could have the same effect of protecting certain minorities (not by any means the most oppressed) against majority rule.

The size of the legislative body, in a representative system, is directly related to size of constituency but may have some independent effects. For the usual reasons one who takes a simple social-choice view would expect size of body to be largely or wholly irrelevant. *The Federalist,* on the other hand, argued that the smaller Senate would be less subject to the violent passions of mob psychology, more responsible, since more susceptible to individual attribution of praise and blame, and (perhaps the most telling point) less subject to internal oligarchy.

To a contemporary observer, however, the most important effect of size is that greater manpower permits greater specialization and expertise. In the twentieth century the House has developed a highly organized system of committees, with each member devoting much of his work to a particular substantive field. The less numerous (even if individually more brilliant) senators, spread over the whole range of legislative subjects, cannot hope to rival the collective expertise of the House. (Yet couldn't Senators compensate with larger or better staffs?) If we believe in deliberative processes, therefore, we might expect the House to play a preeminent role in legislation, a role contrary to the expectations and intentions of the Framers but consistent with their desire to have at least one body highly expert in affairs of state. This is the view of many students of Congress.

The small size of the Senate, together with its formally coequal power, also entails that each individual senator has more power and prestige than his counterpart in the House. This no doubt helps attract the best-qualified candidates, as the Framers intended, or at least the best at getting elected, but the resulting high quality of senators may be counteracted to some degree by the temptations, also arising from prestige, to be a media show horse or to run continually for the presidency.

My examination of the institutional features of the House and Senate indicates some of the effects bicameralism may have, but the magnitude of these effects (already hard to judge) depends also upon how the two chambers interact and which tends to prevail. Here, too, our conclusions will vary depending upon what theoretical view we take concerning the legislative process.

If the policy preferences of citizens and legislators are assumed to be fixed, each body can be treated as a unitary actor attempting to work its legislative will. Policy outcomes will then presumably be limited to those which both chambers prefer over the status quo; otherwise one body or the other would refuse to pass the legislation. If the preferences of the two chambers are substantially different, this requirement of concurrent majorities can significantly restrict possible legislative outcomes and contribute to delay (if the difference between chambers is temporary) or to permanent obstruction of the popular will and protection of the status quo.

Among policies preferred to the status quo by both chambers, which ones can we expect to be enacted? Pursuing the fixed-preference assumption, each chamber presumably pushes for the policies it prefers, but the only real weapon available to each is potentially self-defeating—the threat of imposing the status quo and passing nothing unless the other chamber gives it most or all of what it wants. This situation has the marks of a two-person bargaining game, with partial conflict of interest. Game theory and the microeconomic analysis of bargaining offer some insights into such games, such as the likelihood that the outcome will fall somewhere along a Pareto-optimal "contract curve" which is defined by the property that for any outcome off the curve there is an outcome on the curve that improves things for one actor without hurting the other. Unless there is confusion or vindictiveness or hard bargaining designed to affect future outcomes, one can expect Pareto-optimal results, but exactly which ones, among a plethora of alternatives, is determined by bargaining skill or other factors not encompassed by such theories. The matter is even more complicated, of course, if the president enters the game with a threat of veto, and it is complicated still further if independent actors such as conference committee chairmen defy the will of their chambers. Abandonment of the fixed-preference assumption would also increase theoretical indeterminacy.

It is not easy to determine empirically which body actually prevails. Examination of House-Senate disputes which have gone to conference indicates that the Senate "wins" some two-thirds of the time.[11] But this figure would not accurately represent the influence of each house upon legislation unless conference disagreements reflected the differences between the policies truly desired by the two bodies. This is not likely to be the case: each body engages in strategic behavior and takes account of the other in passing its own bills. The House, for example, may tend to cut appropriations bills more than it wants in the expectation that the Senate will restore some funds; similarly, the Senate may inflate appropriations somewhat in the knowledge that there will have to be compromise with the House. Moreover, the second-acting body (most often the Senate) may simply defer, reluctantly, to the first body on many points when it passes its version of the legislation and may take only its strongest differences to conference; little wonder, then, that the second body seems to prevail at the final stage. Indeed it is the second body—not necessarily the Senate—that usually "wins" in conference; when the Senate initiates legislation, it is the House that prevails about two-thirds of the time in conference committee.[12]

Since one cannot be sure in any particular case what each house really wants, one cannot tell how much influence each actually has on the final product. But the common impression may not be far wide of the mark: that the House generally has more say on the specifics of legislative policy, and the Senate acts mainly as a court of appeals on limited questions. If this is so, and if the small size of constituencies renders the House less subject to public opinion, the restraint upon majority rule is correspondingly increased.

Under the deliberation view of the legislative process the picture is rather different. Interaction between House and Senate involves not only bargaining with fixed preferences but genuine debate over the merits of legislation and the possibility of one chamber's convincing the other to change its stand. From this perspective, House predominance would reflect its greater command of detail and would indicate that the error-reducing function of bicameralism may be particularly important.

I have left in doubt which models of the legislative process come closest to reality, for the good reason that the answer is not known with any certainty. Evidence bearing directly upon the equality or inequality of citizens' influence, or upon the rigidity or malleability of preferences in the course of legislating, is fragmentary and inconclusive. Yet some assessment of what is most probably true is needed in order to sort out the effects of bicameralism.

A belief in equal citizen influence fits nicely with formal theorizing (and with a certain complacency about the workings of democracy); it is embraced, with varying degrees of fervor, by most Western microeconomists and by many others. But the axioms of perfect (or unbiased) information and zero transaction costs upon which it rests are hardly tenable. It is not equally easy for all citizens to vote; some—especially those of lower income—have a harder time finding transportation and getting away from jobs or children to register and cast ballots. Those with money and communication skills can more easily find out what government is doing and write or visit their congressmen or contribute to campaigns. Corporations, trade unions, professional associations, and other groups organized for economic purposes have great advantages in lobbying. The theoretical argument that there are markets for information and organization, that citizens can purchase the means of legislative influence, only reinforces the point that it is money and other unequally distributed resources, rather than equally distributed votes, that largely determine how much different individuals can influence policy.

But if we take the not very daring position that the usual political science models of biased competition and group struggle are probably closer to the truth than some notion of perfect individualistic democracy, we are still left with the question whether it is realistic to regard policy preferences as fixed with respect to the legislative process. Here I would depart somewhat from the conventional view and argue that deliberation and preference change occur, and that their importance has been very much underemphasized. Legislators spend a substantial amount of time and effort working on legislation, and not all of it merely involves ascertaining the preferences of constituents. Considerable attention is devoted to questions of fact bearing upon the likely costs and benefits of particular proposals. How much will it cost to build a nuclear power plant, and how long will it take? How much power, worth how much, will be generated? How much danger is there that radioactive material will be released by an earthquake or other accident, given the geology of the site, the technology of the plant, and various alternative safety precautions? What would be the consequences of such an accident? How can radioactive waste be disposed of, and at what cost? What side effects will the discharge of coolant have upon fish and the natural environment?

Or, to take the case of an income maintenance proposal, how will it affect work incentives? What employment opportunities exist, and how many of what sort would be provided? How available are day-care centers, and what effects do they have upon children? How will benefit levels and other provisions affect family stability? What will be the net effects on income distribution, economic growth, and social harmony?

In every area of legislation, there are many questions of this sort that bear significantly upon the costs and benefits of legislative proposals. The answers are often unknown. Much testimony of a highly technical and expert sort is solicited in the search for answers, and sometimes original reserach is commissioned. Committee hearings and markup sessions, informal discussions among legislators and lobbyists, and floor debates often revolve around issues of fact and evidence. It is not uncommon, when important new evidence is presented, for legislators to change their positions or for legislative bodies to reverse their votes. Nor, when this information is disseminated by the media, is it unknown for public opinion to change. Anyone who watches the course of a major piece of legislation, from the earliest tentative proposals through the drafting and submission of bills, the holding of committee hearings, debate and amendment and passage on the floors of both houses, and (sometimes) final adjustment in conference committee, can hardly doubt that deliberation about the impact of legislation is a vital part of the legislative process.

From this perspective we can judge the main effects of American bicameralism. In the first place, it undoubtedly provides some resistance to public opinion and majority rule. Equal representation of states in the Senate coupled with population representation in the House is of rather little importance in this regard, and the different modes of election no longer apply, but the different effective constituencies entailed by the differing size of electoral districts (counteracted to some degree by the term-of-office effect) probably make a real difference. It seems clear that the House and Senate represent somewhat different constellations of interests, that neither is perfectly responsive to the general public, the House less so than the Senate, and that in their joint operation they provide two separate arenas for the vetoing of popular measures, thereby supporting the legislative status quo against change and protecting certain (presumably propertied or organized) minority interests.

There is some reason to believe that the undemocratic effects of bicameralism, and even the antimajoritarian tendencies of Congress generally, are declining, however. In the face of democratic politics, overtly antipopular institutions are probably fated either to be democratized, as was the US Senate, or rendered impotent, as was the House of Lords, or abolished.[13] The trend toward broader electoral participation, which began some two hundred years ago and has continued ever since—with some temporary setbacks like the progressive "reforms" following changes in US immigration patterns around the turn of the century—has recently been supplemented by procedural changes and growing public interest lobbies, which increase the visibility of the legislative process, and by some tentative moves toward reducing the role of private money in campaigns. It is not unreasonable to suppose that such developments help reduce obstacles against the public will, although they may stop far short of guaranteeing absolute political equality.

Be that as it may, much of the resistance to public opinion that can be attributed to bicameralism (as opposed to antipopular features that are common to both houses of Congress) may be only of a limited or temporary sort. In the end, legislators in both bodies must face similar electoral sanctions. The six-year terms of senators and the small, low-visibility districts of representatives offer only partial protection against the voters, and the net difference they produce between House and Senate is surely a modest one. The delaying aspect of bicameralism, which requires legislation to wend its way through two separate chambers, can at most offer only transient obstruction against urgent public desires; only passions that cool fairly quickly can be resisted. The specialization that has evolved in the larger body, the House, may subject legislation to powerful scrutiny, but scrutiny in itself can stop popular proposals for good only if it demonstrates that the popular passions were in fact based upon error.

It is therefore in the furtherance of deliberation, the production of evidence, and the revealing of error that bicameralism probably has its greatest effects. Bicameralism itself may provide for a measure of deliberation merely by ensuring that proposals are considered by two independent bodies. This effect is much enhanced, in the American setting, by the specialization and expertise that size has made possible in the House, and by the special influence upon legislation that the House has achieved.

It is not necessary to subscribe to the notion that everything about the present has been understood by great men of the past in order to acknowledge that the Founders were very likely correct on this point: while American bicameralism no doubt sometimes keeps us from drinking any tea at all, it may often improve legislative tea which was at the outset excessively hot or ill-brewed.

Notes

I am indebted to Joseph Bessette's work on deliberation for stimulating this essay and to the Institute for Research on Poverty at the University of Wisconsin for giving support. I am also grateful to David Fellman, Barbara Hinckley, Barry Rundquist, and Donald Wittman for a variety of comments and suggestions, not all of which could I respond to here.

1. Jeffrey L. Pressman, *House vs. Senate: Conflict in the Appropriations Process* (New Haven: Yale University Press, 1966).

2. Alexander Hamilton, James Madison, and John Jay, *The Federalist Papers,* ed. Clinton Rossiter (New York: New American Library, Mentor edition, 1961), p. 385.

3. *The Federalist Papers,* nos. 62 and 63, especially pp. 378, 379, 384, 385.

4. Such a view of legislatures is implicit in the first, or perfect information, section of Anthony Downs, *An Economic Theory of Democracy* (New York: Harper, 1957).

Kenneth J. Arrow, *Social Choice and Individual Values* (New York: Wiley, 1963; originally published 1951) and the subsequent social-choice literature demonstrate that the concepts of popular will or majority preference are not always easily defined: in a given group, for example, majorities may prefer A to B and B to C but also prefer C to A. In the following discussion I will continue to speak of the popular will, with reference to those circumstances under which it is defined, and in contrast to preference aggregations in which citizens are unequally weighted.

Some of the game-theoretic aspects of legislative coalitions are discussed in Steven J. Brams, *Game Theory and Politics* (New York: Free Press, 1975).

5. Mancur Olson, Jr., *The Logic of Collective Action: Public Goods and the Theory of Groups* (Cambridge, Mass.: Harvard University Press, 1965).

6. A piece of evidence that legislators do in fact respond more closely to their constituents' preferences when an election is near is James Kuklinski, "Representativeness and Elections: A Policy Analysis," *American Political Science Review* (in press).

7. Robert A. Dahl, *A Preface to Democratic Theory* (Chicago: University of Chicago Press, 1956), pp. 112-118.

8. The fixed-preference analysis in James M. Buchanan and Gordon Tullock, *The Calculus of Consent: Logical Foundations of Constitutional Democracy* (Ann Arbor: University of Michigan Press, 1962), ch. 16, qualifies this conclusion somewhat, but only by treating coalitions and intensities of preference in a manner not generally accepted in economic theorizing. Depending upon how voters are distributed among districts, however, runoff or unit-rule effects might occur.

9. Samuel P. Huntington, "Congressional Responses to the Twentieth Century," in *The Congress and America's Future*, ed. David B. Truman (Englewood Cliffs, N.J.: Prentice-Hall, 1965).

10. E. E. Schattschneider, *The Semi-Sovereign People* (New York: Holt, Rinehart, 1950).

11. Richard F. Fenno, Jr., *The Power of the Purse: Appropriations Politics in Congress* (Boston: Little, Brown, 1966), pp. 616-678; David J. Vogler, "Patterns of One-House Dominance in Congressional Conference Committees," *Midwest Journal of Political Science* 14 (1970): 303-320.

12. John Ferejohn, "Who Wins in Conference Committee?" *Journal of Politics* 37 (1975): 1033-1046; Gerald S. Strom and Barry S. Rundquist, "A Revised Theory of Winning in House-Senate Conferences," *American Political Science Review* 71 (1977): 448-453.

13. Jean Blondel, *Comparative Legislatures* (Englewood Cliffs, N.J.: Prentice-Hall, 1973), pp. 32-35.

Chapter 9

The Carter Congress and Urban Programs: First Soundings

Demetrios Caraley

When the heavily Democratic 95th Congress and the Democratic Carter administration took office in January 1977, city officials and others concerned with the problems of large cities were optimistic about the prospects for expanded federal aid programs, for the past four decades had shown that the federal government had been most responsive to the needs of urban areas in those few years when a heavily Democratic Congress was serving with a Democratic president in the White House.[1]

The significance of the Democratic majorities in Congress was that most Democrats in the House and Senate had been willing to vote for new and expanded urban programs and for greater spending, whereas most Republicans had not. The size of the Democratic majorities in Congress was significant because most southern Democrats voted on urban programs more like Republicans than like their northern Democratic colleagues. This meant that in order to pass significant urban legislation, the number of Democrats in each house had to be large enough to constitute floor majorities even in the face of large southern Democratic defections. Having a Democratic president in office was significant because typically it had been Democrats Roosevelt, Truman, Kennedy, and Johnson rather than Republicans Eisenhower, Nixon, and Ford who had been important sources of legislative proposals and budgetary support for federal aid to cities and who approved rather than vetoed any urban aid programs initiated by Congress.

During the early part of his quest for the Democratic presidential nomination, Jimmy Carter had not shown any special feeling for the drift of many of the nation's older and larger cities, especially those of the East and Midwest, into what I have elsewhere called "underserviced, crime-ridden, bankruptcy-skirting slum ghettoes."[2] Indeed, in the spring of 1975 when there appeared to be a real possibility that New York City might default on its bonds, Carter implicitly identified himself with President Ford's position by expressing opposition to any federal "bail-out" of New York or other cities facing severe fiscal pressures.[3]

By the spring of 1976, however, when he had established himself as the front-runner for the nomination, Carter began making promises of increased urban aid. He continued these in his presentation before the Democratic convention's Platform Committee in June, in the television debates with President Ford, and generally throughout his campaign for the presidency in the fall of 1976. Twice in October Carter took occasion to tell New York City audiences of his commitment to help large cities in general and New York City in particular. It was reported that after midnight on election night, when it was becoming clear that New York City's more than 700,000-vote margin for Carter would overcome the 428,000 deficit he was running elsewhere in the state, give him New York's 41 electoral votes, and thus clinch the presidency, Carter spoke on the telephone with New York City's Mayor Abraham Beame, telling him, "Abe, I love you," and assuring him that the Carter pledges for aid to urban areas would be redeemed.[4]

Yet within months after Carter took office, various big-city mayors at the annual meeting of the US Conference of Mayors grumbled that too little help had been forthcoming from the new administration.[5] In July, the executive director of the National Urban League, who had been one of the black interest group leaders personally closest to Carter before his election, complained publicly that the president had "fallen short on policies [and] programs" for cities and did not appear "to be working as hard to meet the needs of minorities and the poor as he did to get our votes."[6] Just a few days later, Mayor "Abe, I love you" Beame also publicly criticized Carter, saying that the administration's preliminary welfare reform proposals failed to include any provision for federal absorption of the financial contribution that some states (and notably New York) mandated their local governments to make—a reform that Carter had promised at various times during the campaign.[7] By the end of August, fifteen black leaders launched what they called "a counter-attack on the callous neglect of blacks, the poor and American cities."[8] One day later it was reported that President Carter had ordered an urgent review of federal urban policy,[9] apparently in response to these criticisms.

The Carter Urban Program

In the first eight months of 1977, the Carter administration never did announce any "urban program" as such. What it did immediately upon taking office was to ask Congress for an "economic stimulus" package to "stimulate" the economy and reduce unemployment. Central to this was the expansion and modification of three major grant programs that brought federal payments directly to city governments: public works jobs, countercyclical assistance, and public service jobs. In March the Carter administration also proposed an extension and modification of the community development block-grant program whose authorization was due to expire on September 30.

The public works jobs program was originally enacted by Congress over President Ford's veto in July 1976 as Title I of the Public Works Employment Act. It authorized for fiscal 1977 (that is, the fiscal year beginning October 1, 1976, and ending September 30, 1977) $2 billion of grants to local and state governments on a "formula-and-project" basis[10] for public works projects on which work could begin within ninety days of project approval. The grants were intended both to help local and state governments upgrade their physical plants and to create jobs for unemployed construction workers. In December 1976 the Commerce Department awarded grants for 1,988 projects, including 468 for municipal buildings, 473 for water and sewer facilities, 133 for public safety facilities, and 220 for streets and bridges. The Commerce Department reported that about $18 billion of additional project applications were on hand that could not be approved because all funds had been committed.[11]

When President Carter took office he asked Congress for an additional $2 billion in budget authority and supplemental appropriations to approve more projects in the remainder of fiscal 1977 and for a new $2 billion in budget authority for fiscal 1978. President Ford had requested no supplemental appropriations for fiscal 1977 and had asked for no new budget authority in his fiscal 1978 budget, thus indicating his intent to terminate the program.

The countercyclical assistance program was also enacted by Congress in July 1976 over President Ford's veto. It was Title II of the Public Works Employment Act, and it authorized up to $1.25 billion through fiscal 1977 for five quarterly payments to local (two-thirds) and state (one-third) governments, using a formula based primarily on unemployment. The total amount of money available for distribution nationally rose automatically with incremental increases in the unemployment rate above 6 percent. These grants were supposed to help city and state governments avoid cutting back the size of their work forces because of budgetary shortages and thus avoid further depressing the economy and raising the unemployment rate. The program would automatically terminate if in any quarter the national unemployment rate fell to 6 percent or below, and no grants could be made to any local government or state whose own unemployment rate was not at least 4.5 percent.

President Carter requested from Congress an additional $925 million for the remaining two quarters of fiscal 1977 (for a total of $2.175 billion) and proposed a maximum funding level of $2.25 billion a year for fiscal 1978 through fiscal 1982. In his fiscal 1978 budget, President Ford had asked for no funds at all to continue the countercyclical assistance program beyond fiscal 1977.

Public service jobs actually consisted of two formula-based grant programs, one authorized in 1973 as Title II of the Comprehensive Employment and Training Act (CETA) and the other authorized in 1974 as a new Title VI of the same act. Title II provided grants to local governments with unemployment rates of 6.5 percent or more for the purpose of funding new public service jobs on their payrolls. The public service jobs funds would directly reduce unemployment by providing positions for the unemployed and presumably would also help city governments improve their services by employing more workers. The jobs were to be filled by persons who had been unemployed at least thirty days. As originally enacted in 1974, Title VI also provided grants to local governments—larger ones than under Title II—for funding public service jobs for persons unemployed for more than fifteen days. Title VI was reauthorized and expanded in 1976, but very much stricter eligibility rules were added. All new jobs from the expansion of the program and half of any existing jobs that had become vacant had to be filled by persons who had low incomes and had been unemployed at least fifteen *weeks* or were on welfare. In addition, the 1976 amendments directed that new jobs be created in "community employment projects" whose duration could not exceed twelve months, as opposed to permanent jobs in regular city agencies. In fiscal 1976 about 310,000 jobs were being funded by CETA, 50,000 under Title II, and 260,000 under Title VI. Since enactment of the expanded Title VI had come at the end of the 1976 session of Congress, no new funds had been appropriated for fiscal 1977, but a continuing resolution was passed to permit continuation of spending in 1977 at the 1976 level.

President Carter asked Congress for an additional $919 million in supplemental appropriations for fiscal 1977 in order to raise the total number of CETA jobs to 600,000 from 310,000, for a one-year extension of CETA through fiscal 1978 (it was due to expire on September 30, 1977), and for $5.9 billion to fund an overall 725,000 jobs in that fiscal year. President Ford in his fiscal 1978 budget had requested $2.384 billion in supplemental appropriations to continue funding Title VI at its ongoing 260,000-job 1976 level through the end of fiscal 1977 and announced his intent to phase out the Title VI program completely by the end of fiscal 1978. He did however ask for $400 million to continue to fund 50,000 jobs through fiscal 1978 under the Title II program.

Community development block grants to cities, counties, and other local governments were authorized on a formula basis by the Housing and Community Development Act (HCDA) of 1974. These block grants replaced previous separate categorical project grants for urban renewal, model cities, neighborhood facilities, and similar programs intended to eliminate slums and rehabilitate deteriorating neighborhoods. The level of funding for fiscal 1977 was $3.24 billion. The Carter administration asked for a three-year extension of HCDA with an authorization of $4 billion in fiscal 1978, $4.15 billion for fiscal 1979, and $4.3 billion for fiscal 1980. The administration also proposed that there be added to the act an alternate allocation formula that would tend to favor the older, larger cities of the Northeast and Midwest, and that $400 million of the overall authorization be set aside for nonformula, discretionary, project-type "action grants" reserved for "distressed cities."

President Ford had asked for $3.5 billion for community development block grants in his fiscal 1978 budget. He had also called for a three-year extension of HCDA and for an alternative formula along the lines of the Carter administration proposal, but not for its special "action grants."

The Congressional Response

The overall congressional response to the Carter administration's urban proposals was clearly favorable. Not only did Congress approve the supplemental appropriations that President Carter had requested for fiscal 1977 to expand public works jobs and public service jobs, but it also appropriated in the same bill the additional amounts requested for fiscal 1978 so that the entire two-year increase could be available for commitment and/or spending in fiscal 1977; it adopted the increased level of funding for countercyclical assistance grants but extended the program's authorization only for a year instead of for five years as President Carter had requested; it extended for three years and increased the level of funding for community development block grants and added an alternate allocation formula more favorable to the larger and older cities of the Northeast and Midwest and a provision for action grants to distressed cities, as requested by the Carter administration; and it extended the authorization for the public works jobs and for the public service jobs programs (at spending levels accommodating the Carter requests) for a year through fiscal 1978.

Four kinds of voting patterns emerged from the eighteen roll-call votes in the House and the seventeen roll-call votes in the

Senate relating to the Carter urban proposals: bipartisan votes, in which majorities of Republicans, northern Democrats, and southern Democrats voted on the same side; party votes, in which majorities of Republicans voted in opposition to combined majorities of northern Democrats and majorities of southern Democrats; conservative versus liberal coalition votes, in which majorities of Republicans and majorities of southern Democrats joined to vote against majorities of northern Democrats; and northern versus southern coalition votes, in which majorities of Republicans and majorities of northern Democrats voted against majorities of southern Democrats.[12]

Bipartisan Votes

Four of the eighteen votes in the House and six of the seventeen in the Senate were bipartisan. All four bipartisan votes in the House were prourban,[13] supporting

- final passage of the HCDA (CQ House Vote 203);[14]
- approval of the special rule allowing the fiscal 1977 stimulus supplemental appropriations bill to be debated with a waiver of points of order (CQ H 60);[15]
- approval of the conference report on the public works jobs authorization act (CQ H 65);
- approval of the conference report on the fiscal 1977 stimulus supplemental appropriations (CQ H 171).

Five of the six bipartisan votes in the Senate were also prourban and supported

- final passage of the HCDA (CQ Senate Vote 177);
- final passage of the public works jobs authorization act (CQ S 48);
- killing of an amendment to the public works jobs bill to require 10 percent matching funds from local and state government recipients toward the cost of the projects (thus making participation in the program more onerous and reducing its scope (CQ S 47);
- final passage of the 1977 stimulus supplemental appropriations package (CQ S 130).

On one vote, however, majorities of both parties took the antiurban position by adopting an amendment raising the minimum public works grants guaranteed to every state, the District of Columbia, and the trust territories (thus marginally reducing the amount of funds left for the states with the largest, neediest cities but also slightly increasing the incentives for senators from non-urban and/or low-unemployment states to support the bill) (CQ S 43).

What almost all of these bipartisan votes had in common is that they were on final passage or adoptions of conference reports where earlier votes or amendments had demonstrated the bill was certain to pass. They also demonstrated that while majorities of Republicans typically voted to keep urban spending programs as low and restricted as possible, when the choice was between having or not having a community development program or a public works program or additional appropriations for economic stimulus, a majority even of Republicans voted yes. There were some real diehards, however, so that even in these bipartisan votes on final passage and conference reports an average of 39 percent of the Republicans in the House and 32 percent in the Senate voted no, apparently as a symbolic protest to show they preferred no program at all.

Party Votes

Nine of the eighteen votes in the House and four in the Senate were party votes. On all these votes, Democratic majorities took the prourban position and prevailed. Specifically, in the House, majorities of northern Democrats and majorities of southern Democrats combined to defeat majorities of Republicans and

- kill an amendment to the countercyclical assistance program formula to emphasize state and local tax effort rather than unemployment rates (CQ H 211);
- enact an extension and expansion of the countercyclical assistance program (CQ H 212);
- enact an extension and expansion of the public works jobs program (CQ H 24);
- kill amendments to the fiscal 1977 (revised) budget resolution[16] and to the stimulus supplemental appropriations act that would have reduced or restricted spending on various of the urban programs (CQ H 19, 62);

- finally pass those budget resolutions and the appropriations act (CQ H 20, 35, 63);
- approve the conference report on the countercyclical assistance program (CQ H 218).

The Republican opposition was most extreme on the spending increases in the budget resolutions and the appropriations bill and least extreme on the public works jobs and the countercyclical assistance authorization acts. In five of these party votes, majorities of *eastern* Republicans voted with the Democrats.

On the four votes in the Senate, majorities of northern and southern Democrats joined to

- defeat an amendment to the fiscal 1978 budget resolution reducing the funding for public service jobs and approve an amendment increasing spending for community development programs (CQ S 135, 132);
- adopt a budget resolution with new fiscal 1977 (upward-spiraling) spending targets (CQ S 38);
- adopt the countercyclical assistance authorization act (CQ S 127).

Actually, on the fiscal 1977 budget resolution and on the countercyclical assistance act, Republicans were exactly evenly divided, but since they did not provide a majority for the pro-urban position, while the northern and southern Democrats did, the votes were classified as party votes. On all five of these party votes, majorities of eastern Republican senators voted with the Democrats instead of with the other Republicans.

With one minor exception, the party votes were essentially on whether to have programs that were more controversial than those passed by bipartisan majorities and what various spending levels should be. If politics is basically about "who gets what, when, how,"[17] these votes were on the kind and size of the "what" there would be for the various "whos" to try to "get."

Conservative versus Liberal Coalition Votes

Four of the eighteen votes in the House and six of the seventeen in the Senate were conservative versus liberal coalition votes. In the House, majorities of southern Democrats successfully joined majorities of Republicans three times to defeat northern Democratic majorities and impose an antiurban outcome by

- fixing the formula for public works jobs (two votes) in such a way as not to take into account rates of unemployment and hence to reduce the proportion of funds that would go to the large, hardship cities (CQ H 22, 23);
- requiring that 25 percent of the HCDA action grants be reserved for cities under 50,000 in population that were not central cities of metropolitan areas (CQ H 201).

On one occasion, this conservative coalition was unsuccessful, being outvoted by the northern Democrats in its antiurban attempt to try to lower the spending ceiling for countercyclical assistance (CQ H 61). In two of the conservative coalition's victories, majorities of eastern Republicans voted with the northern Democrats. Three of the four conservative versus liberal coalition votes in the House were among the most closely contested of the eighteen votes cast.

In the Senate, a majority of southern Democrats joined a majority of Republicans to outvote a majority of northern Democrats only once, successfully imposing an antiurban outcome by reducing the funds authorized for federally assisted housing in the extension of HCDA (CQ S 171). The conservative coalition did, however, try five more times to impose antiurban outcomes, but failed to

- defeat an amendment to the fiscal 1978 budget resolution raising spending for low-income housing (CQ S 133);
- defeat the preliminary fiscal 1978 budget resolution that provided for increased spending on the different urban programs (CQ S 137);
- cut funds for public service jobs from the fiscal 1977 stimulus supplemental appropriations (CQ S 129);
- extend eligibility for the HCDA action grants from distressed cities to all cities with distressed areas (CQ S 175);
- eliminate application of the new, alternate HCDA formula to cities under 50,000 (CQ S 174).

Five of these six votes in the Senate were among the most closely contested of the seventeen urban votes cast. In each of the conservative versus liberal coalition votes, majorities of the eastern Republican senators voted with majorities of the northern Democrats rather than with the other Republicans. The last vote, on the HCDA formula, was actually also a "snowbelt" versus "sunbelt" coalition vote, as not only a 90-percent majority of the eastern Republican senators but also a 100-percent majority of the midwestern Republicans joined a 79-percent majority of eastern Democrats and a 100-percent majority of midwestern Democrats to outvote a combined 94-percent majority of southern Democrats, 56-percent majority of western Democrats, 90-percent majority of southern Republicans, and 92-percent majority of western Republicans.

While some of the conservative versus liberal coalition votes were, like some party votes, on spending levels—the size of the "what"—the most important conservative versus liberal coalition votes were on the issue of which "whos" were going to "get" how large a share of it.

Northern versus Southern Coalition Votes

One vote each in the House and Senate was a northern versus southern coalition vote. This unusual pattern found majorities of Republicans and majorities of northern Democrats voting together against majorities of southern Democrats. Such a cleavage had previously appeared in the 1960s over major civil rights legislation promoted by the northern Democrats, supported by the Republicans, and opposed by the southern Democrats, but it was not a cleavage that had appeared on urban aid votes.

The House vote was on an amendment to delete from the bill extending HCDA a new, alternate formula that had been added for allocation of community development block grants. The original formula enacted in 1974 was based on the size of a city's population, its amount of overcrowded housing, and its percentage of poor (this last factor weighted twice). A number of studies conducted by the Brookings Institution, the Department of Housing and Urban Development, and others showed that this formula tended to favor the newer and still-growing cities of the western and southern sunbelt at the expense of the older cities of the Northeast and Midwest whose populations were declining and whose fiscal problems were the most acute.

The alternate formula was based on the amount of older, pre-

1940 housing (weighted 50 percent), poverty (weighted 30 percent), and population growth lag, that is, the degree to which a city's population growth rate between 1960 and 1973 was less than the average population growth rate for all central cities of metropolitan areas (weighted 20 percent). If the alternate formula did not remain in the bill, among the cities that would have the size of their grants reduced beginning in fiscal 1978, as the "hold harmless" provisions which had been guaranteeing them at least the average of the payments they had received from the categorical programs in the 1968–1972 base period began their three-year phaseout, were Boston, Detroit, Cincinnati, Cleveland, Minneapolis, St. Louis, Kansas City, New York, and Washington, D.C. Washington, D.C., for example, faced a cut of some 61 percent from $40.9 million to $15.8 million; Philadelphia's grant would drop by 50 percent, from $60.8 million to $30.1 million. Among the large cities that would gain funds by defeat of the alternate formula were Dallas, Memphis, and Houston. Dallas had already profited more than 400 percent by the existing formula, from $2.6 million under the nonformula categorical grants to $13.3 million, and Memphis had gained 121 percent, from $6 million to $13.3 million.[18]

The amendment to delete the alternate formula failed in a vote of 149–261 (CQ H 199). An overwhelming majority of 82 percent of the southern Democrats took the antiurban position and backed the amendment, while 83 percent of the northern Democrats and 66 percent of the Republicans voted against it. A more dramatic split, however, was the snowbelt versus sunbelt sectional one: in the twelve eastern states (Maine, New Hampshire, Vermont, Massachusetts, Connecticut, Rhode Island, New York, New Jersey, Pennsylvania, Maryland, Delaware, and West Virginia) the vote was 110 to 1, and in the twelve midwestern states (Illinois, Indiana, Michigan, Ohio, Wisconsin, Iowa, Kansas, Minnesota, Nebraska, Missouri, North Dakota, and South Dakota) it was 108 to 7 against the amendment, signifying that from these two regions of the country there was almost unanimous opposition despite party and urban, suburban, or rural type of constituency. On the other hand, in the twenty-six southern and western states, a majority of which (Arizona, California, Florida, Georgia, Alabama, Arkansas, Louisiana, Mississippi, Oklahoma, Texas, New Mexico, Tennessee, Kentucky) enjoyed the presence of newer, growing cities, the vote was 141 to 43 in favor of deleting the alternate formula.

The vote in the Senate that generated a north versus south sectional split was also over an allocation formula—the formula for distributing funds under the public works jobs program. As reported by the Senate Environment and Public Works Committee, the formula, which was supported by the Carter administration, would have distributed 65 percent of the program funds among local and state governments essentially according to the absolute number of unemployed in each state. It would have reserved distribution of the remaining 35 percent of the funds, however, for the local and state governments of states whose unemployment rate exceeded 6.5 percent. Once again the 35 percent "set aside" for states with the highest unemployment rates would primarily favor cities of the Northeast and Midwest where not only were there large absolute numbers of unemployed but the rate of unemployment was also disproportionately high.

The amendment, which in effect would have eliminated the 35 percent set-aside for states with unemployment rates above 6.5 percent and distributed all the funds on the basis of the absolute number of unemployed, was defeated 56 to 32 (CQ S 46). A majority of 53 percent of the southern Democrats took the anti-urban position and supported the amendment, while 72 percent of the northern Democrats and 63 percent of the Republicans opposed it. Nineteen of the snowbelt's twenty-three eastern senators, including all sixteen from the six New England states, New York, and New Jersey (ten of whom were Democrats and six Republicans), voted against the amendment. Unlike the vote on the CDA alternate formula in the House, however, only a bare 12-to-11 majority of the snowbelt's midwestern senators voted against the amendment, and they were joined by an overwhelming 17-to-3 majority of the sunbelt's western senators.

Both these sectional coalition votes on allocation formulas—like some of the conservative versus liberal coalition votes—disposed of the critically serious issue of which "whos" were to "get" how much of the "what" available.

Voting Splits and Party Majorities

An examination of the position of party majorities on the urban votes just analyzed shows that in the House a majority of all Democratic members who voted favored the prourban position in sixteen (or 89 percent) of the eighteen votes. By contrast, a majority of the voting Republicans took the prourban position on only five (or 28 percent) of the votes. Similarly, in the Senate a majority of the Democrats voted the prourban position on sixteen (or 94 percent) of the seventeen votes, while Republican majorities supported the prourban position on only six (or 35 percent) of the votes. Thus the 1977 urban votes continued the pattern in which the Democrats were the prourban and the Republicans the antiurban party in Congress.

Bases of Urban Support, and Opposition: Party versus Constituency and Region

In order to identify further patterns of congressional support for and opposition to urban programs, all representatives and senators were classified, in addition to party, according to type of constituency[19] and region and were assigned "urban support scores" based on the percentage of votes on which they took the prourban position. The most significant scores are summarized graphically in figures 1 and 2.

An examination of the House scores shows the following:

- With respect to party, Democrats were strikingly more prourban (with an average urban support score of 78 percent) than Republicans (36 percent), and this held true in every type of constituency and every region.
- With respect to type of constituency, urban representatives (76 percent) were more prourban than suburban ones (64 percent), who in turn were more prourban than rural ones (53 percent). These interconstituency differences were much smaller than the interparty ones, so that the least prourban Democrats, those from rural constituencies, had an average urban support score almost twice as high (66 versus 35 percent) as the most prourban Republicans, those from urban districts.
- With respect to region, eastern and western representatives (81 and

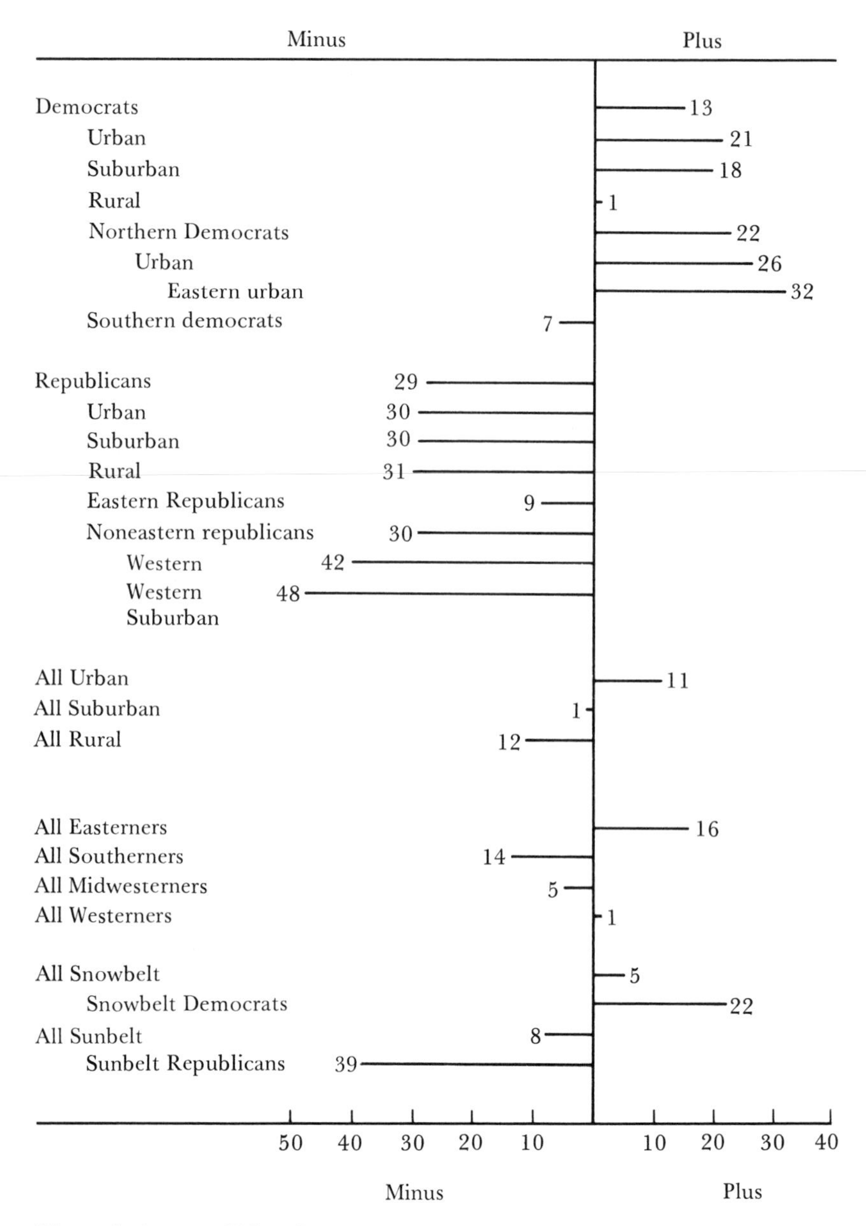

Figure 1. Average Urban Support Scores by Party, Constituency, and Region: House of Representatives (Deviations from chamber urban support score of 65 percent)

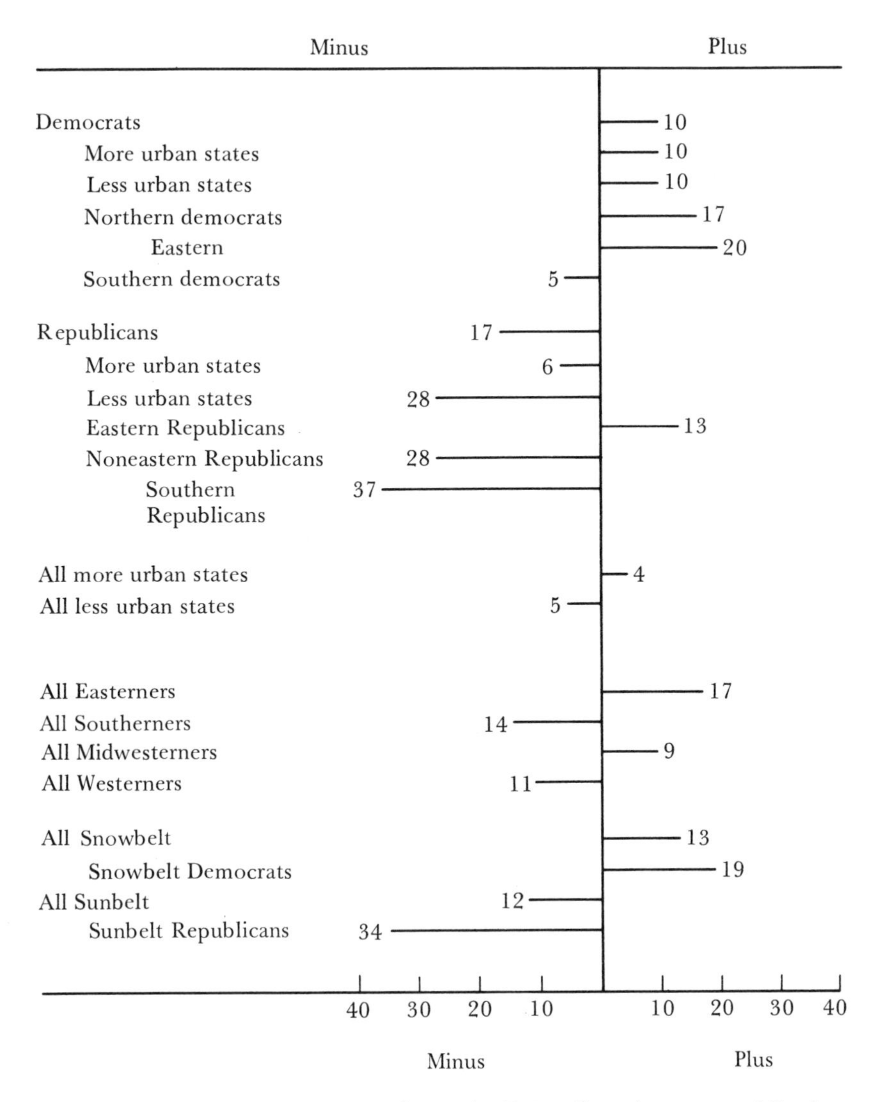

Figure 2. Average Urban Support Scores by Party, Constituency, and Region: Senate (Deviations from chamber urban support score of 68 percent)

66 percent) were more prourban than midwestern and southern ones (60 and 51 percent). The most important regional patterns were, however, those within each party: southern Democrats were significantly less prourban than northern Democrats (58 versus 87 percent), and this held whatever the character of their constituency; eastern Republicans were significantly more prourban than noneastern Republicans (56 versus 30 percent), again whatever the character of their constituency. Indeed, the scores of the southern Democrats and of the eastern Republicans were each closer to those of the opposite party than to the scores of the rest of their party colleagues.

- In terms of party, constituency, and region combined, the most prourban representatives were the northern Democrats (87 percent), within that group, the urban northern Democrats (91 percent), and within that group, the eastern urban Democrats (97 percent). The least prourban representatives were the noneastern Republicans (56 percent), within that group, the western Republicans (23 percent), and within that group, the suburban western Republicans (17 percent).
- In terms of a snowbelt versus sunbelt distinction, the snowbelt representatives were somewhat more prourban than the sunbelt representatives (70 versus 57 percent), but this difference was less than one-third the interparty one between the Democrats and Republicans and thus relatively small. When, however, party was added, the snowbelt Democrats became very much more prourban than the sunbelt Republicans (87 versus 26 percent), with the difference (61 points) being larger than any other interparty, interregional, or interparty and interregional one combined.

Study of the Senate scores shows the following:

- With respect to party, the Democratic senators were significantly more prourban than the Republicans (78 versus 51 percent), and this was true both in the states with or without cities of 250,000 in population and in every region.
- With respect to character of the statewide constituency, senators from the "more urban" states had higher scores than those from the "less urban" states (72 versus 63 percent) but this difference was accounted for exclusively by the Republicans. Democratic senators from the "more" and "less" urban states had the same

scores, and these were higher than those of either group of Republican senators.

- With respect to region, senators from the East and Midwest (85 and 77 percent) were more prourban than those from the West and South (57 and 54 percent), but as in the House, these differences were not as important as the interregional differences within the two parties: southern Democratic senators were significantly less prourban than northern Democratic ones (63 versus 85 percent), being about twice as close to the Republican senators as to their northern Democratic party colleagues; eastern Republican senators were very much more prourban than noneastern ones (81 versus 30 percent). *Indeed, the eastern Republican senators were even slightly more prourban than the Democratic senators as a whole and some ten times closer to the northern Democrats than to the noneastern Republicans.*
- In terms of combined party and regional groups, the eastern Democrats (88 percent) were the most prourban senators and the southern Republicans (31 percent) the least.
- In terms of a snowbelt versus sunbelt regional distinction, the snowbelt senators had significantly higher urban support scores than the sunbelt senators (81 versus 56 percent), a difference almost as large as that between Democrats and Republicans. When party was added, the snowbelt Democrats became, as in the House, very much more prourban than the sunbelt Republicans (87 versus 34 percent), a difference (53 points) larger than any other interparty, interregional, or combined interparty and interregional one.[20]

Finally, two important differences emerged from a comparison of urban support scores in the House and Senate. First, in the House party was clearly more significant than region in accounting for urban support, and either of those two factors alone was more significant than nature of the constituency, whereas in the Senate, party and region were about equally important, though again each was more important than the urban character of the state. Second, while the Democrats delivered the same amount of support in both the House and the Senate (78 versus 78 percent), Republicans were closer to the Democrats and more supportive of urban programs in the Senate than in the House (51 versus 36 percent).

Accounting for Differences in Urban Support

Why the Democratic members of Congress were more prourban than the Republican members, and most strikingly in the House, is a question that cannot be answered definitively here. One aspect of the explanation is that since Woodrow Wilson's administration the leading Democratic national officeholders, in the presidency and in Congress, have been ideologically committed to using the power and funds of the federal government to alleviate widely felt problems. This was so whether the problems were experienced by farmers, businessmen, union laborers, or, more currently, the unemployed, urban dwellers, and city governments. The dominant Republican ideological position for the most part has been that social and economic problems should be dealt with not by the federal government but by the states or the "marketplace," that is, private efforts.

In addition, most Republicans have also been committed to holding down spending by the federal government (especially when the federal government is running sizable deficits and additional spending may further fuel inflation), and federally aided urban programs are usually expensive. Those who select themselves as candidates for the congressional nominations of a particular party, Republican or Democratic, are likely to be people who for the most part find that party's broad ideological image or policy orientation appealing. If elected, they tend to carry to Congress ideological or policy outlooks that motivate them to support their party's traditional positions.

Another part of the explanation for the prourban and antiurban stances of Democrats and Republicans in Congress is that members of the two parties have tended to come from different kinds of constituencies. Since the 1930s the main bulk of at least northern Democratic strength in the House and Senate has been from urban districts and the most urbanized states. The main bulk of Republican strength, on the other hand, has been from more rural districts and states where urban problems are not felt at firsthand and where anti-big-city feelings have traditionally been strong. In 1977 northern Democrats held 86 percent of the seventy-seven northern urban House seats, while Republicans held 51 percent of the northern rural seats. For a substantial bulk of northern Democratic and of Republican members of Congress, therefore, ideological inclinations and the perceived needs of their constituencies neatly coincided to provide mutually reinforcing motivations for prourban and antiurban positions, respectively. It should also be recognized, however, that in 1977 only 30 percent of the northern Democratic House members came from predominantly urban districts, so that the high level of urban support from northern Democrats was no longer, if it ever was, a simple reflection of their constituency characteristics.

The case of the southern Democratic members of Congress is special. From the Reconstruction era after the Civil War to the early 1960s, it was practically impossible for Republican candidates to be elected to the House or Senate from the states of the Old Confederacy. This was the result of a strong tradition of automatic allegiance to the Democratic party among all but a tiny fraction of white southerners. Broadly speaking, that tradition was based on the fact that Republican administrations and Congresses were perceived as being responsible for freeing the slaves and imposing the indignities of northern military occupation on the South in the decades after Appomattox.[21]

Given this overwhelming opposition to anyone running for Congress under the Republican label, any policy differences among aspirants to Congress were fought out not in general elections between party opponents but in the primary election for the Democratic senatorial or congressional nomination, whose victor was virtually guaranteed success in the general election. Accordingly, southern senators and representatives were elected to Congress as Democrats and gave the minimal required support to be counted as nominal members of their party by voting with their northern Democratic colleagues on the organization of the Congress, including the election of presiding officers, floor leaders, and committee chairmen. But most of the time those southern Democratic members of Congress voted on urban legislation the way that persons with their conservative, anti-expansion-of-the-federal-role, anti-federal-spending ideological outlook and from their basically rural and small-town constituencies (in 1977, 42 percent of the southern Democrats still came from rural constituencies and only 20 percent from urban) could be expected to vote—in support of the dominant Republican antiurban position.

The atypically high level of prourban support given by the eastern Republican representatives and senators in part reflects the fact that they tend to have a more liberal ideological outlook toward federal intervention in dealing with serious problems than noneastern Republicans. In the 1976 session of the 94th Congress, for example, all nine of the Republican representatives and all six of the Republican senators who had conservative coalition opposition scores exceeding 50 percent were from the East.[22] The eastern Republican representatives are also heavily concentrated in suburban districts close to the large, older cities that are facing the greatest hardship and thus have varying proportions of constituents who commute to jobs in those cities or want to patronize their specialty shops and cultural facilities. Also, some of those suburban districts contain older suburban municipalities that have themselves begun to feel the effects of poverty, physical deterioration, and budgetary shortages. The eastern senators, of course, have both the older central cities and the close-in suburbs in their statewide constituencies. As the notion has come to prevail that the southern and western sunbelt is profiting at the expense of the troubled East and Midwest, the eastern Republicans' liberal ideology and the needs of their constituencies combine to motivate them strongly to deviate from the typical Republican position and give greater support to urban legislation.

The very low urban support scores provided by the western Republicans as compared even to other Republicans is difficult to account for. In terms of ideology (as measured by 1976 conservative coalition opposition scores), western Republicans were not significantly more conservative than the rest of the noneastern Republicans. The western Republicans may, however, have perceived themselves as special targets of the emerging Northeast-Midwest snow-belt coalition's attempts to rewrite urban aid formulas to benefit those two regions. Accordingly, the western Republicans, who simply as Republicans were already relatively antiurban in ideological inclination, may have suffered a backlash and overreacted in defense of both a preferred ideology and a constituency status quo favorable to their interests.

Outcomes and Prospects

Looking to the future, what can the outcomes of the 1977 session of the Carter Congress tell us about the prospects for any sharply increased federal aid to hardship cities?

An optimistic evaluation would point out that in 1977 Congress extended four important grant programs that sent payments directly to cities, increased their previous levels of authorization and funding, added a new alternate allocation formula to the HCDA that favored hardship cities, and with only two exceptions defeated attempts during floor consideration to change proposed allocation formulas so as to increase their "spread" and thus make them less favorable to hardship cities. The conclusion of this optimistic evaluation would be that prospects for future increases in urban aid are bright.

There is also room for a pessimistic evaluation, however, which can lead to different conclusions. First, the public works jobs, countercyclical assistance, and public service jobs expansions were not sold as procity programs although it was clear that city governments would be recipients of a large share of the grant payments. These programs were promoted, especially by the Carter administration but also in Congress, as means of stimulating what almost everyone conceded was a badly recessionary economy and of reducing what everyone conceded was an excessively high rate of unemployment. Many of the votes identified in this essay as pro-urban may have been cast because members of Congress saw those votes also as pro-strengthening the economy, a consensual goal.

Second, the amounts of new money authorized by the programs were small, both in the eyes of city officials and other spokesmen for the poor and minorities and in relation to total federal outlays.[23] Third, the fact that only a few "more spread" votes carried can also be seen as less a reflection of the voting strength of the pro-hardship city forces in Congress than a recognition that the formulas were already providing for very broad eligibility and spread. Even the addition of the alternate HCDA formula was not expected to raise the size of grants that hardship cities had been receiving under the program. The purpose of the alternate formula was simply to keep those cities from beginning to suffer very large cuts from the previous level of their grants as the "hold harmless" provisions were phased out at the end of fiscal 1977.

The conclusions of this more pessimistic evaluation would be that even under very favorable political conditions, Congress and the Carter administration did not do very much to help hardship cities deal with their serious budgetary, service-delivery, and poverty- and slum-related problems. The prospects for increased urban aid under what might become less favorable conditions in the next few years would thus be dim. Which is the more correct evaluation remains to be seen, but discussion of the key fiscal and political considerations that will obviously bear on the future course of federal aid to hardship cities may give a better sense of what that course is likely to be.

Fiscal Considerations

The most crucial fiscal consideration influencing the prospects for increased urban aid will be the state of the national economy. As long as the economy remains as recessionary and with as high a level of unemployment as in fiscal 1977 and 1978, there will be no budget margins or fiscal dividends (that is, increases in revenues in excess of those needed to meet the cost of existing program commitments) that can be "painlessly" diverted to new or expanded urban programs. Any new funding would thus have to come at the expense of nonurban programs or by increasing the federal deficit from what was already at $45 billion in fiscal 1977 the third largest in peacetime history, exceeded only by the deficits in fiscal 1975 and 1976. Also, even if the deficit began to drop with any sharp strengthening of the economy, significant increases in spending for urban aid programs would interfere with the Carter administration's campaign commitment to eliminate the deficit completely and actually balance the budget by fiscal 1981.

Moreover, under the new congressional budgetary process, Congress can no longer easily disregard a president's concern for a balanced budget and appropriate large additional funds for urban and other programs that it may favor. Before the enactment of the Congressional Budget and Impoundment Control Act of 1974, Congress could simply add appropriations and not have to be explicitly concerned about the resulting size of any deficit. Now Congress must enact preliminary and final budget resolutions for each fiscal year which show total projected spending and how it is allocated by broad program area, total anticipated revenues, and the gap—deficit or surplus—between expenditures and revenues. Consequently, in order to increase spending for urban programs over and above that proposed by the president, Congress must make a reduction in spending somewhere else, provide for more revenue, or explicitly declare a larger deficit. If it does the last, Congress joins the president in bearing responsibility for the possible inflationary consequences.

Of course, if the economy again reaches a prosperous, full-employment level, some measure of "free" budget margins or fiscal dividends may reappear. The Brookings Institution analysis of the fiscal 1978 budget and of the Carter administration's economic and budgetary commitments projected a $10 to $26 billion budget margin for new initiatives by 1981.[24] But even if the assumptions on which this projection was based—the most important being achieving a full-employment economy and an inflation rate not exceeding 5 percent—held true, there certainly would be claims from the military, new energy research and development programs, national health insurance, and a variety of other existing or new non-urban programs competing with city governments for any margin of uncommitted revenues. Undoubtedly there would also be demands for further general tax reductions as inflation forced people to pay taxes at steadily higher effective rates.

The funds needed for substantially improved urban aid are extensive not only because of the large needs of hardship cities, but also because since the Nixon-Ford administration the trend in the design of urban aid has been away from categorical-project grants and toward a reliance on formula grants with broad eligibility.[25] This trend has made it very expensive to deliver a particular amount of dollars to the older, hardship cities. For under formula grants, a very large number of local governments is eligible or "entitled" to a share of the funds appropriated for a program. (General revenue sharing makes all of them eligible.) Thus to increase aid to a few dozen large, hardship cities requires sufficient funding to "spread" to hundreds or thousands of other jurisdictions the additional dollars to which the formula automatically entitles them.

By contrast, funding authorized under the pre-Nixon categorical-project grants did not have to be so widely spread but could be targeted primarily to the smaller number of jurisdictions that demonstrated the greatest need. Project grants also gave advantages to the superior "grantsmanship" abilities of many large cities, which had sizable, experienced staffs to prepare grant applications, extensive contacts in the urban-oriented Washington departments, and a track record of successfully implementing projects in the past.

Of course, additional funds could be targeted to the hardship cities even without increasing total spending, by changing entitlement formulas to weight more heavily the adverse factors found disproportionately in those cities or by returning to project grants. But it will obviously be much more difficult for Congress to narrow the eligibility for formula grants or to shift from formula grants to project grants than it was to shift from project grants to formula grants, because narrowing eligibility would reduce the number of constituencies to which benefits would flow, whereas the shift from project to formula grants expanded it. Admittedly, members of Congress were in the past willing to authorize and appropriate funds for urban project grants on the basis of need, even if they thought their own constituencies or states would get little direct aid. But once the constituencies of large numbers of members already benefit as a matter of legal entitlement, members of Congress will typically refuse to vote for a proposal to reduce their constituencies' share or eliminate it. A "hold harmless" provision for all existing beneficiaries (that is, a guarantee not to get fewer dollars in the future than they were getting in the past) thus becomes a key prerequisite for changing the formula or adding project grants so as to direct more funds to hardship cities.

One ploy for targeting more money to hardship cities that may have a chance of succeeding is to maintain or even slightly increase funds for the existing formula beneficiaries so that no one loses dollars—that is, to hold everyone "harmless"—but also to add funds for new discretionary, categorical project grants. The Carter administration took this tack by proposing in the extension of HCDA not only a slight increase for the regular block grants but also the setting aside of an additional $400 million for action grants to economically distressed cities. But even with the sweetener of increased funding for the regular block grants, the $400 million for action grants proved especially vulnerable. First, by an overwhelming 2 to 1 roll-call vote in the House and by voice vote in the Senate, 25 percent of the $400 million was reserved for suburban and rural cities below 50,000 in population; second, when the Senate Banking, Housing, and Urban Affairs Committee decided to add still another alternate formula for regular HCDA block grants, it provided that the extra funds needed for recipients choosing to take their grants under it would come out of the $400 million for action grants, rather than out of the shares of those staying on the old or first alternate formula. The committee estimated that after these withdrawals, only $288 million would be left for action grants in fiscal 1978, $202 million in fiscal 1979, and $125 million in fiscal 1980.

Political Considerations

The most important political consideration for the prospects of increased urban aid is whether future Congresses can continue to have the heavy Democratic majorities of the 95th Congress and whether the typical Democratic representative and senator will remain as prourban as in the past. The very great importance of the size of the Democratic majorities in the 95th Congress must be stressed: in the House during most of 1977,[26] there were 292 Democrats, of whom 201 were from outside the South and 91 were southerners, and there were 143 Republicans. This meant that the number of northern Democrats alone was not much smaller than the number of Republicans and southern Democrats combined—the maximum voting strength of the antiurban, conservative coalition. This distribution of seats also meant that whenever the northern Democrats stayed solid and picked up even a 20-percent minority of the southern Democrats or a 15-percent minority of Republicans, the northern Democratic, typically prourban position would prevail. Roughly the same situation obtained in the Senate.

Yet for the Democrats to control as large a number of seats in Congress as they did in 1977 is highly atypical: it happened before in recent history only between 1933 and 1938 in the Roosevelt administration, between 1965 and 1966 in the Johnson administration, and in the 94th Congress (1975-76) when, however, President Ford's power to veto frequently raised to two-thirds the majorities required to pass prourban programs. A much more typical distribution of seats in Congress since World War II was represented in the 87th Congress, which was elected with President Kennedy in 1960 and was in session in 1961 and 1962. During most of the 87th Congress, there were 263 Democrats and 174 Republicans in the House of Representatives, making it appear that the House was safely in the control of the prourban Democratic party. And the Democrats did in fact have nominal control, being able to organize the House and elect members of their party as Speaker and as chairmen of the various committees. However, the appearance of control was deceptive, as only 159 Democrats were "northern" and 104 came from the South. The result was that the total number of 174 Republicans plus 104 southern Democrats greatly outnumbered the 159 northern Democrats, so that working control of the House was usually in the hands of the Republican-southern Democratic antiurban conservative coalition, and almost no prourban legislation was passed.

Because the power of incumbents to get reelected is great,[27] there may not be any sharp drop in the number of Democrats elected to the next few Congresses. But as the stigma of Watergate and the Nixon administration fades (and especially if the Carter administration or Democratic members of Congress produce important scandals of their own), the number of Democrats in Congress will probably decrease and move somewhat closer to the post-World War II norm, thus weakening the voting strength of the prourban forces.

The second fundamental political consideration for the prospects of increased urban aid for hardship cities is that in the past two decades a twofold population trend has weakened the political strength of the urban East and Midwest. Within metropolitan areas, large cities, and especially the older cities of the East and Midwest, have been losing population to their suburbs. Within the nation, the East and Midwest have been losing population to the South and West.

It is important to recognize that despite much talk of the United States being an "urban" nation, in 1975 only 29 percent of its population lived in central cities of 50,000 and above and only

20 percent in the really large cities of 250,000 or more. On the other hand, 39 percent of the population lived in "outside central city" or suburban areas.[28] Thus the nation is urban only if that is defined as meaning "metropolitan-area-living" (29 percent in central cities plus 39 percent in the suburbs equals 68 percent) but not in the sense of being "large-city-living."

The decline in the proportion of the population living in large cities results in a steadily decreasing number of members in the House of Representatives who represent urban districts. In the 95th Congress, only 103 (or 24 percent) of the districts were predominately urban, while 138 were predominately suburban, 121 rural, and 73 mixed. In terms of city size, of those 103 urban districts, only 90 included cities of 250,000 or more within their boundaries, either in whole or in part. Even among the seats held by northern Democrats, those that were predominately suburban (70) slightly exceeded the number that were predominately urban (66), and there were also 35 northern Democratic constituencies that were predominately rural.

In the Carter Congress the suburban northern Democrats were almost as supportive of urban positions (88 percent) as the urban northern Democrats (91 percent), and even the rural northern Democrats' votes were substantially prourban (78 percent). How long northern Democratic members from suburban and rural constituencies will continue to share, by and large, the policy outlook of the Democratic central-city representatives while these latter are ceasing to be the dominant contingent in the northern Democratic membership is an open question. But it is difficult to conceive of a rise in the Democratic suburban and rural level of pro-urban support, so the probability is that the level will drop.

The decline in the proportion of the population living in the Northeast and Midwest will result in a decreasing number of representatives with districts from those regions. A major *New York Times* study projected that when Congress is reapportioned after the 1980 census, the states in the East and Midwest will lose, and those in the South and West will gain, 15 seats. Likely losers are New York (4 seats), New Jersey (1 seat), Ohio (2 seats), Michigan (1 seat), Illinois (2 seats), Pennsylvania (2 seats), Indiana (1 seat), and Missouri (1 seat). The projected gainers include Florida (5 seats), Texas (2 seats), New Mexico (1 seat), Arizona (1 seat),

Colorado (1 seat), Utah (1 seat), Oregon (1 seat), Tennessee (1 seat), North Carolina (1 seat), Arkansas (1 seat). Within states the major losers are likely to be districts in St. Louis, Chicago, Detroit, Pittsburgh, Philadelphia, Jersey City, Newark, and New York City. The gainers would be in areas close to or including Phoenix, Albuquerque, Denver, Houston, Little Rock, Orlando, and Tampa.[29] In short, the loss of seats would be in the regions (the East and Midwest) that gave a relatively high level of support to urban programs, and the gains in those regions (the West and South) where except for the western Democrats there have been only low levels of urban support.

How long western Democrats will continue to provide high levels of urban support is a crucially important question. In 1977 western Democrats both in the House and the Senate voted only slightly less prourban than the eastern Democrats, the most pro-urban of all members of Congress. Yet western *Republicans* were shown to be the least prourban group in the House and were within five percentage points of being the least prourban group in the Senate, where their antiurban stance was exceeded only by the southern Republicans. If the eastern-midwestern snowbelt coalition continues to organize and engages in "aggressive regionalism,"[30] western Democrats too might start thinking more in terms of regional constituency interests than ideology or party loyalty and thus provide less voting support for urban aid programs and formulas that specially favor the older, larger, hardship cities.

The impact of present population trends on the Senate is more difficult to nail down. Since the Senate is never reapportioned, the size of its regional groups will remain the same. But senators in general, and even Democratic senators from the more urban states, will inevitably have to recognize the increasingly suburban character of their overall constituencies, and politically they may not be able to afford the reputation of being out-and-out champions of big cities and of the disproportionately large concentrations of poor and of blacks who live there. On the other hand, fifty-four senators *do* represent states that have at least one city of 250,000 or more. These senators will not be able to neglect urban interests completely.

Finally, the increasing suburbanization and the westward and southward flow of the population will probably affect the intensity of presidential leadership in favor of increased federal aid to large cities. In a nation where after 1980 fewer electoral votes will be coming from the East and Midwest and where the suburban population will be in a position to outvote its big city residents, presidents will probably not find it electorally profitable to assign their highest policy and budgetary priorities to programs that can be perceived as basically benefiting large cities. Democratic presidents, however, whose traditional followings have included the poor and the black and others who live in large cities, will no doubt find it much harder to ignore their needs than will Republican presidents. President Carter, for example, received almost two-to-one majorities or better in such cities as New York, Boston, Newark, Philadelphia, Cleveland, Chicago, Detroit, Minneapolis, St. Louis, Oakland, and Baltimore. Substantial parts of those majorities came from black voters, who were estimated as having cast 90 percent of their votes for Carter nationally.[31] The large majorities built up in New York City, Philadelphia, Pittsburg, Milwaukee, St. Louis, and Kansas City accounted for Carter's statewide margins of victory in New York, Pennsylvania, Ohio, Wisconsin, and Missouri without which he would not have had the electoral votes to win the presidency. If Carter seeks reelection in 1980, he would as a Democrat need strong support among large-city and black electorates, and it is doubtful that the turnout and the size of his 1976 majorities among these groups would again be forthcoming if his administration did not show itself significantly responsive to urban interests.

Nevertheless, the most probable long-term impact of the decline in the population living in large cities and in the metropolitan areas of the East and Midwest generally is that Congress will not be enacting dramatically large additions to, expansions of, and increases in spending for urban grant programs. Furthermore, those additions, expansions, and increases in spending that Congress does enact will probably "spread" their benefits widely and thus interest the suburbs (and perhaps even poor rural areas) as much or more than large, central cities. Congressional enactment of urban programs, on the other hand, which would target funds narrowly, primarily to improve the fiscal conditions of hardship city governments and the physical and social conditions of the poor—

especially the black, slum-dwelling poor—will be extremely difficult if not altogether impossible.[32]

Notes

I thank my friends and colleagues Peggy Cuciti, Flora Davidson, Mary Ann Epstein, Gerald Finch, Charles Hamilton, Robert McCaughey, Richard Pious, Robert Reischauer, and Kathryn Yatrakis for helpful advice on this essay; Ralph Nunes, Ronald Susser, David Caraley, and Anne Caraley for research assistance; Columbia University's new Center for the Social Sciences for computing facilities and the services of consultants; and the Barnard College Faculty Research Fund for a grant to help defray the cost of research assistance and typing.

1. See Demetrios Caraley, "Congressional Politics and Urban Aid," *Political Science Quarterly* 91 (1976): 19-45.

2. Demetrios Caraley, *City Governments and Urban Problems* (Englewood Cliffs, N.J.: Prentice-Hall, 1977), p. xi.

3. *New York Times*, May 8, 1975.

4. Ibid., Nov. 4, 1976.

5. Ibid., June 14, 1977.

6. Ibid., July 22, 1977.

7. Ibid., July 27, 1977.

8. Ibid., August 30, 1977.

9. Ibid., August 31, 1977.

10. Federal urban grants are allocated on a formula, project, or combined formula and project basis. In a formula grant, funds are allocated according to the extent a recipient meets certain prescribed numerical factors in the formula, such as relative share of the nation's population, or its poor families, or its unemployed. Project grants are allocated in response to applications that request federal funds for particular proposals or projects. Combined formula and project grants are made in response to specific applications, but a formula sets maximum and sometimes minimum limits on the share of total funds that can be allocated to a state and/or its eligible local governments.

11. See the *Federal Register*, December 23, 1976, pp. 56146-56172; US Senate, Committee on Appropriations, *Economic Stimulus Appropriations Act, 1977*, S. Rept. 95-58, 95th Cong., 1st sess. (1977), pp. 20-21.

12. These categories, which are mutually exclusive, are adapted from but not identical to the distinctions made by the Congressional Quarterly Service. See, for example, its *Congressional Roll Call 1976* (Washington, D.C.: Congressional Quarterly Inc., 1977), especially pp. 27, 32, 37. The term "southern Democrats" is used here to refer to those Democrats coming from the South as defined by CQ: the states of the old Confederacy—Alabama, Arkansas, Florida, Georgia, Louisiana, Mississippi, North Carolina, South

Carolina, Tennessee, Texas, and Virginia—plus the two border states of Kentucky and Oklahoma. The East includes the states of Connecticut, Delaware, Maine, Maryland, Massachusetts, New Hampshire, New Jersey, New York, Pennsylvania, Rhode Island, Vermont, and West Virginia; the Midwest, Illinois, Indiana, Iowa, Kansas, Michigan, Minnesota, Missouri, Nebraska, North Dakota, Ohio, South Dakota, and Wisconsin; and the West, Alaska, Arizona, California, Colorado, Hawaii, Idaho, Montana, Nevada, New Mexico, Oregon, Utah, and Washington. "Northern Democrats" refers to all the nonsouthern Democrats, whether they are from the East, Midwest, or West.

13. The prourban position on a vote was considered to be (1) on the question of having or not having an urban program, to have the program; (2) on the question of having higher or lower funding, to have higher funding; and (3) on the question of allocation formulas, to have the formula that would direct most money to the so-called "hardship cities," those larger and older cities primarily in the East and Midwest with the most serious economic and social problems. For one plausible index of city hardship, see Richard P. Nathan and Charles Adams, "Understanding Central City Hardship," *Political Science Quarterly* 91 (1976): 47-62.

14. Fuller explanations of all these votes can be found in the 1977 *Congressional Quarterly Weekly Reports.*

15. This was necessary because the timing of all the actions required on the stimulus package had gotten out of phase, and without this rule a point of order could have been raised against the appropriations bill being considered before the legislation authorizing the increased spending.

16. Under provisions of the Congressional Budget and Impoundment Control Act of 1974, Congress must pass each year a preliminary (in the spring) and a final (in the fall) budget resolution setting a ceiling on overall spending, estimating a floor for revenues, and projecting the likely deficit of surplus. In order to accommodate the Carter urban proposals, Congress in early 1977 had to revise upward the spending ceiling for fiscal 1977 that it had set in its fall 1976 budget resolution and to approve a new preliminary budget resolution with a high enough spending ceiling for fiscal 1978.

17. See Harold Lasswell, *Politics: Who Gets What, When, How* (New York: McGraw-Hill, 1936).

18. *Congressional Quarterly Weekly Report,* March 5, 1977, p. 418.

19. In the House a constituency was classified as "urban," "suburban," or "rural" according to whether a majority of its population lived in a central city of a standard metropolitan area, the "outside central city" portion of a metropolitan area, or outside a metropolitan area. Constituencies where there was neither an urban, suburban, or rural majority were classified as "mixed" and excluded from analysis with respect to the impact of constituency on urban votes. Since in only one state—New York—did a majority of the population live in central cities, Senate constituencies could not be classified in the same way. The character of statewide constituencies was therefore classified as "more urban" if the state had a city whose population was 250,000 or larger and "less urban" if it did not. No other population cut-off for the size of a state's largest city was found to be statistically significant in accounting

for differences in the urban support scores of senators. The urban character of the state was also classified according to the percentage of its population living in central cities, as follows: 0 to 20 percent, "low urban"; 21 to 40 percent, "midurban"; and 41 to 60 percent, "high urban." There was no statistically significant difference in the urban support scores of senators when their states were classified in this fashion.

20. Those interested in statistics should know that the nontechnical analyses presented in this section are supported by formal multiple classification analysis (MCA). In the House an MCA of party, region, and nature of constituency produced adjusted betas of 0.66 for party, 0.38 for region, and 0.14 for constituency, and a multiple R squared of 0.597. When the nature of constituency was measured in the Senate according to whether the state's largest city was less than 250,000 in population or 250,000 and above, the MCA produced adjusted betas of 0.55 for party, 0.60 for region, and 0.32 for constituency, and the multiple R squared was 0.529. When the nature of constituency was measured in the Senate according to the proportion of the statewide population living in central cities, the MCA adjusted betas became 0.51 for party, 0.47 for region, and 0.16 for constituency with a multiple R squared of 0.484. The F ratio for constituency measured in this fashion (0.116) was not statistically significant at the point 0.05 level.

21. See V. O. Key, Jr. *Southern Politics* (New York: Alfred A. Knopf, 1949).

22. See *Congressional Roll Call 1976,* pp. 37-42. A conservative coalition opposition score exceeding 50 percent indicated that on the liberal versus conservative coalition voting splits, the member voted more times with the majority of northern Democrats than with the majority of Republicans and majority of southern Democrats. The 1976 conservative coalition opposition scores were based on 143 votes in the House and 177 votes in the Senate.

23. The added funds (that were not legally precommitted to state governments) over the Ford budget requests for the four programs analyzed, amounted to approximately $3.5 billion for fiscal 1977 and $9.5 billion for fiscal 1978. As a proportion of the outlays projected by the May 1977 congressional budget resolution, these sums constituted 0.9 percent for fiscal 1977 and 2 percent for fiscal 1978.

24. Joseph A. Pechman, ed., *Setting National Priorities: The 1978 Budget* (Washington, D.C.: The Brookings Institution, 1977), p. 366.

25. To my knowledge, Jeffrey Pressman was the first political scientist to analyze in print the implications of the shift from categorical-project grants to formula grants. See his "Political Implications of the New Federalism," in Wallace E. Oates, ed., *Financing the New Federalism* (Baltimore: Johns Hopkins University Press, 1975).

26. "Most of" because through deaths, resignations, and special elections, the number of northern Democrats, southern Democrats, and Republicans changes slightly over the course of a session of Congress.

27. See, for example, Walter Dean Burnham, "Insulation and Responsiveness in Congressional Elections," *Political Science Quarterly* 90 (1975): 411-435.

28. U.S. Bureau of the Census, *Statistical Abstract of the United States: 1977* (Washington, D.C.: Government Printing Office, 1977), p. 16, table 15; p. 22, table 22.

29. *New York Times,* January 23, 1976.

30. See the remarks of the Texas Senator Lloyd Bentsen during debate on the HCDA, *Congressional Record,* June 7, 1977, pp. S9061-S9062.

31. As students of elections will know, presidential election returns by large city are not reported in any standard reference. I am indebted for the 1976 totals to Alfred Toizer who is conducting a study at Temple University of the impact on the electoral-vote outcome of presidential pluralities in thirty-eight large cities. The estimates of the 1976 black vote are from Joint Center for Political Studies, *Focus*, Vol. IV, No. 12 (Washington, D.C.), p. 4.

32. For an argument, although unlikely, it is at least possible that a broad-based political coalition could be developed to support expanded federal aid for the problems of hardship cities, see Caraley, *City Governments and Urban Problems,* ch. 20.

Chapter 10

The State Legislature as a School of Political Capacity
William Ker Muir, Jr.

[By] the delegation of the government . . . to a small number of citizens elected by the rest . . . the effect . . . is . . . to refine and enlarge the public views, by passing them through the medium of a chosen body of citizens, whose wisdom may best discern the true interest of their country, and whose patriotism and love of justice will be least likely to sacrifice it to temporary and partial considerations.
James Madison

Politics is perhaps the only profession for which no preparation is thought necessary.
Robert Louis Stevenson

What is a legislature? That question has long nagged at me. Legislatures have been outside my personal experience, and while I have found the scientific and fictional literature on Congress and statehouses often informative, no book or article ever gave me assurance that I knew what a legislature was. But every schoolchild knows the answer, you say. A legislature is a lawmaking body. That answer, however, has failed to help me. The reason for its shortcoming has to do with metaphor.[1] Calling a legislature a lawmaking body likens Congress and statehouses to factories. The metaphor asserts that a legislative institution makes statutes the way a factory makes widgets. The analogy, however, fails all three tests of an effective metaphor: (1) familiarity: the audience must be intimately familiar with the analogue, in this case a factory; (2) congruency: the things that are being likened to one another must be significantly similar, so that an audience already familiar with the particulars of the analogue will focus on the essential aspects of the unfamiliar thing; (3) morality: the analogue must act as a guide for action and appraisal, so that the audience will know how to behave effectively toward the unfamiliar thing and will in turn be able to judge its behavior.

In my view, likening legislatures to factories is not going to be of much help by any of these tests. For one thing, a complex manufacturing establishment is not something with which many audiences are intimately familiar. A student, a mother, or a lawyer, to take three examples, rarely having ventured inside a real factory, lacks feeling for the importance of capital and tools, the interplay between formal rules and informal understandings, the moral dilemmas of supervisors and laborers, the interdependency of incentives and admonition, the extreme information problems, and so forth. To liken one thing to another, both of which are unknown, does not help us to grasp the unfamiliar, which is the function of metaphor as an intellectual tool. Because their familiarity makes them accessible to a broader audience, memorable political metaphors tend to fall back on physical nature[2] and youthful experiences like romantic love and athletic competition.

Second, comparing a legislature to a factory does not sharpen insight. It fails the test of congruency. The question is whether an experienced factory operative would focus on important features of a legislature if told to think of one as "like his shop." Of course, even legislators disagree on what is important about their enterprise, but I know few among them, and equally few scholars, who would stress as its essential features its extreme hierarchical accountability procedures, or its preoccupation with profit, or the building of inventories, or the centrality of an authoritative coordinating blueprint, or its hiring lines, or its union-management antagonisms, or its strikes, or the lack of individual discretion. Certainly one does notice in a factory and a legislature such apparent likenesses as a division of labor or the importance of orderly procedures for getting a lot of things done, but such similarities are also common to such very different forms of human interaction as the marketplace, teams, families, universities, and white-collar offices. One is left with the suspicion that the factory metaphor is not uniquely valuable and, worse, may obstruct more than it improves the habits of our eyes.

Third, and most important, the factory metaphor disorients. It leads the uninitiated to a false assessment of legislatures and thus to inappropriate behavior. To begin with the problem of appraisal, a factory that makes widgets "well" produces a lot of them "cost-effectively." When the assembly line breaks down, or a slowdown occurs, or sabotage is practiced, everybody "knows" that the enterprise is doing badly. Analogize a legislature to a widget-making factory, and one quickly concludes that a "do-nothing" Congress is a bad thing. Conversely, a statute factory that produces a lot of laws is a good legislature. A scale of values is built into any metaphor, and we expect things of our institutions according to the analogies we use to acquaint ourselves with them. In my opinion, the moral baggage accompanying the lawmaking metaphor needs careful inspection, especially in a country that proclaims that one of its essential values is individual freedom from governmental intrusion and oppression.

Metaphor in our speech not only indicates what standards we use to measure our institutions, it also suggests how we should behave when participating in them. The lawmaking metaphor tells an audience nothing on this score. The analogy of the factory, if it indicates anything to the average student, mother, or lawyer suggests a passive consumer perspective. In a factory, "employees only" are permitted in the working areas, and the requirements of "safety first" exclude the customer from playing more of a part in the process than deciding whether to take the final product when it finally arrives on the store shelves. The metaphor does not imply that the public might or ought to participate. I would hazard that one reason that the crucial profession of lobbying has fallen so low in public esteem is that the factory metaphor makes the lobbyist a trespasser and a hazard.

A metaphor that fails to satisfy any of the three requirements of familiarity, congruency, or morality is a miscast metaphor. A remote, misshapen, and disorienting analogy leaves us blind and awkward. Because we depend upon metaphor to instruct us in how to relate to things, our personal effectiveness depends upon the quality of our analogies. Thus the fundamental question What is a legislature? which translates into What is a legislature like? is of critical importance, and ignoring it carries a grave intellectual and moral risk.

When it comes to alternative metaphors for a legislature, we confront an embarrassment of riches. A legislature has been compared to an arena, an assembly, a balance, a bawdy house, a brokerage firm, a bunch of horse traders, a branch, a butcher, a card game, a cash register, a circus, a citadel, a club, a cockpit, a collection agency, a conciliator, a congeries of committees, a dance hall, a debating society, a decision maker, an engine, an errand boy, a family, a forum, a group, a house, an inquisition, a judge, a jury, a locus of pressures, a locus of social forces, a machine, a marketplace, a medium, a mender of the social fabric, a mirror, a moral midwife, a nightclub, an organ of the body, a porkbarrel, a pride of lions, a problem attracter, a rat race, a referee, a sausage maker, a school, a seminar, a small town, a stage, a struggle, a theater, and a zoo. Some terms are more familiar to one audience than another, but all the analogies have different implications for understanding and judgment, often contradictory in what they indicate as essential and right.

The test of an intellectual tool comes in its application. What I propose to do in this essay is to take one metaphor and apply it in an exploratory way to the "best" legislature in the country. The analogy most appealing to me is that of the school. The image of the legislature as the academy for a democracy's future leaders attracts me, if only because of the sophistication of its authors, James Madison and John Stuart Mill (ably assisted, as they were, by Alexander Hamilton and Alexis de Tocqueville, respectively).

The Federalist, James Madison's treatise on representative government, was a campaign document supporting the ratification of the Constitution of the United States. The Constitution contained the idea of a national representative legislature—a House of Representatives. Madison's analysis in *The Federalist* began with the first problem of politics, the prevention of governmental oppression. By Madison's lights the best security against governmental oppression was to make government dependent upon the people. However, when the government was a "pure democracy"[3] in which the people "assemble and administer the government in person" by majority vote, the temptation "to sacrifice the weaker party or an obnoxious individual" went unchecked and, hence, enlarged the likelihood of a new form of oppression in which one part of the people would deal unjustly with a weaker part. "Personal security" in a pure democracy was an ever-available hostage to "men of factious tempers, of local prejudices or of sinister designs."

According to Madison, the "valuable improvements" of the new Constitution harmonized the need for government's dependence on the people with the important principle that it should be independent of a momentarily popular but capricious, parochial, or malevolent faction of the people. The constitutional solution was representative government: Exclude the people from direct participation in their collective capacity and delegate the governing of the nation to a popularly chosen House of Representatives, whose members would systematically "refine and enlarge" the opinions and passions of the people. The "chosen body of citizens," the members of the House of Representatives, would then constitute a "medium," an intervening substance through which the forceful "public views" of the people would be conveyed to the organs of government. Passing factious claims through the cool and weighty medium of legislative representation would tend to refract, condense, and synthesize these "temporary or partial considerations" into "the true interest of their country." (In modern terms we would say that the House of Representatives would transform group interests into the public interest.)

But Madison and Hamilton, who collaborated with Madison, felt the need carefully to prepare the legislative medium. The individual representatives, selected as they were from parochial existences, deficient in the theory and practice of public affairs, and lacking "due acquaintance with the objects and principles of legislation," simply would need to be made better.

It is not possible that an assembly of men called for the most part from pursuits of a private nature, continued in appointment for a short time, and led by no permanent motive to devote the intervals of public occupation to a study of the laws, the affairs, and the comprehensive interests of their country, should, if left wholly to themselves, escape a variety of important errors in the exercise of their legislative trust.[4]

The aim of the Founding Fathers was to prevent these legislative representatives from being left "wholly to themselves," and Madison discussed two constitutional devices to force them to be more capable than they naturally might have become. As every schoolchild knows, one was to surround the House of Representatives with three "auxiliary precautions"[5] of an aristocratic stripe—a Senate, an executive, and a judiciary (these precautions, by insulating the nation from the immediate effects of any "important errors," permitted the representatives to be granted a wider scope for experimentation). The second was to make sure that congressmen represented relatively populous districts, on the theory that the bigger the district, the better its representative (the pool of potential competing candidates would be larger, and the influence of any one faction would be diluted by the presence of other factions).[6]

It was to the practical (and extra-Constitutional) maintenance and improvement of the legislative "medium" itself that Madison (and Hamilton) turned in later parts of *The Federalist.* The individual representatives, these "men called for the most part from pursuits of a private nature," had to be schooled in political capacity.[7] Once brought to the capital, they had to be taught discernment—to make good decisions respecting the application of governmental force to a free people's affairs. Madison particularly emphasized three goals of this legislative education:

justice (that is, negotiation with due process): in an open context in which all interested parties were called to participate, learning to undertake patiently the task of drafting, redrafting, and critically appraising legislative proposals;

wisdom (that is, incrementalism and progressive compromise): learning to put together a succession of well-chosen and well-connected regulations, a "train of measures,"[8] which would have a gradual and successive operation, visible only to one who paid "constant attention" to the policy area; and

patriotism (that is, sectional sensitivity): learning how uniform-appearing laws have unanticipated but derivative consequences when applied to the diversity of conditions in which the different citizens of a large nation lived.

Madison only sketchily indicated how these three educational objectives were to be achieved.[9] He insisted that a legislature was a poor school unless it was egalitarian and hence that it must accomplish the education of "the bulk of the members," so that there were many masters of the public business, not just "a few especially skilled" ones.[10] Beyond that principle, however, Madison did not venture but left to John Stuart Mill the task of fleshing out the scholastic metaphor of the legislature as a school.

Considerations on Representative Government, written in the mellowness of Mill's later years, took up Madison's problem of the unskilled democracy. Mill's solution, like Madison's, was to educate democratic leaders. Here he developed the Madisonian theme that legislatures (and particularly the provincial assemblies) functioned as democracy's "school of political capacity."[11] The virtue of Mill's work was that he took the scholastic metaphor seriously and developed its several features.

1. The students, or the "scholars," as Mill called them,[12] should come from all walks of life. When assembled, they should comprise "a fair sample of every grade of intellect among the people." Initial diversity was crucial. The principle of open admission had to apply.

2. The education should be adversary and oral. Rhetorical argumentation, practiced "in the face of opponents," should be the pedagogical method. The representatives should be made to "work . . . against pressure,"[13] pushed to the Socratic hilt, preferably coming to enjoy but at least getting inured to the testing of ideas "by adverse controversy." In short, their minds were not so much to be filled as to be "exercised." Constant classroom attendance had to be required. A norm of sharp criticism had to be established. Performance was to be immediately graded as a "means of making ignorance aware of itself."

3. There were to be two classes of teachers. One was to consist of fellow legislators with "superior" minds. They would be crucial to the learning process of the new students. While these "old boys" would constitute a portion of the student body and would not be a separate faculty, they would play the part of tutors and would be entrusted with the task of teaching their less accomplished schoolmates. As the senior class of the legislative school, they would have an obligation to teach their "enlarged ideas" and "higher and more enlightened purposes" to their tutees.

4. As an incentive to teach, the student tutors would in return be given by their schoolmates the details of lives and occupations to which the tutors might otherwise lack personal exposure. In other words, the "schooling of grown people by public business" would take place in characteristically reciprocal circumstances, with each class of legislator teaching the other as much as it could, in marked contrast to the one-way, more authoritarian methods "of the schooling of youth in academies and colleges."

5. In addition, there would exist a faculty of outsiders not a part of the student body. Some would be part-time and tempo-

rary—"thinkers and writers" whose compensation would be nothing more than the pleasure of "pressing [their] useful ideas" upon the students. Others would be full-time and professional teachers—subject-matter experts whose job would be to teach the students a specific topic and a "defense" of a position concerning it, "cramming" their students' heads with facts, arguments, and reasons.

6. Moreover, on top of the student tutors and outside faculty, there would be a "schoolmaster," the supervisor of the school. Mill quoted approvingly, "As the schoolmaster is, so will be the school." He depicted the schoolmaster's job as one of maintaining standards and moral discipline,[14] developing procedures for effective teaching,[15] and assuring that the subject matter in the classrooms would be sufficiently diverse and challenging to stimulate the interest of the best students and stretch the less able to their utmost. Mill left it ambiguous whether the "schoolmaster" was formally part of or outside of the student body.

Mill added four objectives of legislative education to Madison's original three purposes of justice, wisdom, and patriotism. Mill insisted that a good legislature should also teach the following:

principled thinking: developing the capacity and the habits to think, analyze, and speak in terms of explicit major premises;

the value of facts and information: learning how "to profit by knowledge," knowing when one is ignorant, and learning how to learn;

creative methods: developing devices for being imaginative and insightful, especially by mastering the dual arts of perspective and heuristic, of looking for comparisons and asking questions about them which lead to discovery and invention; and

a set of high standards: understanding the demanding levels of good performance, against which all efforts at legislative thought, speech, and action would be judged—in short, a capacity "to distinguish the best."

Mill never forgot that the metaphor of likening a legislature to a school was only an intellectual tool. The "education of the citizens is not the only thing to be considered; government and administration do not exist for that alone, great as its importance is."[16] A legislature was much more besides an academy. But for one's first encounter with a legislature, for an orienting metaphor, both Madison and Mill insisted on emphasizing the academiclike qualities of the representative institution. Think of it as a school, they would say, and you will see it as individual rational legislators do. Representatives attend their legislative school to get a good education in public affairs. They are using it to advance their life careers. Hypothesize that an education in public affairs is their immediate purpose, and you will observe them getting one by using their resources, their votes in committees and on the floor, their status as bill carriers, and their extant store of political skills and acquaintance to attract teachers who will educate them. The legislature is seen as an opportunity to master the concepts, knowledge, and skills needed to make them more able in future public positions (say, as judges, mayors, executive agency heads, and teachers of the next generation of democracy's ruling class).

This educative notion of Madison and Mill may seem to turn matters on their head, for in the conventional conception a good legislator uses his knowledge and position to realize now his aspiration for the good society. The metaphor of a school is a reversal of the implications of the metaphor of a legislature as a statute factory. Public policy, instead of being the raison d'être of a legislature, simply becomes one of several simultaneous concerns, the social byproduct of the legislature's schooling function. The question is whether the school analogy is productive of better public understanding and judgment about a legislature.

The California state legislature is the best state legislature in the United States. So concluded the Citizens Conference on State Legislatures in 1971.[17] No obvious decline has set in since—quite the contrary: California's legislature has effected significant improvements in the interim between 1971 and 1977.

California's is also the busiest state legislature. In 1976, for instance, it oversaw and directed the expenditure of over $25 billion. In the two-year session, 1975–76, it enacted over 2,750 laws. Many of these bills were of minor moment, making small adjustments to existing legislation. But some were significant in consequence, magnitude of difficulty, or fiscal scale. The legislature enacted the first agricultural labor relations act in the country, a comprehensive juvenile-justice reform act, a complete restructuring of prison sentencing, public-school teachers collective bargaining legislation, a $600 million increase in annual unemployment insurance taxes, a significant tort and professional reform in the area of medical malpractice, a complex scheme for regulating construction within a thousand-mile-long coastal zone, a comprehensive reform of eminent-domain legislation, a pathbreaking and stringent nuclear energy safety act, the first euthanasia (or right-to-die) law in the United States, elimination of the oil-depletion income-tax deduction, a new basis for taxing timber, decriminalization of marijuana use and private adult sex acts, and provision of unemployment insurance to farmworkers, not to mention numerous proposals considered at length but not passed: for example, a statewide prime agricultural land use law.

Being a state legislature, it did not deal with foreign affairs, military defense, and immigration, and it lacked the monetary power of the national government, which meant it had to balance its budget. Otherwise, its agenda was boundless, including every domestic matter except the post office.

But if one walked from the streets of Sacramento onto the grounds of the state capitol, the feeling would not be one of entering a factory but a campus. It was a city campus. The grounds occupied fourteen city blocks, with the main building standing at the center. There were gardens and open spaces. Runners jogged around the grounds. Music—Vivaldi, Bach, and Mozart mainly—threaded down from speakers hidden in the palm trees and sequoias. In the main building educational displays, largely historical, were hung along the corridors. A changing series of art exhibitions was always on display in the public part of the governor's office. On bulletin boards were tacked countless announcements of lectures, meetings, colloquia, films, musical events, and athletic contests. Enter onto the "floors" of the two legislative chambers, and you would see eighty (or forty) desks lined up like schoolchildren's. They were school desks, with hinged tops which concealed pencils and paperclips, gum and candy, and books, lots of books: looseleaf volumes, hardcover treatises, and paperbacks. There was a lecture dais at the front of each of the chambers.

Moreover, scattered throughout the main building were several dozen smaller rooms—"committee rooms"—looking like small classrooms. Here the desks of the legislators were usually elevated above the lecture stand, so that the lecturer stood at the center of a semicircle, in the style of a law or medical school instructor, speaking up to the students arranged in graduated banks so that their faces might be scrutinized more piercingly.

Scurrying around the hallways were men and women burdened with books and briefcases, looking like late schoolchildren, snatching a last look at some hard-to-remember fact before being quizzed on it. People rushed, talked, and rushed on again. There was laughter, gesticulation, concentration, energy, and interest.

Were one to ask the legislators what was happening to them, they would reply:[18]

"This is the greatest education I've ever had."
"I've learned so much up here."
"My class—the class of '66—was the largest and the best they've ever had up here."

The legislators tended to see themselves as students. The "freshmen" wandered about, unsure and raw. The "old boys" played pranks on them, ragged them in debate, and initiated them into the traditions of the house. Freshmen and old boys alike wrote papers and speeches, which they gave to each other for appraisal and improvement. And like students they constantly pondered on the imponderable questions of identity: who were they? what would they do with their lives to fit valuably into the world?

It was a posh school, this California legislature, a rather special kind of school where the students were important, a boarding school like the one in *Tom Brown's Schooldays* or, to Americanize the simile, like the kind Fitzgerald and Auchincloss and Knowles and Salinger might write about, with the unmistakable air of the East Coast prep school to which the sons and daughters of the well-to-do would be likely to go.

Like the scholars of Rugby and Groton, the legislators had left home and their families, and they were often lonely. Since the school year was long—from January to mid-September—they were on their own for extensive periods of time. Some had trouble adapting to their liberation from familiar domestic routine; like college students, a few caroused at first. But soon they found that their best and most valuable friends were their fellow students. Town-gown hostility existed, and rather than continue to face the resentments of the townies, they associated mainly with each other, finding apartments to share and restaurants that were reasonable and congenial. At night they returned to the main building, the capitol, ostensibly to do some homework (which was never-ending) but actually to engage in bull sessions with their colleagues from which much that was valuable could be learned.

It was a good boarding school, and the scholars enjoyed enviable academic privileges. They had individual private suites to do their studies in—elaborate "closets," to use one of Madison's quaint, eighteenth-century terms—with pleasant furniture, staff, secretaries, and telephone systems.

They were also all on scholarships, obviating the need to find part-time employment which would detract from their studies. Room and board and books were "free," so to speak. They got a living allowance (about $26,000 a year, plus $35 a day for the 200-plus legislative days spent each year in Sacramento). It was a school to which many eager candidates applied for admission. Like slots in the military academies, places in the legislature were determined on a strictly geographical basis: one scholar from each of the eighty assembly and forty state senate districts. The admissions and scholarships committee was the electorate, decentralized by district and applying standards of merit through a series of tests administered at service clubs, union halls, political gatherings, press conferences, and radio and television stations. Typically, the qualities examined for were rhetorical ability, digestion of knowledge, trustworthiness, and energy. The candidates for assembly seats were selected every two years, for state senate seats every four years.

The purpose and result of this decentralized and populist admissions and scholarships process were the selection of a rather diverse student body. Most were men, but some were women; some were elderly, but most were younger; some were intellectuals, some persons of action; some self-taught, some elegantly educated; some thing-oriented engineers, some people-oriented humanists; some rich, some poor. It included persons of every religious persuasion, as well as blacks, browns, Asian-Americans, and whites of every European background. While they tended to share what the political scientist Louis Hartz called the liberal tradition in America, their diverse backgrounds, schooling, and professional experience made them about as heterogeneous a student body as any first-rate American college could boast. In John Stuart Mill's words, they constituted "a fair sample of every grade of intellect among the people."

What was the substance of their education? The subject matter was taught in the committees to which the scholars were assigned. In the assembly, for example, the normal load of each member was three committees, selected from an offering of twenty subject-matter committees. The courses dealt with every aspect of life: agriculture, business, labor, law, transportation; criminal justice, education, health, housing, welfare; energy, land, water; appropriations, taxation; elective politics, local government, state government organization, government personnel; and the public administration of the legislature itself.

Able legislators saw the educational possibilities of such a rich curriculum. As freshmen, they would take the courses open to freshmen—say, labor, transportation, and education. In their second terms, however, they would stay on education but shift from labor and transportation to business and welfare. In their third term, they might drop welfare and substitute government personnel. Thus, at the end of six years, they would have mastered six topics, including a major, so to speak, in education (with its labyrinthine formulae of educational finance). Not only would legislators know the subject matter, they would also know the executive agency heads, the labor union representatives, the leaders of commerce, the welfare rights lawyers, and the county supervisors that the topics dealt with.

Most of the pedagogy consisted of the "problem method." For example, a constituent's letter or the testimony of a witness might interject a question like, "Tizzy Lish, a mother of two youngsters, recently divorced and living on alimony, has become very sick and in need of surgery and long hospitalization. Who pays her bill of $15,000?" A problem like that exercised the mind, requiring an examination of the insurance and health laws of nation and state. It set a legislator to thinking about the development of health insurance, the nature of labor-management collective bargaining where the terms of so many Americans' health benefits were determined, the changing nature of the family, the liberal judicial treatment of marital dissolution, the job market for divorcées, and the costs of health care. There was no dearth of challenging and provocative problems. As a fine business school was fed rich suggestions for case studies by outside businesses, so the California legislature attracted to itself provocative problems to nourish its members' education.

There were elementary and advanced courses on most subjects. The elementary courses taught the fundamentals of their subjects. Then a follow-up course would permit an exploration of more subtle aspects of the material. To appreciate these different levels of treatment, one had to acquaint oneself with the difference between the policy (or technical) process of the legislature and the fiscal (or appropriations) process. Briefly, most bills went through two committee examinations in a single house (which meant a successful bill would usually run through four committees in all, assembly and state senate combined). The first examination would raise such questions as Would the bill work? Was it logical? Were the assumptions about cause and effect intelligent? Was there a real problem to be solved? At this level the bill and the problem would be examined technically: the policy committee intended to design as good an "orange" as it could.

After the bill's technical efficiency was perfected, it was subjected to a second examination, the fiscal process. The proposal was appraised comparatively, relative to the competing merits of other perfected proposals: Would the good results of this bill outweigh the good results of some other proposal which would have to be foregone for lack of funds, manpower, or energy? Was a technically good farm labor relations board more valuable than a necessary freeway or a vital land-use planning board? The fiscal committee had to decide whether the good "orange" designed by one policy committee was more desirable than a good "apple" developed by a different policy committee.

The technical process related to the Is, the fiscal process to the Ought. The former was empirical in nature, the latter philosophical. Of course, the distinctions were not so distinct, and each process gamboled from time to time in the other's realm. But the important point was that there were two tasks to be done on almost every bill, and that the second task of choosing between two efficiently designed bills required a comparative focus and judgment, instead of a limited technical skill.

The task of making choices was conducted mainly by one large committee in each house—appropriations, comprising four subcommittees. To it came the handiwork of all the policy committees for review. The appropriations committee consisted predominantly of "old boys." Most of its members already had mastered a half-dozen or so subjects by sitting on that many policy committees. Attentive observers of the legislature would see sitting on the appropriations committee the same legislator he had seen earlier in the week at work on the education committee, or the knowledgeable type who was earlier dominant on the local-government committee, or the legislator who had played such an important part in getting the mentally-and-physically-disabled bill through the health committee. If there was a senior honors seminar in the school, appropriations was it.

The old boys sitting on appropriations were not the only old boys in the legislature. Others, some of them equally competent, were sprinkled throughout the policy committees. The course on appropriations was a time-consuming one because there was so much hard work to be done, but the members who were there seemed experienced and at home with the various topics, more so than the average legislator on policy committees.

The old boys were constantly talking with the freshmen and younger members. They were systematically seated on the floor of each house beside the younger members, in a friendly big-sibling program. They dined together and competed athletically and sat next to each other at party functions. The older members on appropriations had a chance to observe and question younger legislators, who had to bring their own bills to appropriations, where they had to teach their elder brethren about the Is and Ought of their own proposals. And, finally, the several generations would lock horns in debate on the floor. The old boys set high standards; they were not easily beaten. In these several contexts the "enlarged ideas" and "enlightened purposes" of the seniors were handed down systematically to the new membership of the house.

One Republican sophomore summed up his legislative education in this way:

I would like to compare it to post-secondary school education. We live in that kind of climate up here. You can say that at any institution you can get an education. If you choose not to, you can get a degree still. The same is true up here. You can stay in office and perpetuate yourself. But you'll never be a worker, but only be worked on. It all depends on whether you're willing to work. In school you find the guy who makes you work and think. It may be that he's an SOB. But you stick yourself on him, and you learn. Same here: you pick a hard course of action to learn.

I've often said it was like going back to school. I have an apartment right across the street, and at night I used to come on campus, in the evening, to go to the hearings, just to watch the authors and the committee members and learn the subject matters. I've gotten enough of that education by now. I spend more time at Frank Fats Restaurant so as to watch that area of activity of the lobbyists. They say more business is done on the golf course than in business firms. Similarly, more legislation is written at Frank Fats. I've tried to be more social. I'm not one who readily goes to the Firehouse Restaurant for two hours at lunch. I've got to force myself to take these courses, but they're essential to my education.

Last year certain of the bills I introduced I did purposefully just so that I'd come before every committee, every one except the committees I was already on.

And on the floor you can be superficially prepared, or you can know and understand why someone is trying to do something. You can sit in your seat on the floor, press a button, and go off and do your own thing: minimum participation. Or you can read all those forty bills, attempt to understand them, agonize, feel you are as informed as anyone on the floor, and then be pissed off because Willie Brown [a Democratic assemblyman with a superior mind] gets up and describes an impact you never thought of. Then you realize there will always be better people than you at doing the job. But you know you are valuable.

If space and patience were unlimited, the school analogy could be spun out at much greater length. I could talk about the lobbyists who reminded the legislators of good college teachers, the resemblance of the political parties to cliques of jocks and grinds, the "TA" (or teaching assistant) status of staff (a new development since the days of Madison and Mill), the nature of the "author system" by which individual legislators retained personal responsibility for their bills throughout the whole process from inception to the governor's signature (real coauthorship was even less frequent in the legislature than it tends to be on liberal-arts campuses), the importance of the Speaker of the assembly as chief senior prefect, the extracurricular contests with the governor and his veto power, the effect of required attendance on the floor, the subtle but vital importance of floor debate for holding staff and legislators to account, the nature of the final-examination process back in the district,[19] and most interesting of all, the special importance of the "schoolmaster"—the nonpartisan fiscal analyst employed by the legislature (in turn, the analyst had a personal staff of over forty economists helping him). It was this California legislative analyst, A. Alan Post, who gave the state legislature a programmatic perspective independent of the outlook of the governor and his bureaucracy.

But rather than elaborating further, I want to bring the reader back to the question of explanation: What made this school work? What prevented undue slack among its students,[20] that shortfall between promise and delivery with which all schools since Socrates' have been afflicted, but with which some academies contend more successfully than others?

Here I will recall one of Mill's major points, that a legislative education was likely to be characteristically reciprocal and more "indirect" than "the schooling of youth in academies and colleges." Reciprocity, of course, has always been an important notion in descriptions of legislatures. In discussions of statehouse politics, there abound images of horse trading, logrolling, quid pro quo, pork-barreling, political resources, influence peddling, powerbroking, and mutual backscratching—all references to reciprocity. But I believe that an explicit and systematic application of the fundamentals of reciprocity to an analysis of the legislature as a school would bring into focus some important features of legislative life. The following are some features of reciprocity.[21]

1. Parties to reciprocal transactions are both supplicants and suppliers. They must have something they want and something they will give up. The have-nots, those that have nothing valuable to exchange as the price of their desires, are unable to influence others to supply their needs. Unless they develop some scarce talent or taste to exchange with others, the dispossessed are barred from participating in the marketplace and become "invisible." Thus reciprocal institutions produce productive and distinctive attitudes and habits.

2. Complex reciprocal institutions get clogged up unless a currency

gets established. Currency is a medium of exchange, acceptable to most suppliers as payment and often redeemable in and out of any local marketplace. Currency leaps over the limits of time and place to which in-kind exchanges are confined. Furthermore, currency not only facilitates reciprocity, it also permits individuals to store up value in the form of savings, which constitute convenient, non-deteriorating, and readily portable resources to be used in some later context or trade.

3. Reciprocal phenomena are paradoxical and problematic. For example:

Scarcity of goods or services both increases and diminishes values, and new scarcities are constantly upsetting the structure of values, enriching some persons and impoverishing others at the same time.

Abundance has both threatening and pleasing effects, and while the good fortune of one's competitors may excite envy and fear, the good fortune of one's customers may be a cause for jubilation.

Competition can diminish and increase individual choice, depending on whether the competition is *with* or *for* one's supply of goods and services.

Coercion both facilitates and endangers voluntary reciprocity; coercive institutions are essential to the keeping of promises and the maintenance of minimum levels of equality, but abusive persons in coercive institutions can tyrannize over the free marketplace.

4. Three fundamental principles underlie the dynamics of reciprocity:

The rationing principle: attractive goods and services will be consumed by others to the point of exhaustion unless a price is established (sometimes called the law of free goods).

The bottleneck principle: abundant elements will provide a diminishing return if any other element with which they combine to make a product is in short supply (sometimes called the law of diminishing returns).

The satiety principle: people tend to become contemptuous of things they hold in long supply (sometimes called the law of diminishing utility).

With these basics in mind, observers of the California state legislature might be especially interested in the fact that:

1. almost every California state legislator—and certainly everyone deemed to be "effective" by his peers—had a policy specialty, a "turf";

2. every policy area had a specialist legislator working on it;

3. these specialties were self-assigned;

4. the bulk of the legislators rarely traded votes and were rarely asked by others to do so, yet despite their reluctance to trade votes, they were liked and respected, and they had few fears of retaliation for refusing to do so;

5. legislators who had researched a particularly difficult policy area (say, child care) eagerly shared the fruits of their research with other members, irrespective of party, often circulating memos of analysis to every colleague;

6. there was little envy; on the contrary, there was a lot of camaraderie, genuine mutual admiration, trust, and gratitude for the excellence of their fellows;

7. all legislators were responsive to constituent mail, even eager to read it and quick to lend assistance;

8. most Democrats, their party momentarily holding a heavy majority in the legislature, genuinely wished there were more Republicans in the house;

9. the Speaker of the assembly, who was elected by the majority of the lower house, had tyrannical formal powers, could dictate committee assignments, allocation of staff, campaign funds, and office space, and hence was capable of making life miserable for, and a harsh example of, an uncooperative legislator, yet he rarely exercised his power tyrannically and was preoccupied with the problem of appearing "fair";

10. the few legislators who were despised by their peers were mistrusted because they gave their "word" carelessly and their stories dishonestly;

11. the two most valuable tools in the legislature—according to the consensus of legislators—were informational: the nonpartisan analysis of the budget bill completed by the nonpartisan fiscal

analyst (the "schoolmaster"), and a nonpartisan bill analysis compiled in the assembly and distributed to each assemblyman before floor debate (the analysis contained a statement of the problem each bill was intended to alleviate and the pros and cons of the particular solution);

12. in the last two decades the eighty-seat assembly, the lower house elected every two years, has produced 175 "alumni." This group of former members of the assembly, elected in the 1958 election or later and since departed for one reason or another, included at least

20 U.S. congressmen

27 state senators

6 high-level federal agency officials

5 statewide elected officials

4 judges

3 high-level state agency officials

2 high-level elected local officials

2 assemblymen, returned from private life.[22]

These dozen observations made sense if one focused on the significance of knowledge of public affairs as the currency of the California legislature. Within the California legislature there was a market for specialized, high-quality knowledge, and as in all free markets scarcity was the measure of value. The rarer the intellectual handle that a legislator could supply, the more valuably it was regarded by potential supplicants for it. To master a specialty and to teach it reliably to one's colleagues earned their highest respect, gratitude, and obligation to reciprocate by teaching something valuable back. Partisan competition often produced competing specialists in important subjects. At the same time, because the informational machinery of the legislature was basically nonpartisan and academically free and provided an opportunity to specialize to virtually every legislator, no one lacked the capacity to escape a condition of intellectual poverty. Not having to remain in the dark, no legislator had to exchange his or her vote as a way of helping out a colleague; rather, he could pay off any personal indebtedness by sharing his intellectual goods and services. Constituent problems, by suggesting new specialties to master, provided opportunities to build informational resources. (Constituents, because they served on the district admissions and scholarships committees, also provided an element of motivation, prodding legislators into taking full advantage of their educational opportunities.)

Exchange of knowledge made each participant in the legislative marketplace personally richer. The phenomenon of mutual enrichment, of course, was the essential nature of reciprocity: because one party's values or abundance were different from another's, each could give up some piece of knowledge of less value than the intellectual service received in return. So long as legislators were customers of each other, then any individual legislator's intelligence or effectiveness was a cause for jubilation to his or her fellows, not an occasion for jealousy. (The establishment of single-member districts, moreover, meant that no legislator competed for another's seat.) This ambiance of mutual enrichment and of free, open, nonenvious intellectual exchange was highly prized and exhilarating, and any deviant legislator who refused to live by the few reciprocal rules of the intellectual marketplace was treated as a pariah, who would destroy a great thing.

The key to understanding a good legislature like California's was that its members had adopted the vocation of politics: they were professionals. The young men and women who inhabited the assembly, in particular, had a long public career to look forward to, but it was a future full of imminent change and uncertainty. None could reasonably, and few wanted to, count on a dependable future in the assembly. That meant that they had to internalize the benefits of their assembly experience. They had to make the products of their lives there portable, so to speak.

Power—influence based on authority—could not be transported outside the assembly; an assemblyman's vote was tied to his seat and would no longer be his property when he vacated it. Moreover, converting the power of the vote directly into wealth, the currency of a venal legislature, was a legal taboo and in the California state legislature a moral one, too. That left political capacity as the authentic prize of a legislative experience. Knowledge of public affairs was the currency that could be redeemed outside the assembly, convertible into jobs and power and careers of moral and aesthetic satisfaction. That was why knowledge was so important to these individual professional politicians and why, in thinking about legislatures in general, observers could profitably focus on its generation and distribution.

I will end by making six observations:

1. By looking at a legislature as a school of political capacity, one gains insight into the necessary prerequisites of turning a poor or a corrupt legislature into a good one. There must be pedagogical devices to distribute knowledge. The critical element of a good legislature involves the distribution of high-quality learning to "the bulk of the members," irrespective of party, ideology, or clique. In my opinion, every state legislature ought to institute as many of the educational elements of the California state legislature as it can afford, starting with a nonpartisan fiscal analyst, a nonpartisan culminating-bill analysis (called in California the Third Reading File Analysis), a nonpartisan legislative law office, procedures for amplifying the educative opportunities of lobbyists, and staff for members, committees, and parties.

2. If knowledge is made abundantly available to the bulk of the members of a legislature, then reciprocity works in strikingly favorable ways. The lack of something legitimate to trade tempts and even requires legislators to make illegitimate exchanges of votes and money. However, if knowledge rather than something more seamy becomes the currency of legislative exchange, then the character of the legislative marketplace is qualitatively altered.

3. Reciprocity is the essence of liberalism. Unlike authority (whether based on coercion or moral force), reciprocity when employed as the central organizing device of a society expands liberty and encourages individual diversity. Liberalism—the world view that devotes itself to and admires the development of the substantial, self-reliant, self-governing, and skeptical individual—is a complex, paradoxical, and elusive ideology, hard to interpret to any generation that lacks perspective on the alternatives to it. Liberalism, based as it is on the notion of reciprocity, is often marred by its natural by-products of greed and materialism and hence reveals only grudgingly its genius for turning self-interest to good purposes and for sublimating ambition to noble effect.

4. The important thing to remember is that many California state legislators did go on to more critical and difficult jobs and that their careers as public leaders were undergoing a process of consolidation while in the state legislature. The quality of the early stages of their professional development was affected by what happened to them in the legislative institution. In a decade when democrats all over the world have had doubts about the capacity of their public leaders, legislatures have to be seen for what they are or can be, the principal institutions of political learning. When a nation has devices by which those citizens who have chosen the political calling can be made better than they thought they could be, that is a development of great significance.[23]

5. If we turn the analogy around, if we liken formal institutions of learning to legislatures, we can see rich educational implications. If a state legislature like California's has done a good job in educating its "scholars," if there is less slack in it than occurs in our conventional colleges and universities, then perhaps there is a lesson to be learned about education in general. For example, I came away from the California state legislature impressed by the pedagogical efficacy of (1) the problem method, (2) the requirement of universal debate, (3) the vitality that diverse student backgrounds brought to the classrooms, (4) the potential of peer teaching, (5) the utility of written examinations that required students to communicate abstract and complicated ideas to nonexpert laymen in literate and concrete terms, and most importantly, (6) the intellectual energy that reciprocal incentives evoked.

6. From what I have gathered from talking with others, I believe that my initial ignorance of what a legislature was like is widely shared. Legislatures are hard to comprehend. I think it fair to say that our newspapers and other media have added nothing fundamental to our understanding of them. The preoccupation of journalists with the personal eccentricities of a few legislators, their concentration on the investigative function of legislatures to the virtual exclusion of the dynamics of policy development, their detailed attention to the "sexy" personal struggles among legislators for positions of official leadership, and their cynicism, recurrent and unchangeable no matter what the reality, are a tip-off

that news reporters are as confused as the rest of us about this complex but most democratic of our institutions.

In the last twenty years several efforts have been made to upgrade the level of public-affairs reporting. The Nieman Fellowships at Harvard, for example, were established to send journalists back to school to study the American judiciary. That program has graduated such journalistic pioneers as Anthony Lewis of the *New York Times* and Linda Matthews of the *Los Angeles Times.* My recommendation would be that a similar effort be made for legislative reporting. At minimum, a program like the Nieman Fellowships should be established, preferably (alas for Berkeley) at a university located in a state capital. I believe that the benefits of schooling our legislative journalists would be rich and quickly apparent.

Notes

Ken Betsalel assisted me considerably in the preparation of this article.

1. For two stimulating articles on political metaphors, their uses and abuses, see Lewis Dexter, *The Sociology and Politics of Congress* (New York: Rand McNally, 1969), pp. 184-209, and Martin Landau, "On the Use of Metaphor in Political Analysis," *Social Research* 28, no. 3 (Autumn 1961): 331-353.

2. See John Stuart Mill, *Considerations on Representative Government* (New York: Liberal Arts Press, 1958; originally published in 1861), p. 97, on the foolishness of advanced nations' insisting that developing countries immediately adopt democratic and humane governmental practices: "It is like preaching to the worm who crawls on the ground how much better it would be for him if he were an eagle."

3. The quoted phrases all come from *Federalist No. 10,* unless otherwise noted.

4. *Federalist No. 62.*

5. *Federalist No. 53.*

6. *Federalist No. 10.*

7. See *Federalist Nos. 51, 53, 55, 56, 61, 62,* and *63.* The political scientist Robert Dahl, in his brilliant *A Preface to Democratic Theory* (Chicago: University of Chicago Press, 1956), tends to minimize Madison's concern about schooling the political capacity of legislators. For example, instead of discussing the Madisonian case for producing "virtuous" and "enlightened" representatives in order that they may serve as a "medium" for conveying the "public views" to government, he dismisses it abruptly as "an extremely

dubious and probably false set of propositions purporting to show that representation in a large republic will provide 'better' politicians and reduce the probability of success of 'the vicious arts by which elections are too often carried' " (p. 16). Or, again, while Dahl restates the Madisonian problem elegantly, he seems to ignore Madison's argument.

The only remaining possibility, then, is that some specified group in the community, not defined as the majority, but not necessarily always in opposition to it, would be empowered to decide. But if Hypothesis 1 is correct, then any group in the community with such a power would use it to tyrannize over other individuals in the community. Hence, in practice, no one would have the power to decide the question (p. 24).

But the House of Representatives, according to my reading of Madison, having been schooled so as to increase its enlightenment and virtue, was precisely the "specified group" Madison had in mind to resolve popular disagreements.

8. *Federalist No. 63.*

9. *The Federalist* insisted on six conditions of a good legislative school: (1) books and the time and a private "closet" for legislators to read them in, (2) diverse colleagues and the motivation and opportunities to learn from them, (3) lobbyists and the inducements to listen to their "oral" information, (4) specialists from government agencies from whom expertise for particular topics could be obtained, (5) records of the institution's history which would provide, among other things, the opportunity to avoid repeating previous errors, and (6) bill-carrying responsibilities which would provide individual representatives experience by which their understanding and vision could be tested against results.

10. *Federalist No. 53* made a special point of the importance of distributing knowledge to the bulk of the members of a legislature, lest a few especially skilled legislative members corrupt the institution for their own advantage:

A few of the members, as happens in all such assemblies, will possess superior talents; will, by frequent reelections, become members of long standing; will be thoroughly masters of the public business, and perhaps not unwilling to avail themselves of those advantages.

11. Mill, *Representative Government,* p. 219.

12. The quoted phrases all come from chapters 5 and 15 of Mill, *Representative Government,* unless otherwise noted.

13. Mill, *Representative Government,* P. 162.

14. Ibid, p. 219: " . . . due surveillance [of] unscrupulous and stupid pursuit of self-interest."

15. Ibid: " . . . bringing inferior minds into contact with superior. . . ."

16. Ibid, p. 278.

17. Citizens Conference on State Legislatures, *The Sometimes Governments: A Critical Study of the 50 American Legislatures* (New York: Bantam, 1971), pp. 44-54.

18. Quotations from California legislators are drawn from interviews of thirty California assemblymen and assemblywomen. I conducted these interviews during 1976-77 for use as part of a larger study to be completed by 1979.

19. See Richard Fenno's description of congressmen responding to their examinations back in their districts in his splendid "U.S. House Members in Their Constituencies: An Exploration," *American Political Science Review* 71 (September 1977): 883-917.

20. See the discussion of slack and "lapses" in Albert O. Hirschman's ingenious *Exit, Voice, and Loyalty* (Cambridge, Mass.: Harvard University Press, 1970).

21. My notions of reciprocity largely derive from these five social scientists: Peter M. Blau, *Exchange and Power in Social Life* (New York: John Wiley & Sons, 1964); Robert L. Heilbroner, *The Worldly Philosophers*, 4th ed. (New York: Simon and Schuster, 1972; originally published 1953); Hirschman, *Exit, Voice, and Loyalty*; George C. Homans, *Social Behavior: Its Elementary Forms* (New York: Harcourt Brace, 1961); and Frank H. Knight, *Risk, Uncertainty and Profit* (Boston: Houghton Mifflin, 1921).

22. The numbers of "alumni" who have pursued their political vocation to higher office are understated. I have thus far traced fewer than 100 of the 175 "alumni" in their postassembly careers. Furthermore, I have not double-counted any individual: if an alumnus became first a state senator and then a congressman, he was enumerated only as a congressman, not as a state senator. Moreover, these figures do not include assemblymen who left the assembly in 1958 or earlier, older alumni like Congressman Charles Wiggins or Budget Director (and Secretary of the Department of Health, Education, and Welfare) Casper Weinberger.

23. An interesting contrast is Italy, where the members of the national parliament had no chance of getting legislative experience in provincial assemblies (which, until very recently, did not exist). For an absorbing description of a legislature governing without knowledge, see Giuseppe DiPalma, *Surviving without Governing* (Berkeley and Los Angeles: University of California Press, 1977).

Part IV

Urban Politics and Public Policy

Chapter 11

Mayors and Models: Notes on the Study of Urban Politics

Lawrence D. Brown

I could have written longer notes, for the art of writing notes is not of difficult attainment. The work is performed, first by railing at the stupidity, negligence, ignorance, and asinine tastelessness of the former editors, and shewing, from all that goes before and all that follows, the inelegance and absurdity of the old reading; then by proposing something, which to superficial readers would seem specious, but which the editor rejects with indignation; then by producing the true reading, with a long paraphrase, and concluding with loud acclamations on the discovery, and a sober wish for the advancement and prosperity of genuine criticism.
Samuel Johnson,
Preface to Shakespeare

Most of the literature on city politics in the United States presupposes a common conceptual image of how urban political systems work. This image, an eclectic blend of democratic, administrative, and pluralist theories, has grown so integral to the intellectual atmosphere of the field that it has diverted researchers' attention from some less evident but fundamental sources of urban political behavior. The purposes of these notes are to challenge the traditional model (as I shall call it) by outlining an alternative to it and to raise questions about the normative implications of both models for the place of "local control" in the American federal system.

I do not contend that my model (it is developed so sketchily and elliptically that "approach" is a less pretentious and more accurate term) is useful for every explanatory and predictive purpose. In these notes I try to assume the perspective of generalist local political leaders, especially elected local political executives, for whom the term "mayors" will be used as shorthand throughout. My aim is to spell out in a reasonably systematic way the major determinants of mayoral behavior in American cities.[1]

The argument is frankly theoretical and hypothetical, and it does not hestitate to stray into the realm of speculation. The purpose is not to settle arguments but to provoke argument. Complaints against the traditional model are incompletely documented, and my own "constructive alternatives" are supported by insufficient evidence. The former deficiency is attributable mainly to constraints of space; the latter results from the simple fact that political scientists have not done enough research on the topics discussed here to support rigorously the propositions advanced. Of course, I regret these limitations. Yet an argument, like an alcoholic spirit, may grow more potent, if also harder to swallow, with distillation.

A Traditional Model

The traditional model may be reconstructed with five variables (a term used loosely here to denote "things worth investigating"), each of which corresponds to a by now hallowed level of analysis and set of urban research foci. (1) The first variable is the *urban polity* itself—the electorate, "the people"—typically heterogeneous in cities (in contrast to nonurban places, where residents tend to be relatively homogeneous in their social characteristics) and divided along lines of class, race, ethnicity, and neighborhood. Local politics gets underway, so to speak, when the urban electorate conveys political signals and issues instructions (by voting on election day and by exerting various pressures, organized and unorganized, on the electoral stakes of officials between elections) by means of (2) the *local electoral system,* with its various mechanisms and procedures, and thereby selects, instructs, and constrains (3) *local political leadership*—a council (which may appoint and discharge a city manager), a mayor, and some other, lesser officials. These elected officials, behaving like most American politicians who wish to hold onto their jobs or personal popularity, or who wish to advance to higher office, consider their signals, instructions, and constraints and creatively transform them into programs and decisions (or into inaction and nondecisions) transmitted (4) through an *administrative hierarchy,* composed in varying degrees of "political" and "merit" appointees, and variously organized, to (5) *municipal agencies* (bureaucracies) which resolve conflicts, implement programs, and deliver services, thus producing a "feedback loop" to (1), the urban polity.

These five levels of analysis may be called "internal differentiating variables." They are internal because they are confined to actors and events within the city's corporate limits and take no explicit account of the city's broader, external environment. They are differentiating because the literature has been preoccupied with specifying the causes and consequences of different types of political and administrative organization in different cities. They are variables because such concepts as percentage of ethnics or middle-class persons in a city, type of electoral system, role of political parties, form of chief executive, structure of the administrative hierarchy, and extent of civil service coverage have served both as states of affairs to be explained (dependent variables) and as sources of explanation of other states of affairs (independent variables) in city politics.

My point is not that these concerns exhaust the literature but rather that these questions and variables have defined the mainstream of the discipline. Thus urban research has concentrated heavily (though not exclusively) on such topics as (1) the political expression of "natural" group interests such as class, race, ethnicity, and neighborhood within the urban polity. For example, how do blacks attempt to gain their objectives in city politics?[2] How successfully does the ethnic or class composition of a city "explain" its political structure?[3] How do different neighborhoods react to urban renewal plans?[4] (2) the impact of at-large versus ward-based, nonpartisan versus partisan, and direct-primary versus party-dominated electoral mechanisms, and the fitness of these various mechanisms to express the distribution of interests and opinions in the electorate. For example, do at-large elections tend to favor the candidacies and resources of the upper-middle and upper classes? Does removal of partisan identification from ballots encourage candidates to resort to ethnic and racial appeals? Does candidate selection by direct primary constrain or enhance the role of local "machines"?[5] (3) the composition of local leadership (mayor versus city manager; size and selection of council; role conceptions of city officials; and so forth) and the difference this composition makes. For example, is the city manager obliged to be a "politician" after all?[6] Do constituent pressures determine councilmanic behavior, or are "role conceptions" of greater importance?[7] How do mayors conceive of their leadership task and wield influence on behalf of it?[8] (4) the structure of the local administrative hierarchy. What is to be said for greater or reduced civil service coverage for various positions? Should agencies be more fully centralized or should they be decentralized to the neighborhood level?[9] and (5) the organization and behavior of municipal agencies (and bureaucrats) themselves. To what extent do local police reflect the political culture of their community?[10] How do social workers exercise discretion in dealing with public assistance recipients?[11] How do local school officials respond to federally ordered desegregation plans?[12]

The traditional model has influenced public policy as well as political science. Simply to explicate the model is to paint a picture of American politics in miniature, of "democracy in urban America." It is of course always comforting to think of our institutions in this light; yet the image is especially reassuring when local politics are under consideration because it buttresses the highly valued American ideology of local control. From Jefferson to De Tocqueville to the new and creative federalists and revenue sharers of the present day, it has been widely accepted that a large role for local governments in the distribution of public activities is a crucial means to valued ends. Observance of this faith has decisively shaped the development of the American welfare state, which has been peculiarly reluctant to centralize activities, preferring to avoid damaging charges of "federal dictation" by allowing local interests a loud voice in policy formulation and a firm hand in program implementation.

According to the ideology of local control, the "vitality" of local government ensures that governmental power will be divided and checked, that citizens will enjoy a meaningful and comfortable training ground for socialization into democratic processes, and that important governmental decisions will be made "close to the people" affected by them.[13] Clearly these values are dependent upon the proper workings of local politics; unless these politics are reasonably democratic—reasonably consistent with the traditional model, in short—the case for local control grows cloudy. In the United States, a theory of local politics is inherently a theory of American federalism, a commentary on the "proper" areal division of governmental powers. I shall argue that the traditional model is an incomplete and at times misleading way of conceptualizing local politics, that urban political research has undervalued some key variables, and that a more realistic image of local politics is not, on the whole, very supportive of the traditional arguments for local control.

The Metropolis Without

The first and fundamental problem with the traditional model and with the study of modern urban politics generally is the preoccupation with *internal* differentiating variables. Discussions of city politics frequently proceed as if local political systems are somehow self-contained. Explicit attention to the city's place in the larger political world is rare, and extended analysis of the influence of this external environment on internal political life is rarer still. Yet it is worth entertaining the proposition that mayors respond as much to external as to internal forces.[14] it may be argued that two external conditions—the city's position within a decentralized metropolitan political economy and the city's place within the American federal system—explain more about urban politics than do any truly "endogenous" variables.

The first and basic fact of urban political life—and of local leadership behavior—is that most cities exist within what Oliver P. Williams has called a decentralized "metropolitan settlement."[15] The city (meaning not only the largest cities, but also medium- and small-sized ones, and suburbs) is usually one semiautonomous governmental jurisdiction within a metropolitan area composed of several such jurisdictions. (A central city, of course, is apt to be an urban core surrounded by these other jurisdictions.) Each incorporated place competes with its immediate and more distant neighbors for valued resources—jobs, economic activity, tax revenue, cultural distinction—and therefore for the types of residents (largely middle- and upper-class and white) and the types of institutions (especially businesses) that provide these resources.[16] Because the city is an atomistic participant in competitive processes within a decentralized metropolitan setting, the mayor is not only the chief executive of a political system but also in some measure the manager of a local political economy.

At the very top of the list of concerns of most local leaders are taxing and spending (their sources, their levels over time, their distribution within the city); the physical condition and socioeconomic and racial composition of the city as a whole and of individual neighborhoods; and the levels and rates of growth of employment, industry, and local economic activity in general.[17] If the city faces high and rising taxes, increasing demands on the budget, a sizable poverty population, high or growing unemployment, rapid inflation in the costs of conducting local government business, or slow economic growth, these problems force their way to the top of a mayor's political agenda. The task of managing the local political economy will lead a mayor forcefully in certain directions: some form of urban redevelopment, with federal or private funds, is little less than imperative if a mayor is to give the impression that he is dealing with local decline. So, too, intrametropolitan competition may prevent him from pursuing some options, because (as Hunter and the "neo-elitists" recognized) these options—particularly ones calling for locally funded redistribution of services to groups below the middle class—will appear illegitimate or infeasible.[18] The main "engine" of local politics is not the polity within but the metropolis without.

Yet try as he may to deal with these economic constraints, a mayor generally discovers that local trends are determined by forces over which he has no control and little influence. A central task, whether the mayor likes it or not, is often to grapple with what economists have called the "cycle of cumulative deterioration" that metropolitan decentralization inflicts in some form on most American cities.[19] This cycle (so called for its mutually interacting and reinforcing elements) begins when city residents of the middle and upper classes (usually white) move across the city's legal boundaries into more desired locations in the suburbs. Simultaneously, business and industry—manufacturing, wholesaling, retail, service, and other firms—move out too. Economists disagree whether business tends to follow population or vice versa, but it makes little difference to the present point, which is that unless a city can either annex or otherwise incorporate the areas into which population and business are moving or generate appeals of its own strong enough to retain or reattract the migrants—and most can do neither—it must adjust to the consequences of these movements.

If the decline in population and jobs is not offset by new gains—and it usually is not—the city's tax base declines over time and a heavier tax burden falls upon those remaining behind. Outmigration seldom reduces a city to a "ghetto" or "reservation" or "sandbox"[20] inhabited only by the poor and lower class. Those remaining generally include a modest number of well-off people who prefer to live in the city or who need to be there for business reasons, and who can afford "Gold Coast" housing within its confines, and a much larger number of middle- and working-class people for whom it is impracticable to move for one or another reason. Nonetheless, the proportionate increase over time of poor and black residents as affluent whites leave is likely to cause a mayor and other civic leaders considerable anxiety. Their concern tends to be intensified by continuing immigration of less well-off, often quite poor, people who settle in the city because low-skilled jobs, low-cost housing, and social services are there, because family and friends are already there, or because class and race discrimination prevents them from settling elsewhere. Problems of personal adjustment, family breakup, and crime reduce the employment potential of these new residents; outmigration of business, and of low- and semiskilled jobs with it, adds insult to injury. Because the city's poorer residents tend to have unusually high unemployment rates, large families, and severe needs for city services, they constitute a bad bargain for a city in competition for the good things of metropolitan life. They contribute little in taxes but absorb a good deal of municipal revenue.

As the city's class composition shifts downward, the working- and middle-class city dweller (especially the home owner, who bears the property tax bill) suffers a tax "squeeze" as city hall attempts to balance expenditures with revenues. Local taxpayers find themselves paying more and more over time in order to maintain constant (or even declining) levels of public services. This squeeze may alienate residents with the strongest personal stake in local politics (those who remain in the city and pay taxes) from the local leaders presumed to represent their interests so "closely." It may provoke class and race antagonism. It also progressively strengthens one of several incentives to suburbanize for those who are or become able to leave. This development, in turn, pushes the cycle of cumulative deterioration a step further.

I should point out that this ideal type of the cycle of cumulative deterioration is subject to many qualifications.[21] It is not certain that outmigration of business has a devastating impact on the number of low- and semiskilled jobs in the city. Immigration of the poor (especially of poor southern blacks) to large northern cities has slowed dramatically since the middle and late 1960s. Some cities (Washington, D.C., for example) are retaining and attracting upper- and middle-class residents in large numbers. The importance of property and other taxes for the locational decisions of individuals and firms has long been debated. Some cities (Chicago, for example) have benefited from elements of economic revival led by but not limited to increases in public-sector and service employment. The federal government has increasingly taken the burden of caring for the poor off the shoulders of localities.

A refined and meticulous version of the cycle would require very lengthy elaboration. It seems fair to say, however, that enough deteriorative processes are present in sufficient strength in a large enough number of cities to support the hypothesis that the task of managing intrametropolitan competition and of dealing with the cumulative deterioration this competition encourages stands high on local political agendas.

Urban mayors confront throughout their tenure roughly a dozen areas of economic (and therefore political) vulnerability. As head of his local jurisdiction, a mayor is expected by some part of his constituency to "do something" about: negative or low rates of growth in major economic sectors; loss of affluent contributors to the tax base; immigration of people who tend to be poorer and needier (on the whole) than those moving out; high and persistent levels of unemployment, much of it impervious to cyclical improvements in the local economy; increased demands on the city budget—particularly in the areas of public assistance, education, health care, and police services—by needy populations; very high inflation in the costs of capital equipment, routine maintenance, and other expenses involved in running a city; severe payroll (and other) pressures from growing numbers of increasingly well-organized and politically aware public employees; depletion of the property tax base, ironically because of tax abatements offered to, and less intensive land utilization by, the service enterprises and office buildings that constitute the main sources of employment growth in the larger cities; the presence of sizable stretches of tax-exempt land and, in some cities, spreading "zones of abandonment"—blocks of vacant and vandalized buildings, unwanted by developers or commercial entrepreneurs; increased pressures on city services (and therefore on city budgets) from suburbanites who work and play in the city; and last but far from least, the extreme susceptibility of local economies to cyclical trends in the national and regional economy—rates of inflation, building slumps, unemployment trends, growth of GNP, and so forth. Most of these problems are external: they come from outside a city, are not of a city's or a mayor's own making, and remain for the most part outside a mayor's effective control. Although these factors seldom find their way into the texts of urban politics, it may be that careful research would support the proposition that these external political-economic forces fashion the municipal agenda more strongly than any other single set of explanatory variables.

Confronted with these problems, a mayor may resort to three general strategies. First, he can attempt to bring expenditures and revenues into balance by increasing existing taxes, imposing new taxes, borrowing money (at high interest rates and contingent upon state approval), forwarding budget items from one year to the next, sneaking operating expenses into the capital budget, refusing to fill jobs that become vacant, cutting municipal services (close a hospital here and a library branch there, pick up the garbage less often), and so on. From a political standpoint these approaches are painful nonsolutions and will be tried on a significant scale only if two other approaches prove clearly inadequate.

The second strategy is a vigorous mayoral effort to win more and more state and federal aid for more and more of what the city wants done. This strategy may subject a mayor and his aides to inconvenience and worse when multiple copies of documents must be transmitted and intentions clarified for the benefit of middle-level bureaucrats in federal or state agencies. Yet these difficulties tend to involve procedure more often than substance and usually appear to be a tolerable price to pay for fiscal relief.

Third, a mayor may and usually will pursue some form of urban redevelopment, encouraging land-use patterns that increase tax yield to the city. This strategy entails a commitment of the city's money, legal authority, and legitimacy to the quest for new luxury apartments, convention centers, department stores, sports arenas, hotels, banks, insurance and other office buildings—whatever will "revitalize" the central business district and adjacent areas and attract or retain business and the middle and upper classes.

The strong bias of this strategy toward the interests of the middle and upper classes and of business may be (and usually is) rationalized in two ways: first, in the long run, the benefits of more rapid local growth (or less rapid decline) may "trickle down" to lower-income citizens. Second, the fact that federal categorical programs increasingly address the needs of the less well-off allows a mayor to devote local politics to business and upper-class interests with a clear conscience.

The redevelopment imperative may be seen in many forms: in mayors' affection for federal urban renewal programs and the familiar success stories built upon it (the mayoral careers of Lee of New Haven and Collins of Boston were prime examples);[22] in the ongoing quest for private redevelopment funds in city after city across the nation now that categorical federal renewal aid is being phased out; in the routine utterances of mayors, such as one in a small city in upstate New York who declared publicly that the decision of a department store chain not to open a branch in his city was his biggest disappointment in one recent year.

If the reader discerns an argument not unsympathetic at points to the elitists and neo-elitists in the community power structure debate, he is partly correct. Local politics *are* pervasively biased toward business and toward middle- and upper-class interests. This bias results, however, not (as Hunter thought) from the back-room machinations and string pulling of *community economic elites* but rather from the amorphous and impersonal forces of *metropolitan political structure.* The customary focus on community power and its "structure" (or lack of it) is, as Oliver Williams has remarked, too narrow, and it concentrates on the wrong structures.[23] The standard elitist argument that economic interests within the community determine political outcomes is similarly misleading. Favored class and business groups need not participate in politics, lift a finger, or utter a word to get their interests served. Their influence derives mainly from political leaders' preoccupation with the competitive economic position of their jurisdictions vis-à-vis those around it. This preoccupation in turn derives from the decentralized political structure of the metropolis (that is, from the presence of differentiated, competitive, legally separate jurisdictions within metropolitan areas). A more sophisticated formulation, then, would view metropolitan political structures as "preconditions" for the influence of local economic interests, which in turn strongly affect local political outcomes. Political structures do make a difference after all. But no less misleading than the elitists' narrow analysis of the power of local economic elites is the pluralists' image of American democracy in miniature played out by vigorous political executives in city hall. Both approaches suffer from the same handicap: an undue preoccupation with internal processes and variables. In fact, it is probably not too much to say that the most important "actors" in city politics are suburbs, although they do not "act" in city politics at all.

The second external constraint on city politics is the American federal system itself, for the state and federal governments influence the workings of cities in many ways. The urban-politics literature recognizes this general point but careful studies of the actual workings of federal influence are few, and of state influence, close to nonexistent.

To point out that the federal government plays an important role in contemporary city politics verges on the banal. The charge that "the feds" have implanted themselves squarely in city affairs and have attempted to "administer cities from Washington" has become a commonplace among commentators on urban affairs.

Although the federal presence has certainly grown since the early 1960s and has achieved undeniable importance in urban politics, research that traces in detail the workings of federal policies and their enduring consequences for local political life in a range of cities is scarce. At risk of oversimplification, it appears that most federal urban programs fall into one of two categories: those that substantially reflect city politicians' own conception of what is good for the city (the major examples are urban renewal and general revenue sharing), and those that express the federal government's conception of what cities should be doing on behalf of disadvantaged groups in the city. (The best examples are the Great Society programs of the Johnson administration.) The first type tends to command the gratitude and occasionally the active involvement of the mayors;[24] the second type tends either to be exploited as a source of patronage or shunned by city hall and delegated rapidly to local agencies (both public and private) into whose ongoing operations they are assimilated, their antipoverty goals displaced with hardly a protest from the supposedly domineering "feds."

The overwhelming weight of the (admittedly limited) empirical evidence on federal urban programs is at odds with the image of aggressive federal bureaucrats invoking the letter of federal law and regulation to manipulate timid and inwardly resentful local officials. For the most part, the federal government hands over the operations of grant-in-aid programs (whether largely unrestricted, allocated by formula, or distributed on a "project" basis) and stands by passively even as their purposes are ignored or defeated. Title I of the Elementary and Secondary Education Act of 1965, intended to support innovative educational programs for disadvantaged pupils, was in fact often used by school systems to cover routine expenses in school budgets[25]—a fact of which HEW and White House officials were well aware. Community action agencies found that they must either enter into competition with established local service agencies and grow weak and isolated or lend support and funds to those agencies as the price of toleration.[26] The Model Cities program, set up to win the support of city hall for innovative programs planned by the poor but delegated to local agencies, found that local commitment went no further than the final federal dollar.[27] Federally encouraged "hometown plans" in which cities were asked to work out their own approaches to promote local hiring of minorities in the construction industry were repeatedly sabotaged by local unions.[28] Section 235 of the National Housing Act of 1968, which provided some improved housing for the poor, also permitted shady operators to market substandard dwellings to lower-income purchasers in some cities.[29] In none of these cases did the federal government take decisive action to constrain local processes and set the program on its intended course. It is of course in the nature of mayors to complain loudly in the press and in after-dinner speeches about the paperwork, photocopy bills, and "strings" that federal aid forces upon them. Unfortunately, political scientists have tended to give more weight to these pronouncements than to empirical evidence on implementation when generalizing about the federal role. In the meantime, careful investigations of the systematic (as distinct from the short-lived and program-specific) effects of federal policy on local politics remain to be carried out.

Whereas the influence of the federal government in urban politics appears to be largely ad hoc and (from the city's viewpoint) inconvenient, the effects of state government on local politics are deeply rooted, persistent, and structural. The states, of which the city is by judicial doctrine a mere "creature," exert influence on the ongoing workings of city politics at least equal in importance to that of the federal government. Unhappily, because the literature contains very little of value on city-state political relations,[30] I must limit my defense of this proposition to a laundry list of major modes of state influence on cities,[31] accompanied by the customary appeal for more research.

First, the states may determine, limit, or manipulate the structure of local government. The state constitution (or acts of the legislature) may grant cities "home rule" (the right to organize their own charter commissions and adopt their own charters, electoral forms, and administrative organization). Or they may prescribe various options in governmental structure for different categories of cities (usually defined by size). Or they may spell out local governmental structure in detail.

Second, state constitutions and laws set conditions for municipal incorporation, consolidation, and annexation. State government is therefore the major constraint on a city's power to deal by political and legal means with the movement of population and business.

Third, states limit local administrative organization in many ways. They may reorganize local agencies (in all cities, certain cities, or individual cities) by statute, may require that local administrative reorganizations be submitted to them for approval, and may even retain the power to appoint local personnel. Boston's chief of police was appointed by the governor of Massachusetts until 1962, for example, and the St. Louis police department is still governed by a board of commissioners appointed by the governor of Missouri.

Fourth, states may and do restrict a city's fiscal options by limiting both the types of taxes cities may impose and the amounts of tax revenue they may raise.[32] State government may place limits on maximum rates of taxation (by setting a maximum taxable percentage of assessed value of real property within a locality, for instance); on amounts of tax imposed per capita; on the actual dollar amounts of taxes to be levied; and on the ratio of general property tax revenue to other sources of revenue; and so on. They may forbid cities to tax revenue sources tapped by the state itself (for example sales, income, or commuter taxes). They may limit a city's discretion over the uses of city revenue (prohibiting municipal support for private institutions, for instance).

Fifth, states often impose stringent limits on the city's ability to borrow money. They do this, for example, by legislating a fixed amount or fixed percentage of assessed valuation of local real property as an upper limit on debt. States may also limit cities' local debt by restricting the terms and types of debt that may be incurred (especially long-term debt) and the purposes for which it may be used.

Sixth, state governments limit and prescribe local personnel practices, often in considerable detail. Officials in local health, welfare, education, housing, and other departments often must meet minimum state standards (as must the health and housing codes, welfare criteria, and educational programs they administer). Local public employees may have to meet general statewide merit standards. States may establish ground rules and procedures for local collective bargaining and may directly legislate public-employee benefits, including holiday and vacation schedules and pension levels, areas of increasing concern to many municipalities. Public-employee unions may therefore find the state legislature a useful ally against their nominal local superiors in the collective bargaining process.

Seventh, states influence local educational practices—by tradition, the most local of locally controlled functions—in many ways. They may establish teacher certification standards (examinations, specific college-course requirements, and the like). They may set curriculum standards in greater or less detail and may even prescribe specific textbooks for classroom use. They regulate school record keeping, building safety, and more.

Eighth, states affect local land-use patterns in a great variety of ways. State courts may become deeply involved in settling land devleopment disputes within and between localities. State planning agencies may attempt to enlist the governor, legislature, and executive departments behind one or another local development pattern or proposal. State housing agencies may subsidize local housing projects or even act as developers of local projects. State departments of commerce and economic development sell state bonds and use the receipts to subsidize businesses wishing to locate or relocate within the state, including in-state businesses moving from a central city to the suburbs. In this way state government may subsidize the cycle of cumulative deterioration.[33]

Ninth, states generally require that standard budgeting and accounting formats be used by local governments, and state examiners (usually reporting to the state comptroller) audit local books.

Tenth, states may set up pretty much at will broad-ranging investigative inquiries (blue-ribbon appointed panels, legislative committees, and the like) into local affairs. Charges aired by such bodies may break (and have broken) mayors and local political regimes; at a minimum, they win headlines and shape local residents' attitudes toward their government.

Not all states use all of these powers to the fullest; however, all states make some use of most of these powers. On balance it seems fair to say that state governments are major (external) "participants" in local politics, that they are at least as pervasive and influential participants as the federal government (whose reach is largely limited to, and limited in, the sixth, seventh, and eighth areas listed above), and that the state role in urban politics deserves far more research attention than it has received.

I have been arguing that the overreliance of the traditional model of urban politics on internal variables leads it to neglect the importance in city politics of forces originating outside the city itself. From a mayor's standpoint, these external forces are givens with which he must come to terms but which he cannot hope to change fundamentally. Obviously, the argument that the civic agenda is established in large part by external forces sharply challenges the preconditions and the presumed social benefits of local control, the former requiring polity-based agenda setting, dominant roles for electoral mechanisms and processes, and creative, vital local leadership, and the latter a wide sphere of local autonomy, meaningful citizen training in political participation, and the resolution of salient issues within political confines close to the people themselves.

The Polity Within

Even if the importance of external forces in city politics is acknowledged, the traditional model and ideology of local control have not been refuted or laid to rest. One should not assert too much on behalf of these external constraints. Although they help set a mayor's agenda, they are not the sole source of local political energy. However insistently external considerations force their way into a mayor's political calculations, he retains a reasonably wide range of choice about how to deal with them. Downtown redevelopment, for example, may be concentrated in some parts of the central business district more than in others, may seek to attract some types of commercial establishments and not others, may displace some businesses and residents more readily than others. The quest for federal aid may pursue some programs and avoid others, and the implementation of these programs may vary greatly from place to place according to the local political climate. Taxes may rise quickly or slowly, cutbacks may strike some neighborhoods and some public-employee groups more severely than others, and so forth. In other words, although external forces help to establish the general nature of the municipal agenda, the major determinants of the political translation from agenda to programmatic decisions work themselves out "endogenously." It is therefore necessary now to look not at what the traditional model leaves out but rather at the adequacy of what it offers. Do the relationships that the model (as I have reconstructed it) postulates among the five internal differentiating variables in fact capture the processes of city politics in a realistic and useful way?

The starting point of the traditional model, as of most variants of democratic theory, is the electorate. Because any student of urban sociology and indeed any casual observer of cities knows that the principal difference between urban and nonurban populations is the heterogeneity of the former,[34] it is not surprising to find much emphasis in the city politics literature upon attachments and cleavages between groups. Four cleavages (used hereafter as shorthand for "cleavages and attachments") have received special attention: class (defined as socioeconomic status, position within a prestige hierarchy, and in other ways);[35] race (black or white);[36] ethnicity (native or parental homeland); and area (neighborhood of residence).[37] Because each of these groups may be expected to perceive and express interests of its own, it is also not surprising that two questions have preoccupied researchers within the framework of the traditional model: first, what political demands do these groups make? and second, how adequate are the city's electoral (and other political) processes to express and channel these demands? (Do different class and ethnic groups expect different governing styles and public programs of city government? Do at-large elections weaken neighborhood political consciousness and organization?)

By setting the issue of local participation in this framework, the traditional model pictures a vigorous political life shooting up from the grass roots. The standard normative arguments for local control both presuppose and reinforce this image—an image sharply at odds with the low levels of attention and involvement of local electorates.[38]

If one postulates an ideal type of the urban resident and then reconstructs theoretically his calculus of political participation,[39] the most striking elements are the disincentives and obstacles to it. First, a "rational" citizen will opt to participate only if the activities of local government are sufficiently salient to him to make participation worthwhile. If the importance I have assigned to external constraints on local government is justified, then the range of important matters that can be resolved by local political processes is narrow. (Whether local residents perceive the situation in this way is or course another question.) But even a citizen who acknowledges a stake in participation may conclude, after a preliminary glance at the political environment or from experience, that the fragmented, chaotic, and archaic structure of his local government raises the frustrations of participation above his level of tolerance. Indeed, one would expect those local residents most concerned about the character of civic life to be the first to "vote by moving van"[40] and select a (suburban) community of more like-minded coparticipants.

Even within the universe of potential participants—those who are concerned, long-suffering, and settled—urban heterogeneity will, ironically, inhibit participation at least as much as it will stimulate it. Social identity does not automatically confer political identification; the latter is something to be chosen and affirmed. In the heterogeneous urban milieu, many citizens share in a range of potential political roles, grounded in a range of class, racial, ethnic, and neighborhood allegiances which point in different and sometimes contradictory directions and with which the more homogenous suburban, small-town, and rural populations need concern themselves less.

In the heterogeneous city, individual political choice is strongly conditioned by the collective political environment, that is, by the complex range of institutional allegiances available to the citizenry. Discussions of urban heterogeneity too seldom linger over the implications of the fact that urban politics are riddled not simply by diverse cleavages but also by crosscutting cleavages. Thus superficially "natural" opportunities for political expression may in reality evoke cross-pressures. An urban working-class black may find that black politics and union politics do not mix easily. The lower-class resident's allegiance to neighborhood "turf" may block identification with ethnic ties and with economic interests shared with others of his class. Effective neighborhood politics (concerted action against a highway or renewal project, for instance) may require suppression of class, ethnic, and racial identifications.[41]

Contemplating political action, the member of the narrow circle of potential participants may ponder the tensions in his social identities, admit that he feels mixed emotions about the trade-offs that political action requires, conclude that the life of homo politicus is not for him, and withdraw from the ongoing political game, perhaps into alienation, into voting alone, or into deference to the political "stratum."[42] On the other hand, he may ignore or resolve the tensions in his political identity, affirm a personal political agenda, conclude that his goals are important enough to justify a commitment to more than occasional activism[43] in the local arena, and seek entry to the political stratum himself.

Those who have traveled this far on the rocky road to participation—those who are concerned about local politics, willing to endure its frustrations, planning to stay in the city, and undeterred by the cross-pressures of social identities and roles—are hardly likely to limit themselves to the simple act of voting, which is a highly inefficient means of advancing focused and deeply valued ends. Instead, the most direct course is to join (or even to form) a voluntary association, a special-purpose organization that loudly proclaims its commitment to specific ends, invites and enlists the united strengths of the like-minded on behalf of them and in support of each other (thus acting as the functional equivalent of the suburban or small-town political system?), and is staffed for sustained advocacy and monitoring in defense of its goals.[44]

This speculative reconstruction of the calculi of participation points toward a two-tiered local polity consisting of (1) nonactivists and very occasional activists (including those whose participation is limited to voting), and (2) organizational adherents and enthusiasts, active or at least present in a large number of special-purpose bodies, most with small memberships. In short, political signals are conveyed not only and indeed not mainly by electorates expressing "natural" social attachments and cleavages, but also by the leaders and supporters of special-purpose organizations. Students of city politics ought therefore to be at least as interested in organizational representation as they are in electoral representation.[45]

The importance of formal organizations in local politics derives not only from the supply of political communications, so to speak, but also from the nature of demand in city hall. This may be seen from another hypothetical construction, this time of a mayor's calculus in searching for cues about politically advantageous behavior. A mayor taking office may, in essence, take his cues from four general sources: (1) his election and its "mandate"; (2) his personal priorities and values (his "feel" for the community and his own beliefs about its needs); (3) external forces and considerations (the city's competitive metropolitan position, the conditions attached to state and federal aid, and so on); and (4) the focused and refined demands and positions of organized groups.

The first two sources of cues (which represent the contending positions of the famous debate about whether representatives view themselves, or ought to view themselves, as instructed delegates or as free agents) are dear to the heart of the traditional model but easily overemphasized. A mayor's electoral mandate and sense of the community give him at best vague, highly general, and even platitudinous directions as to the course he ought to follow. In the nature of the case, what he needs as chief executive (as distinct from candidate for office) is a refined, workable, programmatic agenda. The fact that certain appeals worked on election day tell him next to nothing. The same limitations that make voting inferior to organizational representation for activists seeking to convey clear-cut signals make it similarly inferior for political leaders in search of such signals. A mayor's election plurality is an aggregation of thousands of individual votes; each of these votes by itself represents the outcome of inscrutable individual aggregations and trade-offs across many specific issues, grievances, and intangible considerations ("image"); most voter-aggregators may be described, by themselves and by political observers, in terms of several complex social identities; and in any case the electorate's concrete views about practical tradeoffs are largely unknown. As Wallace Sayre pointed out in a discussion of the mayoral office in New York City: "No mayor ever knows with any certainty what mix of subelectorates produces his victory, nor which of his appeals was central to its aggregation. His electoral mandate is therefore always highly ambiguous."[46]

Because they lack a clear election-based agenda, and because few mayors think it wise or proper to try to implement, ex nihilo, their personal values and priorities, the dependable cue-giving elements of a mayor's situation tend to be the last two of the four types I have listed. A mayor feels compelled to respond, first and above all, to threatening, externally created problems. He also solicits (and is freely offered) advice, often quite detailed, about dealing with these and other problems from various formal organizations which want to be consulted or have a stake in the outcome. Even in Mayor Daley's Chicago, where an unusually strong leader stood at the head of a uniquely powerful political machine, Banfield found that formal organizations took the largest role in initiating action on issues of citywide importance.[47] Unfortunately, there has been little recent, sustained research on the political activities of formal organizations at the local level.

Voluntary associations (chambers of commerce, unions, the Urban League, the League of Women Voters, taxpayer and homeowner groups, and so on) are not the only formal organizations exerting influence in local politics. Municipal bureaucracies, public agencies which owe their existence and budgets to elected officials and are charged with administering public laws, also play important roles, although these too are not those envisioned by the traditional model.

Traditional democratic and administrative doctrine expects public agencies to play a tightly circumscribed role, receiving directives from political superiors and embodying them in regulations and procedures that faithfully reflect the outcomes of the political process. Although the inescapable presence and utility of administrative discretion has long been acknowledged, the emergence of local public agencies as constant and influential participants in the policy-making process, with expertise, discretion, stakes, and perspectives distinctively their own—what Samuel Beer calls "public sector politics"[48]—remains a relatively unexplored development.

In sum, the traditional image of elected political leadership receiving signals from a heterogenous, politicized electorate and creatively transforming them into instructions to be carried out in a neutral spirit by local administrators does not accurately capture the complexities of urban politics. A more realistic image pictures local leadership soliciting and receiving signals from heads of and spokesmen for formal organizations, both voluntary associations and public agencies. These organization heads purport to speak for sizable numbers of politically conscious members, articulate and argue for focused goals, and in a word give the mayor what he needs most—concrete advice about where he stands with the "electorate," about how a contemplated course of action will affect his political stakes.

Conclusions

The alternative model of urban politics I have sketched regards three forces—the political logic of local competition within decentralized metropolitan areas, the constraints and requirements of the state and federal governments, and the influence of formal organizations active at the local level—as the major determinants of local outcomes. If this argument is correct, then, as Wilson put it several years ago, urban researchers ought to consider whether we have been preoccupied with the wrong questions and the wrong variables.[49] If the approach outlined here is on the right track, then an urban-politics literature preoccupied with the internal variables of the traditional model—and therefore with such questions as the correlates of ethnicity and class with reformed governmental structures; the relationship between indices of "reform" in local government and budgetary outputs; the consequences of opting for city managers and at-large and nonpartisan elections rather than mayors and ward-based and partisan elections; and the effect of appointing public officials on grounds of politics rather than "merit"—cannot be said to have identified variables and questions of primary importance.

The image of urban politics developed here also argues for skepticism about the ideology of local control among policymakers attempting to arrive at a "proper" distribution of functions among the various levels of the American federal system. Obviously, my approach does not endorse the time-honored vision of vital local governments, close to the people, ever-active in fulfillment of grass-roots democracy. Arguments about appropriate distributions of functions among levels of the federal system usually boil down to disagreements about the identification and weighting of benefits and costs—in this case, the benefits and costs of defining a wide scope for the play of local politics in the American system. My argument is that several misconceptions of the nature of local politics have produced corresponding misperceptions of the benefits of local control.

The American commitment to decentralization is filled with deep irony. In the name of democracy, anticentralism, popular control, and accountability we divide power among three levels of government. We fragment it still further at each level of the federal system, distributing it among independent executives, legislatures, courts, and other special agencies. In the name of liberty, we retain major private, market-based power centers too. And then, because we believe in popular control, government close to the people, and all the rest, we mark out a large field for local governments in our system—failing to recognize that the cumulative effect of all this decentralization assuredly deprives local political leaders of the power they need in order to be truly accountable and to exercise leadership in any meaningful sense. Asked to play a major role in our federal system but caught up in external and internal forces largely beyond their effective control or management, American local governments are at once very important and very weak.

The discrepancy between capacity and expectation may be resolved in one of two ways: either by increasing the powers of local government and enhancing their "vitality" or by asking them to do less (that is, by centralizing some prerogatives and functions that are now locally "controlled" at higher levels of government). This issue, which deeply divides American conservatives and liberals, cannot be explored properly here. In opting for the liberal alternative, however, I would point out that over against the presumed benefits of local control, many of them questionable, stand a range of social costs that derive from reliance upon a large number of semiautonomous municipal jurisdictions and can only grow more severe with greater local autonomy. These costs include fiscal imbalance within metropolitan areas (political fragmentation permits a high degree of residential separation according to income, and heavy reliance on local governments for public services therefore carries the consequence that "the low-income subdivision both needs more and has less");[50] municipal underinvestment in "human capital" undertakings such as education and manpower training because individual local units are unable to reap the rewards of their investment if the locally trained resident exercises his option to take his skills elsewhere;[51] encouragement to stratification within metropolitan areas by race and class as communities specialize in catering to the values and prejudices of those who can afford to act upon them in the housing market;[52] economic inefficiencies such as failure to take advantage of economies of scale in government organization and service delivery at a time of very sharp inflation in the costs of running local governments; a persistent political bias within localities toward the interests of business and of residents of middle-class and higher status, groups that hold the key to a city's competitive position within metropolitan areas; incapacity of city government to pursue significant redistributive programs on behalf of the poor (a population whose condition has improved in cities in recent years, thanks largely to general economic conditions and to the generosity of federal transfer payments and categorical programs, and thanks very little to local political processes); and a general contraction of civic life so profound that many communities—especially older central cities, demographic stepping-stones on the road to higher social standing—become "communities of limited liability,"[53] in which the major form of political expression is "voting by moving van"; and a domination of such civic life as remains by the organizationally adept and well-connected, a category that seldom includes the urban disadvantaged.

The true nature and extent of these social costs is of course highly debatable and much debated; so too is the degree to which more centralized arrangements would overcome them. The point here is simply that American society continues to incur these costs (whatever may be their true nature and extent) in good part from conviction that a large scope for local governments and the politics that move them entails more than offsetting social benefits. Part of a political scientist's business is to assess the validity of such convictions. Perhaps theorists of American federalism should again ponder, and with different conceptual foci and differently targeted research, the balance of benefits and costs that American society accepts by embracing so tightly broad local discretion and the traditional image of urban democracy from which it gains strength.

Notes

I wish to thank Martha Derthick and the editors of this volume for helpful comments on an earlier draft of this paper.

1. I confess to some uncertainty about the precise universe of local officials to whom my arguments apply. I do suspect that the political forces I describe might be generalized in a theory not simply of mayoral behavior but of "generalist local leadership." However, obvious differences among mayors, city managers, and councilmen in recruitment, tasks, constituencies, and role conceptions persuade me to dodge this difficult question by confining my argument to mayors.

2. For example, James Q. Wilson, *Negro Politics: The Search for Leadership* (Glencoe, Ill.: Free Press, 1960).

3. This issue is discussed at length in Edward C. Banfield and James Q. Wilson, "Public-Regardingness as a Value Premise in Voting Behavior," *American Political Science Review* 58 (December 1964): 876-887; Raymond Wolfinger and John Osgood Field, "Political Ethos and the Structure of City Government," *American Political Science Review* 60 (June 1966): 306-326;

Robert L. Lineberry and Edmund P. Fowler, "Reformism and Public Policies in American Cities," in James Q. Wilson (ed.), *City Politics and Public Policy* (New York: John Wiley & Sons, 1968), pp. 97-123; and James Q. Wilson and Edward C. Banfield, "Political Ethos Revisited," *American Political Science Review* 65 (December 1971): 1048-1062.

4. For example, James Q. Wilson, "Planning and Politics: Citizen Participation in Urban Renewal," in James Q. Wilson, ed., *Urban Renewal: The Record and the Controversy* (Cambridge, Mass.: MIT Press, 1966), pp. 407-421; and Langley Carleton Keyes, Jr., *The Rehabilitation Planning Game: A Study in the Diversity of Neighborhood* (Cambridge, Mass.: MIT Press, 1969).

5. Edward C. Banfield and James Q. Wilson, *City Politics* (Cambridge, Mass.: Harvard University Press, 1963), chaps. 7-12, passim, and references cited there.

6. Karl A. Bosworth, "The Manager is a Politician," in Oliver P. Williams and Charles Press, *Democracy in Urban America,* 2nd ed. (Chicago: Rand McNally, 1969), pp. 246-255.

7. For example, Kenneth Prewitt, *The Recruitment of Political Leaders* (Indianapolis: Bobbs-Merrill, 1970); Heinz Eulau and Kenneth Prewitt, *Labyrinths of Democracy: Adaptation, Linkages, Representation, and Policies in Urban Politics* (Indianapolis: Bobbs-Merrill, 1973).

8. For example, Edward C. Banfield, *Political Influence* (New York: Free Press, 1961); Jeffrey L. Pressman, "Preconditions of Mayoral Leadership," *American Political Science Review* 66 (June 1972): 511-524.

9. For example, Alan A. Altshuler, *Community Control* (New York: Pegasus, 1970).

10. James Q. Wilson, *Varieties of Police Behavior* (Cambridge, Mass.: Harvard University Press, 1968).

11. Martha Derthick, "Intercity Differences in Administration of the Public Assistance Program: The Case of Massachusetts," in Wilson, *City Politics and Public Policy,* pp. 243-266.

12. Robert L. Crain et al., *The Politics of School Desegregation* (Garden City, N.Y.: Doubleday Anchor Books, 1969).

13. See Anwar Syed, *The Political Theory of American Local Government* (New York: Random House, 1966); Alexis de Tocqueville, *Democracy in America,* vol. 1 (New York: Vintage Books, 1945), especially pp. 89-101; Robert C. Wood, *Suburbia* (Boston: Houghton Mifflin, 1958), chap. 2.

14. See the argument that mayors are growing increasingly oriented toward external "audiences" instead of internal "constituencies," in James Q. Wilson, "The Mayors vs. the Cities," *The Public Interest,* no. 16 (Summer 1969): 25-37.

15. Oliver P. Williams, *Metropolitan Political Analysis* (New York: Free Press, 1971), chap. 7. The argument developed in this section owes much to Williams's ideas.

16. Although my argument concerns the competition between central cities and their surrounding suburbs within individual metropolitan areas, jurisdictions also engage in regional, national (and even international) competition for desired resources.

17. For illustrations from three cities, see Lawrence D. Brown, "Coordination of Federal Urban Policy: Organizational Politics in Three Model Cities" (Ph.D. diss., Harvard University, 1973), chap. 3.

18. Floyd Hunter, *Community Power Structure* (Chapel Hill: University of North Carolina Press, 1953); Morton S. Baratz, "Two Faces of Power," *American Political Science Review* 56 (September 1962): 947-960, reprinted in Edward C. Banfield, ed., *Urban Government*, 2nd ed. (New York: Free Press, 1969), pp. 454-464.

19. For a lucid exposition of the cycle, see William B. Neenan, *Political Economy of Urban Areas* (Chicago: Markham Publishing Company, 1972), chap. 1. See also William J. Baumol, "Macroeconomics of Unbalanced Growth: The Anatomy of Urban Crisis," *American Economic Review* 57 (June 1967): 415-426, and Stephen M. Miller and William K. Tabb, "A New Look at a Pure Theory of Local Expenditures," *National Tax Journal* 26 (June 1973): 161-176. For an important earlier treatment of the political economy of metropolitan fragmentation, see Robert Wood, *1400 Governments: The Political Economy of the New York Metropolitan Region* (Cambridge, Mass.: Harvard University Press, 1961).

Because the terms "urban," "local," and "city" are used throughout this essay with considerable abandon, indeed as if they were interchangeable, some effort to define the universe of incorporated places in which these external constraints exert themselves may be helpful. Put simply, I hypothesize that political-economic constraints of an "external" nature are of major importance in all types of American localities except (perhaps) small towns. Obviously my summary of external constraints has been framed with the largest cities—New York, Detroit, Baltimore, and so on—and metropolitan areas in mind. Yet similar processes are at work in "declining" and even stable medium- and small-sized cities throughout the nation—Lowell, Massachusetts, Binghamton, New York, and Jackman, Maine, for example.

Suburbs, especially affluent ones, do present a problem. There must, of course, be net gainers in the atomistic competition described here, and suburbs are foremost among them, but the fruits of success present problems of their own—heavier traffic, enlarged police and fire forces, and crowded schools, leading to larger budgets, higher taxes and exacerbated disputes about zoning and land use—which may be described as problems of "political economy" and which are "external" from the localities' standpoint. Thus I contend that the general line of argument applies to suburbs too, although it stands in need of particular modifications too complex to explore here.

In fact, I consider the arguments sketched here to amount to a model of fairly general application—not merely to the largest cities, but to "cities" and indeed to many "localities," down to (and perhaps even including) the level of the small town.

20. George Sternlieb, "The City as Sandbox," and Norton E. Long, "The City as Reservation," *The Public Interest*, no. 25 (Fall 1971): 14-38.

21. See Bennett Harrison, *Urban Economic Development* (Washington, D.C.: Urban Institute, 1974), a thorough review and critique of the urban-deterioration literature, from which most of the propositions in this paragraph are taken.

22. See Robert A. Dahl, *Who Governs?* (New Haven: Yale University Press, 1961), and Raymond E. Wolfinger, *The Politics of Progress* (Englewood Cliffs, N.J.: Prentice-Hall, 1974), chaps. 5-10, for the politics of renewal in New Haven. See also Brown, *Coordination of Federal Urban Policy,* chap. 3, for Boston and two other cities.

23. Williams, *Metropolitan Political Analysis,* pp. 7-11.

24. On the crucial role of organized mayors (and of the intergovernmental lobby in general) in securing enactment of general revenue sharing, see Samuel H. Beer, "The Adoption of General Revenue Sharing: A Case Study in Public Sector Politics," *Public Policy* 24 (Spring 1976): 127-195.

25. Jerome T. Murphy, "The Education Bureaucracies Implement Novel Policy: The Politics of Title I of ESEA, 1965-72," in Allan P. Sindler, ed., *Policy and Politics in America* (Boston: Little, Brown, 1973), pp. 160-198.

26. Peter Marris and Martin Rein, *Dilemmas of Social Reform* (New York: Atherton Press, 1967); James L. Sundquist and David W. Davis, *Making Federalism Work* (Washington, D.C.: Brookings Institution, 1969), chap. 2.

27. Brown, *Coordination of Federal Urban Policy,* chaps. 4-6.

28. See, for example, "Boston Plan Comes Apart," *Boston Globe,* August 6, 1971; "Boston Plan is Dead," *Boston Sunday Globe,* October 24, 1971; "39 End Training in Construction, Can't Get Jobs," *Evening Bulletin* (Philadelphia), October 25, 1971.

29. United States Commission on Civil Rights, *Home Ownership for Lower Income Families: A Report on the Racial and Ethnic Impact of the Section 235 Program* (Washington, D.C.: Government Printing Office, June 1971).

30. The best account of city-state political relations in the literature remains the discussion of relations between New York City and the state of New York in Wallace S. Sayre and Herbert Kaufman, *Governing New York City* (New York: Russell Sage Foundation, 1960), chap. 15. See also Martin A. Shefter, "City Hall and State House: State Legislative Involvement in the Politics of New York City and Boston" (Ph.D. diss., Harvard University, 1970).

31. This section draws heavily on Frank P. Grad, "The State's Capacity to Respond to Urban Problems: The State Constitution," in Alan K. Campbell, ed., *The State and the Urban Crisis* (Englewood Cliffs, N.J.: Prentice-Hall, 1970), pp. 27-58.

32. On the importance of city-state politics in the prelude to the recent New York City fiscal crisis, see Martin Shefter, "New York City's Fiscal Crisis: The Politics of Inflation and Retrenchment," *The Public Interest,* no. 48 (Summer 1977): 108-109, 111.

33. James Dumont, "The Policies and Politics of State Economic Development" (senior honors thesis, Government Department, Harvard College, 1975).

34. The classic statement, of course, is Louis Wirth, "Urbanism as a Way of Life," *American Journal of Sociology* 46 (July 1938): 1-24, reprinted in Albert J. Reiss, Jr., ed., *Louis Wirth on Cities and Social Life* (Chicago: University of Chicago Press, 1964), pp. 60-83.

35. For example, James Q. Wilson, *The Amateur Democrat* (Chicago: University of Chicago Press, 1966); William Kornblum, *Blue Collar Community* (Chicago: University of Chicago Press, 1974), especially chaps. 6-8; and Harry Brill, *Why Organizers Fail* (Berkeley: University of California Press, 1971).

36. Wilson, *Negro Politics*; Banfield and Wilson, *City Politics,* chap. 20.

37. On ethnicity and area see William Foote Whyte, *Street Corner Society*, 2nd ed. (Chicago: University of Chicago Press, 1955), chaps. 4-6; Nathan Glazer and Daniel P. Moynihan, *Beyond the Melting Pot,* 2nd ed. (Cambridge, Mass.: MIT Press, 1970); Wolfinger, *Politics of Progress,* chap. 3 and Keyes, *The Rehabilitation Planning Game;* Stanley B. Greenberg, *Politics and Poverty: Modernization and Response in Five Poor Neighborhoods* (New York: John Wiley and Sons, 1974).

38. Electorates in the United States are, of course, famous for their low levels of attention to and involvement in politics at all three levels of government. The ideology of local control, however, rests precisely upon supposed reasons for exceptions to the rule, namely, the heightened salience of local issues and the superior accessibility of local governments.

39. In the following section I intend the term "political participation" to denote ongoing and sustained, not sporadic and ad hoc, involvement. For example, the citizen whose political activities extend no further than occasional (or even regular) voting or helping a friend or neighbor win election to office every five or ten years does not qualify as a "participant" in this sense.

40. Williams, *Metropolitan Political Analysis,* p. 30.

41. Federal antipoverty programs of the late 1960s and early 1970s, especially those that made an explicit effort to change the nature of participation in local politics, furnish useful illustrations of the effects of crosscutting cleavages. When these programs were being contemplated and enacted, the assumption of natural group interests gave rise to slogans like "black unity," "class consciousness," "ethnic solidarity," and "community organization." The image of group interest and action implicit in these utterances found their way into federal policies aimed at spurring political participation of the "poor" and the "black community" and directed at promoting "community organization" of "poverty neighborhoods."

The implementation of these federal programs soon demonstrated how misleading was this image of the urban polity. Diversity of interest by class and by neighborhood fragmented the so-called "black community" and set organizations and areas against one another for control of federal funds. The poor of different races, ethnic groups, and neighborhoods found cooperation on behalf of supposedly shared class interests to be difficult if not impossible. Meaningful community action repeatedly foundered on contradictory class styles, race antagonisms, and ethnic tensions. As for ethnic solidarity, often highly overrated as a local political force, although it may stand intact on election day, the day after the election it too usually shatters into divisive interests of class, generation, and neighborhood and usually remains divided until (and sometimes at) the next election. In each case, the urban "masses" tend to refrain from involvement or soon withdraw from it, leaving the spokesmen and loyalists of organized groups to battle with one another (and among themselves) for power and funds.

42. The term is taken from p. 90 of Dahl's *Who Governs?* a work that heavily influenced this section. See also Samuel J. Eldersveld, *Political Parties: A Behavioral Analysis* (Chicago: Rand McNally, 1964), pp. 451-452.

43. The term is taken from David Nexon, "Asymmetry in the Political System: Occasional Activists in the Republican and Democratic Parties, 1956-1964," *American Political Science Review* 65 (September 1971): 716-730.

44. The "true" participant might instead run for office or become a party "regular" or "professional." (Concerning the latter alternative, it is suggestive that when asked "if they were to become more active in politics, they would prefer to work through political parties or other groups," only 23 percent of Eldersveld's sample chose parties. See *Political Parties,* pp. 91-92.) On the relationship between local discretion and incentives for organizational formation and activism, see James Q. Wilson, *Political Organizations* (New York: Basic Books, 1973), chap. 5.

45. This is certainly not an original insight. The local political activities of voluntary associations, municipal bureaucracies, and business firms have been explored by Banfield, Wilson, Dahl, Norton Long, Sayre and Kaufman, and others. My point is that an organizational perspective has yet to find its way into the mainstream of urban politics studies; important recent works along these lines are remarkably scarce.

46. Wallace S. Sayre, "The Mayor," in Lyle C. Fitch and Annmarie Hauck Walsh, eds., *Agenda for a City* (Beverly Hills, Calif.: Sage Publications, 1970), p. 573.

47. Banfield, *Political Influence,* chap. 9.

48. Beer, "Adoption of General Revenue Sharing," pp. 127-129.

49. James Q. Wilson, "We Need to Shift Focus," in Banfield, *Urban Government,* pp. 21-33.

50. Wilbur R. Thompson, *A Preface to Urban Economics* (Baltimore: Johns Hopkins Press, 1965), p. 116.

51. Dick Netzer, *Economics and Urban Problems,* 2nd. ed. (New York: Basic Books, 1974), pp. 232-238

52. See Williams, *Metropolitan Political Analysis,* chaps. 6-7.

53. The term is from Morris Janowitz. See the excerpt of his *The Community Press in an Urban Setting* (Glencoe, Ill.: Free Press, 1952) reprinted in Williams and Press, *Democracy in Urban America,* pp. 134-142. The quotation is from p. 141.

Chapter 12

The Paradox of Power: Mayoral Leadership on Charter Reform in Boston

Philip B. Heymann and Martha Wagner Weinberg

Americans have always had extremely complicated attitudes toward their elected chief executives. Public regard for the executive branch and optimism about its ability to take initiatives and to move the other institutions of government seems to be cyclical: times of crisis may lead to a focus on the executive, and the public's demand for unitary leadership at such times justifies some optimism about its prospects. But our interest in and judgment of chief executives is also affected by a lasting ambivalence, one that has colored our view of elected executives since the Founding Fathers wrote the Constitution. We expect chief executives to provide leadership, to take initiatives, and to be skilled operatives in the complex environment in which they work. At the same time, we distrust those who amass too much power, those who depart from the policy "merits" to cajole and bargain with other centers of power to get what they want, and those who seem to relish the exercise of authority.

During the 1960s and early 1970s, many scholars and observers of politics looked to elected chief executives to shape the political agenda, to take initiatives, and to provide leadership in government.[1] Because of popular concern with the "urban crisis," big-city mayors were special targets for public attention and concern. Students of urban politics began to look beyond the textbook description of mayoral powers and to ask how mayors accumulate power. In his classic article on mayoral leadership, Jeffrey Pressman suggests that mayors must learn to behave as astute politicians who value power and know how to use it.[2] He recognizes that the political environment in which a mayor must make and carry out policy profoundly affects and constrains him, but he also urges mayors to come to understand that environment and to be willing to accumulate the formal and informal resources to affect it in turn.

Work by Pressman and others that stressed the need for mayors to be adroit politicians in order to carry out policy added a new dimension to the study of mayoral leadership. But exercising mayoral leadership is more complicated than even these studies would lead us to believe. It is true that mayors, like other elected chief executives, must build their political resources if they hope to accomplish significant goals. They must attend to three basic sources of strength—authority in the city or the party, the influence on other powerful actors that can flow from effective use of that authority, and public support for the mayor and hostility to his opponents—trading one for another and each for actions and decisions important to the city. The task of protecting and enlarging these sources of strength, however, has dilemmas built deep within it.

If a chief executive's attempt to build authority and influence is widely recognized, it is likely to set off the public distrust awaiting those who seek concentrated power, and it will activate political opponents who are both fearful for their own influence and responsive to the public's desire for political opposition to the attempt. The same sort of resistance awaits any attempt to win some margin of freedom from the pressures of public accountability at the polls. (The reaction is not entirely unhealthy, for power sought for civic goals is not easy to distinguish from power sought for its own sake and may be just as much a source of concern even if the motivation for it is pure.) In addition, the means for garnering and exercising power—bargaining and cajoling and threatening—are not widely accepted, so they are often carried out in a secrecy that, if penetrated, magnifies distrust.

Big-city mayors are faced with a paradox. They must understand power and seek to use it, for urban problems will not be solved without strong leadership. At the same time, because of our ambivalence about concentrating power and about using the means that are required to build influence and affect results, they must recognize that there is a political price to be paid for attempting to accumulate power—that one step forward may mean two steps back.

Boston Charter Reform as an Example

This essay will focus on the implications of this ambivalence for big-city mayors, particularly for Kevin White of Boston in his attempt to change the city's charter. First elected in 1967, by 1977 White was one of the few survivors of the class of young, liberal, big-city mayors who were elected in the 1960s. Because each individual who holds the office of mayor brings to the job different personal traits and a different style, and because each big city is different, it would be incorrect to assume that White's experience in Boston was typical of that of all other mayors. However, he is a good individual to study in order to make some generalizations about the obstacles faced by big-city mayors in the 1960s and 1970s as they attempted to make policy and to exercise leadership.

In many ways White represents a prototype of the activist chief executive, sensitive to the need to shape the political process in order to achieve his own goals. He had won office with the support of a coalition of groups who had opposed the candidacy of Louise Day Hicks and her stand against desegregation of the Boston schools. Many saw him as the Boston equivalent of John Kennedy or John Lindsay. But in addition to espousing liberal causes and social reforms, White made it clear from the beginning of his term that he believed it was necessary for a good mayor to build a strong bank of political power and resources in order to govern. He often referred to himself as pursuing "Lindsay's goals with Daley's methods." In addition, he was a winner. Even after the trauma of court-enforced school busing, he managed to win reelection with the aid of well-financed, thoroughly professional campaign machinery and a record of effective urban management. Still, as White began his third term, shortly after Watergate, it was clear that the press and much of the public—even those who agreed with his ends—had grown critical of his use of a mayor's resources, especially patronage, and resentful of the independence with which he could and did exercise the power he had accumulated.

Just as it would be incorrect to label White a typical mayor, so it would be distorting to suggest that charter reform is a typical case involving an attempt by a mayor to exercise leadership. But for several reasons it is a good case to look at in trying to understand the paradoxes of mayoral leadership. First, an important part of White's charter proposal involved an attempt to strengthen the office of the mayor, something that many of those who argue for leadership in the executive think would help mayors manage their cities.[3] White already had a great deal of formal authority, as well as a strong, well-supported staff, discretion over substantial sources of funding, and access to voters. He lacked few crucial assets of mayoral power. The charter reform promised to increase the mayor's freedom to pursue even unpopular goals for the city by making reelection of an incumbent more likely. At the same time, it would help increase his influence with other political actors by creating a supportive political party and by augmenting mayoral authority over the Boston school system.

In addition, the proposal included an intricately intertwined mix of organizational changes felt by many to be necessary for the good of the city and increments in resources designed to enhance both the mayor's prospects for reelection and his political and governmental powers. White saw the charter reform package as a means to help him cement the necessary and natural connection between a mayor's power and his ability to achieve the social good. For others, however, charter reform represented an abuse of power undertaken for self-serving reasons.

Charter reform is also a revealing case because of the kind of symbolic issue that it became. The literature on reorganization and government reform suggests that proposals for restructuring government are generally uninteresting to the public.[4] However, White's proposal for charter reform aroused considerable public controversy and a great deal of public debate. The battle was not restricted to the provisions of the proposal; both proponents and opponents saw charter reform as representing a set of basic principles that were at stake. For White there was no reason to divide the provisions into those that increased his powers or job security and those that promised reduced school costs or black representation on elected bodies, although he of course recognized that others might see a sharp distinction. The proposals designed to increase his authority and to enhance his electoral prospects seemed as healthy and desirable as the others; as he saw it, all would ultimately serve the city's welfare. Opponents of White's proposal, on the other hand, characterized it as a devious attempt to conceal a power grab under the mantle of other social reforms. They focused not on the question of the desirability of a strengthened mayoral office but on the desirability of a strengthened White. As a result, the issue for them was not only charter reform but also Kevin White himself and his style and methods of governing.

The Issue: History and Strategy

On September 23, 1976, Kevin White was the host at a dinner at the Parkman House, the old Beacon Hill mansion that White uses for official entertaining. The purpose of the dinner was to talk about changes in the charter of the city of Boston. The majority of the guests were academics from several of Boston's universities who were familiar with the city and with its problems. Among the others present were several members of the mayor's staff and Edward McCormack, the chairman of the newly formed Committee for Boston (CFB), a group of Boston community leaders, businessmen, and prominent citizens appointed by White to address the problems of violence and unrest in the city.

At the dinner White spoke of the need to revise the city's charter in order to ensure minority representation on the school committee and the city council. He also suggested that the charter should be changed to give the mayor greater control over school department fiscal affairs and personnel practices. He spoke movingly of the need to accomplish these changes not only because they would allow for increased accountability and efficiency but also because they would serve as an important symbol of the city's recovery from the trauma of court-enforced busing. "I can feel that the city is ready to turn around," he said,

I really can feel it. We need to change the charter to show minorities that they have a voice, that they are represented. And we need to show the voters and taxpayers that we understand their concern with taxes and their frustrations with living in Boston, We can do it—we can turn the mood of the city around.[5]

White then asked the guests to discuss his proposals and to serve as an ad hoc committee to provide him and his staff with help and technical advice.

The mayor's presentation at the Parkman House was not the first occasion on which he had proposed charter change. In 1974 White had formulated what became known as "Plan 3," a charter change that would have made the school department a line department of the city and that would have provided for district elections of school committee members.[6] Plan 3 had been presented to the voters as a referendum and had been soundly defeated, but neither White nor his staff had given up on charter reform. Improving education—or even achieving the necessary precondition to improvement, a slowdown in white flight from the schools—required doing something about the school committee, which continued to devote almost all its attention to jobs and contracts and all its words to a futile attack on busing. In addition, White wanted the charter changed to include a provision for partisan mayoral elections. A surprisingly close election victory in 1975, combined with resentment of the extent of campaign attacks on his use of patronage and his sources of funds, had led White to see partisan elections as both a way out of the uncertainties, divisiveness, and ugliness of "personality politics" and a way to ensure party control as an alternative to patronage for dealing with those whose support he needed. A huge school tax bill provided the perfect opportunity to use a popular school reform as an occasion for a less popular electoral reform.

During the summer of 1976, several members of White's staff had contacted many of those who attended the Parkman dinner and had had individual conversations with them about the changes the mayor wanted. In addition, on September 16, the week before the dinner, White had sent a letter to the Committee for Boston asking it to make recommendations for structural changes in the school committee and the city government. The committee members had agreed to respond to the mayor's request, with the understanding that they were free to reach their own conclusions and would not necessarily come to any final agreement on charter change. McCormack's presence at the Parkman dinner provided the link, carefully fostered by the mayor's staff, between the work to be done by the Committee for Boston and the deliberations of the technical advisory panels of academics.

Boston's city charter, the general and special laws that provide for the governing structure of the city, can be changed in three ways: by establishment of a charter commission; by enactment of a home rule petition; or by change in the general state statutes. White and his staff had decided to try for change by using the home rule petition because for them it was the simplest, surest, and quickest way of getting what they needed. Change by establishment of a charter commission requires two referenda, one on the formation of the charter commission itself and one on the charter that it produces. Trying to effect change through referenda is both extremely time-consuming and, because of the difficulty of achieving a positive vote on a referendum question, difficult to manage. White feared that issues of race might infect the consideration of a referendum. In addition, the referendum could turn out to be an unwanted test of the mayor's popularity.

The alternative route of changing the charter by passage of a general law would not have required local initiative or a referendum. Since general laws must apply to a class of not fewer than two cities and since the type of law necessary to reform Boston government might not be suitable for Springfield and Worcester, the two next largest cities in Massachusetts, the reformers did not consider change in the general laws an appropriate mechanism. Instead, the mayor and his staff decided to file a home rule petition, which requires approval of the proposed changes by the city council, the mayor, both houses of the state legislature and the governor. Charter change by home rule petition does not require a popular vote and can therefore be accomplished quickly if all the bodies necessary for approval agree. It was because of these features that White and his staff decided to file a home rule petition to achieve the structural changes they wanted. Most such petitions provide for a ratifying referendum, but for the reasons already discussed this was not to be included.

The plan of the mayor and his staff was a relatively straightforward one. The Committee for Boston and the academic panel would consider the question of what changes needed to be made in the city's charter and would conclude that they should recommend what White wanted for the schools and the electoral structure. By asking both the blue-ribbon Committee for Boston and a prestigious panel of experts to consider the question of charter change, the mayor hoped to be able to provide a double layer of insulation for himself from charges that charter reform was designed to serve his personal interests. Both bodies were clearly independent of White. Yet because they would rely on work done by White's staff, both the issues on their agenda and the recommendations they made could be influenced. The mayor, with the backing of these two committees, would then file a home rule petition which would be passed quickly by the city council and the legislature and signed by the governor. The procedure might be attacked by purists for lack of public participation, but it was far more likely to succeed than any more open and deliberate one. Members of the council, for example, who could be induced to cast a quick favorable vote would find it far harder to urge conservative constituents to support White on the too-liberal, too-pro-White side of a referendum question.

The Defeat of Charter Reform

The only major problem with White's plan to achieve a change in the city's charter was that it did not work. On November 18 the Committee for Boston issued its report. Among the recommendations were most of the measures that White and his staff had talked about with both the CFB and the panel of academic experts who had testified before the committee. These included recommendations that the current system of electing members of the school committee and the city council at large be abolished and that fifteen new electoral districts be set up, with a member of the school committee and a city councillor to be elected from each district.[7] These measures would virtually guarantee minority representation on both bodies. In addition, the CFB recommended that the terms of city councillors and school committee members be extended from two to four years, that municipal elections be held in even-numbered years, and that the mayor be given more control over the school budget and the appointment of the school superintendent.

In his press conference announcing the committee's recommendations, Chairman McCormack made it clear that the CFB's report was distinctly the product of the committee. "We did not concern ourselves with what the Mayor finds palatable or unpalatable," he said. "This is an independent committee."[8] And indeed it had behaved independently on one issue that was to become crucial in the whole battle over charter reform—the issue of reintroducing partisan elections in Boston. During the time that the committee was deliberating the question of what changes should be made in the charter, White, through his staff, had suggested that the current system of nonpartisan mayoral elections, with a runoff between the two candidates making the strongest showing in the preliminary election, be changed to a partisan race with the winners of the Democratic and Republican primaries facing each other in the November election. He and his staff and one of the academic experts, Doris Kearns of Harvard, argued that partisan elections would increase participation and would lend new life to the two-party system, thereby increasing electoral choice and accountability.

The Committee for Boston rejected the White argument for partisan elections, though it did include Kearns's spirited defense of the proposal as an appendix to its report. The arguments that White made about the benefits of partisan elections had been made elsewhere and had some credence among political scientists. But to the committee the most immediate beneficiary of such a reform seemed to be Kevin White. Boston voters are overwhelmingly Democratic, and White's strongest challenges in previous general elections had been other Democrats. Turnout in primaries is generally low and consists of the party faithful. Those on the CFB who opposed the provision for partisan elections argued that White as an incumbent with a tight organization could easily dominate a Democratic primary and then easily defeat any Republican or Independent in the November election.

Despite the CFB's refusal to include a recommendation for partisan elections, White decided to include that proposal in the home rule petition that he presented to the city council on December 6. He also added several "sweeteners" to make the plan acceptable to the council, including an extension of the terms of those councillors who were currently serving and no mention of district elections for council members; instead, the proposal increased the size of the council from nine to fifteen, with all councillors to be elected at large. White had decided, after much debate within his staff, to sacrifice some of the advantages of the insulation the CFB provided to try to obtain the increments in mayoral power he thought necessary and, sacrificing additional CFB support, to use old-fashioned horse trading to turn the offer into one the council could not refuse. White's plan was to move the proposal quickly through the council with the aid of the sweeteners and intensive lobbying of councillors and then, during the Christmas holidays, to send it to the legislature, which could only vote it up or down.

The first stage of the White plan seemed to go smoothly. In mid-December the city council's Committee on Laws and Ordinances held hearings on the proposal and, after canceling the final set of hearings scheduled for December 28 and 29, referred the bill to the full council. Though several councillors characterized the White package as a "tank job" and as "completely devoid of popular input,"[9] after an all-night session on December 27 the council passed an amended version of the White proposal. A "White coalition" of five councillors was carefully assembled by White and his staff, and they lobbied the other councillors intensively. On January 5 White signed the council's charter package and began to prepare to send the proposal to the legislature.

White's strategy called for moving the package swiftly through the legislature and to the governor for his signature by January 20. The assumption underlying this strategy—that the leadership of the legislature would support the plan and would be able to ensure its passage—seemed to be a good one. The leadership of the Massachusetts legislature is extremely powerful and on most issues is able to control the fate of legislation. Before introducing the legislation, White had had conversations with House Speaker Thomas McGee and White's close ally, Senate President Kevin Harrington. Having just denied White new taxing authority to meet the mounting city bills, they told him that they would guarantee the passage of the charter reform proposal if he could show the support of the thirty-three-member Boston delegation. Although the Boston delegation included some of White's political opponents, White had always been influential with the majority. In addition, he had reason to believe that many Boston legislators would be especially inclined to support this particular piece of legislation. Several members of the State House of Representatives were faced with the possibility that they would lose their seats because of legislation mandating a cut in the size of the House in 1977. If the charter reform proposal were to pass, the city council and the school committee would increase in size, offering the possibility of new jobs for deposed representatives. White also controlled the city services in legislative districts and a large number of jobs with the city of Boston, both of which he could make more or less available to legislators.

Because of White's agreement with the leadership and his relationship with the Boston delegation, most observers assumed that the package would pass swiftly through the legislature. However, it was as he prepared to introduce his package in the legislature that the mayor's plan began to unravel. On January 6, the chairperson of the Boston Finance Committee (FinCom) announced that the commission, an independent body with the power to investigate the finances and administration of the city of Boston, would hold its own public hearings on the charter reform package because the package had "clearly not been given a public debate."[10] During the five days of hearings, representatives of fifty neighborhood groups spoke, forty of whom opposed passage by the legislature. After concluding the hearings, the FinCom recommended that the plan be defeated in the legislature unless it was amended to include greater participation in the charter reform process and exclude the provision for partisan elections.

At the same time, other opposition to the plan began to mount, from several different sources and for several different reasons. Among the earliest and most vocal opponents of the package were members of the school committee, who stood to lose power because of the part of the proposal that was aimed at school committee reform. The plan was also opposed by several of White's long-standing political opponents. Perhaps the most important of these was State Senator Joseph Timilty, who had lost to White by a narrow margin in the last mayoral election. Timilty characterized the package as having "something for every single politician in the Commonwealth, but nothing for the people."[11]

In addition to those who opposed the plan because they had personal political gains and losses to consider, other groups and individuals began to come out against the proposal. These included several neighborhood and citizen groups, among them "good government" groups such as the League of Women Voters and CPPax, who had traditionally been White's allies. Barney Frank, an influential liberal representative and former White chief of staff, criticized the plan because it included the proposal for partisan elections which, he argued, would mean that fewer people would determine the outcome of the mayoral race and there would be a disproportionate loss in the number of liberal voters. In addition, several prominent spokesmen for minority groups, whom the plan was supposedly designed to help, spoke out against the plan because they felt that it did not go far enough; it provided an opportunity for black representation on the school committee but at the same time transferred much of the committee's power to the mayor and the superintendent. Others criticized the plan because they said it was inconsistent; the school committee was to be elected by district, in a nonpartisan election, while the council and the mayor would be elected at large, in a partisan contest. Still others opposed the plan as a political power play, designed to increase White's power and to benefit incumbents. Finally, many opponents called the proposal "secretive" and characterized the manner in which the package had been moved through the council as "hasty" and "under cover and under-handed."

Toward the end of January, the White plan for moving charter reform through the legislature had begun to come apart. By February 9, when the legislature's Joint Committee on Local Affairs held hearings on the measure, large numbers of individuals and groups had begun to express themselves on the issue of charter reform, most of them voicing strong opposition to the plan. The mayor's strategy of moving the plan quickly and deftly through the legislature no longer seemed viable. The press, which had reported on the issue all along on the back pages of the newspaper, began to feature the issue prominently. Individual legislators in the Boston delegation began to receive mail and phone calls from constituents urging them to oppose the bill.

Feeling the heat of the opposition to partisanship, one of the five city councillors supporting the package announced that he would prefer it without partisanship. On February 12, the Boston City Council held a meeting to consider eliminating that provision, which no longer commanded majority support. The mayor and his allies on the council were able to prevent the council from presenting him and the city with an attractive alternative reform proposal that simply eliminated partisanship, but only by turning a nineteen-hour session into a widely reported farce that produced a package containing inconsistent and patently undesirable amendments. No one expected or wanted White to substitute for his proposal the hastily conceived and inconsistent product of these unseemly deliberations. But the maneuvers had been costly. The support of the council came to mean less than it had before; its process and product were widely ridiculed. White stood almost alone.

The opposition forces had organized. The bias of the political system toward slowing down initiatives such as charter reform became evident. White's support in the Boston delegation began to disintegrate. Several individual representatives reported to the House leadership that charter reform was an issue on which they could not "go along" because of pressure from their constituents. White believed the leadership would not stand for this, but they did not claim and seek to enforce any prior commitments. On February 17, shortly after it became clear that the Boston delegation would not vote with White, the charter reform bill died in the legislature.

Mayoral Leadership in Charter Reform

According to the most sophisticated academic analysis of the factors leading to the successful mayoral leadership, Kevin White should have been able to win on the issue of charter reform. The most astute practical politicians in Boston—from White to Barney Frank to White's long-time opponents—agreed with this assessment. The array of resources and powers that White had to draw on was formidable.

The formal authority of the mayor of Boston is great. Boston is one of the strongest of the "strong mayor" governments in the country. The mayor is elected directly and serves a four-year term, while the council has only a two-year term. There are no other individuals who hold municipal offices filled by a citywide election. Almost all city departments are headed by a single commissioner rather than by a board of commissioners, and the mayor has direct appointing authority over most department heads. In addition, the mayor controls over 2,000 appointments, some to full-time jobs and some to positions on boards and commissions. His staff is exempt from civil service and is not limited in number. Finally, the checks on his power to control the city budget are not nearly as severe as those under which mayors in other big cities operate. He does not have to deal with a Board of Estimate or an independently elected comptroller. The city council has limited control over the mayor's budget: by law they are able only to cut appropriations, not to increase them.

In addition to having strong formal authority, White was proceeding in an environment characterized by several features that should theoretically have operated in his favor.[12] Charter reform could have been achieved at little financial cost to the city. The case for doing something about a heavily criticized, patronage-ridden school committee that was delivering less and less at sharply increasing costs was widely acknowledged. The mayor had clear jurisdiction to initiate the home rule petition. He had considerable staff support to enable him to carry out the project. He also had access to the media, the majority of which supported his proposal when he first initiated it. He had a strong political organization, a sympathetic press in the *Boston Globe,* and ties to a variety of politically oriented citizen groups.

Finally, and perhaps most important, White had all of the personal characteristics and political instincts that according to the most sophisticated analysts of mayoral leadership would lead to his success. White is not a purist, unwilling or unable to try to use his political resources to get what he wants. A liberal mayor in a conservative city, throughout his tenure in office he had had practice in using his accumulated influence to bring others to accept unpopular actions involving busing or tax increases or revaluation of residential property.[13] In this case, too, White demonstrated a capacity and willingness to pyramid his resources and to devise a strategy to use them to his advantage. He had used his staff to lay the groundwork for both the Committee for Boston and the work of the technical advisory panel. He was willing to bargain with the city council on the plan in order to move it through as quickly as possible. As one councillor put it, "Depending on a guy's point of view, he'd have to be a statesman or a fool to turn down the sweeteners."[14] White personally engaged in heavy lobbying throughout the process. In addition, he nailed down the commitment of the legislative leadership to pass the charter reform proposal on the condition that he hold the Boston delegation. He poured his time and energy into lobbying with the representatives. He did not remain above the fray, maintaining a statesmanlike posture, but instead actively bargained, negotiated, and used his political capital.

White brought to charter reform a characteristic that many would argue is a prerequisite to exercising mayoral leadership—an understanding of the rules and a love of the game of politics. In a city and a state where politics is highly personal, he relied on his relationships with the legislative leadership and with some state representatives to seal commitments of support. He also was willing to bargain with city councillors who were initially opposed to the plan. He took the time to plan carefully. Rather than letting events unfold at their own pace and by their own momentum, White had formulated a strategy early. As he put it, "I operate in such a way that I can sometimes see a whole complex process laid out like a chess game. The fun comes in seeing this and in being able to calculate each move of each individual chess piece."[15]

The Failure of Charter Reform and the Paradox of Mayoral Leadership

In many respects, White behaved like a model "new breed" political leader on the issue of charter reform. He understood politics and how the game was played. He recognized that his success at initiating programs and at influencing policy hinged on his ability to maximize his own power and, at the same time, that maximizing his own power was not the only end worth pursuing.[16] Yet although all of this was true, he was unable to get the changes that he wanted in Boston's charter. An analysis of his loss tells us a great deal not only about White and charter reform but also about the exercise of political leadership.

There is some disagreement about precisely which individual or groups did the most damage to White's plan for charter reform. Some observers have suggested that the activity of the media and the organized groups that eventually opposed charter reform was so influential that Boston legislators had to vote against it, or wanted to, because they perceived it to be a widely unpopular change. A local poll showed that a substantial majority of those with an opinion on the issue were opposed, and in the end the question in the daily press had become whether White should be allowed to wrangle more power or job security for himself.[17] Many observers feel that citywide polls do not affect legislators, however. Some of these felt that the death knell was sounded by a few influential citizens in the neighborhoods who were able to persuade their particular representatives in the Boston delegation of the unpopularity of the White proposal in their wards and among their supporters. Individuals powerful in the city or state were crucial in convincing the leadership to release commitments to support the proposal.

In any case, about some things there is no disagreement. The proposal evoked a response from individuals who White believed would play no major role in the consideration of charter change, and at least some of the legislators involved acted more independently than they normally did on other issues. There is also no disagreement about why charter reform became the public issue that it did, and why it aroused so much opposition. The battle over charter reform became a battle over a much larger matter, whether the mayor should be allowed to increase his own power and reduce his electoral risks. The way people reacted to the charter proposal, and in particular to the provision for partisan elections, often depended on the way they felt about White himself.

In trying to assess what went wrong for Mayor White, it is well to ask three questions. Was the objective well chosen? Why did the public react as it did? Could White have brought charter change about despite an unfavorable public reaction? Since all observers agree that the changes White proposed for the schools could have been enacted without difficulty, we shall focus on the widely disputed provisions of the package, those that would have increased the mayor's power and job security. Of these the most controversial was the issue of partisanship.

The Decision to Seek Partisanship

The effects of concentrated power and secure tenure for the chief elected executive are in fact ambiguous. They allow executives a means to accomplish crucial common purposes, but they make it difficult for others, including the public, to thwart actions that are unwise or self-interested. How one balances these considerations in appraising a move to increase a mayor's power or electoral security obviously depends on three factors: how much confidence one has in the individual in power; how pressing is the need for unified action; and how adequate are the present mechanisms for dealing with the need. In practice, the determination of the merits of a proposed increase in executive power is complicated by the fact that the right to judge its appropriateness is widely shared and depends on the individual decisions of many people about whether the need for more unified action is truly pressing and whether suitable mechanisms for checking a fortified executive are also in place. For White, favoring an increase in the power of his own office was relatively straightforward, for he did not fear an abuse of concentrated power. However, for many others with a stake in the outcome, neither the objective of increasing mayoral power nor the means White chose to accomplish that objective—establishing a system of partisan elections—were clear-cut "goods."

Wanting greater powers was not, in itself, a sufficient reason for White to seek the electoral changes. In deciding on the objective of partisanship and in formulating his proposal, White had to take into account four additional factors: the costs of the attempt in terms of the public suspicion of crass self-interest that it might generate; the risks of losing and the possible damage to a valued reputation for skill and power that such a loss might inflict; the possibility that the inclusion of partisanship might lead to the sacrifice of the other valuable objectives in the charter package and of the prestige that would flow from accomplishing them; and the extent to which the benefits of partisanship to White and the city could be realized, even if with some effort, with the resources

White already enjoyed. Judgment of the first factor depended on a prediction about the saliency of partisanship as an issue; the second and third required an assessment of his chance of winning.

As to the last factor, Mayor White insisted that the issue was broader and more significant than the question of whether it heightened his prospects for reelection.[18] The real issue, he argued, was the question of whether factionalism and the politics of personality were interfering significantly with the needs of Boston and whether, if they were, he could solve the resulting problems by the informal use of the powers he already had. His answer was clear:

I came of age in the sixties and was taking political science courses when people really believed in political parties as mechanisms for holding the political system together. To understand my own desire to centralize power in the mayor's office, you must understand how much the city needs to be held together. This city has been saved by a strong executive. When I was re-elected in 1975, I tried to galvanize the city against the forces that were hitting it from outside—the suburbs and the federal government . . . but what I didn't really realize was how little psychological pressure there was for the city to hold together as a constituency against the forces that were killing it. I couldn't control that unless I had power and a lot of it.

You may think that this explanation is only a way of making myself look good on charter. But I couldn't let political power loose in the neighborhoods and in the districts. That would only fragment us. I wanted a strong party as a way to hold power in the center, to keep all the bright young guys who will succeed me from killing each other off. I wanted a process to centralize power that would go on after me—and I felt that partisan elections and strengthened political parties might lead to that.[19]

The Public Reaction

The link between granting the executive more power and receiving concrete benefits in return is a difficult one for citizens to make. But the public is very sensitive to the connection between proposals for increasing executive power and the individual interests of the executive that that power might serve. White understood this and formulated his strategy accordingly. He recognized that only a mood of crisis could win the support of those who did not otherwise feel comfortable with the mayor's style and goals. But there was no crisis, and many of the city's voters were not satisfied with the goals or style of a liberal, sophisticated, "national" mayor in a conservative, ethnic, often parochial city. The nearest thing to a crisis was the soaring price of the city's schools, a matter dealt with in the charter reform package but unrelated to partisanship. White's strategy called for associating partisanship closely with his other reform proposals and for convincing those whose support he needed that the whole package of reform proposals would be good not only for him but also for the city.

White wanted partisanship and believed in partisanship; he also knew that he could not make a case for it strong enough to persuade the public. These facts account for his choice of procedural strategy. There was to be no referendum. There were to be no prolonged public hearings, no separate meetings in the districts and neighborhoods. White recognized that other parts of the package would be acceptable and perhaps even popular. The time for school reform was right. His strategy was to link partisanship inseparably with school reform.

White's plan for dealing with the public reaction to his proposal depended on his assumption that he could capitalize on the need to do something about a public crisis and that the proposal to increase his own power would be seen as incidental to measures to deal with that crisis. The widely felt need for reform would carry the day. In fact, exactly the opposite happened. Public perception of White and of his objectives submerged the question of the merits and demerits of the reforms themselves. A Becker poll taken at the height of the controversy showed that respondents who were favorable to the mayor approved of charter reform by a five-to-three margin, but citizens who had a low opinion of White opposed the plan by a margin of two to one.[20] The poll also showed that very few respondents had knowledge of any of the specifics of the proposal and that those who knew anything about it said that the crucial issue was the question of how much power the mayor should be allowed.

White correctly recognized the "direction" of public reaction to the partisanship issue. He underestimated the breadth and the strength of the reactions of both citizens and officials to his efforts to concentrate power and to change the electoral system. He was wrong in thinking that despite the efforts of opponents there would be relatively little public attention to partisanship and in assuming that what attention it did get would be overwhelmed by favorable reaction to other aspects of the proposal.

The Effect of the Public Reaction on the Outcome

Though he had thought about public reaction, White had not focused his strategy on winning over the public. He did not expect popular support, even if he underestimated the public opposition. He thought the decision could be kept within those centers of power where his own resources could be brought to bear effectively on behalf of the proposal and where public reactions could not. If he made a crucial mistake, this was it. He threw his own resources into what other political actors took as a test of his power. What White did not recognize was that the issue was one where his resources were uniquely vulnerable. Because the controversy revolved around whether or not White should be allowed to secure his position and enhance its resources, the knowledge that he already had both substantial electoral advantages and real power over other political actors served only to heighten suspicion of the proposal and of his steps to win support for it.

Legislators were particularly sensitive on this issue. One of the leading legislative opponents of the charter proposal later complained that because White had provided support for legislators on a number of occasions and because he had the power to grant or withhold support in the future, he felt that he could make even major legislative decisions unilaterally, relying on his power to call in debts and to bestow favors to control representatives regardless of their views of the merits.[21] If this was White's assumption, certainly he was often correct. On many issues affecting Boston, representatives were more than willing to be influenced by the formidable array of resources that the mayor could bring to bear to persuade them that he should get what he wanted, despite the fact that following the mayor's lead diminished both the reality and the public perception of their own independence as politicians. But this was no ordinary issue. It cut unusually deeply in terms of both public suspicion and public consciousness of a supportive legislator's dependence on the mayor. Thus the incentives for representatives to oppose the charter reform proposal were especially strong. Once it became clear that the issue had some salience for the public and that the legislative leadership would not insist on passing White's proposal, legislators had good reasons, as well as the authorization of other powerful actors, to stray from the White fold. At the same time, in refusing to go along with a measure that would increase White's power, they could resist a change that might increase their own dependence on a powerful chief executive.

There are occasions when having substantial resources may constitute a disadvantage for a chief executive. The dispute over charter reform was one of these. The mayor's obvious power in Boston, even without charter reform, itself constituted an argument against the need for increased powers. The proven effectiveness of his electoral machinery enhanced opponents' fears of the advantage he would gain from partisan elections. The regular reports that he was powerful with legislators and could thereby win even on the manifestly unpopular partisanship issue made it necessary for some legislators to prove their independence. For White, having a large number of resources was not always an advantage when the issue was a salient one involving an increase in the mayor's power.

Conclusion

Mayor White almost won; the legislative margin was very close indeed. The costs of the loss to White in terms of his reputation for power and skill were significant but not overwhelming. Other parts of the package may still be enacted separately. One cannot say that his gamble was a foolish one. He did miscalculate the odds; he thought he had a nearly sure thing. What he missed—what the teaching of the 1960s about mayoral power missed—was an important paradox that elected chief executives face.

In order to exercise leadership, elected executives need to understand political power and know how to use it. They must be bold even with some unpopular initiatives. Chief executives who are seen as trying to amass political resources or to reduce the electoral costs of acting independently, however, are viewed with fear or cynicism by a citizenry that has a healthy distrust of concentrating power in the hands of single individuals and a natural suspicion that self-interest motivates politicians as much as the rest of us. This "damned-if-you-do and damned-if-you-don't" paradox is especially salient for mayors. Unlike presidents or even governors, they have jurisdiction over very few issues on which they can take the posture of statesman, thereby softening their images as power-hungry politicians who are concerned only with their electoral futures and with amassing political resources. Perhaps Mayor White could have won despite the fear of concentrated power had he been able to eliminate the accompanying suspicion of self-interest. But he could have accomplished this only by announcing that he would not run again, and that would hardly have served his purposes.

Jeffrey Pressman laid out the conditions for mayoral leadership and argued that elected chief executives must understand the nature of the political environment and attempt to control it in order to be effective at what they do.[22] Analysis of the case of charter reform in Boston leads us to add a corollary to Pressman's general theorem. The theorem is that in order to be a successful leader as a mayor, especially to be able to pursue important goals on which there is not a broad consensus among political leaders, it is necessary to amass power. The corollary is that it is equally necessary to recognize that increased power to pursue disputed goals will not, and perhaps should not, be readily granted to any powerful leader, except perhaps in time of obvious crisis. Political resistance to increases in power heightens as power grows and as the taste for it, however well motivated, becomes more apparent. The implications are clear. The public more readily accords to leaders the powers that come from an ability to persuade and to bargain than the less easily checked force of authority. Great powers are more freely allowed to those who show the least zest for exercising them vigorously. Public fear of, and reaction against, measures designed to concentrate power and to insulate chief executives from public accountablity is widespread and, if circumstances seem to warrant, may become intense.

What are the practical lessons that White or other mayors who seek to lead effectively and independently and want to accomplish substantial goals can learn from looking at how the case of charter reform unfolded? Any mayor needs a powerful office and some security in occupying it; yet as it becomes obvious that he is working to build either power or security, he is likely to generate opposition, distrust, and skepticism about his motives. If there is no popular support for granting the powers he seeks, he has only two choices: either to pursue increased powers secretly, keeping his hand well hidden until the powers are his; or to reduce his expectations and limit his goals to those that he can attain by using those powers he is freely granted. He may seek to build popular support for increasing his powers, but this involves overcoming the public's traditional fears and healthy skepticism and requires accomplishing this herculean feat despite the persuasive opposition of all those who would lose influence.

Our ambivalence about executive power creates a Hobson's choice. A mayor can try to accumulate power in such a way that he effectively conceals what he is doing from the public and, in so doing, assume all the moral and political risks of secretly altering an accepted balance of democratic powers; or he can decide not to risk the public disapproval and censure that often accompany the quest for power and by that decision sacrifice achievement of what he perceives to be important and pressing city needs. To recognize that there is no easy way to resolve this dilemma is at least to begin to understand why the careers of big-city mayors are not often triumphant ones.

Notes

1. The most influential of the studies produced by these analysts is Richard Neustadt's *Presidential Power* (New York: Signet, 1960). In it Neustadt argues that presidents must learn to amass resources, to bargain, and to accumulate as much power as they can in order to further their goals.

2. Jeffrey Pressman, "Preconditions of Mayoral Leadership," in Richard Leach and Timothy O'Rourke, eds., *Dimensions of State and Urban Policymaking* (New York: Macmillan, 1975).

3. See Pressman, "Preconditions of Mayoral Leadership," pp. 280 ff. It is unclear whether the reform in the charter proposed by White actually would have strengthened his chances for electoral victory or his ability to control the machinery of government.

4. See, for example, Harold Seidman's excellent chapter on reorganization of the federal government in *Politics, Position and Power* (New York: Oxford University Press, 1970).

5. Both authors of this article were present at the Parkman dinner.

6. For further description of this proposal, and for a more detailed description and analysis of the mayor's plan for charter change, see the three cases on charter reform in Boston prepared for the John F. Kennedy School of Government under the supervision of Philip Heymann.

7. For a more detailed description of the proposed changes and the rationales for them, see the committee's report, *Increasing Accountability to the Neighborhoods: The Committee for Boston's Plan for Charter Reform* (1976).

8. "City Council, School Committee Revamp Urged," *Boston Globe,* November 18, 1976.

9. "Reorg Plan Calls for Ballot Box," *Herald American* (Boston), December 21, 1976.

10. "FinCom Votes Study of Charter Change," *Boston Globe,* January 7, 1977.

11. "White's Plan Hit by Timilty," *Boston Globe,* January 10, 1977.

12. Pressman, "Preconditions of Mayoral Leadership," p. 280.

13. For an excellent extended discussion of Kevin White's background and career, see Alan Lupo's *Liberty's Chosen Home* (Boston: Little, Brown, 1977).

14. "Hub City Council Faces 'Temptations'," *Boston Globe,* December 8, 1976.

15. Interview with Kevin White, October 12, 1977.

16. Though the conventional wisdom suggests that most mayors seek only those goals that will help them get reelected, Paul Peterson and J. David Greenstone have made a convincing argument that political ideology and personal beliefs also enter into the calculations of mayors in pursuing policy. See their article, "Two Competing Models of the Policy-Making Process: The Community Action Controversy as an Empirical Test," in Willis Hawley and Michael Lipsky, eds., *Theoretical Perspectives on Urban Politics* (Englewood Cliffs, N.J.: Prentice-Hall, 1976).

17. "Public Disapproves Reform Plan But Likes Some Things in It," *Herald American* (Boston), February 22, 1977.

18. Interview with Kevin White, October 12, 1977.

19. Ibid.

20. "Public Disapproves Reform Plan," *Herald American,* February 22, 1977.

21. Interview with a representative from Boston, February 14, 1977.

22. Pressman, "Preconditions of Mayoral Leadership."

Part V

Implementation

Chapter 13

Implementation: A Theoretical Perspective

Martin Rein and Francine F. Rabinovitz

Between Intent and Action

In the past social scientists interested in public policy directed their attention to looking at how policies develop. More recently they have concentrated on determining whether policies actually accomplish what they are intended to accomplish. Therefore, they are investing a good deal of intellectual capital in the problem of how to evaluate the outcomes of governmental actions. But between the inputs and the outputs, there lies a terrain that is still fairly unexplored: the question of how policies change as they are translated from administrative guidelines into practice. This paper is about that process, what we call "the politics of implementation."

We do not intend to test a theory but to develop for the first time a comprehensive perspective of implementation at work. Practitioners—those who carry out policy—have accumulated whatever wisdom on implementation exists, but the advice they offer and receive is incomplete and often inconsistent. Thus, "Implementers are often faced, on crucial matters, with principles leading to divergent alternatives and inadequate information (and understanding) to choose among them."[1]

In our perspective on the processes of implementation we intend not only to sum up existing experience but to provide a framework for understanding such departures from legislative intent as became apparent to the people who were charged with evaluating the social legislation of the 1960s. The "nothing works" interpretation of governmental intervention that arose from such evaluations led many observers to conclude that the scope of government should be reduced because it lacks the capacity to translate its lofty ideas into effective programs of action. Such an indictment may be too sweeping; indeed, the liberal response to this assault is that some programs, judged to have failed, may never have been tried at all.[2] Attending to the implementation process permits us to consider the point at which intent gets translated into action and where and why slippage and reformulation occur. Our purposes for doing this are practical as well as theoretical. We hope to state the perspective of imperatives of the implementation process in such a way that they can be taken into account during the formulation of new policies. Then, perhaps, we can avoid the appearance of impotence that seems now to haunt us.

The Imperatives of Implementation

If implementation is understood as (1) a declaration of government preferences, (2) mediated by a number of actors who (3) create a circular process characterized by reciprocal power relations and negotiations, then the actors must take into account three potentially conflicting imperatives: the legal imperative to do what is legally required; the rational-bureaucratic imperative to do what is rationally defensible; and the consensual imperative to do what can establish agreement among contending influential parties who have a stake in the outcome.

There is a striking relationship between each imperative and one of the interpretations of democratic theory.[3] The legal imperative corresponds to the first view of implementation, which stresses the importance of subordinate compliance to rules that derive from, and are presumed to be consistent with, legislative mandates.[4] The law itself becomes the referent for all the actors in the process. The rational imperative corresponds to the process by which the executive and his bureaucracy engage in problem solving. The criteria for an acceptable solution encompass what, from a bureaucratic point of view, is morally correct, administratively feasible, and an intellectually defensible course of action. The consensual imperative takes as its central concern agreement among contending perspectives as they are represented by the principal actors—the legislature, the executive, and the administrative agency, together with their respective constituencies.

We argue that implementation involves drift from declared purposes where all three imperatives operate together in translating policy into practice. However offensive this may seem to those who prefer an orderly division of labor among politicians, interest groups, and bureaucrats, we need to accept the reality that the implementation process exists precisely because no acceptable trade-off rules can be formulated in advance of practice, and because we cannot assume that the legal imperative will always dominate. In other words, in order to understand how legislation is implemented, we need to appreciate how the legal, rational, and consensual principles manage trade-offs, first by considering the underlying logic of each imperative, and then by examining implementation as a process during which the conflicts among the three imperatives are resolved.

The Legal Imperative

Legislation embodies a process of barter, compromise, and accommodation together with its own rationality, that is, the judgment of what is politically possible when at least most of the interests affected by the law have their say. (The voice of politically weak groups, however, is often not heard. When interested groups become systematically excluded from the discussion process, the view that the legislative outcome is a measure of the intelligence of democracy is greatly undermined.) Implementers must consider the outcome of this process and assume that when they authorize legislation, one of the formal imperatives for civil servants is obedience to the law as stated. When lawyers dominate the implementation process, they try to act as strict constructionists who faithfully interpret legislative intent according to historical precedent. In contrast, when scientists are responsible for implementing legislation (as they do at the Atomic Energy Commission), they may be more inclined to challenge the legislative will when it conflicts with their interpretation of how best to protect the community. However, such simple generalizations are really not adequate. We know, for example, that there are some lawyers who are more preoccupied with rule changing than with rule compliance, but what the circumstances are that lead bureaucracies to recruit one type or another is an intriguing but neglected question.

The interplay between the legislative process and the legal imperative as a guide to implementation is not well understood. There are a number of factors relevant to understanding when legal compliance is strict; however, their importance in relation to one another has not been studied systematically. The following list provides a beginning: (1) the strength and prestige of the legislative committee in which a bill originates; (2) the expertise of the committee's members, hence the presumption that the bill is technically sound; (3) the extent to which areas of disagreement are squarely faced and clarified during legislative debate; and finally (4) the level of support for the law, among both lawmakers and the local communities where the legislation is implemented. In a case such as tax legislation, when all these factors are positive, those who are responsible for implementation will try faithfully to reflect the intent revealed in the bill's legislative history. This process is facilitated by the fact that, as Stanley Surrey explains, "Government personnel . . . involved in the drafting of the tax legislation are also involved in the preparation of Regulations . . . it is understood that explanatory material contained in the Committee Reports on the floor debates will usually be included in the Regulations. . . ."[5] In large part the same persons and interests (whether inside government or outside) involved in the legislative process are equally involved in the implementation process.

The fact is, however, that explicit, tightly organized legislation also limits political maneuverability in the legislative arena and makes coalition building difficult. Thus we may at the outset assume that when clarity, consensus, prestige, and expertise reinforce each other, the legal imperatives will be most binding during implementation. However, fully resolving disagreements early in the legislative process so that clear statutory guidelines will follow is not possible most of the time. Controversial issues are often left open and ambiguous in order to avoid confrontations that could threaten support for and successful passage of a bill. When this happens, guideline writing becomes most important, and implementation is only partially controlled by legal redress through the courts.

Frequently, legislation is left very vague when time for passing it is short and the means to a particular end are poorly understood. The Economic Stabilization Act, for example, authorized the president "to issue such rules and regulations as he may deem appropriate to stabilize prices, rents, wages and salaries. . . ." President Nixon passed the authority delegated him by this act to the Cost of Living Council and the Pay Board. Kenneth Davis[6] points out in a discussion of this situation that Congress was forced to provide a law that simply stated that the administrators responsible to the president should "as rapidly as feasible supply the standards" because no one had a clear idea of what measure stabilization would involve.

The Rational-Bureaucratic Imperative

Even when all the conditions demanded by the legal imperative have been satisfied, the law still will be put into effect only if it does not violate the civil servants' sense of what is reasonable or just. Bureaucratic rationality embraces a number of different perspectives, the first of which includes "consistency of principles." Consider a concrete case. In 1968 Congress included statutory guidelines in the Economic Development Act (EDA) that are internally contradictory. The bill authorized loans only to businesses in sound financial condition. However, it also required that loans be granted only when firms were unable to secure money from any source other than EDA and when there was clear need in the local areas for the firms' products. A business applying for the loan could not hope to advance its position if by doing so it created a possible loss of business for someone else. However difficult it may have been logically to reconcile these principles, we can surely appreciate the motives that inspired businessmen eager to protect local firms from unwanted competition who insisted that they be included in the legislation.

The head of the Business Loan Division in Washington had little recourse but to ignore the legislation as it was written. But how did he reconcile the contradictions? He sought principles that he felt were based on reasonable bureaucratic criteria for disbursing loans. He developed a new set of goals inspired by a variety of purposes that were not in the original legislation: speed in approving projects, which not only made administration easier but also avoided a large unexpended budget for the division at the end of the year; the desire to build a local constituency, which would lend political support for EDA if it ever became necessary; and the wish to protect against the charge of fiscal irresponsibility in supporting businesses that were likely to fail. This strategy specifically called for loans to businesses that could immediately create jobs, encourage entrepreneurship (at a time when the concept of black capitalism was much in vogue), and demonstrate their economic viability (thus protecting EDA's investment).[7]

A second aspect of bureaucratic rationality is "workability." In the legislation that created Health Maintenance Organizations (HMOs), the statute clearly required that employers in certain firms offer their employees the choice between an HMO or some other form of health care. The law also required doctors who participated in the HMO program to practice in a group, not alone, and to be reimbursed on a capitation basis. These stipulations had the perverse effect of alienating both consumers and providers. The unions felt that the "dual choice" requirement weakened their position as sole collective bargaining agent, and doctors opposed the narrow insistence on group practice as the only form of providing care and capitation as the exclusive system of reimbursement. Without the cooperation of the unions and the doctors the program was unworkable. Because the legal and the bureaucratic imperatives conflicted, those responsible for implementing the legislation were confronted with a dilemma. Ultimately they ignored the legal imperative and designed new regulations that would minimize the opposition of the two major interest groups.[8]

Another example where workability was an issue arose in legislation on education. The Federal Bureau of Elementary and Secondary Education felt it had a clear mandate to disburse automatically funds allocated by a formula prescribed in Title I of the Elementary and Secondary Education Act. Instead of monitoring the funds directly to see whether they actually reached their targets, those at the bureau decided to rely only on the original applications to judge whether the applicants' intent was to conform to the requirements. They made this decision in light of the stormy debate about federal control of education that surrounded the legislation. Moreover, the recipients of funds comprised the fledgling bureau's major constituency, as in the health case. Thus bureaucratic rationality dictated that directly confronting the major source of support should be avoided whenever possible if the program was to be workable.[9]

A concern for institutional maintenance, protection, and growth is the primary inspiration for bureaucratic rationality. But such a rationale is more complicated than the simple posture of self-regard by which members of an organization defend their domain. It is also a sense of what professionals and managers who administer the program believe is correct policy; a judgment about what is administratively feasible, which draws on experience accumulated in the collective memory of the bureaucracy; and the determination of the forces that make legislation operationally untenable.

The Consensual Imperative

Finally, one must take into account the interest groups affected by the legislation. Under the consensual imperative, implementation is governed entirely by the preferences of these groups at the same time that the legal and the bureaucratic imperatives are both subordinated.

When a bureaucratic agency is new, weak, and under pressure to produce visible results, the outside interest groups it is supposed to affect actually manage implementation almost by themselves. HUD's Office of New Communities provides an extreme case in point. The office was supposed to develop guidelines for determining what constituted new communities and how they should be distributed across the nation. Inexperienced, understaffed, faced with 200 inquiries by applicants, it came under congressional criticism because no grants had been made a year after funds became available. In its desire to respond quickly, the office had developed guidelines by generalizing principles from material in applications already in for review. Then, once the office had sent the guidelines out to client constituent industries for comment, it adjusted and published them. From the $240 million in loan guarantees controlled by these guidelines, the office awarded grants to the large private companies whose priorities and definitions had themselves already set the standards for judging the qualities desirable in new towns.

When an agency owes its existence to outside interests that also control the legislative process through which its programs develop, it has to pay substantial obeisance to these groups. For example, the origin of environmental policy as well as its administration through the Environmental Protection Agency (EPA) developed out of the very political movement that made environmental quality a public issue. The agency, as a result, faced activist, informed, educated constituencies whose pressures accounted for its very being. Therefore, any opposition to the regulations that exist has come from outside interests attached to oil and energy industries that are in competition with the EPA.

When the consensual imperative dominates, a power shift among the different outside interest groups produces a corresponding shift in the implementation process. Consider the case of regulating the radiation from power plants. About 1971, at a time when the environmental lobby enjoyed a position of maximum influence and power, the authority to set standards was assigned to the Environmental Protection Agency. The agency, in turn, set strict standards for individual plants and tried to intervene at each step in the radiation cycle in order to ensure that nuclear power plants were guarding against the potential dangers of radiation. When the energy crisis later shifted the source of power to the producers of energy, the Nixon administration, without a change in legislation, reassigned the responsibility for radiation control to the Atomic Energy Commission, which, presumably, held a more relaxed attitude toward radiation protection.[10]

In this situation, when the environmentalists lost control of implementation, they turned to seeking change via the initiative process (a procedure by which citizen groups can petition for legislation).

When Imperatives Conflict

Tension among legal, bureaucratic, and consensual imperatives can and often does surface. This is hardly surprising since the power of government is after all cooperatively exercised. When tension occurs, different government bodies have different ways of dealing with it. For example, Congress can sometimes pass laws based on executive policies with which it substantially disagrees. Its usual device for dealing with such a problem is the attachment of riders.

We used to believe that this conflict among imperatives was our protection against the arbitrary exercise of government power. As Paul Appelby wrote in 1949, "The very complexity . . . the often unclear intermingling of responsibility, the fact that various roles in government compete, intervene and engage in conflict, is assurance of the existence of checks and balances more pervasive than those formally defined by the Constitution. . . ."[11] When the demand for action is high and the effects of influence on the results of that action are obscured, the general result is not a sense of protection against arbitrary behavior but primarily a widespread sense of frustration.

The Stages of Implementation

Thus far we have treated implementation as if it were a unified process. But in fact implementation proceeds through three major stages—guideline development, resource distribution, and oversight—with the legal, rational, and consensual imperatives operating at each stage along the way.

First, guidelines are developed at the point where legislative intent is translated into administrative prescriptions for action. Once developed, guidelines are promulgated to those individuals in departments who must ultimately administer the program. In the case of federal legislation the new regulations and their guidelines are printed in the *Federal Register,* and these are often modified after interested parties get a chance to challenge them.

Second, resources are allotted to the administrative agencies responsible for carrying out the legislation. However, the amount of resources available is not entirely set beforehand because there are usually discrepancies between appropriation and authorization. Furthermore, the time when resources become available is also crucial for implementation.

Third, some process of oversight must be started as a way of promoting accountability at the lower levels of the bureaucracy. This procedure follows Kaufman's interpretation of how noncompliance threatens democratic principles: if guideline evasion is rampant, the legitimacy of legislation is threatened. The three most commonly used forms of oversight are monitoring, auditing, and evaluation. (Monitoring how legislation is put into practice is different from evaluating its outcomes. The former is concerned with whether practice complies with guidelines, the latter with whether practice produces results.)

It should be noted that to discuss these three stages of implementation separately is only a heuristic device, since the process is not linear but circular. Thus the legislature monitors the guidelines developed by the administration; those who must implement the guidelines monitor and attempt to influence that administration; those who develop guidelines must determine whether the lower reaches of the bureaucracy comply with them.

Guideline Development

Guideline development—normally the responsibility of an administrative agency—is the first stage in the process of implementation. Administrators, by demonstrating the conformity of guidelines to legislation, often will try to reassure the legislature that their programs are neutral in terms of their legislative intent. In testifying on the administration of the revenue-sharing program, John Ehrlichman, then chief counsel to the president of the United States, said that "in developing revenue sharing guidelines we merely converted the requirement of the law into administrative regulations."[12] Nevertheless, this is the stage in making legislation consistent with the bureaucracy's interpretation of what is reasonable where the scope for the administrative initiative is actually enormous. For example, the legislative committee investigating the California Welfare Department's implementation of the 1971 reform act criticized the former director for issuing regulations which "in general conflicted with legislative intent and which specifically conflicted with understandings reached in executive-legislative negotiations on the bill." The director of the State Welfare failed, according to the report, to implement *all* the provisions of the act particularly favored by the legislature.[13] Then there is the recent conflict between Congress and the administration over guidelines developed to implement social services. Congress intended to make social services available across the board, even to those who might potentially become welfare recipients in the future, but the existing guidelines restricted social services primarily to those who were already receiving welfare. By concentrating on those in severest need, the guidelines prohibited the broader spectrum of the lower-middle-income population from receiving welfare and made access to services very highly selective. This conflict between the administration and Congress was bitter and acrimonious, with the Senate Finance Committee threatening at one stage to overturn the regulations and to report out of committee a program that had no federal regulations on how the states should spend social service funds.[14]

Some states' governments have recognized explicitly in their own procedures that guidelines have the power to modify legislative intent. Michigan, for example, has a standing joint committee that regularly reviews administrative regulations and can bring them before the entire legislature for new action.[15] In the national government, on the other hand, there is no mechanism other than Congress itself for resolving disparities between legislation and guidelines. The Office of Management and Budget (OMB) is mandated to act as arbiter when conflicts among regulations by administrative agencies become rampant.

There is more to the guidelines process than the mere reinterpretation of legislation. Buried in guidelines are numerous decisions about how to make a program work. For example, an agency often must decide whether it should prescribe specific requirements or simply indicate the type of result it favors. The Model Cities administration commissioned studies of citizen participation and concluded that it preferred "maximum expression," which involved citizens at eight different parts of the decision-making process. Although some bureaucrats within Model Cities' local agencies argued that such citizen activity should be prescribed at each stage along the way, the central agency felt it had issued this finding as information only and had set broad standards for participation.

There are also decisions to be made at this stage on whether new policies should be either retro- or proactive. For example, in developing the guidelines for the density and height of buildings under the 1961 revision of New York's zoning ordinance, a choice had to be made between on the one hand requiring the existing industrial establishments to conform to new standards or allowing a "year of grace" so that all buildings in progress could be completed under old regulations, and on the other deciding that the new law should not cover existing arrangements at all.

Despite its substantive impact, the guidelines-development process rarely has been analyzed by students of policy and administration. Perhaps they have neglected this stage because it seems at first glance so simple and so technical: Congress passes a law, and then administrators write rules that provide detailed instructions for carrying out that law. But once one examines the whole process in detail, such an interpretation is hard to sustain. In fact, once we had recognized that policy is defined first in law form, which in turn is translated into guidelines, we decided to commission a set of detailed cases on guideline development in order to better understand that process.[16]

Resource Distribution

The second stage in the implementation process is characterized by negotiations over the amount of resources and the timing of their availability as the process moves from appropriation through authorization to the ultimate release (or possible impounding) of funds. In the American federal system the congressional committees alone do not actually control the flow of resources with one exception, the administration of formula-grant programs such as welfare. In these cases, funds are awarded through an open-ended grant formula and then disbursed by the Office of Management and Budget, an arm of the executive branch. In 1970 only about 65 percent of funds authorized were appropriated, in contrast with a rate of 80 percent in 1966. The divergence that had grown up between authorization and appropriations was particularly dramatic in the Department of Health, Education, and Welfare, where appropriations as a percentage of authorizations fell from 80 to 50 percent.[17] Roy Ash, former OMB director, indicated in response to questions about an impounded item that "it was never intended that all authorized funds could be spent."[18]

The authorization-appropriation-disbursement split can affect the implementation process itself. This can happen when there are time delays in making authorized funds finally available. One outcome is the well-known, end-of-the-year fund dumping—a not-uncommon feature in the operation of many programs. Why should scarce resources be casually dumped to prevent their reverting back to the government? One explanation is the fear that spending less than was requested will be interpreted as having overestimated what was needed, and this could threaten the next year's appropriations. However, the only time appropriations committees, which are by nature anxious about the cost of programs, actually become directly involved in their implementation is when, for example, they commission special investigations to ferret out possible abuse.

Timing, that is, when the resources really become available to an administrative agency, may be as crucial for implementation as their actual amount. The fact that the legislative and executive branches reckon time differently—one by the fiscal, the other by the calendar year—creates problems. In the interim between presidential budgeting and congressional action, agencies with routine programs do better than new programs. New programs, "subject to sudden shifts in workloads or demands for speedy action, are condemned to inauspicious starts, so that their managers are seen to be failures before they have a chance to act. More energy in Washington is consumed, more frustration generated, more constraints placed on effective management by apparent conflicts in legislative and executive calendars than by any other single condition."[19]

Timing arrangements for financing also provide enormous bureaucratic leeway. An example from HUD experience is indicative. When it was first organized, HUD set aside millions of dollars of its program funds for cities to cover their projects from inception to completion. Angered by the inflexibility this created within cities, the next administration's officials asked cities to plan on a short-term basis, a year at a time, but still using funds from the committed long-term allotments. Impounding stopped the shell game—and left most cities with half-finished projects and no future funds.

Normal OMB procedure permits the program's office to dole out the funds appropriated by the standards it sets itself. In one instance, this power led to very rapid spending, without debate, of money set aside for the Highway Trust Fund. Owing to such occurrences, Congress has now reserved for itself the privilege of "reserving" or "apportioning" the money for the fund. However, the effect of this move on policy is still not very clear.

Of course not all programs have the degree of flexibility allowed the Highway Trust Fund. Many operate with a time constraint that by law controls the flow of funds, and when fiscal time schedules are rigidly routinized, implementation naturally has a different history.

The Oversight Process

Program oversight takes three forms: monitoring, auditing, and evaluating. Of the three, monitoring is the least publicized. The American government has always had procedures for monitoring departmental compliance, and the agency responsible for it is the OMB. Normally the OMB issues numbered circulars that establish what the monitoring process will be for particular departments. However, it happens that agencies often do not conform to the circular's directions for setting up communications systems needed for continuous monitoring.

The process of auditing traditionally refers to the monitoring of financial accounts and is quite complex because of the many agencies that perform the service. A special unit within an agency that administers a program can audit that program (as in the case of HEW). However, an independent agency such as the General Accounting Office also performs audits. Either way, unlike the monitoring procedure, auditing is kept organizationally separate from the implementing departments of the agency being audited. This practice was established to assure disinterested review. Even so, one might speculate that the internal audits are undertaken as a way of warding off or dealing with the external audits. As such, they are not devices for learning but a defense of established practice.

Of course, both kinds of audits may languish for want of subsequent action. For information acquired in audit to be used, it may be necessary to leak the findings to persons outside the process so they can feed it back as pressure on those within. The audit, through such indirect routes, may serve as the handmaiden to guideline development. This gives rise to one very intriguing question: Under what conditions does the audit function in the political game of attack and defense, and when does it serve as a mechanism for collective learning?

A certain program may call for a highly standardized auditing procedure, where each audit, internal or external, is expected to conform to the same rules. On the other hand, there may be room in an audit for considerable discretion. When allowed discretion in their review, some auditors will probe the relationship between operations and legislative intent. When this is the case, audits perform functions similar to those performed by evaluations.

Evaluation traditionally refers to the assessment of a program's achievements. The recent emphasis on evaluation has emerged from the discovery that even when monitoring confirms that proper procedures are being adhered to, there is still no guarantee that they will achieve the desired outcome. Evaluation is in principle a logical and appealing idea because the emphasis on results allows Congress to assess whether its policies are working. However, evaluations are often not precise enough instruments to determine whether a program has failed and should be ended.[20]

The distinctions between these three types of oversight processes are becoming quite blurred. This is evident, for example, from the way in which the General Accounting Office, the government's principal auditor, conducts its audit programs. GAO's own figures provide an idea of the scope of its activities. It estimates that over the past five years about 30 percent of its professional staff has become involved in actually evaluating federal programs under the authority granted it by the Legislative Reorganization Act of 1970. Under this act, the GAO has considerable scope and can initiate evaluations (aside from audits) on its own as well as respond to congressional requests for evaluations.

No matter how well oversight mechanisms such as these work at the outset, they all tend to wear down with time. Usually, the overseer starts taking into account mitigating circumstances that could endanger performance or required procedures. Eventually, the laxity he perceives becomes the object of criticism. The old procedures for oversight are nonetheless retained, but now the overseer creates a new institution to check on those who do the checking.[21] Thus the process of oversight is just as subject to criticism as the guidelines-development process. When during the sixties government relied chiefly on the guidelines process for control, administrators complained that procedures were unrelated to results. Now in the seventies they complain that the achievement is thwarted by the preoccupation with measuring progress!

The Principle of Circularity

We have pointed out that all the stages of implementation are interdependent. The process is not one of a graceful, one-dimensional transition from legislation to guidelines and then to auditing and evaluation. Instead it is circular or looping. For example, in the tax arena we find that civil servants affect legislation even before it is drafted. They take account of the law's potential for implementation by trying to anticipate the reactions and preferences of those for whom the program is designed. Guidelines are not simply imposed on new tax legislation. The law requires that they be drafted and published in the *Federal Register* to give interested parties a chance to react to the new proposals. Then interest groups and the bureaucracy responsible for implementation have an opportunity to intervene. Obviously the more negotiation with and accommodation to the groups that are to be affected by federal guidelines, the greater the disparity between legislation and practice.

The postwar American experience with gasoline rationing provides a good example of the circulatory process at work in legislation initiated from the bottom up. Local boards, out of a sense of moral obligation, began on their own to give returning veterans extra gas allotments. This maneuver became popular with the public, though it was not within the legislation or the national guidelines for gas rationing. Regional boards then requested the national board to legitimate the policy. The national board ultimately changed its guidelines, bowing in part to the preferences of local subunits and in part to the fear of the regional boards that they would lose control over the local boards through these ad hoc decisions.[22] The politics of accommodation, in this case, did not cease after the legislation had been developed.

Again, no one participant in the process ever really is willing to stop intervening in the other parts of the process just because his stage has been passed. Thus Congress sometimes insists on participating in the implementation process. Recognizing that different agencies have characteristically different approaches to programs in the same subject area, Congress also frequently attempts to influence implementation at the outset by specifying which department will administer a new program.[23] But Congress's choice of a unit does not assure its wishes will prevail. A case in point is Section 7 of the enabling legislation for the Department of Transportation (DOT). Initially Congress asked that the department develop its own standards for federal investment in transportation. Dissatisfied, it later decided on stricter controls. It modified the bill so that the department had to submit its proposed guidelines to Congress for ultimate approval. There have been times when Congress has gone even further in certain fields by expressly prohibiting various departments from researching their own implementation standards.[24]

Congress has sometimes demonstrated that it does not understand that it operates under the principle of circularity. It has tended to resist proposals for simplifying implementation such as the OMB-backed idea of combining joint funding for categorical grants into single packages or the proposal of the Advisory Commission on Intergovernmental Relations for consolidating certain grants. Its argument has been that legislative prerogatives should not be confused with executive initiative, although in fact such mixtures are a regular occurrence.

Oversight and Circularity

Programs have both an exchange value and a use value. Some scholars have argued that new programs are valued primarily as a medium of exchange for politicians, bureaucrats, and interest groups.[25] Their very existence provides legislators with an activities list to justify getting elected again, bureaucrats with similar rationales for continuing their appointments, and groups outside the executive arena with tangible evidence of service to particular interests. But for the overseers of social programs it is the use value that is of primary importance. Therefore the result of monitoring, auditing, and evaluating should be to stimulate the process of circularity by altering legislative intent and administrative practice.

When oversight is taken seriously, it generates pressure to develop indicators of program performance, which are not only in-process measures of service activities but also outcome measures of program achievement. Surprisingly, the most complex arguments have developed over the meaning of specific performance measures as outcome indicators: Are police arrest figures useful as measures of officer performance or must arrest/conviction rates be computed? Do complaint clearance rates tell us about the efficiency of fraud prosecution offices or do the rates need to be weighted for types of consumer crime? These questions may be complex, but they are clearly relevant. There is a danger, however, that the search for objective outcome measures may obscure the initial assumptions about the program and preempt the legislative function. The very assumption that programs are designed to achieve measurable ends may itself be unwarranted.

In order to elucidate how the oversight process stimulates the principle of circularity, we believe that it is necessary to establish a somewhat broader list of potential program outcomes than currently exists. Let us concede that legislation is designed to bring about some level of change, once implemented. However, in the case of social legislation, there is often no clear consensus of what overall social goals the legislature is aiming toward. This is where a broader set of possible outcomes would be helpful. Limiting our comments to the evaluation process, we propose three different ways in which evaluation may influence legislation and administration: by producing changes in program activities, changes in purpose, and changes in the climate of opinion.

By a change in program activity we mean a shift in something like the volume of resources available, the character of the program in question, or the distribution of beneficiaries or costs. When these shifts occur, as they often do, a program evaluation can detect them and thus provide clues for understanding how purpose evolves from practice.

For example, there are programs that have more than one ultimate goal. Often the success of one part of the program may not mean that another has succeeded as well. A medical care program like Medicaid was designed to improve the access of low-income groups to medical resources as well as the health of the population. Evaluation has demonstrated that Medicaid did in fact improve access to good care, but to date it has not necessarily improved the health of our low-income citizens. There are other programs that have not only multiple but also ambiguous, uncertain, and evolving goals. Confronted with these circumstances, evaluators find it difficult to ferret out purpose without imposing their own interpretation.

By a change in purpose, we mean simply that a program has accomplished its critical mission even though somewhere along the way its content has changed. Consider the case of manpower programs. By the late sixties a marked change of purpose in the programs emerged, in which priority was given to disadvantaged groups rather than to middle-income workers, as before. Consequently, the volume, programmatic character, and clientele of these programs changed dramatically. An evaluator typically might ask if a manpower program provided its graduates with jobs that represented an economic improvement over their past circumstances and if they had been able to hold onto these jobs, thereby improving their net position over time. He would find that despite the changes that did occur, the program's central thrust of securing stable and adequate jobs did not change.

The case of a change in the climate of opinion is one in which a program contributes to altering the context or atmosphere in which policies are developed. A program may fail to capture substantial resources or achieve its mission but nevertheless contribute to altering the political climate in which issues are discussed. For example, voter registration programs failed to achieve their objectives because they ran into stubborn opposition from local political parties fearing that the inclusion of new groups in local politics would threaten their established position. However, their actions created a climate of opinion that made government more willing to experiment with other forms of participation less threatening to established institutions. The idea of community control of school and medical care likewise may be understood in this context. In other words, a program may fail in the short run while still influencing the trend of future developments.

Environmental Conditions

We have sketched out a broad framework from which to consider the imperatives, stages, dynamics, and outcomes of the process of implementation. It seems clear that the way in which legislation is actually implemented also depends on environmental conditions. There are three crucial environmental conditions that influence the implementation process: goals saliency, complexity of the process itself, and the nature and level of available resources.

These conditions have different impacts on the various levels of government that exist within our system.

Goals Saliency

Legislation can be classified in terms of how clear it is about what it wants to accomplish; whether it wishes to accomplish its stated purposes immediately or whether it is to some extent a symbolic process; and, finally, how urgent the sponsors feel the legislation's implementation is compared with their other goals. For example, Congress has passed various pieces of legislation to bolster the economy of depressed areas, but it has chosen as its modus operandi the coordination of federal agencies with other goals to pursue and for which area redevelopment is peripheral. Thus the Defense Department has always resisted paying the cost premiums incurred when using suppliers in depressed areas because it is under greater pressure to keep costs down and to sustain the plants erected by its captive suppliers than it is to encourage suppliers to move to depressed areas.[26] In the new communities program, HUD has argued that the slow pace of its work is not principally caused by vague and conflicting goals but by the fact that "most of the original provisions of the Act designed to achieve these goals have not been funded." Administrative action terminated all of those provisions, a good indication of unwillingness to incur the costs of reaching a program's original goals.

Ambiguous, symbolic, low-saliency programs are characteristically implemented in a very complex, circular fashion. Programs whose goals are clear, instrumental, and urgent are generally more centrally and hierarchically implemented.

Implementers of newly created programs having little past precedent may try to deal with goals uncertainty by developing weak and general guidelines. Alternatively, they may rely upon blue-ribbon panel reviews designed to observe the program and guide it through its formative years. However, older programs that have benefited from institutional learning about what their goals are may rely more on solid guidelines and less on monitoring and review.

We believe that a comparison of some aspects of foreign policy to similar aspects of domestic policy, would show that the process of implementation in the former is much more straightforward and direct and interest groups are much more limited in their ability to intrude their preferences. We therefore conclude, as common sense would dictate, that purpose should and does affect process. But under what conditions is it possible to enjoy clear purposes that have been agreed upon and in this way to limit the complexity of the implementation process? Galbraith explains the phenomenon in terms of the decline of power of the legislature: Just as public bodies can become the captives of the firms they seek to regulate, so too have the Armed Services and Appropriations committees become the ally of public bureaucracies that enjoy substantial amounts of power because of the influence of the constituencies supporting them. The members of these committees "derive power in Congress, patronage, and prestige in the community at large by identifying themselves fully with the interests of the military bureaucracies of which nominally they are the watchdogs."[27]

When analyzing the question of clarity of intent and priority of purpose, we need to ask, Clear for whom? A bill may, after all, have clarity and saliency for the particular person in Congress who heads an influential committee and who can thereby affect the resources of the program as well as the peace of mind of the civil servants who administer it. We expect that a bill that has a close and influential guardian will have a different history of implementation than legislation that has no such overseer.

In addition, each new administration selects legislation to symbolize the main philosophy of the newly elected government. We should therefore expect that some programs would have higher urgency and enjoy higher priority than others. Under these circumstances the executive office will review the regulations, set down clear deadlines for developing the guidelines, and assign loyal and able civil servants to the task of implementation, all the while bypassing the established bureaucracy if necessary. Clarity, consistency, sincerity, and saliency of goals should lead toward greater centralization of the process of implementation. The fewer the loops between legislation, guidelines, and practice, the more will be done, and the less urgent will be the need to monitor and review the process.

Complexity

Implementation is also a function of the number of levels, the number of agencies, and the number of participants who have a say in the process or are able to veto any stage along the way. A study by Hawley illustrates this point.[28] From an analysis of urban renewal decisions, he concluded that the wider the range of participation, the less likely were urban renewal programs to be implemented in the community. Similarly, Greenstone and Peterson conclude that more poverty funding was received and distributed in cities where community participation was low than where maximum feasible participation was emphasized.[29]

Participation, according to this last study, inhibits decision making. The idea is that the more open the system is and the greater the number of actors with decision and veto power, the less likely decisions are to be made. An open and complex decision process that functions at many levels is always in danger of eroding consensus and distorting its initial priorities.

However, one can also argue that complexity itself is a protection. For example, urban renewal generally takes quite a long time. A HUD management study conducted in 1969 reported that the process for approving an urban renewal project had come to contain some 4,000 steps. Saying no at any point was impossible because the several thousand preceding steps locked the reviewer in!

Another aspect of complexity is the nature of the policy environment in which particular programs are to be carried out. In the absence of uniform, coherent objectives and overriding principles, an environment overcrowded with various legislative mandates may create a situation where the multiplicity of programs may cancel each other out.

Consider an example in housing policy which is not atypical in many countries. The value of tax relief to aid home purchases rises in proportion to the individual's tax rate and hence income. But construction subsidies for rented units bear no relation to the income of tenants. Rent controls do provide a way for low-income families to find accommodations at prices they can afford, but at the same time they may provide disincentives for building privately constructed housing. Subsidized public housing offers high housing standards and relatively low rents that the poor can afford. All these programs in combination represent a substantial expenditure for public aid to home owners and tenants. However, because they have no clear rationale for distribution behind them, they not only distort housing markets considerably but also create an arena where the mandates may come into open conflict and undo each other.

Resources

Implementation is also a function of the type and level of resources required for action. Not all legislation requires that resources take the shape of a direct outlay of expenditures. For example, if a law is passed that requires all utilities to use coal for 25 percent of their energy, no new spending is required by government. (There are obvious beneficiaries of such a policy, although who pays the final costs may be more obscure.) Removing the legal obstacles to clinical abortions or requiring that all applications for airports and sewers by cities be approved by an areawide planning agency are other examples of laws that do not need direct outlays of funds. Still another example of legislation that does not require a direct outlay of money is legislation that makes it worthwhile for middle-income families to own their own homes in order to take advantage of tax concessions. Although intermediaries may be necessary to notify people of their rights and their potential eligibility for such benefits, nonetheless, one should not expect such legislation to require elaborate machinery for monitoring and review.

We expect that the pattern of implementation will vary according to the nature of the resources required. Therefore it may be useful in line with the different examples just cited, to distinguish between types of legislation by resource requirements—those designed to regulate the standards of products or the performance of individuals, firms, or agencies, and others that provide incentives or distribute public largesse in the form of services or cash. Kaufman has written on a similar theme, in which he studied administrative feedback.[30] He selected various federal bureaus where, as he explained, feedback ought to be well developed because the functions performed by these bureaus require accountability and control. Accordingly, he tried to classify bureaus by function (whether they directly administer programs, disburse funds, regulate behavior, or service clientele) and administration (whether they administer their own or intergovernmental programs). But his classification seems unsatisfactory to us, because he found widely different behaviors within the same categories. For example, in his classification of service bureaus administering their own programs are the Forest Service with tight feedback as well as the Bureau of Elementary and Secondary Education with lax feedback. Missing in his design is a theory about how the operations of the bureau would effect their use of feedback procedures. Unfortunately, the classification we have developed is vulnerable to the same criticism.

The level of resources to be distributed also influences the way in which implementation takes place. When the stakes are high, pressure for a piece of the pie will accordingly be strong. For example, every consultant to EDA recommended that projects be concentrated in a single growth center in each district, but because congressmen had to gain support from constituents all over their districts, the resources were spread out. Similarly, the original Model Cities program was to be limited to just a few towns. Congress eventually halved the appropriation for this program, but not before it had doubled the number of cities receiving grants from the original 75 to 150. Of course, the effect of these new pressures diluted the amount of resources available to perform the functions of monitoring, review, audit, and evaluation and thus reduced oversight and vigilance.

Implications

For years Americans have operated with a paradigm of pluralism. The heart of the pluralism theory is that government responds to those public demands that are exerted through formal associations. Because of the great number of interest groups, some in competition with each other, the power to direct policy is quite dispersed. Policy, then, is the result of compromise among these various interest groups. In the course of the negotiations toward compromise, every contender gets some benefits, for no interest is altogether forsaken.[31] Along the way, membership overlaps among these groups and a general process of socialization to a set of overriding values help to reduce polarization. Whatever conflicting demands remain are reconciled by government, which then assigns priorities for them.

Along with others, we have tried to argue that such a conception based on pluralism is incomplete. Both groups and governments act not simply in terms of the input of demands and pressure but in terms of their own perception of future requirements. Government bureaucracies do not simply respond to external pressure but vigorously attempt to create constituencies to support their agenda for reform. Efforts to impose standards of behavior on a reluctant or indifferent community go beyond the view that government only reacts to pressure.

Incrementalist theories were designed (in some sense) to correct for this oversight in group theory. Incrementalism captures the separate importance of large formal organizations rather than the role of individuals and groups. But incrementalism is past-oriented. It encourages the view that what happens in one period is pretty much determined by what happened earlier, because administrators rarely depart significantly from what they are already doing. They muddle through as best they can, making only marginal changes in the established operations of government.[32]

However, when government's view of the future shapes its present action, one must conclude that it is not merely acting in response to old habits and decision rules, as the marginal, incremental, adaptive view would imply. One must take into account administrative and legislative initiatives in order to understand how the civil service implements and in the course of implementation develops policy. An impartial account of the process can not take the view that an integration of competing views is based solely on the principle of marginal adjustments, which helps to bring about a consensus. Some notion of instrumental rationality is needed as well, where implementation takes place in relation to a purpose. In other words, although the Simon-Lindblom satisficing scheme can adequately describe the cognitive processes of decision implementers, policies and programs vary dramatically in longevity, resources, and associated struggles for scarce funds.[33] Thus the process is less one of slow incremental change than of bureaucratic entrepreneurship, some more and some less successful.[34] But that is not to say that the accumulation of slower changes, which incremental descriptions tend to underemphasize, is not important to implementation.

The question that arises is, of course, Whose purpose? The

liberal critique has traditionally been that bureaucracy works, all right, but only toward its own purposes. Robert Wood, for example, notes, "The real difficulty is that public agencies often achieve goals and carry out objectives that political observers or the public have come to feel are out of date, inadequate in scope or plain wrong. (Alternatively we feel that the objectives are in fact set internally by the public organizations themselves; hence, they are self serving, not serving us)."[35] The radical critique disagrees; it has traditionally argued that such organizations are instruments of one or another part of the private sector.

We believe either position is oversimplified. The process of implementation and who or what is being served at any one point in time or on any level are often quite unclear. The implementation process, related as it normally is to narrowly defined goals and outcomes, muddles the question of whether the functions of bureaucracies are in fact narrowly confined to policies with the most potential. Radicals would have us believe this mystification is deliberate. Conservative thinkers would take this very ambiguity to buttress their own argument. For example, Edward Banfield has argued that since implementation can be a complex process, open to change at every level, governments should adopt only those policies that can be easily implemented. In domestic welfare policy, this point of view has led to the support of an income strategy and the repudiation of services or indirect-subsidy approaches. But a clear, easily implemented, but limited policy is not without its own costs. There may be a conflict between what can be implemented and what is useful. It is not that the poor do not need money but that a small marginal increase in money may not be enough to prevent the poor from being victimized by the private market. Difficult as service strategies may be to implement, government may have to develop and improve upon them. We believe that changing the performance of institutions is an aim government cannot altogether forsake.

In summary, then, we are suggesting that the politics of implementation is governed by at least three formal imperatives: (1) respect for legal intent (legal rationality), which is (2) mediated by the concern for instrumental rationality as it is defined by civil servants yet (3) informed by the knowledge that action requires internal and external consensus. The politics of implementation may be best understood as an attempt to resolve conflicts among these imperatives. The way in which conflicts are resolved is a function of the purposes (their clarity, saliency, consistency), the resources (kind, level, and timing), and the complexity of the administrative process of implementation.

In general, one ought to be able to expect that clear and salient nonsymbolic goals, with as little complexity as possible in the stages of implementation, a low degree of circularity among them, and a large amount of resources will create programs where there is a minimum of discretion, a low level of slippage, and a maximum degree of consensus. In some instances clear goals emerge from initially ambiguous purposes. For that to happen, it takes a consensus among the competing interests to help clarify over time the ambiguous, vague, and indefinite programs. But the process does not always work this way. Some governmental purposes are forever mired by uncertainty of commitment, ambivalence, and contradiction. Under these circumstances, consensus is always fragile, and intent can be inferred only retrospectively, in the course of implementation

Notes

1. Paul Berman and Milbrey W. McLaughlin, "*Implementing Innovations: Revisions for an Agenda for a Study of Change Agent Programs in Education,*" Rand Corporation Working Note WN 8450-1-HEW (Santa Monica, Calif., November 1973).

2. Robert Weiss and Martin Rein, "Input Analysis in Program Evaluation," MIT Department of Urban Studies and Planning, mimeo (1978).

3. For a fuller discussion of the interplay between democratic theories and the process of implementation, see Martin Rein and Francine Rabinovitz, "Implementation: A Theoretical Perspective," Harvard-MIT Joint Center for Urban Studies Working Paper No. 43, March 1977.

4. Stanley Surrey, "Treasury Department Regulatory Material under the Tax Code," in Jeffrey Pressman, Francine Rabinovitz, and Martin Rein, eds., *Guidelines, Policy Sciences* 7 (December 1976), special issue.

5. Herbert Kaufman, *Administrative Feedback* (Washington D.C.: Brookings Institution, 1973).

6. Kenneth Davis, *Discretionary Justice* (Baton Rouge: Louisiana State University Press, 1969).

7. Jeffrey Pressman and Aaron Wildavsky, *Implementation* (Berkeley: University of California Press, 1973), chap. 4.

8. Drew Altman and Harvey Sapolsky, in Pressman, Rabinovitz, and Rein, *Guidelines,* pp. 417-439.

9. Jerome T. Murphy, "Title 1 of ESEA: The Politics of Implementing Federal Education Reform," *Harvard Educational Review* 41 (1971): 35-64.

10. Richard D. Lyonds, "EPS Loses Its Authority to Limit Plant Radiation," *New York Times,* Dec. 12, 1973.

11. Paul Appelby, *Policy and Administration* (Birmingham: University of Alabama Press, 1949).

12. Juergen Haber, "Revenue Sharing Report: Ehrlichman Promises Audits and Strict Evaluation of Local Programs," *National Journal Reports* 5 (7), Jan. 1973.

13. Senate-Assembly Subcommittee on Implementation of Welfare Reform, California, *Report to the Legislature* (March 17, 1972).

14. Judith Turner, "Welfare Reform: HEW Sidesteps Showdown with Congress over Revamping Social Service Regulations," *National Journal Reports* 5 (1973): 1132-1138.

15. Malcolm E. Jewell and Samuel C. Patterson, *The Legislative Process in the U.S.* (New York: Random House, 1966), chap. 19.

16. Francine Rabinovitz, Jeffrey Pressman, and Martin Rein, "Guidelines: A Plethora of Forms, Authors and Functions," *Policy Sciences* 4 (1976), pp. 399-416.

17. Advisory Commission on Intergovernmental Relations, *The Gap Between Federal Aid Authorization and Appropriations: Fiscal Years 1966-1970,* Report M-52, in cooperation with the Council of State Governments (Washington D.C.: Government Printing Office, 1970).

18. *New York Times,* January 19, 1974.

19. Robert Wood, "When Government Works," *The Public Interest* 17 (Winter 1970).

20. Genevieve J. Kelezo, "Program Evaluation: Emerging Issues of Possible Legislative Concern Relating to the Conduct and Use of Evaluation in the Congress and the Executive Branch," Congressional Research Service, Library of Congress Publication no. 74-78SS (Washington, D.C., 1974).

21. H. L. LaFramboise, "Administrative Inspection and Methods Analysis in the Department of Veterans' Affairs," *Canadian Public Administration* 2 (1959): 195-201.

22. William H. Riker, "The Veterans' Gas Ration," in Harold Stein, ed., *Public Administration and Policy Development* (New York: Harcourt Brace, 1952), pp. 744-759.

23. James A. Noone, "New Federal Programs Seek to Aid State in Control of Coastal Area Exploitation," *National Journal Reports* 4 (1973): 1889.

24. B. W. Barsness, "Policy, Challenges and Objectives of the Department of Transportation," *Quarterly Review of Economics and Business* 9 (1969): 63-76.

25. Robert R. Alford, "The Political Economy of Health Care: Dynamics without Change," *Politics and Society* 2 (1972): 127-165.

26. Anthony Downs, "Testimony on National Public Works Investment Policy," U.S. House of Representatives, November 1, 1973.

27. John Galbraith, *Economics and the Public Purpose* (Boston: Houghton Mifflin Co., 1973), p. 174. See also Harvey M. Sapolsky, *The Polaris System Development: Bureaucratic and Programmatic Success in Government* (Cambridge, Mass.: Harvard University Press, 1972).

28. Amos Hawley, "Community Power and Urban Renewal Success," *American Journal of Sociology* 68 (1963): 422-431.

29. J. D. Greenstone and P. E. Peterson, "Reformers, Machines and the War on Poverty," in J. Q. Wilson, ed., *City Politics and Public Policy* (New York: Wiley, 1966), pp. 267-293.

30. Kaufman, *Administrative Feedback*.

31. For a criticism of this view based on survey data see Richard Hamilton, *Class and Politics in the United States* (New York: Wiley, 1972), pp. 34-36.

32. O. Davis, M. Dempster, and A. Wildavsky, "A Theory of the Budgetary Process," *American Political Science Review* 60 (1966): 529-547.

33. Charles Lindblom, "The Science of Muddling Through," *Public Administration Review* 29 (1959): pp. 79-88.

34. Peter B. Natchez and Irvin C. Bupp, "Policy and Priority in the Budgetary Process," *American Political Science Review* 67 (1973): 951-964.

35. Wood, "When Government Works."

Chapter 14

What Ronald Reagan Can Teach the United States about Welfare Reform

Frank Levy

Introduction

As this essay is being written in the autumn of 1977, the Carter administration is finishing legislation for its proposed comprehensive welfare reform. The legislation will receive congressional consideration during the remainder of this year and most of 1978.

The administration's proposal is regarded as liberal in that it raises benefits for some recipients while it extends benefits and jobs to a number of people not now covered by welfare.[1] But welfare liberalization and welfare reform are not synonomous. Many legislators criticize the administration's proposal on the grounds that welfare reform should take a more conservative tack. Other legislators argue that the proposal is far too ambitious. These legislators—really latent policy analysts—insist that any reform must minimize problems of administration and implementation.

In their search for alternatives, both the conservatives and the analysts refer frequently to "what Ronald Reagan did in California." Governor Reagan, in the summer of 1971, obtained passage of the California Welfare Reform Act (CWRA), an act whose primary purpose was to slow the state's explosive welfare growth. In 1963, the state's major assistance program, Aid to

Families with Dependent Children, paid benefits to 375,000 people. By 1967, the number of recipients had more than doubled, to 769,000, and by the time CWRA was passed, the number of recipients had more than doubled again, to 1,608,000. But in the three years following the act's passage, the number of recipients declined to 1,330,000. This reduction suggests CWRA was a conservative policy, yet at the same time it suggests CWRA was an example of successful implementation. It is my purpose in this essay to present a brief history of CWRA in order to assess the validity of these suggestions.

A history of CWRA is intriguing because its apparent success contrasts so sharply with most recent studies of the policy process. Governor Reagan himself has made much of this success, and it is instructive to consider a sample of his language:

> Three years ago, in a determined effort to get control of California's runaway welfare system, this administration developed a detailed blueprint for reform.
>
> The state's welfare and health care system had become a $3 billion a year moral and administrative disaster leading us down the road to bankruptcy. . . . Welfare rolls were going up at a dizzying rate—40,000 per month. The truly needy . . . were receiving too little because others were abusing the system by claiming, and getting benefits they didn't deserve. . . .
>
> Our 1970 task force worked for months to pinpoint the reasons for this gloomy state of affairs. After systematically going through a maze of state and federal laws, regulations, and procedures with a fine-toothed comb, the task force was able to recommend a detailed, comprehensive welfare reform program. . . .
>
> We had already begun to put many of these reforms into effect administratively. Others required legislation. As a result of long negotiations between my office and certain legislators, some 70 percent of these reforms were enacted into law a half year later in the Welfare Reform Act of 1971.
>
> . . . we would have been delighted three years ago to merely accept no increases in the case load. Yet the reforms have achieved much more.
>
> Today, there are 350,000 fewer persons receiving Aid to Families with Dependent Children in California than when we began three and a half years ago. Had the rolls continued to spiral upward at the same 40,000 per month rate during the years since, California today would have about 1.5 million more people on welfare than there actually are.[3]

Fifteen years ago, the governor's statement would have served as a textbook example of policymaking. A problem materializes; a task force diagnoses the problem; appropriate legislation is drafted and passed; the legislation and complementary administrative changes are implemented; the desired result is achieved. Today, textbooks are different. Fifteen years of large government programs have shown the resistance of the policy environment to radical change. At the beginning of the New Frontier, we imagined we could build social policy as we would build a Polaris Missile. Today, we understand that not even the Polaris was built like the Polaris,[4] and new textbooks vie with each other in explaining why the policy process moves so slowly.

This new view of policy suggests that Governor Reagan was mistaken in his appraisal of CWRA—no policy could have been that successful. Alternatively, CWRA could have been the one-in-a-thousand example where many of the standard obstacles to new policy did not exist or were overcome. In fact (or perhaps alas) we shall see that both views are right. To begin with, CWRA did not have the massive impact the governor described. Governor Reagan is a man who works very hard, but he is also blessed with abundant good luck. In the case of CWRA, he had the luck to institute a fairly moderate policy just at the time when demographic factors would cause the "welfare explosion" to end both in California and the rest of the country. By intention or by design, his claims of eliminating 350,000 recipients from the AFDC rolls are an example of *post hoc ergo proptor hoc.*

At the same time, CWRA was a one-in-a-thousand policy success. The combination of CWRA and associated regulations mandated a large number of changes in a one-billion-dollar program involving thirty-five counties and numerous local personnel. With one major exception, these changes were successfully implemented. The result was a welfare program that, as the Governor intended, was reoriented toward fiscal considerations and away from clients—particularly clients with earned income. On balance, however, more recipients appear to have been helped than hurt by the changes, and there is general agreement that the post-CWRA system was improved in efficiency and equity. The impact of these changes on the size of the caseload was quite modest—far less than the governor desired or claimed. But by any realistic standard, the changes represented a significant redirection of a large social program.

In what follows, I will be discussing only CWRA's most important aspects. Readers interested in a more detailed discussion are directed to two superb sources, the first by Mark Neal Aaronson and the second by Frederick Doolittle and Michael Wiseman.[5] But even a brief discussion of CWRA serves to illuminate its specific provisions. This is no small benefit, for while many people approve of "what Ronald Reagan did," relatively few can describe "what Ronald Reagan did." Understanding mechanics of CWRA will help to clarify exactly what Ronald Reagan can tell the United States about welfare reform.

A Brief Tour of AFDC

Before one can understand anything of welfare reform, it is first necessary to know something about welfare itself. When most people speak of "welfare," they mean Aid to Families with Dependent Children (AFDC). AFDC began life as a minor title in the Social Security Act of 1935. Its purpose was to strengthen the states' "Mothers' Pensions" programs—programs designed to aid children who had lost the income of their father through disability or abandonment. In keeping with the practice of the time, the legislation for AFDC left the control of many program parameters with the states. Thus, states were encouraged to set decent benefit levels through a cost sharing formula, but Congress specifically refrained from requiring states to pay at least a minimum benefit. State administration continues through the present time, though with somewhat diminished discretion. The resulting interstate variation created a situation in which AFDC is best thought of as fifty-one separate programs.

In California, the AFDC system in 1970 (before CWRA) could be characterized by seven parameters which are conveniently grouped into two functions: program eligibility and benefit calculation. Program eligibility depended on three parameters: the Needs Standard, the Assets Test, and the Hours Rule.

1. The *needs standard* was the state welfare department's estimate of the minimum income required by a family. Each family's standard was constructed from a state-supplied table which took

into account the number of family members, the sex and age of each family member, a separate allowance for the cost of housing (based on the family's actual payment, up to a maximum), the cost of utilities, and so forth. The state prepared separate tables for different regions of the state to reflect variation in the cost of living. For a mother and two children, the needs standard in a typical California urban county (such as San Francisco) was $271 per month.[6]

2. The *assets test* defined the maximum amount of property a family could own if it was to be eligible for AFDC. In 1970, a family could own real estate not exceeding $5,000 in net value (market value minus outstanding mortgage) and $600 of personal property other than household furnishings. Other property like a truck or a car could be owned if it were part of a "plan for achieving self-support."

3. The *hours rule* applied only to families headed by an able-bodied father. The original 1935 AFDC program was designed for female-headed families and included male-headed families only where the father was disabled. This restriction led to the charge that AFDC was encouraging fathers to desert their families in order to qualify the families for aid. In 1960, the federal government offered states an option of establishing an AFDC-U program, a variant of AFDC for two-parent families where the father is unemployed (hence the U). To date, twenty-seven states, including California, have established such a program. To be defined as unemployed, the father must be working less than a specified number of hours (which originally varied from state to state). If the father worked more than this number of hours, the family was ineligible for AFDC-U, no matter how low its income. In 1970, California's limit on hours (or hours rule) was set at 153 hours per month. No such test applied to families headed by women or disabled men.

To establish eligibility for AFDC, a family had to simultaneously have income below the needs standard, satisfy the assets test, and satisfy the hours rule (if the family was headed by an able-bodied father). Once eligibility was established, benefits were calculated according to the following formula:

Procedure for Calculating AFDC Benefits

$$\begin{array}{c}\text{Actual AFDC}\\\text{monthly benefit}\\\text{for eligible family}\end{array} = \begin{array}{c}\text{maximum}\\\text{payment}\end{array} - \text{tax rate} \times \left(\text{earnings} - \begin{array}{c}\text{work-}\\\text{related}\\\text{expenses}\end{array} - \begin{array}{c}\text{earnings}\\\text{disregard}\end{array}\right)$$

(If the term in parenthesis is negative, it is treated as zero.) Benefit calculation according to this formula depended on four parameters:

4. The *maximum payment* was the AFDC benefit paid to a family with no other income. It was calculated using a standard table which was similar but not identical to the table for the needs standard. The maximum payment table included fewer variations for individual circumstances (for example, rent was treated on a uniform basis without regard to the actual amount paid). More important, the dollar amounts in the maximum payment table were lower. The mother with two children described earlier could receive a maximum payment of $172 per month, $99 per month less than her needs standard. This divergence between the needs standard and the maximum payment may seem surprising, but even today the AFDC needs standard exceeds the AFDC maximum payment in over half of the states.

5., 6., 7. The *tax rate, work-related expenses,* and the *earnings disregard* were three parameters whose joint function was to provide incentives for AFDC recipients to work. The principle of the work incentive required that if a recipient earned a dollar, she should lose less than a dollar of benefits—that is, a recipient who worked should have more disposable income than one who did not. In practice, this incentive was first established by examining only net earnings—gross earnings minus work-related expenses. These expenses include actual paycheck deductions like Social Security taxes, but they also include items like transportation expenses, expenditure on required uniforms, day-care costs, and so on. In theory, every California county AFDC office permitted the same items to qualify as expenses, but in practice, the county offices varied substantially in what they would permit.

The second part of the incentive was established by ignoring all net earnings up to the limit of the earnings disregard. In California in 1970, this disregard was the sum of two terms. One was a flat $30 per month, mandated by federal law. The other was the difference between the family's needs standard and the family's maximum payment. In this way the state allowed the family's earnings to "fill the gap" between the needs standard and the maximum payment with no loss in benefits. Thus the mother with two children already described could receive ($30 + $271 − $172) =

$129 of net earnings before she would lose any benefits at all.

The final part of the work incentive was the tax rate. When a family's net earnings exceeded the earnings disregard, each additional dollar of net earnings would reduce the family's AFDC benefit by the amount of the tax rate. In California this rate stood at .67, so that a $1.00 increase in net earnings above the disregard would reduce the family's AFDC check by 67¢ and increase spendable income (net earnings plus benefits) by 33¢, providing a continuing incentive for work.

Once one masters the jargon, the system appears straightforward. To become eligible for aid, a family had to have income less than the needs standard and assets less than the assets test. If the family was headed by an able-bodied father, he had to be working less than the hours rule. Once a family established eligibility, actual AFDC payments were calculated according to the benefit formula just described. Eligibility was retained as long as the formula continued to yield positive payments (and the assets test and hours rule were satisfied).[7]

Note in this process that the work-incentive parameters had the unintended (and unavoidable) consequence of substantially expanding welfare eligibility. In order to encourage work, the combination of the earnings disregard, the tax rate, and deductions for work-related expenses translated gross earnings into reduced benefits at a slow rate. This translation was so slow that the mother with two children might have gross earnings as high as $600 per month or more and still receive some AFDC payment.[8] Given typical low-skilled wages, this level of earnings was unlikely, and so was it unlikely that the woman could "work her way off of welfare."

While I have described the 1970 AFDC system in California, similar procedures and formulas (though not similar dollar amounts) were used in most other states. Despite my protests to the contrary, many readers may still find the system to be complex. Upon reflection, however, it is clear that the system must have been more complex than my description, for in many respects, a state's welfare system is like a tax system in which even the simplest words are potentially open to a variety of meanings. How does one define income? Over a month? Over six months? If it is over a month (as it is), which month do we choose? Actual income received last month? Expected income for next month? And how, if at all, do we count the income of a grandmother who lives in the same city, or of a stepfather who has obligations from a previous marriage?

Similarly, the system raises numerous administrative questions. How much information is required on the application form? How is the information verified, and how often is it reverified? Who has responsibility for reverification—the recipients or system personnel? All of these definitions and administrative questions were handled through a multiplicity of regulations, most of which were designed by the states within federally imposed limitations.

Finally, AFDC in all states contained a set of characteristics best described as restraints. By restraints, I refer to any factor that kept legally eligible families from applying for or receiving benefits. In some cases, restraints and administrative practices overlapped—for example, a particularly long and complex application form. But the ultimate restraints were attitudes among system administrators and among potential recipients themselves. Particularly in smaller towns, administrators could make it their business to "know the circumstances" of all applicants and to render judgments, independent of formal regulations, that were unlikely to be appealed. Moreover, large segments of the public felt that to apply for welfare was to come to an extremely low pass in one's life. It was a public admission of failure that was to be avoided at all reasonable cost.

The total effect of these restraints was quite strong. In 1960, perhaps one-third of all households legally eligible for AFDC were receiving benefits. As late as 1967, benefits were received by less than two-thirds of those eligible.[9] But in this regard the 1960s marked the end of an era. Increasing urbanization and individual anonymity, the civil rights revolution, the organization of welfare recipients, and the linking of medical assistance to welfare receipt[10] all worked to create a significant change in attitude. By 1971, most of the restraints were gone, and over 90 percent of those eligible for AFDC actually received aid.[11] In the process, AFDC had become a kind of negative income tax for female-headed households[12] in the sense that eligible families accepted benefits as a matter of course and not only in the most extreme of emergencies. This then was the welfare system which Governor Reagan attempted to reform.

Setting the Stage

When Ronald Reagan campaigned for governor in 1966, he often told the following joke concerning a telephone conversation between a welfare recipient and her caseworker:

Recipient:
I need an emergency supplement to my grant this month. I have a new baby who has no place to sleep and I need the supplement to get a new crib.
Caseworker:
Oh, my goodness. I'll get you the grant right away. But tell me, where is the baby sleeping now?
Recipient:
The baby? He's sleeping in the box the color television came in.

It was a cruel joke, meant to establish the candidate as someone who would fight welfare growth. But surprisingly, when the candidate became the governor, his antiwelfare posture was not translated into any immediate action.[13]

Upon taking office, the governor sent a quickly constructed set of AFDC changes to the legislature. By 1970, he had proposed the same package three more times, but his efforts were desultory at best. As time went on, it became clear that stronger efforts would be required. When the governor had entered office, the number of California AFDC recipients had stood at 769,000. By 1970, the number of recipients had risen to 1,490,000, certainly not the outcome the voters had expected.

In understanding the period, it is important to appreciate the fiscal terror caused by this growth in the rolls. Today we see the growth for what it was: a sharp increase in the proportion of eligible families who chose to apply for aid. While the AFDC rolls were dramatically increasing, the *number of eligible families* was growing very slowly. And when most eligibles had signed up for benefits, the growth in the rolls would stop. But this explanation became clear only after the fact. At the time, the air was filled with hypotheses ranging from lax administration of AFDC to the disintegration of black families, and to the total breakdown of society. No one could be certain of the truth, so it was all too natural to simply extrapolate current trends. From the perspective of the state or county official charged with raising funds for the increasing rolls, the situation was truly frightening.

The governor's plan of attack began in the summer of 1970, the end of his first term, with the appointment of a task force to develop recommendations for welfare reform. In keeping with the governor's desire to emphasize fiscal management in the AFDC program, the task force was comprised of people with management backgrounds and specifically avoided any social work professionals. The task force delivered its recommendations in December, after the governor had won a second term by a large margin.

One member of the task force was Robert Carleson, the top deputy director in the State Department of Public Works. In January 1971, the governor appointed Carleson to be the director of social welfare. The appointment marked the beginning of a period in which the top and middle management of the State Department of Social Welfare was to be purged of people with social welfare backgrounds. One key administrator died. Others were transferred. Still others were forced out by the department's new direction. Lawyers and fiscal personnel, picked by the governor and Carleson, took their places.

This transformation of the state's social welfare management was an attempt to reinstitute some of the "restraints" described in the previous section. The governor and Carleson knew they could maintain direct control over a big-ticket item like reform legislation. But they also knew that the state's AFDC policy depended on many other day-to-day items handled by lower-level officials: the writing of regulations; the structuring of recipient appeal procedures; the extent to which the department challenged the suits brought by legal aid attorneys. The level of activity in all these areas would result from the department's "tone," and tone was a function of personnel. A change in tone might also serve as a signal to prospective AFDC applicants to stay away. No one could guarantee these changes would reduce the welfare rolls, but they seemed like a sensible first step. Their enhancement of the governor's antiwelfare image was an added benefit.

The governor's success in shifting personnel was the first indication that CWRA would not follow a "new view" policy scenario. Compare, for example, Jeffrey Pressman's description of a somewhat different personnel policy in Oakland, California: "Even the mayor's own office in City Hall is not necessarily friendly terrain. When Mayor Reading discovered in the fall of 1967 that his receptionist was openly critical of him and his policies, the mayor decided to transfer her to another department. But the city manager, fearing the wrath of the employees' association, advised caution, and civil service moved slowly in arranging the transfer. It was not until the spring of 1969—a year and a half later—that the change was made."[14] Such a policy would have brought tears of laughter to Mayor Daley's eyes. But Pressman's point was that Mayor Daley was the exception: most people charged with designing new policy act under restraints similar to those limiting Mayor Reading. In the case of CWRA, the governor had sufficient interest and power to begin a new policy by reshaping the staff who would be charged with its implementation. Few policies begin life with similar advantages.

Throughout early 1971, the governor, Director Carleson, and Carleson's staff formulated reform proposals. But even as they worked, they gained an understanding of another powerful tool—the broad area of discretion they could carve out of federal authority. In 1968, the Congress required states with AFDC payment systems similar to California's to update both their needs standard and their maximum payment to reflect changes in the cost of living. The changes were to be instituted by July 1, 1969. California, like most other states, failed to meet the statutory deadline. Over time, however, other states came into compliance and after a year had passed, only California and two other states had made no changes. In the summer of 1970, the state was found out of compliance with federal legislation in a conformity hearing conducted by the Department of Health, Education, and Welfare (DHEW). In September, a federal court judge made a similar finding in a suit brought against the state by California AFDC recipients. The judge gave the state sixty days to comply. During the fall, the state responded by proposing an increase in the maximum payment in combination with certain other changes in the benefit calculation formula. In fact, most of these formula changes required new state legislation—they were not simply administrative decisions—and so they were immediately enjoined by a state court.

In January 1971, DHEW announced that because California was in continued violation of federal legislation, it would order all federal assistance for California's AFDC program to be suspended on April 1. This was the agency's trump card and as such it indicated the weakness of the federal position. Under current law, AFDC is funded jointly by the federal government, state governments, and in some cases local governments. In California, the federal government provides approximately fifty cents out of every AFDC dollar, so the federal official was talking about withdrawing approximately $500,000,000 per year. Had the money been withheld from something the state valued intensely—an irrigation project or a highway—it would have represented a clear penalty. But in the case of AFDC, the withholding of funds might well have been translated into reduced benefits, which would hurt precisely the people the action was supposed to help. Thus the cutoff of funds was massive retaliation—too big a threat to be taken seriously. Whether DHEW was serious will never be known. The governor contacted the vice-president, who in turn had the secretary of DHEW retract the order.

Ultimately the matter was settled, but not before the governor won additional advantage. In March, he met with the president in San Clemente. With respect to welfare, three issues were on the table. The first was California's continued noncompliance with the law. The second was the governor's own proposals for welfare reform, which he had just outlined in a message to the legislature. The third was the president's proposal for welfare reform—the Family Assistance Plan (FAP).

The president wanted California to come into compliance with federal law, and more important, he wanted the governor's support (or at least lack of open opposition) for FAP. The governor knew that some aspects of his own welfare proposals would be in violation of existing federal law and so would require DHEW to grant waivers of the law if the proposals were to be implemented.

A deal was struck. The president and the governor would agree (at least temporarily) on certain principles of welfare reform. The necessary waivers for the governor's plan would be granted, and California would increase welfare benefits effective July 1, 1971, two years after the original date of compliance.

In theory, this delay might have left the state with a huge bill for retroactive payments, that is, payments dating back to the time when the cost-of-living adjustment was required by law. But the state pleaded in federal court that such a settlement would ruin its finances. The same judge who originally held the state in violation of the law ruled, reluctantly, that retroactive payments were not required. Thus the two-year delay was not only costless—it actually saved the state a significant amount of money.

The state's technique in this case is best described as catch-me-if-you-can. The technique is quite old, but it was refined into a high art by southern school districts as they tried to avoid desegregation in the 1960s. It assumes that any court decision will be a long time in coming and when it comes will require nothing more than was required in the first place. Thus nothing is lost by attempting "remedies" that are illegal.

In the new view of policy, it is common to assume that federal-state conflicts lead to policy failures, not policy successes. Pressman captures the relationship well: "When the problem of conflict has been addressed by designers of intergovernmental structures, it has been treated as a matter of disagreement over goals—to be remedied by collaborative discussion during the formation of the policy, with implementation presumably following in the wake of that initial agreement. This strategy is a perilous one, for, as some recent studies have shown, there are many ways in which initial policy agreement can dissipate during the process of implementation."[15]

Here, too, CWRA (or rather, CWRA's prehistory) was an exception. Intergovernmental conflicts may lead to a standstill, but in this case a standstill—a freeze on AFDC benefit levels—was exactly what the governor wanted. Moreover, the nature and size of the AFDC program guaranteed the standstill would not be mutual. The state refused to comply with the federal government, but the federal government continued to pay its share of AFDC costs to the state. In the end, the conflict had given the governor everything he wanted, including a new resource—the promise of federal waivers to enhance CWRA's prospects.

The California Welfare Reform Act

In March 1971, the governor introduced CWRA to the legislature. By October 1971, CWRA had become law. Because the act is little understood, it will be useful to review its major provisions.[16]

CWRA had three major themes. First, AFDC was too easy to obtain, and the program needed tighter eligibility requirements. Second, the program needed to increase its ability to deal with fraud. The third theme was more complex. It held that AFDC work incentives (such as the tax rate and the earnings disregard) were a failure. They did not encourage work; they only discounted income in a way that allowed those who would have worked anyway to remain eligible for benefits. The governor and Carleson believed recipient work was something that should be required rather than encouraged through incentives. Moreover, they believed a program based on work requirements could be "sweetened" by more generous benefits and still result in savings. These three themes provide a framework in which to discuss CWRA's provisions.

Tightened Eligibility

I have shown how AFDC eligibility depended upon a needs standard, an assets test, and an hours rule. CWRA tightened each of these restrictions and added two new restrictions as well.

The needs standard was simplified into a uniform, statewide schedule which depended only upon family size. Intrastate variations in the cost of living, separate calculations for rent actually paid, and other case-by-case variations were no longer considered.

The assets test was tightened by counting as assets a variety of household furnishings, subject to a limit of $1500. In addition, trucks and other items that were part of a "plan for achieving self-support" were no longer automatically exempt from assets limits.

The hours rule was tightened for the second time in a year. The spring 1971 increase in AFDC payments had been accompanied by a reduction in the hours rule from 153 to 130 hours per month. CWRA proposed a further reduction to 100 hours per month. This reduction brought California's AFDC-U program into line with AFDC-U programs in other states.

CWRA also proposed supplementing eligibility restrictions with a residency requirement and a gross income limitation. The residency requirement permitted counties, under certain general conditions, to deny AFDC benefits to otherwise eligible families who had not lived in the county for one year prior to application. The gross income limitation denied eligibility to any family whose gross income exceeded 150 percent of their needs standard. The limitation was aimed at families who had large gross earnings but who qualified for AFDC on the basis of large work-related expenses for day care, transportation, and so on.

Antifraud Provisions

CWRA proposed several antifraud provisions, including an increase in financial incentives for counties to collect support payments from absent fathers. A second provision established an earnings clearance system in which the State Department of Social Welfare would run cross-checks between county AFDC records and employer earnings records. The checks were to ensure that a recipient's entire earnings were being reported.

Increased Benefits and the Substitution of Required Work for Work Incentives

In the spring of 1971, the governor had raised a family of three's maximum payment from $172 per month to $204 per month. CWRA raised this amount again to $235 per month. At the same time, CWRA proposed reducing work incentives, first by standardizing work-related expenses. As I have shown, AFDC benefit calculations were based on net earnings—gross earnings minus any allowable work-related expenses. CWRA standardized these expenses (except for child care) to a flat $25 per month for those who worked ten days or less and $50 per month for people who worked more. The act also proposed reducing the earnings disregard—the first portion of net earnings that resulted in no benefit reduction. Prior to CWRA, the disregard was the sum of $30, mandated by federal law, plus the difference between the needs standard and the maximum payment. Under CWRA this second term was eliminated, and the disregard was set at a flat $30.

Work incentives were reduced not because the governor opposed work but because he and Carleson believed the incentives were ineffective and only served to increase eligibility. If, for example, 1970 work incentives were combined with the $235 monthly payment, a three-person family could have retained eligibility with gross earnings as high as $750 per month. CWRA's stricter work incentives translated earnings into reduced benefits at a faster rate, and under CWRA the family would lose eligibility with gross earnings of about $550, an even lower limit than in the smaller-benefit, pre-CWRA system.

The governor and Carleson could propose reducing work incentives in this way because they simultaneously proposed a work requirement under which counties containing about half of the state's AFDC caseload would participate in a work demonstration project. This project, entitled the Community Work Experience Program (CWEP—pronounced "see wep") required fathers on AFDC-U and mothers on AFDC without young children to "work off" their AFDC grants through public service jobs to be created by the counties. The recipients were to receive their AFDC grants in lieu of wages and would work no more than it would take them to earn their grant if they were working at the minimum wage.

When assessing CWRA's provisions, it is important to keep two dimensions of the act in mind. The first is its complexity—the number of changes the act imposed upon a large public program. The second is the act's tone—the political direction in which it tried to push the system. CWRA was certainly complex, for it mandated a large number of changes in budget calculations, eligibility tests, and other aspects of the AFDC program. Even without the job creation implied by CWEP, the act required a substantial amount of implementation. CWRA's political tone is harder to define. CWEP, to be sure, was "punitive," but it was offered only as a demonstration project with little indication of substantial prior thought (for example, job creation was left to the counties). With CWEP excluded, the act looked conservative but in fact was fairly moderate. The rearrangement of work incentives and the tight hours rule appeared important until one realized that only 20 percent of AFDC-U fathers and 15 percent of AFDC mothers were working at any given time. The gross income limitation would have affected only 1 to 2 percent of all AFDC families. The residency requirement hurt some families, but even at the time it was passed there was a feeling that it would be declared unconstitutional. Moreover, any harmful aspects of the law had to be weighed against the 10 to 15 percent increase in benefits (compared to the spring of 1971) received by most recipients. Other aspects of the act, like the standardized needs standard, could legitimately be described as marginally increasing the system's efficiency and equity.[17]

In summary, CWRA as passed by the legislature was a complex act which could create numerous administrative problems. But with the exception of CWEP the act was not drastically conservative, nor was it radical in any other sense. Rather, it was a series of incremental adjustments which "tilted" the system away from recipients with earnings and toward recipients who did not work, while it tightened administrative procedures. A political moderate might well have called it an improvement.

The Process of Implementation

The heart of the new view of policy is a recognition of the implementation process. Legislation is important, but politics continues well after the legislation is passed. New regulations have to be written, and new administrative procedures have to be designed; each of these changes must be translated into new behavior at ground level.[18] Normally, the implementation of a new policy involves a number of people who at worst oppose the policy directly and who at best have many other things (besides the policy) on their minds. For this reason, the new view of policy makes implementation synonymous with the delay and deflection of the policy's original goals.

Again, CWRA proved to be an exception. To be sure, one important aspect of the act—CWEP—was destroyed in the implementation process. But most other aspects of the act went through as planned, and they were supplemented by several important administrative changes. The end result was quite impressive.

It is now standard practice to begin an implementation scenario by listing the players. In the case of CWRA, a short list of players would contain four names: the state government, the US Department of Health, Education, and Welfare (DHEW), the county welfare offices, and a limited number of organized welfare recipients. But four different players did not mean four major sources of contention. I have shown how the governor and Director Carleson maneuvered to hold DHEW at bay. In practice, the county welfare offices offered the state equally little resistance. It was not that they were so weak—rather, on most issues their interests and the interests of the state honestly coincided. In California, counties paid for 13 percent of all AFDC costs. The welfare explosion had forced county governments continually to raise property taxes—an extremely unpopular situation. Moreover, some people charged that the counties themselves were the root of the problem because of their lax welfare administration. By 1971, there had been several instances of irate suburban matrons applying successfully for AFDC benefits. Needless to say, they went to the newspapers before they received their first check. In this climate, the counties were more than willing to implement most of the governor's program. I shall describe the major exception—CWEP—more fully below.

DHEW was weak, and the counties were favorable, but welfare recipients were a different story. In some cases, the recipients were organized in formal groups, including chapters of the National Welfare Rights Organization. In other cases, their organization was more ad hoc, but most organizations of either kind had access to legal representation through legal aid attorneys. Aaronson notes that the existence of these attorneys helped shape the strategy of legislators opposed to CWRA. The legislators knew that many of the governor's provisions, like the residency requirement, were almost certainly unconstitutional and that active legal aid attorneys were ready to pounce on the provisions as soon as they were passed. Thus the legislators could afford to yield such provisions in legislative bargaining, safe in the knowledge that they would not survive.[19]

But as Doolittle and Wiseman note, even the success of this strategy may have played into the governor's hands. Soon after CWRA was passed, groups of welfare recipients challenged the residency requirement, the standardization of work-related expenses, and the gross income limitation as violations of the federal authorizing legislation for AFDC. All cases were won by the plaintiffs, but in the process they painted a picture of AFDC recipients similar to the picture painted by the governor: people who moved around to receive benefits, and who looked for maximum deductions—people who played the system.[20] Moreover, many other recipient challenges to CWRA—the constitutionality of the earnings clearance system, the reduction in the earnings disregard—were not upheld by the courts. In summary, the state found itself implementing CWRA with relatively little opposition, and in most ways it used this freedom effectively.

The state had two principal implementation tools: the writing of CWRA's regulations and the promulgation of administrative changes. In 1976, Jeffrey Pressman, Francine Rabinovitz, and Martin Rein edited an important issue of *Policy Sciences* devoted to case studies in the writing of regulations and guidelines. In their summary, the three editors emphasized the importance of regulations and guidelines in shaping program policy. They further noted that this importance is enhanced when the regulations refer to measurable outcomes that can be monitored.[21] Because CWRA referred primarily to fiscal matters like the calculation of benefits, it offered an opportunity to write such "measurable" regulations. Director Carleson controlled this opportunity tightly and wrote a number of regulations for two somewhat conflicting purposes: the actual implementation of CWRA and the reinforcement of the state's hard-line image.

An example of this second purpose was a regulation involving the budget treatment of unborn children. Prior to CWRA, it had been the state's practice to treat the unborn fetus as a child and to increase the family's AFDC benefit accordingly. With the passage of CWRA, the state wrote a new regulation that amended the procedure by counting the fetus as a child but also counting the services received from the mother's body (that is, her womb) as in-kind income. Initially, this in-kind income was assigned a dollar value equal to the cost of housing and utilities for a single person. In fact, such an imputation could have caused a woman's grant to decrease when she became pregnant. In August 1972, the state modified the regulation so that, in effect, having an unborn child would leave her grant unchanged. This regulation, too, was ultimately overturned by the California Supreme Court, but the occasional publicity generated by the regulation and the court fight helped portray the state as a defender of the public treasury. Similar battles were fought over regulations governing the treatment of supplemental grants for special circumstances, the obligations assumed by a man who married a woman on AFDC, and so on.

As the regulations were being written, the state also announced a series of administrative changes. The changes did not flow directly from CWRA but they helped substantially in implementing the act's emphasis on tighter administrative control. The first change involved requiring county welfare officials to assign eligibility functions and service functions to separate individuals. Traditionally, county welfare departments had used professionally trained social workers both to provide services such as counseling and to compute recipients' monthly benefits. As the welfare explosion began, federal and state officials became concerned that these workers were too "prorecipient" in their calculations and perhaps were even recruiting new recipients to the rolls. To deal with this charge, Congress in 1968 mandated that local AFDC offices give the two functions to different groups of people. California implemented this separation in 1971, but the governor spoke of the separation from time to time as if it were part of CWRA.

The second administrative change involved the introduction of a new, fairly complex, nineteen-page application form for AFDC. Some counties held short classes for clients to fill out the forms, but on the whole the form and the documentation it required shifted much of the burden of application from the social worker to the client.

The third change involved the establishment of monthly income reporting. AFDC eligibility is determined on the basis of a family's income in the month it applies for aid. Subsequent benefits are recalculated on a month-by-month basis. Prior to 1972, if a recipient had a change in income or family circumstances, she was expected to report it to the welfare department. If no reports were received, a caseworker would initiate contact to verify the case only at intervals of six months or more. Many administrators felt this infrequent verification encouraged recipients to collect benefits illegally. For example, a recipient might never swear to a false statement, but she might fail to initiate a report on a temporary job expected (perhaps incorrectly) to end shortly. In early 1972, the state required several counties to switch to a system of monthly reporting in which a recipient had to mail in a signed card each month describing what, if any, changes in income or family circumstances had occurred. Later in the year, the system was mandated statewide.[22]

While none of these changes was directly part of CWRA, they were perceived as part of "the governor's program" and were implemented just as easily. Even monthly income reporting—potentially a large headache for county AFDC administrators—was accepted because of the fiscal savings it promised.

The state's one implementation failure was its demonstration program of required work, CWEP. In fact, California's AFDC program already had a federal work requirement, the Work Incentive Program (WIN). WIN had been established by Congress in 1967 and had been expanded significantly in 1971. It required most AFDC recipients (except women with young children) to register for work or training. But a work registration program that does not actually supply jobs is bound to have limited impact. CWEP was supposed to provide jobs (or at least have the counties supply jobs), so it was to be a dramatic departure from existing practices. As such, it stimulated a maximum of opposition. The opposition began in the Department of Health, Education, and Welfare, which ultimately granted waiver approval for CWEP but in the process managed to scale CWEP down to a maximum of 30,000 participants for the first year. In practice, DHEW need not have bothered. At the local level, resistance to CWEP ran so high that few counties were willing to participate. The counties saw CWEP as a source of intense controversy, and they were reluctant to take on the cost and administrative problems of creating recipients' jobs. The DHEW waiver giving CWEP demonstration-project status expired on July 1, 1975. After three years of operation, CWEP had assigned only 9,600 persons to jobs.[23]

Since CWEP clearly failed is it still fair to call CWRA an implementation success? I believe it is. Both CWRA's regulations and the parallel administrative changes created substantial opportunities for program failure. The switching of half a million AFDC cases to monthly reporting was no small job. The new budget calculations, the revised personnel assignments, and other program aspects involved similar potential problems. Even if CWRA was not as complex as the governor first intended, it was nonetheless quite complex, and its implementation was a substantial achievement.

What Did CWRA Really Accomplish?

We now come to an apparent contradiction. I have argued that CWRA—particularly when stripped of CWEP—was a politically moderate program. But the governor, in the statement I quoted in the introduction, suggested that CWRA was responsible for large numbers of AFDC recipients leaving the rolls. His claim of 350,000 exaggerates the raw data only slightly. In January 1971, the date he chose as a starting point, the state's AFDC and AFDC-U recipients totaled 1,608,000. In August 1974, when he was writing *California's Blueprint for National Welfare Reform*, the state's recipients totaled 1,330,000, a drop of 278,000 or 17 percent. The drop is all the more remarkable when one recalls that through the 1960s the number of recipients in the state had more than doubled every four years.

But the question remains: How much of this reduction was due to CWRA? Analysis suggests that CWRA, particularly the associated administrative changes, accounted for a part of this reduction but that most of it was caused by three other factors.[24]

Smaller family size. Beginning in the 1960s, the average number of children per AFDC family began to decline sharply nationwide. The decline was due in part to younger women coming onto the rolls but more generally to the declining birth rate in the population as a whole. Between 1971 and 1974 alone, the average number of children in a California AFDC case declined by 10 percent, and this decline exaggerated CWRA's impact: between 1971 and 1974, the number of AFDC and AFDC-U *recipients* declined by 17 percent, but the number of *cases* declined by only 9 percent.

The end of the recession. In 1970, California had led the nation into recession, but by 1971 it was leading the nation in a short-lived economic recovery. There is substantial evidence that improving economic conditions helped reduce the states' welfare rolls, particularly through the AFDC-U program for families headed by able-bodied fathers. This conclusion rests on three main pieces of data. First, the overall 1971–74 welfare reduction was highly concentrated among AFDC-U recipients.[25] Second, the AFDC-U rolls began to fall in January 1971, ten months before CWRA was passed. Third, between 1971 and 1974, California's AFDC-U caseload declind by 56 percent, but the total AFDC-U caseload in the rest of the country also declined, by 34 percent. Part of California's greater decline was undoubtedly due to CWRA through its monthly reporting and other program changes. But the evidence suggests that economic recovery played the dominant role both in California and the rest of the country.

The exhaustion of the eligible pool. I have shown how the national "welfare explosion" represented a process in which most female-headed families who were eligible for AFDC chose to apply for benefits and receive aid. This process seems to have ended around 1971. Using the 1970 census, Cynthia Rence and Michael Wiseman constructed estimates of the number of female-headed households eligible for AFDC in Los Angeles and Alameda Counties.[26] They then compared these estimates to actual AFDC caseloads. They found that while in 1970 caseloads in both counties were significantly below the eligible population, by 1971 caseloads and eligible populations roughly coincided. It is this factor—the absorption of almost all eligible female-headed households onto the rolls—that most accounts for the leveling off of the AFDC caseload.

When these three factors are taken into account, it appears that CWRA reduced the number of California welfare recipients by perhaps 6 percent below what it otherwise would have been.[27] Six percent is not very dramatic—it sounds like an "incremental change." But this should not be surprising since I have shown that the change was the result of a complex but fairly incremental policy.

Conclusion

I opened this essay with two related questions. First, how could

CWRA have been so big a policy success? Second, what can Ronald Reagan teach the United States about welfare reform?

Success, of course, is defined by many standards. A politician calls a policy successful only if it creates dramatic changes on the face of the earth. A policy analyst uses a more modest standard by which a policy is successful as long as it is not a complete failure.

CWRA falls somewhere below the first standard but well above the second. The act appeared to create great reductions in the welfare rolls but this, as I have shown, was an accident of timing. Nonetheless, the act and related administrative directives created a number of more modest changes which pushed California's AFDC system toward greater fiscal control, the governor's desired result.

Because the governor couched the act in highly punitive language, there is a tendency to write it off as something equivalent to midnight raids on recipients' homes.[28] To do so would be a mistake. Every bureaucratic system makes errors, and errors, as John Mendeloff has noted, have at least two dimensions. One is their frequency.[29] The other is their direction. When the welfare department denies AFDC to an eligible family, that is an error, but when the welfare department overpays a recipient who has an unreported job, that is an error too. There is a legitimate argument to be made that when the governor took office, California's AFDC system made too many errors, and its errors were too skewed toward recipients. Changes like the longer application form, monthly income reporting, and the uniform needs standard all served to reduce the number of errors and redirect those that remained in favor of the system. The proper direction of errors is open to debate, but reducing their number was clearly a good thing. Even CWRA's antifraud provisions—for example, facilitating the counties' ability to collect child support from absent fathers—is something of which most people (including most recipients) would approve.

The sources of this policy success are clear enough. They began in the federal AFDC law which gave every state broad discretion and gave the federal government weak sanctions even when violations occurred. They were enhanced by the attitude of the county welfare departments—potentially a serious obstacle—who were more than happy to introduce any administrative and procedural changes that might hold down increasing welfare costs. Finally, there was the governor himself, who put a sufficiently high priority on the issue to follow it well after legislation was passed. To be sure, he had his reasons. From the start, he saw a successful, conservative welfare policy as a key element in an eventual run for the presidency. But whatever his incentive, it was his continued interest that kept CWRA relatively intact during implementation. These conditions were unusual, but the case of CWRA suggests that policy is possible, at least once in a while.

Does Ronald Reagan have anything to teach the US about welfare reform? The question may be too late. To any objective observer, President Carter's current welfare reform proposal contains a good deal of the "California Experience." The president's proposal emphasizes tight record keeping, including the institution of monthly income reporting and standardized work expenses. Recipients who can work are expected to work, and the president's proposal mandates the creation of public service jobs to absorb those recipients who cannot find work elsewhere. Differences certainly exist: the president proposes to extend benefits where the governor wanted to limit them, and the president's proposal is free of the governor's harsh insults to the poor. But the heart of a proposal is in the details, and here Ronald Reagan appears already to have taught the United States more than he or we are likely to admit.

Notes

I have benefited substantially from conversations with six colleagues. Michael Wiseman and Frederick Doolittle patiently led me through the intricacies of the California Welfare Reform Act. Eugene Bardach and Martin Levin taught me half of what I know about implementation. Jeffrey Pressman and Aaron Wildavsky taught me the rest.

1. However, most of those who would be newly covered by the Carter proposal are already eligible for food stamps.

2. For a review of many of these studies, see Eugene Bardach, *The Implementation Game* (Cambridge, Mass.: MIT Press, 1977); and Martin A. Levin, *The Political Dilemmas of Social Policy Making* (forthcoming).

3. Office of the Governor of California, *California's Blueprint for National Welfare Reform: Proposals for the Nation's Food Stamp and Aid to Families with Dependent Children Programs* (Sacramento, September 1974), pp. iii-iv. Medi-Cal is California's health care program for the indigent. In subsequent

speeches, the governor reduced his estimate of recipient reductions to 300,000.

4. See Harvey M. Sapolsky, *The Polaris System Development* (Cambridge, Mass.: Harvard University Press, 1972), in which the author shows that the famed PERT system in fact had little to do with the actual Polaris development. I am indebted to Martin Levin for this reference.

5. For a more detailed discussion of CWRA, see the superb studies by Mark Neal Aaronson, "Legal Advocacy and Welfare Reform: Continuity and Change in Public Relief" (Ph.D. diss., University of California at Berkeley, 1975); and Frederick Doolittle and Michael Wiseman, *The California Welfare Reform Act: A Litigation History,* Working Paper no. 71, Income Dynamics Project, Institute of Business and Economic Research, Department of Economics, University of California at Berkeley (August 1976).

6. Doolittle and Wiseman, *California Welfare Reform Act,* pp. ii, 30 ff.

7. The sharp-eyed observer will note I have said nothing about the needs standard. The earnings disregard and the tax rate were work incentives that went into effect only after a person qualified for aid. To qualify for AFDC, a person had to have net earnings below the needs standard. Once on AFDC, eligibility was maintained as long as the benefit formula yielded positive payments. But since the benefit formula contained the tax rate and the earnings disregard, it was possible for a person's earnings to rise above the needs standard without his losing all benefits.

8. Doolittle and Wiseman, *The California Welfare Reform Act,* chap. 3. The large disregard was due in part to the fact that the needs standard had been periodically updated for changes in inflation, while the maximum payment had remained unchanged since 1976.

9. The figure for 1960 is an educated guess. The figure for 1967 is based on tabulations of the Current Population Survey developed by Barbara Boland. See Barbara Boland, "Participation in the Aid to Families with Dependent Children Program (AFDC)," in *The Family, Poverty and Welfare Programs: Factors Influencing Family Instability,* paper no. 12, (p. 1), in US Congress, Joint Economic Committee, Subcommittee on Fiscal Policy, *Studies in Public Welfare* (Washington, D.C., November 1973), pp. 139-179.

10. Medicaid (Medi-Cal in California) is the federally sponsored health care program for low-income citizens. In many states, Medicaid benefits were limited to recipients of AFDC. Even in states that extended some care to non-recipients, AFDC recipients often received broader coverage. Thus, the existence of Medicaid implicitly raised the benefits of being on the AFDC rolls.

11. Boland, "Aid to Families with Dependent Children."

12. On two counts, AFDC was not a negative income tax for males. First, nearly half the states precluded male-headed families from any AFDC benefits. Second, states that aided male-headed families through an AFDC-U program determined eligibility both through the family's income and through a limit on the father's hours of work (the hours rule). A negative income tax would have considered income alone.

13. For the description of events in this section, I draw heavily on Aaronson, "Legal Advocacy and Welfare Reform," chap. 5.

14. Jeffrey L. Pressman, "Preconditions of Mayoral Leadership," in *American Political Science Review* 66, no. 2 (June 1972) :517. The mayor attempted to pursue an open-door policy in which Oakland's citizens—particularly minorities—would feel free to come to his office and discuss their problems with city policies. The secretary in question was openly hostile to minorities and acted effectively as a barrier between individuals and the mayor.

15. Jeffrey L. Pressman, *Federal Programs and City Politics* (Berkeley: University of California Press, 1973), pp. 10-11. The theme of agreements coming apart is also explored in Jeffrey L. Pressman and Aaron B. Wildavsky, *Implementation* (Berkeley: University of California Press, 1975).

16. The summary in this section draws heavily on Doolittle and Wiseman, *The California Welfare Reform Act*, chap. 3.

17. See ibid., chap. 4, for a discussion of the relative numbers of winners and losers under CWRA.

18. For a discussion of the implementation process, see Bardach, *The Implementation Game;* Levin, *Political Dilemmas;* and Pressman and Wildavsky, *Implementation.*

19. Aaronson, "Legal Advocacy and Welfare Reform," chap. 6.

20. Doolittle and Wiseman, *The California Welfare Reform Act*, pp. iii-53.

21. Francine Rabinovitz, Jeffrey L. Pressman, and Martin Rein, "Guidelines: A Plethora of Forms, Authors, and Functions," in *Policy Sciences* 7 (1976): 399-416.

22. Another administrative directive instructed counties to switch to prior-month budgeting, in which a recipient's AFDC benefits would be computed on the basis of last month's actual income. Previously, the benefit had been calculated on the basis of the recipient's estimate of income for the next month, a process which state officials claimed led to a variety of errors. It is interesting to note that this kind of retrospective calculation has been included as part of President Carter's welfare reform proposal.

23. California State Legislature, Joint Legislative Audit Committee, *Auditor General's Report on the California Work Experience Program*, (Sacramento, May 6, 1974).

24. This analysis is contained in Frank Levy and Michael Wiseman, "The California Welfare Reform Program: An Overview of the Numbers," Institute of Business and Economic Research, Department of Economics, University of California, Berkeley (December 1976), mimeo.

25. In January 1971, AFDC-U had 0.3 million recipients, while AFDC had 1.3 million. But between January 1971 and August 1974, the AFDC-U rolls declined by 197,000 people (−62 percent), while AFDC declined by only 77,000 people (−6 percent).

26. Construction of these estimates is detailed in Cynthia Rence and Michael

Wiseman, "The California Welfare Reform Act and Participation in AFDC," *Journal of Human Resources*, in press. Alameda County contains Oakland and Berkeley, California. Together, Alameda and Los Angeles account for about half of the state's welfare caseload.

27. Levy and Wiseman, "The California Welfare Reform Program," pp.24-27.

28. Midnight raids refer to the practice in which a social worker demands entrance to a recipient's home late at night or in the early morning to search for an unreported man in the house. This practice was outlawed by the Supreme Court in a case arising in Alameda County, California.

29. See John Mendeloff, "Welfare Procedures and Error Rates: An Alternative Perspective," in *Policy Analysis* 3, no. 3 (Summer 1977): 357-374.

Chapter 15

Reason, Responsibility, and the New Social Regulation

Eugene Bardach

In a well-ordered society, people would be willing and able to take responsibility for protecting themselves against the annoyances, the petty injustices, and the perils of everyday life. They would not allow themselves to be cheated by door-to-door salesmen, injured by faulty home appliances, or tyrannized by bosses and supervisors. They would also take responsibility for protecting family members, particularly the very young and the very old, not only from these everyday hazards but from the special dangers that beset the inexperienced and the physically weak. Measures would be taken to scare off schoolyard bullies or to fend off neighborhood vandals. In a well-ordered society, furthermore, people would take at least some responsibility for protecting individuals with whom their associations were more indirect and indeterminate. Householders would refrain from abandoning old refrigerators in vacant lots, lest children lock themselves inside; managers of firms that manufactured dangerous drugs or chemicals would see to it that their products were packaged safely and with adequate warning labels; and businessmen would discourage their colleagues or subordinates from pursuing racist policies in promoting and hiring personnel.

In a society that is not well-ordered by such natural, spontaneous, and informal means, government is wont to step in with rules, regulations, and laws. Whether or not our society is thus disordered, during the last ten or fifteen years we have experienced a wave of government programs seemingly predicated on the assumption that it is, programs known (mainly to their critics) as "the new social regulation." Merely to name a few of the relevant federal statues suggests the scope of the phenomenon:

Food and Drug Amendments (1962)
Civil Rights Act (1964)
Fair Packaging and Labeling Act (1966)
Child Protection Act (1966)
Traffic Safety Act (1966)
Flammable Fabrics Act (1967)
Wholesome Meat Act (1967)
Age Discrimination in Employment Act (1967)
Consumer Credit Protection Act (1968)
National Environmental Policy Act (1969)
Clean Air Amendments (1970)
Occupational Safety and Health Act (1970)
Lead-Based Paint Elimination Act (1971)
Consumer Product Safety Act (1972)
Equal Employment Opportunity Act (1972)
Federal Water Pollution Control Act Amendments (1972)
Agriculture and Consumer Protection Act (1973)
Employee Retirement Income Security Act (1974)
Privacy Act (1974)
Federal Trade Commission Improvement Act (1974)

Other indicators of the scope of the phenomenon are the accelerating expenditures for social regulation agencies in the federal budget and the growing volume of regulations. Lilley and Miller estimate a nearly threefold increase in expenditures by major federal social regulatory agencies in the period 1970-1975, during which they went from $1.5 billion to $4.3 billion. They report a corresponding increase in the number of pages in the *Federal Register* devoted to social regulatory programs, from 20,036 in 1970 to 60,221 in 1975.[1]

This new wave of social regulation has undoubtedly produced certain beneficial results, even if considerably lesser results than its many and varied originators had hoped. At the same time, the sheer assaultive force of this new wave of legislation has been greater than anticipated, and the sentiment grows in many quarters that the mass of regulation must at least be contained and perhaps substantially reduced. I share this sentiment. Yet I believe that few if any critics of the phenomenon have adequately understood the nature of the social regulation movement or grasped its possible implications for important shared values, like the role of reason in social affairs and the maintenance of numerous autonomous institutions deserving of social trust and responsibility.

My main arguments are as follows:

1. Although there are many problems with the usual governmental approach to social regulation, the principal ones are that it institutionalizes and legitimizes instrumental irrationality—what I call "unreasonableness"—and that in doing so it corrupts the idea and undermines the practice of social responsibility.

2. This corruption and undermining occurs because government shifts responsibility for many instrumental and also for certain moral choices to centralized bureaucratic units and away from local settings and institutions.

3. Many different—but often untested—policy instruments are potentially available that would permit more centralized control over ends but would leave the choice of means to decision makers in local settings and institutions.

4. Even though there is probably more receptiveness now to these alternative policy approaches than there has been in the last ten to fifteen years, certain political and ideological barriers might still block their adoption.

Some Costs of Regulation

What is new about "the new social regulation" is mainly that it is undertaken by the federal government. State and local governments have been administering social regulation programs for many decades. These governments regulate occupational licenses: hospitals, nursing homes, and other health facilities; business and trade practice; land use; restaurant sanitation; construction materials and practices; housing conditions; and so on. In recent years there appears to have been some increase in the scope and intensity of state and local regulation, though it is hard to assess how much. In California, for instance, auto repair and TV repair facilities have recently come under (rather loose) state regulation. Nationwide, district attorneys and state attorneys general have been discovering that consumer fraud prosecutions are politically popular, at least in middle-class constituencies. Minimum deposits for beer and soda containers are now required by law in at least four states. In California there is talk of state-supervised "energy audits" of commercial and industrial plants to reduce energy waste.

The hallmark of both the newer and the older social regulation is its reliance on the "enforcement approach." This approach essentially involves setting standards, authorizing penalties for deviation from the standards, and mobilizing some sort of inspection or audit force to detect such deviations. I shall leave aside the question of how effective this strategy is,[2] and examine only the other side of the coin, the adverse social consequences of the enforcement strategy. Although it is very difficult to estimate the magnitude of these consequences, I do not doubt they are substantial. Equally important, though, is the difficulty in even saying what they are.

One adverse consequence is that more enforcement leads to "big government," widely regarded nowadays as problematic. At present the budgetary outlays on social regulation are very modest. If they amounted to $5 or $6 billion in the federal budget for this fiscal year (a very rough estimate), then they represented under 2 percent of the total. The percentage is probably higher for state and local governments, but not so high that reducing it would make anyone feel he had struck a blow for smaller government. The real problem, though, is in the future. A regulatory agency can always use more inspectors, supervisors, regulation writers, and coordinators, as well as travel budgets and technical apparatus (in some cases). There is no reason to think that in the long run regulation will be cheap.

For the time being, at least, more germane than direct government expenditures are the financial costs that government regulation imposes on the private sector. One of the politically attractive features of social regulation is that the financial costs of programmatic innovations do not show up immediately in the government budget.[3] But these costs are genuine nevertheless. More safety costs real economic resources, as does more sanitation, more environmental protection, and more record keeping to show compliance with antidiscrimination statutes. Murray Weidenbaum estimates, for instance, that purchasers of new 1974 automobiles paid approximately $3 billion extra for governmentally imposed safety features and cites an OSHA estimate that compliance with noise standards proposed by the US National Institute for Occupational Safety and Health (NIOSH) and supported by the EPA will cost $31.6 billion.[4] Pollution control investments to comply with the Clean Air Act and the Federal Water Pollution Control Act will cost business and consumers a few hundred billion dollars.[5]

Another economic cost of regulation is paid in economic inefficiency. This cost shows up neither in public nor in private ledgers, for it is the product of consumer benefits delayed or suppressed owing to interference with the market. As Weidenbaum states the case,

> Yet, the critical price we pay for government regulation is the attenuation of the risk bearing and entrepreneurial nature of our private enterprise system—a system which, at least in the past, has contributed so effectively to rapid rates of innovation, productivity, and growth. A hidden cost of governmental restrictions of various kinds is a reduced rate of innovation. The longer that it takes for some change to be approved by the federal regulatory agency—a new or improved product, a more efficient production process, et cetera—the less likely that the change will be made. In any event, innovation will be delayed.[6]

For instance, Weidenbaum cites the results of a statistical study by Peltzman that estimates the costs of the FDA's delaying approval of new drugs while they are being tested for effectiveness (not safety) at $200 to $300 million annually.[7]

A somewhat more traditional objection to government regulation is the simple resentment at having to play host to a persistent and unwelcome intruder. While the tangible financial costs of government-required paperwork are probably high, the intangible costs to many firms and institutions simply of being subject to regulation might be higher. These costs include the uncertainty introduced into the operating environment, time and aggravation involved in fending off proposed or contemplated regulations and reporting requirements, and the stigma attached to being treated as though one were irresponsible and not to be trusted.[8]

Having acknowledged all these costs, I would nevertheless conjecture that in the long run none is quite as significant as certain subtle effects having to do with the shift in the locus of social judgment from decentralized sites, where it is possible to act informally and with sensitivity to the local context, to centralized governmental agencies, where this possibility is much less. It is important to emphasize that the target of social regulation is not only private business firms, though to be sure the most publicized new programmatic initiatives have been aimed at safety regulation, and safety problems have been associated primarily with private sector manufacturing activities. Social regulation aims also at not-for-profit private institutions and at many of the "line" agencies of government itself. For example, whoever receives federal grant or contract money–whether it be Lockheed or Columbia University or the Boston Redevelopment Authority–is subject to the antidiscrimination provisions of the 1964 Civil Rights Act and of related federal legislation; and unions as well as businesses are subject to ERISA, the Employee Retirement Income Security Act.

Many intergovernmental financial assistance programs are the vehicle for regulatory efforts as well, in that the donor government, through the promulgation and enforcement of regulations, tries to shape the programs and practices of the recipient governmental agencies.[9] By contrast, within a single level of government, a regulatory agency like the Office of Federal Contracts Compliance Programs or the Council on Environmental Quality may be given at least nominal influence over certain practices of the line agencies.[10] If we want to understand the deeper nature and implications of governmental social regulation, therefore, we must certainly take note of its broad swath across such a diversity of targets. The only difficulty in doing so is in finding a suitable term to refer to these diverse targets of regulation. Here I generally refer to them as "local settings and institutions" or "decentralized decision sites" and contrast these with "centralized bureaucratic units."

The shift in the locus of social judgment from local settings to centralized units is of small concern when the judgments of the two parties happen to coincide reasonably well, and this will happen often enough. However, when they do not coincide, the local party will necessarily regard the central enforcement agency as being "unreasonable." Because enforcement agencies are armed with the power and authority of the state, the chances are that they will win most such encounters. But for a number of reasons, the chances also are high that they are in fact being unreasonable. The irony here is that the regulatory agency's unreasonableness is not necessarily the product of stupidity, incompetence, inappropriate political influence, or arrogance, but of sincere intentions well executed.[11] As is often the case when public policy produces a poor outcome, it is not because evil has triumphed over good but because the pursuit of one or more goods is carried on at the expense of others.

Regulation and Reason

To put the matter in its simplest form, when an enforcement agency pursues effectiveness while also upholding principles of procedural due process and of equal and uniform application of the laws, reasonableness is the loser—if not necessarily in the case of every single entity under the agency's jurisdiction, then probably in enough cases to cause concern.[12] The principal reasons are these:

1. The more diverse the local settings and institutions being regulated, the harder it is to write reasonable rules and standards.[13] Rules that are reasonable for one subclass of regulated organizations will be unreasonable for another. Normally an agency (or a legislature) tries to take such variations into account in developing the rules, but there are distinct limits on how much differentiation is possible.[14]

2. Given that the problems of insufficient differentiation cannot be wholly solved, an agency's best strategy is to design its regulations so as to be fairly certain of catching the "bad apples." Now in any normal distribution of apples, the "bad" ones are by definition in only one tail. The implication is that the great majority of good apples, by virtue of being subjected to the same regimen as the bad apples, are treated unreasonably. For the "good apple" firms and institutions subject to regulation, the most obvious sort of unreasonable treatment is that they must bear the added financial (and other) costs of compliance without receiving much in the way of offsetting benefit. From the viewpoint of society at large, it is conceivable that the benefits of successfully regulating the few substantially outweigh the unreasonable costs imposed on

the many. Yet from the viewpoint of these latter parties, the costs are in fact unreasonable.[15]

3. As if the variety and diversity in today's world were not trouble enough, an agency must deal with constant technological and social change as well. Plastic pipe displaces cast-iron pipe in plumbing systems, and sterilized packaging threatens to make refrigeration obsolete in the retail dairy industry. How rapidly can the building codes and the health codes be changed to reflect these shifts? More to the point, can they be written so as not to retard them unreasonably in the first place? To take another example, will the regulatory apparatus now being created to regulate research into recombinant DNA be able to keep up with advancing scientific capabilities and techniques? There are grounds to think it will not.

One problem is that regulatory officials are more likely to be penalized for mistaken haste and enthusiasm in embracing an innovation than for mistaken caution and delay, quite independently of how much damage either sort of mistake actually causes. What official wants to be blamed for a "highly improbable" conflagration or epidemic that nevertheless occurs? Another problem officials have in accommodating technological and social change is that they find it hard to ignore the adverse economic effect likely to be felt by certain commercial interests, like the manufacturers of iron pipe and of refrigeration equipment in the two examples just mentioned.[16]

4. For an enforcement strategy to work, noncompliance must be detectable and measurable. This requirement sometimes leads agencies to overemphasize standards that have dubious relevance to the problem at hand. In community-care homes for the mentally ill, for instance, the attitudes of the proprietor and staff are probably much more important factors in producing a "therapeutic" or even "comfortable" living environment than the number of square feet of space per occupant. Yet licensing codes emphasize physical measures like the latter because it is almost impossible to assess intangibles like motivation and attitude.

5. The inflexibility and unreasonableness that inevitably afflict the standard-setting process are to a certain extent mitigated by the inspection process. Field-level compliance officers learn to overlook a great deal and to substitute bargaining and persuasion

for the application of sanctions. There are limits on how far this drift toward informality can go, however. Discretion is potentially very dangerous. It invites corruption and, more importantly, the suspicion of corruption or corruptibility. Nursing home inspectors in California must administer a checklist survey with hundreds of items in the course of one inspection visit, yet this task is dutifully heeded by most inspectors, who say, "Given the political environment we work in, we really have no alternative but to 'go by the book.' "

Government Unreason as a Social Problem

If government enforcement efforts treat people unreasonably, does it matter? It is not obvious that it does. Although I know of no survey evidence on the point, I suspect most people are prepared to accept a certain amount of fallibility in government and even have a pretty fair understanding of why the regulatory mistakes of government are inescapable. If they are inescapable, then in a certain sense they are forgivable. Bureaucratic unreason has its own special niche beside the unreason we expect from young children, dotty old relatives, and sanctimonious clergymen. We can tolerate their being unreasonable because they are all, in their own ways, essential to the larger scheme of things. Indeed, we make room for them in our jokes, folklore, and literature. Still, there are limits to our good humor and tolerance. The broader and deeper the reach of regulation, the more often more of us will be touched by its unreasonableness. Our tolerant attitudes toward the seeming foibles of "petty bureaucrats" and the like could shift dramatically if we perceived them as prevalent rather than as deviant.

One direct implication of such a shift would almost certainly be greater skepticism about government in general. Skepticism about government as social regulator could lead to misplaced skepticism about government as redistributor of income and wealth or as provider of traditional public services or as overseer of the nation's defense. Indeed, an undiscriminating skepticism about government might curtail or preempt regulatory programs that are or might be genuinely useful and appropriate. For instance, the justifiable backlash against safety regulation by OSHA is also likely to hurt occupational health regulation, an area in which aggressive regulatory intervention is almost certainly needed.

Another consequence of skepticism about government would be an erosion of respect for legality per se. At present "compliance" is normative. Whatever law is at issue, by virtue of being law it gets the benefit of the doubt. For this presumption to be reversed would be a serious blow to society. In this context it is important to remember that the direct impact of unreasonable social regulation on the citizenry is bound to be selective, even if broad. It is experienced directly mainly by the stratum of persons who hold positions of social responsibility and trust: plant managers, shop foremen, personnel directors, union leaders, architects and engineers, sales representatives, liability lawyers, insurance claims adjusters, hospital and university administrators, physicians and surgeons, and line-agency officials at all levels of government. This is a relatively articulate and influential stratum of society. Significant resentment on their part toward administrative law and law enforcement could ripple outward with effects we cannot imagine but should definitely not want to experience.

All this would occur only if this "trusteeship stratum" resented and resisted regulatory unreason. But a worse outcome is conceivable. Many might become simply the equivalent of privately paid functionaries of public regulatory agencies.[17] Others might take on a legal advisory role: business firms and nonprofit institutions would hire them to act mainly as advisers on how to deal with government (and lower-level governments would hire them to deal with higher-level governments). In this capacity they would find their talents had gained them positions not as responsible "trustees" with productive social functions to perform but as paper shufflers, memo writers, and "liaison" personnel with government. In the most extreme conceivable development of this kind, complaining customers or workers or job applicants or just plain bystanders would complain directly to government compliance officials if they thought they had cause, and the private "trustee" class would act mainly as buffers, trying to keep their institutions from being injured by a combination of unfriendly forces.

In this scenario, the only people who would be deserving of trust would be certain government officials and the judges who arbitrate among their competing claims about the concept of the public interest. If this extreme development seems unlikely, the tendencies in that direction are not. Responsibility does, more and more, tend to become professionalized, specialized, and concentrated. And since trustworthiness follows responsibility, its character and social distribution are undergoing the same evolution. There are several reasons to deplore these tendencies. One is that opportunities to take meaningful responsibility, being personally fulfilling, ought to be distributed as widely as possible. A second is that opportunities to feel trusting ought, for the same general reasons, to be as rich and numerous as possible. Finally, the contradictions that inhere in the very concept of "social responsibility" guarantee that centralizing and bureaucratizing it will diminish it. It is a mistake to think that self-interest is the only barrier to fulfilling a social responsibility. Frequently it is another more pressing or more fundamental social responsibility. As Thomas Schelling has put it,

> Often the question is not, "Do I want to do the right thing?" It arises in the form, "What is the right thing to want to do?" The choice is not always between some selfish temptation and some obvious responsible course. The choice is often a policy decision. What should a business do about drug addiction among its employees? What should it do about admitting men to jobs that have been traditionally women's—secretaries, receptionists, or file clerks? Or smoking on the job? Or eliminating some hazard in the product by producing it more expensively and selling it at a higher price? Or letting a black organization dictate policy toward blacks, letting a woman's organization negotiate on behalf of women? Consider the business that is under pressure to discontinue operations in South Africa, throwing people out of work there. What is the right thing to do? Is there a "right thing" in this case or just a choice between equally unsatisfactory options?[18]

Reason and Responsibility

Without choice there is no responsibility, and without reason there is no true choice. Because there is a pronounced tendency in social regulation to remove both choice and reason from local and decentralized settings to more centralized bureaucratic units, whatever responsibility remains to localized decision makers can become a hollow sort of thing. The very idea of responsibility is corrupted. Consider a firm in one of the predicaments posed by

Schelling, facing not only the social dilemma itself but also a government regulatory agency strongly pushing it to grasp one horn of the dilemma rather than the other. The path of least resistance is to acquiesce in this choice. But even if this is, by some definition, the "right" horn to grasp, such a choice process is morally dubious.

Just how often and to what extent one social responsibility comes into conflict with another is an empirical question without a ready answer. Schelling's examples of conflict within a business enterprise are probably most likely to turn up in large-scale corporations with complex internal structures and sufficiently diverse operations to allow exposure to a broad range of customers, suppliers, taxing authorities, and so on. One suspects that a more typical and far less interesting conflict for a firm is between fulfilling some social responsibility and increasing the firm's profits.

It is not in the world of business, however, so much as in the world of public and not-for-profit institutions that the dilemmas of conflicting responsibilities show themselves most readily. For one thing, such institutions derive their legitimacy, and often their legal status and their funding, from their dedication to fulfilling some valued social responsibility, like caring for the sick or educating the young or sustaining the arts. They are therefore that much more susceptible than the typical profit-oriented firm to a potential conflict of responsibilities. Secondly, short-run constraints on revenues (imposed by the budget process and by limited borrowing authority) often make the trade-offs between socially valued objectives or "responsibilities" especially visible as well as acute. A county hospital, for example, may have to choose between upgrading its emergency room and upgrading its affirmative-action hiring program. In addition, the same resources needed for these responsibilities might be needed for renovations to meet new local fire codes or for investments in energy-saving capital equipment.

Pressure to move in some particular direction might be exerted by a central government regulatory agency, in which case the hospital administrator's decision would be affected by the principle of least resistance, as in the case of the private firm. But suppose, for either a profit or a nonprofit entity, that each responsibility is spoken for by competing regulatory agencies. And indeed, as social regulation increases and regulations multiply, the opportunities do grow for different agencies or objectives to contradict one another. The Federal Energy Administration can order a utility to shift from oil to coal, but the Environmental Protection Agency can require just the opposite. OSHA can mandate that lounge facilities must be provided adjacent to women's rest rooms, but the Equal Employment Opportunity Commission can then require that men be given equivalent facilities, something employers would obviously be loath to do.[19] The Freedom of Information Act can require disclosure, while the Privacy Act can forbid it. To be sure, one might argue that such conflicts will create conditions in which conscientious administrators and managers will carve out new areas of responsible autonomy, for if whatever they do is wrong according to someone's lights, they are no worse off for doing what is right according to their own.

Decades of overuse and ideological abuse have made the idea of moral fiber almost too quaint for serious discussion. But if one does take it seriously, as one should, then it should be recognized that doling out "welfare" to the poor and other forms of largesse to the rich and the middle class is not the only way to weaken the moral fiber of the citizenry. Converting moral dilemmas into exercises in dealing with bureaucracy trivializes the experience of choosing and in the long run degrades society's capacity both to see and to resolve moral issues. If moral fiber is harmed when government usurps individuals' responsibilities for themselves, might it not also be harmed—and perhaps even more so—if government degrades people's ability to take responsibility for significant choices affecting others?

Toward Greater Responsibility

It is ironic that the long-run tendency of the social regulation movement, therefore, is to destroy what it has sought to create. For if there is an underlying unity to the programs loosely referred to as "social regulation," it is the theory—usually implicit rather than explicit—that because private and line-agency responsibility is weak or decaying, more centralized governmental units must assume responsibility.[20] Fortunately, though this theory is very crude, it is not hopeless. Its basic thrust is correct, and I would guess that ultimately it is capable of refinement to the point where it would probably do more good than harm. The task of refinement is long and arduous, however, and I wish here to offer only some preliminary observations and suggestions.

As I have already argued, if responsibility must be tied to reason, and if reason, to be efficacious, must be exercised as close to the particulars of a localized situation as possible, then responsibility should be as localized—or as decentralized, if you will—as possible. But reason is not the only precondition of responsibility. Social role also counts: one must see the assumption of particular responsibilities as being entailed by one's social role and therefore, in a very broad sense, making it in one's interest to fulfill them. In a rapidly changing society, however, social roles are often ambiguous, and in a society of great complexity the constant reorganization of institutionalized role relationships sometimes permits certain responsibilities simply to "fall between the cracks."[21] Under these circumstances the general moral duty to "act responsibly" must inevitably be underfulfilled.

The inability of localized and decentralized social processes to guarantee that "responsible" roles will be created, endowed with appropriate resources, and successfully filled argues for more centralized governmental oversight and even management. Oversight and management need not entail compulsion and coercion, however. A variety of policy approaches should be considered, and particular remedies should be tailored to particular problems. Because we as a society have little experience with such approaches, the following list of possibilities is intended to be no more than suggestive:

1. Much social irresponsibility derives from a lack of resources. For instance, most parents accept the customary responsibility to protect and nurture their children, but some lack the financial means or the emotional stability to discharge it. Programs dealing with such problems almost never rely on regulatory strategies. They provide money, counseling, education, and the like. The only form in which a hint of regulation is apparent is the very restricted right of the state to remove children from the custody of "unfit" parents into its own custody.

2. If responsibilities are very expensive to fulfill or are in other

ways inconvenient or burdensome, people may acknowledge them in principle but ignore them in practice. This often occurs because the sanctions for ignoring them are too low or are nonexistent. Government can try to remedy such situations by facilitating the private application of higher penalities. These penalties can take several forms: claims for common-law damages (tort, property, contract); facilitating or even mandating higher insurance premiums for poor safety or malpractice records; and generating adverse publicity targeted on unscrupulous merchants.[22] Public penalties can also be invoked in the form of performance-conditioned taxes; for example, many economists have advocated substituting "injury taxes" for the present system of OSHA standards, inspections, and fines.[23]

3. In many areas of social life responsibility has to be thought of as "shared." Industrial accidents, for instance, may be produced by the joint action of many parties, such as the designer of unsafeguarded equipment, the foreman of the crew, the plant manager, the company safety engineer, and, of course, the worker-victim himself. The nuisance effects of smoking in public places are produced by the simultaneous presence of smokers and persons who are sensitive to smoke.[24] The more complex (and technological) our society becomes, the more parties are likely to share in a collective responsibility. Unfortunately, what belongs to all belongs to none. In such situations the most effective government role might be to clarify or to allocate responsibilities. This occurs, for example, when the legislature codifies, or modifies, common-law doctrines of tort or contract liability.[25]

4. The utility of a reputation for being responsible—and conversely, the disutility of a reputation for being irresponsible—may motivate socially desired conduct. In a transient and mobile society a reputation for responsibility may be hard to earn and a reputation for irresponsibility easy to avoid. Government could facilitate the production of deserved reputations. It might do this by rating, grading, and measuring goods or services, say, or health hazards associated with certain jobs.[26] Or it might register and validate complaints and periodically issue some of the statistical results, as in "Brand X has a 20 percent higher complaint rate than brand Y."

5. Akin to the problem of deficient resources as a cause of ir-

responsibility is the problem of incompetence. The regulatory approach to this problem is licensure, which is ineffective or counterproductive in a great many circumstances.[27] For ongoing quality assurance, for example, it is virtually worthless, as license revocations are exceedingly rare. Publicly subsidized training and "continuing education" might be a partial remedy here. In addition, a "systems" view of the problem is appropriate: if the incompetence cannot be remedied, perhaps exposure to it can be minimized, such as by warning the public to avoid medical quacks or setting up educational voucher schemes so that students can avoid incompetent teachers.

6. Sometimes the critical problem is in the way a private organization manages its quality-control system. Large and wealthy organizations usually have ready access to professional assistance, but smaller organizations may not. In such cases government might furnish free or low-cost consultative services, as it does for nursing homes in California (on a somewhat limited basis). Even in the case of large and wealthy organizations, external intervention might be useful to give the quality-control unit higher status or more leverage within the organization. This intervention can be done by government directly or indirectly through a trade association, say, or a labor union.[28]

7. Government can prescribe and protect the documentary record of transactions. In the event that disputes or difficulties arise subsequently, the record should help to determine responsibility. Knowing this, parties to the transaction are more likely to act responsibly in the first place. California requires auto repair facilities, for example, to save auto parts for which replacements have been furnished and to return them to customers for their inspection. (That the "documentary record" in this case is literally a physical object is beside the point, of course.) Physicians and nurses are required by law to make certain entries on patient charts in certain situations. Many compulsory registration systems, like those for guns, have this same character.

8. Government can subsidize research and development into methods that private parties can use to carry out various social responsibilities. In the field of mine safety, although probably too little has been done over the years and at too great expense, government research and development has been fruitful. Govern-

ment can also facilitate, by subsidies or other means, the diffusion of worthwhile innovations.

9. Finally, it should be noted that none of these essentially reinforcing and facilitative approaches absolutely precludes the addition of a coercive regulatory strategy. Indeed, the shadow of coercion might be a necessary condition for the full realization of facilitation. Enforcing documentation requirements as called for in (7) is one example. Another example would be requiring "continuing education" as in (5) or allowing private complaint-processing organizations, like unions or consumer action groups, to trigger investigative or other harassment activities as an auxiliary to the approaches in (4) and (6). How coercion might be gingerly applied at the boundaries of facilitation in order to enhance the latter while being itself diminished is an idea that I have only barely begun to explore.[29]

The Social Responsibility of Government

Americans are the fortunate heirs of a normative political tradition that insists on the primacy of questions about "the proper sphere" of government. Unfortunately, the tradition has been concerned very little with questions about how government should carry out activities that are acknowledged to be in its proper sphere.[30] Although it is the tradition of Burke rather than of Locke that might furnish answers to such questions or convince us to think them important at all, it is Locke who has schooled us. Consequently it is hard for us to think of "government" as an organic part of society rather than as some sort of independent and barely controllable machine. Yet an organic theory of government is needed to help us answer important questions concerning governmental method and technique. We must learn to see governmental institutions as being wrapped in a web of social responsibilities, part of a network that connects them with all the rest of society.[31] Otherwise it will be hard for us to conceive of "duties and responsibilities" that the government owes to "society" as a whole—not to individual citizens and interest groups, for these may be transient and short-sighted, but to those "trusteeship" institutions that have some legitimate stake not only in the long-run survival of the society but in its good health as well. The only responsibility

Lockean theory recognizes toward such institutions is to leave them alone. However, as these institutions themselves begin to falter, primarily under the onslaught of technological change but secondarily under unreasonable pressures from government, a more up-to-date theory is required. The principal elements in such a theory have already been suggested and may be restated as follows:

Government is rightly expected to intervene to protect individuals from irresponsible conduct that leads to serious physical or social harm and that the affected individuals are unable to prevent.[32]

Government should not, however, intervene without seriously considering whether protecting people from these harms is worth the costs that society will have to bear. These costs are tangible and economic but also intangible and psychic, such as having to put up with meddlesomeness, intrusions on privacy, and unreasonable coercion.

A distinction should be drawn between the government's assumption of a duty to prevent harm by the direct prescription and enforcement of legal obligations, and its assumption of a duty to facilitate the execution by private parties of their responsibility to prevent harm. Government should accept the latter duty a lot more readily than the former.

In the choice of strategies, methods, and techniques, government must weigh the adverse side effects of alternative approaches along with their intended benefits. In particular, government should act so as to preserve respect for the idea of reasonableness and the habit of law-abidingness, and so as to preserve opportunities for private parties and local institutions to take and fulfill responsibilities.

Blocking acceptance of these principles, however, and of a normative political theory that might be developed from them, is the ideological residue of an upper-middle-class political movement that may be called "the New Protectionism." The old protectionism meant tariff policies to protect domestic producers against competition from foreigners. The New Protectionism means a great array of regulatory policies to protect us from ourselves. For each group (or object) to be protected there is of course some counterpart group that is believed, owing to its supposed irresponsibility, to require regulation and constraint. Yet this fact should not obscure the deeper truth that the risks and the complexities of everyday life spring from inadequacies in our technology, our laws, customs, and mores, and, indeed, our biological makeup. We might find it convenient to blame certain alleged malefactors like "greedy corporations" or "the medical establishment" or "fly-by-night sales outfits," but in reality the origins of the problems are much more fundamental and widespread.

Toward this fact one can adopt either of two basic attitudes. One can feel concern and sympathy for a society with such problems and seek ways to help it correct itself, or one can adopt a more punitive attitude and recommend laying on the scourge. The long and continuing association of Ralph Nader and his auxiliary organizations of "public interest" lawyers, physicians, and scientists with the cause of social regulation guarantees strong support for measures that are more prohibitory and punitive than corrective, that is, that enforce rather than reinforce or facilitate. In Nader's view, business is not to be trusted because it is profit-motivated; nor government, because it is the seat of compromise and the ingenious manipulator of mirrors to avoid scrutiny or accountability; nor the common man, because people are slothful, wasteful, and addicted to technology.[33] According to Nader, "There are real collective suicidal tendencies in this country.... It's expressed in our institutions, it's right there to see. There ought to be a clinical psychology built up on institutional insanity. They are generally insane or tending toward it. The Russians have the best satire around because they realize it."[34] This, to be sure, is hyperbole, but it does reflect the underlying disgust with bourgeois and technological society that runs through much of the Naderite movement. In the face of an enormous popular outcry over the decision by the FDA to ban saccharin, to take another example, Anita Johnson, an attorney with the Nader-affiliated Health Research Group, airily dismissed the wave of complaints: "It's nothing more than a taste.... There is hysterical support for the benefits, without evidence that there are any."[35]

Here is Lockean liberalism stood on its head: when there is conflict between society and government, society, not government, is guilty until proven innocent. Standing Lockean liberalism back on its feet would not help much either, for questions of guilt and blame are, if not irrelevant, terribly misleading. Yet they are the stuff on which movements of social protest feed, and there is no question that the social regulation of the last dozen years has in many ways resembled and even aped the classic style of social protest. It has denounced remote "monied interests" and the "concentration and secretiveness of economic and political power," and it makes abundant reference to citizen helplessness, frustration, and vulnerability to manipulation.[36] To be sure, it has been a pallid version of the classic social movement, housewife boycotts of meat being a lot less dramatic than a general strike or a march through the streets of Selma. But the essential style is the same.

Because the style of the movement serves the psychological needs of many (though by no means all) of its adherents, there is no prospect that they would be willing to strip the policy issues of their moralistic overtones. Even if it is not as effective, the accusatory finger, for these individuals, is preferred to the helping hand. There is reason to hope, though, that the number and influence of such individuals will decline in the coming years. For one thing, the protest style in social regulation was borrowed in some degree from the adversary politics of the 1960s antiwar movement and of the minority-group "liberationist" movements of the same period. As the general political culture shifts back toward the center, the social regulation movement is bound to shift as well. Second, the movement has already uncovered and dramatized the most mediaworthy (and probably serious) social ills. The next wave of social regulation, I predict, will deal either with more esoteric problems, like residential energy waste and weather modification and the alleged overabundance of junk food, or with more commonplace problems, like industrial concentration and the (declining?) quality of repair services.

Unfortunately, the residue of New Protectionist fervor from the late 1960s and early 1970s will persist in the regulatory bureaucracies that were set up at all levels of government to implement the legislative mandates of that period. It is possible that some of these regulatory bureaucracies would look favorably on the development of new facilitative approaches to accomplish their social objectives, since agency effectiveness would, after all, probably increase and agency budgets could conceivably expand. The more likely prospect is resistance, however. Generally, the agencies will not favor a contraction of their regulatory authority, for a host of standard "bureaucratic" reasons. Added to these, moreover, is the fact that many persons recruited to these agencies in their formative years are still there. Their roots were in the New Protectionist movement, and they continue to relish the adversary mode of governmental activism.[37]

The decisive struggles over the reshaping of social regulation will not, however, be narrowly bureaucratic or political. They will be intellectual. Elite, and particularly liberal elite, attitudes must become more enlightened. A new synthesis is required of the liberal humanitarian outlook, which is so quick to identify social problems and personal troubles, and conservative realism, which hastens to add up the manifold costs of having government try to do anything about them. The synthesis must work at two levels, the programmatic and the philosophical. I have sketched the rudiments of such a synthesis at each level, though obviously much conceptual and empirical work remains to be done.

Notes

This paper is a part of a larger study of social regulation being directed by Robert Kagan and myself for the Twentieth Century Fund. I wish to acknowledge support from the Ford Foundation in the earlier stages of the work. Able field research has been conducted by Jerome Bayer, Kenneth Block, Donna Leff, and John Scholz. I also would like to thank the following individuals for their helpful comments on an earlier draft: Michael Dempster, A. Lawrence Chickering, Frank Levy, Martin A. Levin, John Mendeloff, Arnold Meltsner, Allan Sindler, Peter Siegelman, John Scholz, Aaron Wildavsky, Suzanne Weaver, and of course Robert Kagan.

1. William Lilley III and James C. Miller III, "The New 'Social Regulation,' " *The Public Interest*, no. 47 (April 1977): 50, table 1. They also count a total of 30 new regulatory statutes in the 1970-1975 period and an increase in the number of agencies from 12 to 17.

2. We all know that in general there is much displeasure over the alleged ineffectiveness of many government enforcement programs. The conventional criticisms are that the budgets are too low, that the policymakers are "captured" by the regulated institutions, that the standards are perforated by loopholes, that the inspectors are corrupt or lax, that the penalty structure is capable of inflicting only minor wounds, and so on. Many of these criticisms are well justified.

3. Mark V. Nadel, *The Politics of Consumer Protection* (Indianapolis: Bobbs-Merrill, 1971), pp. 38-42.

4. Murray L. Weidenbaum, *Government-Mandated Price Increases: A Neglected Aspect of Inflation* (Washington, D.C.: American Enterprise Institute, 1975), p. 51.

5. Allen V. Kneese and Charles L. Schultze, *Pollution, Prices, and Public Policy* (Washington, D.C.: Brookings Institution, 1975), pp. 69 ff.

6. Weidenbaum, *Government-Mandated Price Increases,* p. 101.

7. Ibid., p. 102. Weidenbaum also cites an estimate by Peltzman that "if the drugs that combat tuberculosis had been delayed by two years, the average delay now imposed by the Food and Drug Administration, the result would have been 45,000 additional deaths." On the topic of drug regulation, see Richard L. Landau, ed., *Regulating New Drugs* (Chicago: University of Chicago Center for Policy Study, 1975); Sam Peltzman, "An Evaluation of Consumer Protection Legislation: The 1962 Drug Amendments," *Journal of Political Economy* (September-October 1973); David Seidman, "The Politics and Economics of Pharmaceutical Regulation," in *Public Law and Public Policy*, ed. John A. Gardiner (New York: Praeger, 1977), pp. 177-203; and references cited therein.

8. Said one plant manager, "OSHA doesn't need to tell me what to do. I look out for these workers—they're friends of mine."

9. See Eugene Bardach, *The Implementation Game: What Happens After a Bill Becomes a Law* (Cambridge, Mass.: MIT Press, 1977), chap. 5, especially pp. 119-124.

10. Generally this influence is quite weak (see James Q. Wilson and Patricia Rachal, "Can the Government Regulate Itself?" *The Public Interest,* no. 46 [Winter 1977]). Possibly an interesting exception is the Council on Environmental Quality, whose guidelines for the preparation of environmental impact statements are taken seriously by the federal courts and hence by the federal agencies that risk being sued by private citizens for failing to prepare "adequate" statements. See Eugene Bardach and Lucian Pugliaresi, "The Environmental-Impact Statement vs. the Real World," *The Public Interest*, no. 49 (Fall 1977).

11. Of course, if agency personnel are picayune or stupid or lazy or excessively "political," the results will be a lot worse than I suggest here.

12. Unfortunately, there has been almost no useful empirical work on the statistical prevalence of "unreasonableness" (or "reasonableness") in the impacts of any regulatory program. The explanation for this vacuum, I believe, is that even a modest undertaking of this kind, say in one program in a limited geographical area, would be very time- (and money) consuming and would involve very complex measurement problems. Nearly all the empirical work on bureaucratic interaction with citizens deals with service programs, not enforcement programs. Housing code enforcement is a small exception to this proposition. One could debate whether antidiscrimination programs, which have to some extent been studied empirically (for example, Leon Mayhew, *Law and Opportunity* [Cambridge, Mass.: Harvard University Press, 1968]), qualify, for insofar as they serve complainants, they may be not so much regulatory as service programs.

13. One important dimension of variability is size. There is a general presumption—though it has not been adequately tested—that large firms are better behaved than small firms with respect to safety issues, let us say, because they can more easily afford to be. Another potentially important dimension of variability is the structure of ownership and control, with franchises and department stores tending in some respect to exercise better quality control than independent merchandisers. Market structure is another variable of interest: it appears that firms facing greater competition tend to be less well behaved—the important exception perhaps being government institutions, which enjoy both monopoly power and political power (see Robert H. Nelson, "The Economics of Honest Trade Practices," *Journal of Industrial Economics* 24 [June 1976] : 281-293, and references cited therein). In some cases locale or regional culture or ethnic factors might be significant variables (see Robert E. Lane, *The Regulation of Businessmen* [New Haven: Yale University Press, 1954] ; James Q. Wilson, *Varieties of Police Behavior* [Cambridge, Mass.: Harvard University Press, 1968]).

14. For instance, certain classifications simply cannot be recognized under law. We cannot say that halfway houses for the mentally ill run by nuns or by Mexican-Americans or by young idealists should be treated differently from each other or from the great majority of such facilities, even if for some reason we knew such differentiation would be reasonable. Second, differentiation makes for complexity, but beyond a certain point complexity itself becomes unmanageable and therefore unreasonable. Who knows how to comply with a set of regulations for restaurant sanitation that looks like the tax code? Finally, there is the fact that preparing differentiated rules is time-consuming and difficult if it is done well. Information must be gathered from the field and processed intelligently. (An excellent case study of this process is Robert Kagan, *Regulatory Justice: Implementing a Wage-Price Freeze* [New York: Russell Sage, forthcoming]). Organizational resources are thereby consumed, resources that could perhaps more profitably be devoted to other activities.

15. This problem is aggravated by the traditional division of labor between the public sector and the private sector in their joint production of more "social responsibility": public-sector officials define society's aspirations, while private parties bear the costs. The obvious dangers inherent in this arrangement are not diminished when public officials, acting in what they certainly regard as a high-minded way, assert or strongly imply that costs are not to be given much (if any) weight. This has clearly been the attitude underlying the Clean Air Act, the Federal Water Pollution Control Act, and the Occupational Safety and Health Act. Even if one regards such an attitude as inspiring, or as the manifestation of a noble ideal of public policy, this is not the same as saying it is reasonable, which it surely is not. When it is expressed in the context of a particular regulation enforced on a particular firm, it must look even less reasonable.

16. Although of course political pressure is often brought to bear by such interests to retard change, the basic problem is that officials can yield to it while at the same time feeling and believing that they are serving the public interest. From the point of view of those would-be innovators who are

frustrated by the system, the officials are acting unreasonably and in opposition to the public interest.

17. Tocqueville refers to the "immense and tutelary power" of the democratic state that "takes upon itself alone to secure [the] gratifications and to watch over [the] fate" of its citizens. This power "is absolute, minute, regular, provident, and mild." But "it every day renders the exercise of the free agency of man less useful and less frequent; it circumscribes the will within a narrow range and gradually robs a man of all the uses of himself." Alexis de Tocqueville, *Democracy in America*, 2 vols., ed. Phillips Bradley (New York: Knopf, Vintage Books, 1945), 2: 336-337.

18. Thomas C. Schelling, "Command and Control," in *Social Responsibility and the Business Predicament,* ed. James W. McKie (Washington, D.C.: Brookings Institution, 1974), pp. 79-108.

19. Weidenbaum, *Government-Mandated Price Increases,* pp. 88-90.

20. Many commentators on the new social regulation have tried to define it by comparing it with old-style economic regulation or with welfare-type subsidies and services. In my view, while all of their observations are useful and relevant, none quite gets to the heart of the matter. Lilley and Miller, in "The New 'Social Regulation,'" note that it "affects the conditions under which goods and services are produced and the physical characteristics of products that are manufactured [and] . . . extends to far more industries and ultimately affects far more consumers than the old-style regulation, which tends to be confined to specific sectors . . . [and] often becomes involved with very detailed facets of the production process" (p. 53). Weidenbaum, in *Government-Mandated Price Increases,* refers to a "second managerial revolution" that makes government "assume or at least share many of the key aspects of decision making of all firms" (p. 98). And, "the more recent regulatory efforts . . . cut across virtually every branch of private industry" (p. 7). Cornell, Noll, and Weingast think of the definitional question rather more politically: "So dramatic has been the appearance, if not the reality, of increased government control over product and worker safety that these activities, along with environmental controls, are called the 'new regulation'" (Nina W. Cornell, Roger G. Noll, and Barry Weingast, "Safety Regulation," in *Setting National Priorities: The Next Ten Years* [Washington, D.C.: Brookings Institution, 1976], pp. 457-504, at p. 457). Schultze is perhaps closest to the mark: "In a short space of twenty years the very nature of federal activity has changed radically toward much more complex and difficult objectives. . . . The term *social* (or *collective*) *intervention* assumes a good deal. It implies the rebuttable presumption that the desirable mode of carrying out economic and social activities is through a network of private and voluntary arrangements—called, for short, 'the private market'" (Charles L. Schultze, "The Public Use of Private Interest," *Harpers*, April 1977, p. 44). "Private," "voluntary," and "network" are the key ideas here. Schultze's error is to neglect nonmarket institutions, like the family and grade schools, that have many of these "private and voluntary" features.

21. Schelling, "Comand and Control," pp. 94-95.

22. The institution of small claims courts is one such facilitating strategy that

comes to mind, as is a statutory provision for awarding litigation fees in claims settlements. The potential for the use and abuse of adverse publicity has hardly been explored. The Federal Trade Commission has ordered firms found guilty of deceptive advertising to run ads disavowing their previous claims. An interesting, if abortive, attempt was once made by the US Department of Transportation to shame states into complying with federal highway safety standards by issuing "report cards," complete with numerical scores, on the states' performance.

23. Cornell, Noll, and Weingast, "Safety Regulation," p. 503; Robert Stuart Smith, *The Occupational Safety and Health Act* (Washington, D.C.: American Enterprise Institute, 1976). See John Mendeloff, "Costs and Consequences: A Political and Economic Analysis of the Federal Occupational Safety and Health Program" (Ph.D. diss., University of California Graduate School of Public Policy, Berkeley, 1977), pp. 64-83 and chap. 8, for a critique of the injury tax as conceptually attractive but impossible to implement.

24. Ronald Coase, "The Problem of Social Cost," *Journal of Law and Economics* 1 (1960).

25. Statutory modifications of the negligence or "fault" test in liability cases are relevant in this connection. The movement is toward "strict" liability for more and more enterprises in a variety of areas, but it has been slow and decentralized. Various proposals to hasten the movement through statutory change have been put forward. See Jeffrey O'Connell, "Expanding No-Fault Beyond Auto Insurance: Some Proposals," *Virginia Law Review* 59 (May 1973): 749-829. Ellickson explores ways in which the laws of trespass and nuisance might be modified in order to clarify responsibility for adverse, third-party "environmental" effects. Robert Ellickson, "Alternatives to Zoning: Covenants, Nuisance Rules, and Fines as Land Use Controls," *University of Chicago Law Review* 40 (1973): 681.

26. See, for example, Eugene Bardach, "Where to Get a Good Fix," *Policy Analysis* 3 (Spring 1977): 273-275.

27. Bardach, *The Implementation Game*, appendix B.

28. With respect to industrial accidents, the government has done this already. The existence of OSHA strengthens the hand of a union in bargaining over job safety; the union's strength in turn increases the organizational leverage of the safety experts on the rest of management. See also Christopher D. Stone, *Where the Law Ends: The Social Control of Corporate Behavior* (New York: Harper and Row, 1975), especially pp. 184 ff.

29. See David L. Kirp, "Proceduralism and Bureaucracy: Due Process in the School Setting," *Stanford Law Review* 28 (May 1976): 864-870, for a cogent analysis of possible scenarios in a school context. Note that none of the above ideas applies to the regulation of governmental or public institutions. Good ideas on this subject are in short supply, except perhaps for that of Wilson and Rachal: "It may become necessary for those who wish to broaden the scope of public intervention and regulation to favor leaving the day-to-day management of affairs in private hands. [For] *large-scale public enterprise and widespread public regulation may be incompatible*" ("Can Government Regulate Itself?" p. 14).

It is an open question whether such reinforcing and facilitative strategies (with or without buttressing by coercive methods at the fringes) would be as effective as straight regulation. There are reasons to think they would be more so. A principal impediment to the regulatory approach is its misallocation of agency resources to places where they are unproductive. From the viewpoint of the regulated firm or public institution, the enforcement agency's intrusion is, as I have said, often unreasonable. The corollary is that from the agency's viewpoint its intrusion is unnecessary and largely a waste of time and energy. These resources might be better spent on the minority of true miscreants than on the majority of relatively tolerable firms and institutions. Alternatively, the agency might be better off practicing a form of triage: ignore the organizations that will perform well no matter what and those that cannot be improved no matter what and concentrate on those for whom the agency's efforts will make a difference. Such strategies, however, presume that the agency can persuade the public, its legislative overseers, and itself that diminishing its enforcement efforts in certain areas will not leave them wholly unattended. The availability of facilitative strategies could furnish the needed reassurance. Thus facilitative strategies can not only add to overall effectiveness on their own but can enhance the effectiveness of supplementary regulatory strategies.

It should be noted that facilitative strategies impose their own costs too. There are bound to be direct budgetary expenditures. In some cases there might be substantial record-keeping costs imposed on regulated entities, as in (7). There are also many problems that come from "delegating" governmental authority to private entities, though these seem to me overrated. See Theodore Lowi, *The End of Liberalism* (New York: W. W. Norton, 1968).

30. "Effectively and efficiently" is the standard answer to implicit or explicit questions of this kind. But these are normative only in a very narrow sense.

31. Much has been spoken and written about "the social responsibility of business." Three outstanding works are those by Schelling, "Command and Control;" Roland N. McKean, "Collective Choice," in *Social Responsibility and the Business Predicament*, ed. James W. McKie (Washington, D.C.: Brookings Institution, 1974), pp. 109-134; and Stone, *Where the Law Ends*. Neither the issues nor the answers are very clear, however. In any case, I am in effect proposing a comparable dialogue on "the social responsibility of government." The late Alexander Bickel was a pioneer in this regard. The philosophical—specifically, Burkean—questioning that Bickel directed toward the judiciary now needs to be extended to the legislative and executive branches.

32. In this context the scope of protection should also include certain animals, plants, and other "environmental" values like landscapes. I use the term "individuals" for simplicity.

33. Charles McCarry, in *Citizen Nader* (New York: Saturday Review Press, 1972), quotes a line from a speech by Nader to an audience in New Jersey: "As long as this country is populated by people who fritter away their citizenship . . . watching TV or playing cards or Mah-Jongg, or just generally being slobs, it will never be the country we should want it to be" (p. 135). The "should" in this sentence suggests that we slobs do not even *want* the country to shape up.

34. Ibid., p. 314.

35. Linda E. Demkovich, "Saccharin's Dead, Dieters Are Blue, What is Congress Going to Do?" *National Journal Reports*, June 4, 1977, p. 857. The FDA decision against saccharin might be justifiable—I demur on this point. The point is that even if it is justified, the loss of saccharin is still a loss, especially to the vast majority of consumers who would not have suffered any ill effects.

36. Andrew S. McFarland, *Public Interest Lobbies: Decision-making on Energy* (Washington, D.C.: American Enterprise Institute, 1976), p. 11; Rudolf Heberle, *Social Movements* (New York: Appleton-Century-Crofts, 1951); William Kornhauser, *The Politics of Mass Society* (Glencoe, Ill.: Free Press, 1959); Daniel Bell, ed., *The Radical Right* (New York: Doubleday, 1963).

37. Lilley and Miller, "The New 'Social Regulation,' " p. 58.

Chapter 16

Standing the Study of Public Policy Implementation on Its Head

Michael Lipsky

The critical potential of the study of politics is tied to understanding the impact of political activity. A profound knowledge of the effects of political activity on the lives of citizens is a prerequisite for both radical inquiry and a democratic politics. Both depend upon knowing who gets what, when, and why from public life. Thus recent efforts to study policy implementation are ultimately critical because they attempt to explain better the relationship between what political authorities intend and what actually results from efforts to intervene.[1]

This essay is concerned not with the implementation of any particular policies but rather with the implicit model of the policy process by which implementation is currently understood. The model has two complementary elements: first, that the hierarchical structure of organizations provides a useful map of the policy process; second, that organizations charged with implementing policy are associated with each other in a policy "system." These assumptions, while undoubtedly useful in some cases, in many others detract from an understanding of policy processes. They do this by providing the impression that policy implementation problems are primarily ones of coordination and control, or of negotiations among diverse organized and self-conscious interests. At times, this leads to mystification of the policy process, which makes comprehension and resolution of implementation problems more elusive than necessary. In this essay I want to suggest an alternative approach to policy implementation and discuss the circumstances under which it is likely to be applicable.

In general, studies of policy development and implementation tend to work from assumptions of hierarchy in organizations. In plain language, they tend to take the perspective that the closer governmental units are to policy formulation, the greater their influence is on policy development. Conversely, the closer governmental units are to putting policy into practice, the weaker their influence is on policy.

The same assumptions tend to hold for policy development within organizations. Most studies tend to assume that greater influence over policy is exerted by those who formulate it than by those who carry it out. In the case of an agency required or requested to perform by another governmental unit, most studies tend to assume that policy is set by those at the top of the agency, who then are thought to pass down responsibility for the policy to subordinates for refinement or implementation.

Simply put, policy is conceived in these studies as being made at high levels of government and then passed down to other levels, where it is implemented. It is conceived as consisting of the original statement of objectives and intent, a plan to achieve the objectives, and the results of trying to carry out that plan.[2] In such a conception the problem of policy is thought to be to minimize the distortion between the articulated intent of the policy declarers and the organizational behavior that follows. Distortion may arise from such factors as subordinates' misunderstanding or ignorance, personal incompetence, or local resistance.

It is obvious why these assumptions of hierarchy are pervasive. Organizations are virtually always hierarchically structured to some degree, so long as there is a division of labor. Moreover, this is the way policy *should* develop. Systems of hierarchy are congruent with formal responsibilities. Power and status normally are associated with people at "higher" organizational reaches. In addition, policy development does take place this way in enough instances to appear to confirm the validity of such thinking.

However, the hierarchy assumption is not always or entirely

valid. When there are two or more organizations involved in policy development and implementation, it is not clear that the policy declarer (a federal agency that distributes grants, for example) is more powerful than the agency supposed to implement policy (say a local agency). The presumptive subordinate agency's influence over policy results may more than match that of the policy declarer. Indeed, federal grant-in-aid programs are designed precisely to sustain a high degree of local agency autonomy and in this respect succeed all too well at times.

When implementation tasks fall to two or more levels within a single agency, the same problem surfaces. It is far from obvious that an agency head is consistently more powerful in policy development and implementation than presumptive subordinates. For example, in many respects a police officer has much more influence in determining policy on the street than his captain, although the captain has authority over the officer and responsibility for the entire precinct.[3]

The grip of the hierarchy assumption is perhaps most evident in studies in which the analysis depends upon the gap between the expectations of policy declarers and the final results of policy. Implementation studies which find that urban development projects were not built, even though President Lyndon Johnson (in one case) or the director of the Economic Development Administration (in another) entirely favored them, show that policy implementation is indeed more complicated than simply wishing it were so.[4] Similarly, a study of the efficacy of riot commissions demonstrates that what commissions want is not what they get, although here the emphasis is on the structural discontinuities of commissions as policymakers.[5] These studies have made a considerable contribution toward explaining the complexities of the implementation process. Nonetheless, they turn on the reader's (and writer's) assumption that circumstances should be otherwise. By setting up the analysis using assumptions of hierarchy, they focus attention on the possibilities of constructing or reconstructing policy processes that would operate with less slippage between processes as they should work and processes as they actually do work.

For example, if a study of the implementation of the work-incentive program "reforms" in public welfare was based on assumptions of organizational hierarchy, it would very likely focus on issues of command and coordination. Recommendations to eliminate discrepancies between policy objectives and policy in operation would probably focus on ways to tighten coordination between Washington and the states, the states and local offices, and local administrators and line workers. There is another approach to understanding the problem of implementation in this instance, but before turning to it I will examine another assumption that guides most perspectives on policy implementation.

A second assumption implicit in the model of policy development and implementation is that organizations charged with implementing policy are associated with each other in a policy system. The "system" metaphor originates in the analogy to an organism, with two implications significant for our purposes. One is that changes in part of the system (or in a subsystem) will affect the other parts (or the other subsystems). Thus we infer from systems models that the interests of one part of the system are bound up with the other elements in the system. The second implication is that there is relatively direct transmission of stimuli, or in our case, of commands, between parts of the system, so that messages can indeed flow and parts can indeed be affected by the other parts.

Contemporary policy studies are often explicitly based on systems assumptions in statistical models utilized to study policy outcomes on a comparative basis. Less obvious are the implicit assumptions that there ought to be congruence of interest among elements in a policy "chain" and that at some level all elements in a policy development process tend to have a stake in their mutual health and persistence.

The popularity of a model with assumptions of hierarchy and systems linkage may be explained in part because it reflects an element of truth and appears to fit closely a widely shared impression of the way the relevant world operates. The scope of policy declarers' general powers and responsibilities are usually so broad in comparison to the scope of the units required to implement policy that assumptions of hierarchy appear confirmed. Units of the federal government "decide" to introduce or cut off a federal program, to raise funds or not. In comparison, the range of responsibilities of local implementing units is often smaller. Moreover, it is the case that the varied elements of the world of policy declarers, processors, and implementers (whether federal-state-local or within single jurisdictions) are often mutually dependent.

These assumptions may also be promulgated for heuristic purposes. Policy analysis may incorporate these assumptions because they seem to provide an orderly way to discuss complex phenomena. Assumptions of hierarchy and system linkage contribute to ordering observations. Journalists and scholars alike thus begin their analyses with power and purpose and then consider units of lesser authority which are close to the enactment of "results."

The best recent studies of policy implementation demonstrate that various actors and agencies in a policy "chain" have such widely differing stakes in the outcomes of policy and are motivated so differently that the results diverge sharply from the stated intentions of the policy declarers. This perspective, however obvious once it has been stated, contributes significantly to understanding the overarching general conclusion that emerges from implementation studies, namely, that federal policies, at least those that have gained attention through detailed analysis, cannot be put into place or do not work.[6] These studies also call into question the assumption that the stated objectives of policy declarers can usefully be considered authoritative. If different participants, all with some authority over the policy world, have different objectives, then there can be no single policy objective. From this perspective it makes little sense to seek to understand why policy outcomes tend to be distortions of grand expectations.

Still, these studies communicate implicitly that the intentions and hopes of the policy declarers ought to be realized; orderly government and democratic theory demand it. Whatever their merits in demonstrating the multiplicity of participants and variety of objectives, they still start with a declaration of policy intention by the participant highest up in the chain of information and authority, and they proceed to detail the departures from a theoretical norm of compliance by a responsive bureaucracy.

Those analysts who describe conflict and dissent in policy implementation at lower levels but continue to utilize a systems perspective are caught in a dilemma. If there is a policy implementation system, then lower-level dissent cannot really be very great. If lower-level dissent is so great as to obscure or negate the intentions of policy declarers, of what heuristic value is it to say that there is a policy system? The analytic crux of the dilemma is to determine at what point a strong disposition of lower-level participants to dissent from policy declarers' intentions is significant enough to cancel the utility of a systems perspective.

Predictably, the lessons one learns from policy analysis of this sort are implicit in the model employed to create order from the data. A hierarchical, systems-linked model directs analysts' attention to criticisms of command, control, and coordination in government agencies. Proposals for greater rationality and simplicity in the political system, and greater coordination and accountability within public agencies, are the sorts of insights that this kind of analysis yields. Recommendations based upon this approach are unlikely to be very potent, at the very least failing to take into account the political functions served by delay, poor coordination, incoherence in policy, and conflict among objectives.

Common use of the word "policy" contributes to these conceptual difficulties. In common usage, as here, "policy" refers both to official intentions of public agencies and to what actually happens. Perhaps the ambiguity persists because ordinarily no one doubts that there are significant connections between official intentions and actual practice. Attempting to reduce this ambiguity, Pressman and Wildavsky suggest that "policy" be used to designate a more or less implicit hypothesis about what will happen if certain specified actions are taken. Thus "policy implementation" becomes both the theory of action and the behaviors undertaken to achieve the projected goal. This conception is extremely useful in analyzing the fit between theory and practice in some contexts.[7]

But what if we start with the assumption, confirmed by so many implementation studies, that the relationship between the objectives of high-level officials and the manifest actions of the agencies they direct are at best problematic? What if, in other words, the operational reality of hierarchical integration in organizations is so problematic that the intentions of the policy formulators cannot be assumed to guide policy-oriented behavior very much? If this should be the case, then we are bound to continue to by mystified by the failure of policy implementation because we take for granted something that cannot be taken for granted—

the relationship between higher and lower levels of organizational authority.

There are many contexts in which the latitude of those charged with carrying out policy is so substantial that studies of implementation should be turned on their heads. In these cases policy is effectively "made" by the people who implement it. Where considerable discretion characterizes the jobs of people who implement public-agency activities, people "make" policy in hidden concert with others in similar positions through their patterned responses to the situations and circumstances in which they find themselves.

Examples of high discretion in implementation are readily available. Do FBI bureau chiefs, acting zealously, engage in questionably legal behavior? Do building inspectors regularly take bribes to speed construction certification? Do life-insurance industry mortage and repair funds, allocated to assist ghetto development, flow primarily to relatively prosperous people and enterprises? Do special-education personnel, newly charged with making assessments of children's needs on an individualized basis, persist in programming for them in large part on the basis of their own capabilities, the relative disruptiveness of the child, and the financial resources? Do legal-services lawyers respond to clients in highly routinized fashion despite the injunction to serve as their advocates and to respond fully to their legal needs? They do indeed.[8]

These observations of implementation are contrary to "official" policy proclaimed at higher levels of administrative authority. They are not best understood by studying an organization's failure to develop tight organizational compliance structures or more effective coordination mechanisms. These are organizations whose participants have considerable discretion and who tend to carve out areas of discretion when orders from above conflict with other responsibilities and preferences on the job. They will find ways of doing things they want to do if they have any discretion at all, are not closely supervised, or if the penalties for acting contrary to administrative directives are not highly salient.

An alternative approach to the study of policy implementation is available if analysis focuses on those who are charged with carrying out policy rather than those who formulate and convey it. Rather than analyze interference with the "flow" of compliance in policy studies of this sort, one should focus on how the work is experienced by policy deliverers. One should concentrate on those pressures generated by the agency, such as rules and inducements, and those that prevail for other reasons. Rather than considering them at the end of a policy chain, the policy deliverers would instead be seen as primary actors; others in the policy arena provide the context in which they make their discretionary judgments. In contrast to other approaches to policy implementation, this would be appropriate where the hierarchy of influence over policy is not congruent with the hierarchy of authority in the organization, and where the elements of the policy process are not so closely linked as to warrant saying that they are part of the same policy system.

There are many situations in which this approach is already favored and clearly acceptable. For example, the study of taxicab drivers' treatment of minorities would not start with an explication of the law prohibiting discrimination in public carriers. Instead it would correctly start with an analysis of the behavior of drivers toward passengers of different backgrounds and would then proceed to explore the structural and personal factors that account for the observed behavior.[9]

The study of the behavior of doctors and lawyers toward patients and clients also conventionally proceeds from an analysis of policy as it is being made and then investigates the pressures and inducements—structural and personal—that may account for the behavior. When these matters become issues of public policy—for example, in the amount of time private lawyers spend on the cases of indigent clients in comparison to the amount of time spent by public defenders and publicly paid private attorneys—the organizational context in which the lawyer works becomes one of the key variables under investigation. It would be inefficient to start such a study with the framers of the local statute authorizing the establishment of a public defenders' office, since the critical issue—decision making about time allocation—is manifestly not a matter of statutory design.

Study of the behavior of professionals begins with the training, peer socialization and pressure, and work setting of professionals and treats the organizational context of the job—assuming the professional works for an organization—if appropriate to the analysis. Similarly, study of public workers with some degree of professionalism, such as teachers, policemen, and nurses, also properly proceeds from this perspective.[10] The common element of these work contexts is the wide discretion among policy implementers. They also have in common a degree of independence and diversity of objectives vis-à-vis other policy-implementation participants.

The proper model of policy implementation should not assume that the participants are linked together with common objectives and assumptions but should leave the system assumptions as problematic. Herbert Kaufman's study, *The Forest Ranger,* is to the point here. His rangers are policy implementers with considerable field discretion who through particular personnel policies have been induced to remain tied to the Forest Service system; those who would resist this connection are never hired or are mustered out. Thus the powerful systems linkage in the Forest Service becomes an important finding rather than a guiding assumption.[11]

In sum, this approach is recommended when assumptions of hierarchy and systems linkage are relatively inapplicable. There are at least three conditions that lead people at the bottom rather than the top to make policy although they do not have formal authority in organizations. First, the jobs of policy implementers may simply be defined in terms of wide discretion. Most jobs in the human services, such as social worker, teacher, and police officer, jobs that require public employees to interact with citizens in delivering services, require wide discretion on the part of the policy deliverers. Virtually all public work that requires the mediation of professionals and semiprofessionals also calls for a degree of discretion. (Why else would professionals be called upon to do the work?)

Public policies in which local autonomy and decentralization are part of governmental-process objectives also fall into this category. Revenue-sharing programs and federal categorical grant programs that honor a degree of local initiative are examples. This category alone encompasses a substantial portion of public expenditures.

Second, policy implementers are likely to make policy when they have multiple objectives or work tasks and the policy in question is not of the highest priority to those with superior authority. When tasks compete, resources are limited, and the capacity of those in authority to monitor compliance in all aspects of performance is limited, policy implementers have latitude to choose among objectives.

The greater the volume of decisions that constitute policy implementation, the more is the perspective likely to be useful. The fewer the decisions that need be made in a given time period, the more likely it is that extraneous or idiosyncratic factors—personality, political favoritism, taste—will account for the decision. If there are many decisions to be made, the problem of dealing with the job's problems will likely overwhelm such special factors. Contemporary examples include situations in which public agencies are expected to follow equal opportunity standards in hiring or monitor work safety guidelines while still pursuing other objectives.

Third, people who carry out policy are likely to make policy when they are engaged in implementing policy shifts in ongoing practices. In contrast to the prevailing situation when a new agency is established or a new project is slated for construction, attempts to change ongoing practices must confront the web of relationships and expectations that have previously been developed in workers' roles and in the workplace. In most circumstances extraordinary efforts must be made to overcome the set of previous practices if the policy to be implemented contradicts or interferes with priorities that form part of the expectations of the workers, or with practices on which the workers depend in order to cope with their jobs. The more policy declarers can influence the work structure of policy implementers, the more influential they will be from this perspective.

The work structure approach tends to be more useful in explaining policy developments in established agencies than in new ones and in explaining changes in old policies rather than in new ones. It is significant from this point of view that in the past the subjects that have captured the attention of students of policy implementation have tended to be new and discrete projects and programs, although political scientists have long characterized American policymaking taken as a whole as incremental and highly distributive.[12]

To be sure, a synthesis of the two approaches is indicated in some instances. (And, to repeat, in some instances this approach is not warranted at all.) To the extent that the work context is determined by rules and guidelines promulgated from above, the analyst may want to know how these constraints and influences were derived. Moreover, from a normative point of view the analyst may want to know what the official policy is in order to establish at least one of the standards against which the observed policy may be measured as it is implemented. (There are other standards: community values, the policy preferences of middle-range administrators, and professional ethics, for example.)

But in many instances it will not do to focus exclusively on the translation of law into administration from the top down. Analysts who continue to pursue a policy-chain approach will continue to conclude that the system is ineffective in its own terms. Or they will continue to observe that the system is unresponsive to policy recipients and ultimately to itself, without having recognized that the articulated policy, in never addressing issues of the environment in which policy implementers practice, never addressed the critical issues of implementation.

A focus on the work structure, in contrast, is a focus on what people do, not on an abstraction called "policy" and its fate. This approach to policy implementation may in some circumstances be more conducive to generating useful insights into what actually happens in public agencies and into the ways that policy may be made more responsive to public intervention.

Notes

The author would like to thank Brett Hammond, Richard Weatherley, and Martha Weinberg for their assistance in sharpening the discussion in this essay.

1. The literature on policy implementation is considerable and growing rapidly, in testimony to the attractiveness of implementation as a concept around which to organize research and analysis. This literature is reviewed in Erwin C. Hargrove, *The Missing Link: The Study of the Implementation of Social Policy* (Washington, D.C.: Urban Institute, 1975); Donald Van Meter and Carl Van Horn, "The Policy Implementation Process: A Conceptual Framework," *Administration and Society* 6 (1974): 445-488. See also the excellent discussion of the conception of implementation employed by different authors in Eugene Bardach, *The Implementation Game* (Cambridge, Mass.: MIT Press, 1977), chap. 2.

2. Erwin C. Hargrove puts it this way: "The academic political scientists . . .

begin with a policy as it was initially shaped by the politics of reaching agreement and then chart the continuing politics of program administration in which politicians, bureaucrats, interest groups and publics vie for control over the direction of the program." (*The Missing Link,* p. 3). This description, of course, fits some works better than others.

3. James Q. Wilson treats the problem of police discretion effectively in *Varieties of Police Behavior* (Cambridge, Mass.: Harvard University Press, 1968).

4. See Martha Derthick, *New Towns In-Town* (Washington, D.C.: Urban Institute, 1972); Jeffrey Pressman and Aaron Wildavsky, *Implementation* (Berkeley, Calif.: University of California Press, 1973).

5. Michael Lipsky and David J. Olson, *Commission Politics* (New Brunswick, N.J.: Transaction Books, 1977).

6. See Bardach, *The Implementation Game,* introduction.

7. See Pressman and Wildavsky, *Implementation,* pp. xi-xvii.

8. On the life insurance industry, see Karen Orren, *Corporate Power and Social Change* (Baltimore: Johns Hopkins University Press, 1971). On special education, see Richard Weatherley and Michael Lipsky, "Street-Level Bureaucrats and Institutional Innovation: Implementing Special Education Reform," *Harvard Educational Review* 47, no. 2 (May 1977): 171-197. On legal-services attorneys, see Carl Hosticka, "Legal Services Lawyers Encounter Clients: A Study in Street Level Bureaucracy" (Ph.D. diss., MIT,1976).

9. See James M. Henslin, "Trust and the Cab Driver," in Elihu Katz and Brenda Danet, eds., *Bureaucracy and the Public* (New York: Basic Books, 1973), pp. 339-356.

10. See especially Eliot Freidson, *Profession of Medicine* (New York: Dodd, Mead, 1974), chap. 5; Amitai Etzioni, *The Semi-Professions and Their Organization* (New York: Free Press, 1969).

11. Herbert Kaufman, *The Forest Ranger* (Baltimore: Johns Hopkins University Press, 1967).

12. Excellent studies taking this departure include Pressman and Wildavsky, *Implementation;* Derthick, *New Towns In-Town;* Jerome Murphy, *State Education Agencies and Discretionary Funds* (Lexington, Mass.: D. C. Heath, 1974); Harvey Sapolsky, *The Polaris System Development: Bureaucratic and Programmatic Success in Government* (Cambridge, Mass.: Harvard University Press, 1972).

Index